BLUEGRASS, NEWGRASS, OLD-TIME, AND AMERICANA MUSIC

BLUEGRASS, NEWGRASS, OLD-TIME, AND AMERICANA MUSIC

CRAIG HARRIS

PELICAN PUBLISHING COMPANY
Gretna 2018

*The word "Pelican" and the depiction of a pelican are
trademarks of Pelican Publishing Company, Inc., and are
registered in the U.S. Patent and Trademark Office.*

Library of Congress Cataloging-in-Publication Data

Names: Harris, Craig, 1953 December 20- author.
Title: Bluegrass, newgrass, old-time, and Americana music / by Craig
  Harris.
Description: Gretna : Pelican Publishing Company, 2018. | Includes
  bibliographical references and index.
Identifiers: LCCN 2017051123 | ISBN 9781455624010 (pbk. : alk. paper)
  | ISBN 9781455624027 (ebook)
Subjects: LCSH: Bluegrass music—History and criticism. | Bluegrass
  musicians—United States—Interviews.
Classification: LCC ML3520 .H37 2018 | DDC 781.6420973—dc23 LC
  record available at https://lccn.loc.gov/2017051123

*All quotes are from author interviews unless otherwise indicated. All photographs
are by the author. Front-cover photograph 1984. Back-cover photograph of
fiddle 2012.*

Printed in the United States of America

Published by Pelican Publishing Company, Inc.
1000 Burmaster Street, Gretna, Louisiana 70053
www.pelicanpub.com

To Petey, Bamboo, Tu, and Marys everywhere,
with appreciation to all who shared their time and memories

Contents

Introduction

"Bluegrass is the music of the people, not just the South. The songs come from all over America; they come from Europe. They tell about people's lives and experiences, their loves, heartbreaks, happiness, joy, mama, daddy, grandma, grandpa, farming, coal mining, moonshining, and prison. Anything people go through, there's a bluegrass song."

Five-time IBMA (International Bluegrass Music Association) "Female Vocalist of the Year" Dale Ann Bradley

"It's a living and breathing art."

Banjo player/Compass Records co-owner/producer Alison Brown

The instrumentation—fiddle, banjo, guitar, and bass—is often the same, but old-time Appalachian music and bluegrass have followed different paths since the 1930s. The "Father of Bluegrass," Bill Monroe, "gave everybody an opportunity to shine, but old-time music has a wall of sound," said banjo player Frank Lee, whose Freight Hoppers sparked an old-time revival in the 1990s. "You take the melody and glorify it. You're not trying to show the world what you could do. You play the melody, play it again, and play it again. It's easier for me. I can zone out into what some people call a trance."

"You play a tune for fifteen or twenty minutes," added fiddler Judy Hyman, of the neo-trad Horse Flies, "letting it build and evolve, not through improvisation but a more subtle movement, related to the pacing that minimalistic music moves."

A variety of traditions converged to create the "old-time" or "old-timey" music of Appalachia. Germans settled in Virginia's Shenandoah Valley in 1730, followed by English Quakers, Scots-Irish, French Huguenots, Welsh, Czechs, and Polish. After the Revolutionary War, thousands of Irish arrived as indentured servants. Ireland's potato famine of the 1840s increased immigration. Once the ancestral home of the Cherokee and

Shawano tribes, 40,409 square miles that would become part of Kentucky opened to settlers in the 1850s, after the Indians were relocated to west of the Mississippi River.

At the turn of the twentieth century, Appalachian women still sang a cappella ballads from the Old World. Cecil Sharp and Maud Karpeles collected 1,600 versions of 500 ballads and dance tunes in Virginia, North Carolina, Kentucky, and Tennessee between 1916 and 1918. Nearly all were variants of songs and fiddle tunes collected by Francis James Child in England, Scotland, and Ireland a half-century before. Sharp's rejection of anything other than Anglo-Celtic music, however, prevented him from collecting hundreds of additional songs.

Music and dance intertwined. Reels, jigs, waltzes, and polkas were popular. "You can't separate the music from the dances," said caller/ clawhammer banjo player Phil Jamison. "Reels done by early settlers from the British Isles, primarily Scots-Irish, were the foundation for our square dances, but in square dancing, there are elements of French cotillions and quadrilles, as well as Cherokee and African-American influences. The same is true with step dancing or clogging."

The heart of Appalachian music was the fiddle. "Every fiddle player plays the same notes," said Frank Lee, "but the syncopation, because of their bowing, is different. Sometimes we hook up note for note but at other times, I'll play a countermelody."

Italian fiddles replaced hornpipes, tabors, and harps at Scotland's country dances by the sixteenth century. Their portability and ability to solo or play with other musicians made them the instrument of choice in the Americas. Members of the Cherokee tribe played fiddles and danced "English dances" as early as 1809.

With the exception of a white fiddler in Charlottesville, Cecil Sharp noted that only African-Americans sang while playing banjo or fiddle. The *Western Sentinel* referred to "an old-time colored fiddler from near Iredell" in 1908. A year later, the *Statesville Landmark* mentioned an "old-time fiddler of the colored race." The "old-time" appellation spread to mountain music of both races. "Whites and blacks were certainly playing music together for a long time," said Jamison.

Scottish fiddler Niel Gow's short bow saw-stroke provided the cornerstone of old-time fiddling, but other influences were present as well. By the beginning of the eighteenth century, African-Americans were the primary dance fiddlers in New Orleans. Thomas Jefferson's brother frequented Monticello's slave quarters to dance and learn fiddle from slaves. African-Americans flocked to the Appalachian Mountains, in the 1880s, to lay track and drill tunnels for railroads needed by logging and mining companies.

Trains brought new settlers, along with mandolins and guitars. The blending of cultures intensified after the introduction of phonograph records and radio. "Don't tell me old-timers didn't play jigs," said Rhiannon Giddens. "They played songs from vaudeville, minstrel shows, anything they felt like playing."

Playing with African-American banjo players since the 1840s, white fiddlers became aware of syncopation. Banjo players learned to adapt to Western music's established keys and scales. The banjo "was the first instrument in the black community," said Dom Flemons, "something people made at home thinking of African traditions. People got through hard times with song."

Banjos were "definitely an American instrument," added Giddens. "There were banjo-type instruments in Africa (ngoni, kontigo, gimbri, and gurkel) but the culmination of these instruments, the synchronization of African culture, was the banjo in the Caribbean. It made its way to North America."

The first documented white banjo player (and perhaps the first to add a droning fifth string), Joel Sweeney (1810-60), performed at the Broadway Circus, in NY, in April 1839. An African-American circus worker taught Ohio-born Daniel Decatur Emmett (1815-1904), composer of "Dixie," to play banjo. "Every first-generation white banjo player had to learn from a black banjo player," said Giddens, "and perform in blackface."

The banjo's popularity spread. Automated, coin-operated, banjo-playing machines appeared in the 1890s and inspired violinist Louis Stepner's easily played tenor banjo. By the end of the century, formally attired women were playing parlor music in banjo orchestras.

The winner of the first Banjo Championship of the World, at NY's Chickering Hall in 1887, Stamford, CT's Reuben R. Brooks repeated the next two years. Hyde Park, NY-born Sylvester Louis "Vess" Ossman (1868-1923) transformed hundreds of marches, jigs, and ragtime piano tunes into banjo tours de force, influencing succeeding virtuosos, including Somerville, NJ-born Fred Van Eps (1878-1960), Piqua, OH's Harry Reser (1896-1965), and Reading, MA-born Edwin Ellsworth "King of the Banjo" Peabody (1902-70).

(Adam) Manly Reece (1830-64) introduced the banjo to North Carolina's Piedmont before the Civil War. Banjo-playing Appalachian women included his sister, Julia Reece Green (1842-1911), Cynthia May "Cousin Emmy" Carver (1903-80), Lily May Ledford (1917-85), and Lois LaVerne "Molly O'Day" Williamson (1923-87). Dillsboro, NC-born Samantha Biddix "Aunt Samantha" Bumgarner (1878-1960) cut fourteen tracks for Columbia, in April 1924, backed by fiddler Eva Smathers Davis. She would appear at Bascom Lamar Lunsford's Mountain Dance and Folk Festival, in Asheville, from its 1928 inception until 1959.

Early banjo players played in the downward-stroke clawhammer, or frailing, style, but there were numerous approaches to clawhammer playing. A McMinnville, TN-born farmer who plowed his field with a mule, David Harrison "Uncle Dave" Macon (1870-1952) "had a way of twirling his banjo," said Mac Benford, "and juggling it while he played."

On November 6, 1925, Macon and fiddler Sid Harkreader appeared on *An Evening with WSM*, an on-air fundraiser for Nashville's police department. Three days later, the radio station hired George Dewey Hay, an ex-newspaper reporter who had hosted the predecessor to *The National Barn Dance* in Chicago, to host its new *WSM Barn Dance*. Premiering on November 28, the show's name changed after Hay opened its December 27 broadcast by telling listeners, "For the past hour, we have been listening to music taken from Grand Opera. From now on, we will present the 'Grand Ole Opry.'"[1]

Macon would be one of the *Opry's* top stars for more than a quarter-century, but he clung to the banjo player's traditional comic role. After watching Earl Scruggs' debut with Monroe, he pointed out, "That boy can play the banjo but he ain't one damned bit funny."[2]

In an antecedent of the Scruggs Roll, Moran Lee "Dock" Boggs (1898-1971) picked upwards on the first two strings with his index finger while plucking the other three strings with his thumb. More than three decades separated the two eras of the West Norton, VA-born coal miner's musical career. Tracks between 1927 and 1932 included "Prodigal Son," "Country Blues," "Sugar Baby" (recorded by the Youngbloods as "Sugar Babe"), and "Oh, Death" (covered by David Lindley's fusion-folk band, Kaleidoscope; Ralph Stanley sang it in *O Brother, Where Art Thou?*). During the Great Depression, Boggs gave his banjo to a friend and returned to the coalmines. He wouldn't record again until being "rediscovered" by Mike Seeger in 1963. Continuing to record until 1968, he performed until shortly before his death on February 7, 1971, his seventy-third birthday. "It had been my heart's desire to put my old songs on records," he told Curwood Garrett, "so the younger generation could learn them if they wanted to, and I could make a little extra cash as my pension and social security isn't too much."[3]

Hailing from Fannin County, GA, in the Blue Ridge Mountains, Fiddlin' John Carson (1868-1949) was already a seven-time state-champion fiddler when he traveled to Atlanta, in 1923, to record "The Little Old Log Cabin in the Lane," a nostalgic minstrel tune from 1871, and "The Old Hen Cackled and the Rooster's Going to Crow." Missouri-born Ralph Peer (1892-1960), who produced the session for OKeh, called Carson's fiddling and grizzly singing "pluperfect awful," but the disc sold half a million copies and became country music's first hit. Along with Eck Robertson's fiddle tune recordings of the previous year, Carson's success set off an era of old-time rural music that wouldn't subside until the Great Depression a decade later.

Traveling uninvited to New York in March 1923, Henry Whitter (1892-1941), a Grayson County, VA textile worker who played harmonica and guitar, persuaded the General Phonograph Corporation (owners of OKeh) to audition him. Invited back six months later, he cut nine tracks with fiddler Gilliam Banmon Grayson (1887-1930), including "Lee Highway Blues," "Handsome Molly," and "Little Maggie." Grayson and Whitter's murder ballad, "Tom Dula," helped to ignite the late-fifties folk revival when the Kingston Trio covered it as "Tom Dooley." Grayson and Whitter's "The Wreck of the Old 97," set to Henry Clay Work's "The Ship That Never Returned" (1865), recalled a fatal 1903 mail-train accident near Danville, VA. Covered by Vernon Dalhart (Marion Ty Slaughter), a classically trained singer, it became country music's first million seller (selling more than seven million copies).

Inspired by Grayson and Whitter's success, Ernest Van "Pop" Stoneman (1893-1968) sent a demo tape to Peer, who signed the Monarat, VA-born guitar, autoharp, and harmonica player and songwriter. Stoneman's "The Sinking of the Titanic" (1924) sold over a million copies.

Despite the music's popularity, misinformed outsiders had a scornful view of southeast Appalachia's populace. Envisioning them as "barefoot [with a] long scruffy beard, suspender-clad overalls, shapeless oversized felt hat, a moonshine jug or flask, and long-barreled rifle,"[4] they used derogatory words such as white trash, cracker, redneck, tar heel, swamp rat, and hillbilly to describe them. "A Hill-billie," declared the *NY Journal* in April 1900, "is a free and untrammeled white citizen . . . who lives in the hills, has no means to speak of, dresses as he can, talks as he pleases, drinks whiskey when he gets it, and fires off his revolver as the fancy takes him."[5]

"It signified ignorance, backwoods-ness, and stupidity," said Western KY University professor and author (*Hillbilly: A Cultural History of an American Icon*) Dr. Anthony Harkins.

The stereotype spread through the novels of KY-born John Fox, Jr. (*A Cumberland Vendetta*, 1895; *The Little Shepherd of Kingdom Come*, 1903; and *The Trail of the Lonesome Pine*, 1907), and GA-born William Nathaniel Harben (*Abner Daniel*, 1902). It infiltrated films including *The Cub* (1915), *Rainbow Riley* (1926), *The Big Killing* (1928), *Tobacco Road* (1941), the Ma and Pa Kettle series of the 1950s, and Abbott and Costello's *Comin' Round the Mountain* (1951), as well as radio programs such as *The Judy Canova Show* (1943-55) and comic strips. Billy DeBeck's *Barney Google and Snuffy Smith* (originally *Take Barney Google, F'rinstance*) debuted in 1919. Launched fifteen years later, Al Capp's *Li'l Abner* was adapted for film in 1959. The prejudice persisted. "The way hillbillies were portrayed in movies like *Deliverance* was sad," said Béla Fleck. "*Bonnie and Clyde* was about criminals and murderers. The Beverly Hillbillies appeared foolish but they were smart in their own way. Then you had *Hee Haw*, where they acted stupid and it was supposed to be funny."

"People think traditional people are quaint," added Rodney Dillard. "They don't realize we have values, integrity, and intellectual capacity. Just because we're from the mountains doesn't mean we're chasing our sisters or drinking out of a jug with *XXX* on it."

The deprecation carried over into music on January 15, 1924. At the end of a recording session, Peer asked bandleader Al Hopkins for the group's name. The Watauga County, NC-born pianist responded, "We're nothing but a bunch of hillbillies . . . call us anything." Seizing the opportunity, Peer dubbed the band "Al Hopkins & the Hill Billies." As the educated sons of a former state representative, the Hopkins brothers resisted. "Hillbilly was not only a funny word," Hopkins told Archie Green, "it was a fighting word."[6]

Convincing them of the moniker's commercial potential, Peer persuaded Hopkins and his cohorts to accept not only the name but also the stereotypical garb, dialogue, and exaggerated persona. Their success would inspire similar "hillbilly music" bands such as the Beverly Hill Billies, Gid Tanner & the Skillet Lickers with Riley Puckett and Clayton McMichen, Whitter's Virginia Breakdowners, Carson's Virginia Reelers, and Charlie Poole's North Carolina Ramblers. "Hear, folks, the music of the Hill Billies," proclaimed OKeh in its April 1925 catalogue. "These rollicking melodies will quicken the memory of the tunes of yesterday. The heart beats time to them while the feet move with the desire to cut a lively shine . . . these mountaineers sure have a way of fetching music out of the banjo, fiddle, and guitar that surprises listeners, old and young, into feeling skittish. Theirs is a spirited entertainment and one you will warm to."[7]

Working with Peer and the Victor Talking Machine Company, Stoneman helped to arrange a historic nine-day recording session in Bristol, TN during the summer of 1927. On the first day, Stoneman and his wife, Hattie, recorded in a variety of formats. After a newspaper reported that Stoneman had earned $3,000 in royalties that year, musicians flocked to Bristol. Peer would record seventy-six songs by nineteen acts, including the Carter Family and Jimmie Rodgers on August 1. Hailing from Scott County, VA, twenty-six miles from Bristol, the Carter Family sang songs of the mountains with authenticity. Alvin Pleasant Delaney "A. P." Carter (1891-1960), traveling with African-American guitarist Lesley Riddle (1905-80), mined the mountains for material. With A. P.'s wife, Sara, singing lead and her cousin Maybelle (Addington) (who married A. P.'s brother Ezra in 1926) singing harmony and playing guitar, the trio recorded over three hundred songs, including "Wabash Cannonball," "Can the Circle Be Unbroken," "Wildwood Flower," and "Keep On the Sunny Side" before disbanding in 1943.

Continuing to perform with her daughters, Helen, Anita, and Johnny Cash's second wife, Valerie June, until the late 1970s, "Mother" Maybelle set the foundation with her "Carter Lick" guitar picking. Also known as the "Thumb Brush," "Church Lick," and "Carter Scratch," the technique, which she learned from Riddle, combined melody on the bass strings with rhythmic strumming on the treble strings.

Guitar fingerpicking developed slowly in the Appalachian Mountains. One of the earliest examples, and possibly the first blues recording, Sylvester Weaver's "Smoketown Strut" (1924) "demonstrated the basic elements of country fingerpicking with its syncopated bass, clearly articulated melody line in the key of C, and the use of a roll similar to that later popularized by Earl Scruggs and Merle Travis."[8]

A second-generation brakeman who left the railroad after contracting tuberculosis in 1924, Meridian, MS-born James Charles "Jimmie" Rodgers (1897-1933) arrived in Bristol as a member of the Tenneva Ramblers. It's not clear if they split over an argument, or at Peer's direction, but singer/guitarist Rodgers and the band recorded separately. "He was singing blues," Peer explained, "and they were doing old-time fiddle music. Oil and water . . . they don't mix."

Rodgers' solo tracks would be the beginning of modern country music. Recording a few months later in Camden, NJ, he scored his first hit with "Blue Yodel No. 1 (T for Texas)." Selling half a million copies, it propelled him to stardom, further established by live shows and film appearances. Encouraged to write songs by Peer, who had a publishing deal with Victor, Rodgers penned such classics as "In the Jailhouse Now," "Peach Picking Time in Georgia," "Miss the Mississippi and You," and "Blue Yodel No. 8 (Mule Skinner Blues)." As influenced by blues and jazz crooning as by traditional country music, he recorded "Blue Yodel No. 9 (Standin' on the Corner)" with Louis Armstrong (trumpet) and Armstrong's wife, Lillian (piano). A desegregated recording, in 1930, was groundbreaking.

Rodgers' modern approach made old-time music seem antiquated. The economic downturn of the Great Depression added to the music's collapse. Record sales of $75 million in 1929 plummeted to $6 million in 1933.

Overshadowed by Western swing and crooning movie-cowboy balladry, old-time music came close to extinction. Someone needed to inject new spirit into the mountain sounds and transform them from the realm of nostalgia into a new kind of music worthy of respect. That person turned out to be Bill Monroe.

Bill Monroe, 1989

Chapter 1

Blue Moon of Kentucky

William Smith "Bill" Monroe (1911-96) was no hillbilly. Immaculately groomed, the Rosine, KY-born mandolinist/tenor singer and his Blue Grass Boys wore tailor-made suits, ties, and hats. Their music wasn't carefree jamming but masterfully executed virtuosity. "[Monroe] brought dignity to bluegrass," said former IBMA (International Bluegrass Music Association) president and Hot Rize/Red Knuckles and the Trailblazers founding member Pete "Dr. Banjo" Wernick.

Monroe's music was new and exciting. "People didn't want to hear what their grandmothers sang," said Brooklyn-born and San Francisco-based Jody Stecher. "They could hear that for free."

Combining right-hand chops and left-hand melodies, Monroe summoned "some of the most delicate tones, chimes, and special riffs and flourishes"[1] on his mandolin. Bought in a FL barbershop, around 1945, for $150, his 1923 Gibson F-5 (signed by designer Lloyd Loar) would become, according to Vince Gill, "the Holy Grail."[2]

Monroe's "high lonesome" vocals were as striking as his mandolin playing. "It's hard to sing Dad's songs," said James William Monroe (1941-), "unless you have a high voice. He'd go from straight voice to falsetto and take it up again. I've never seen anybody like him."

"Monroe's singing was as powerful as Louis Armstrong's trumpet," added ex-Carolina Chocolate Drop Dom Flemons. "They both played with gusto and used their instrument to push things further."

Inducted into the Country Music (1970), Bluegrass (1971), and Rock & Roll (1997) halls of fame, Monroe fused country and blues more than a decade before Elvis Presley covered "Blue Moon of Kentucky" on his 1954 debut single. "Elvis gave my father credit," said James Monroe. "Jerry Lee Lewis listened to him on the *Grand Ole Opry*. B. B. King and James Brown were fans. Little Richard loved my father's singing."

"Buddy Holly was a fan," added Wernick, "and Paul McCartney recorded 'Blue Moon of Kentucky.' Jerry Garcia loved bluegrass."

"The difference between rock and roll and music before it," said Ron Thomason, the Dry Branch Fire Squad mandolinist/singer who inducted Monroe into the Rock & Roll Hall of Fame, "is that backbeat—that mandolin chop—that beat that happens when your foot's in the air."

"Monroe took the string-band format—guitar, fiddle, banjo, mandolin, and bass," explained Laurie Lewis, "and created music personal to him out of Appalachian fiddle tunes, church music, rural blues, and everything else he heard. He wrote songs and used the bluegrass idiom to do other people's songs. I like that definition; it fits me."

The youngest of Grundy County, MO-born John Buchanan "J. B." or "Buck" Monroe and the former Melissa Ann Vandiver's six sons and two daughters, Monroe suffered from a severely crossed left eye and poor vision (his eye wasn't straightened until his teens). Eighteen years separated him and oldest brother Harry. He was closest to ten-year-older Birch (named after an uncle), eight-year-older Charles or "Charlie," and three-year-older sister Bertha. The Monroe family had experienced hard times before he was born, but his father had remained determined, cutting trees, hauling timber, operating a mill, and mining for coal. By the time of his youngest son's birth, he owned a 320-acre farm (that would grow to 600 acres), additional property, and various livestock.

With a windup Victrola playing into the night, J. B. buck-and-wing (clog) danced. The youngest of TN-born farmer Joseph M. Vandiver and the former KY-born Manerva Farris's ten children, Melissa was not only a superb backstep dancer but also a proficient fiddle, harmonica, and accordion player and a clear, high-pitched singer. "Melissa was tall and attractive," said Monroe biographer Richard Smith, "with blue eyes, red hair, and freckles. She grew white roses and wore them in her hair from the first buds of spring to the last flowers of fall."[3]

Thirteen-year-old Birch started playing his mother's fiddle in 1914. Charlie and Beatrice followed on guitars. At eight or nine, Bill (or Willie, as the family called him) joined on mandolin. Farmhand Hubert Stringfield (1894-1980) showed him the basics.

Monroe absorbed a wide variety of musical influences. "Rosine is on the Ohio River," explained Don Rigsby, "and people were coming through all the time. There was music that [Monroe] wouldn't have been exposed to otherwise."

The "hollering" yodel of farmhands and railroad workers flavored many of Monroe's recordings. Taught to read shape notes, he sang with the Rosine Methodist Church's youth choir for six months. His poor eyesight made it difficult for him to read music and forced him to give up the choir, but spirituals remained essential to his repertoire.

Melissa's brother, Birch Vandiver, fascinated her youngest son with precise bowing on cello. Another brother, James Pendleton "Uncle Pen" Vandiver (1869-1932), was a country fiddler with "a repertoire of tunes that sank into Bill's aurally trained memory and a sense of rhythm that seeped into his bones."[4]

"He was one of KY's finest old-time fiddlers," Monroe recalled in the liner notes to *Uncle Pen* (1972), "and he had the best shuffle of the bow I've ever seen, and kept the best time. That's one reason people asked him to play for the dances."[5]

"Uncle Pen taught my dad fiddle tunes, waltzes, the ancient tones, and the timing," added James Monroe, "the foundations of the bluegrass music to come."

Immortalized in Monroe's 1950 hit "Uncle Pen," Vandiver lived alone in a hilltop cabin overlooking Rosine. His wife had left him and taken their daughter. Their son died at a young age. Injured when thrown from a mule, Vandiver was unable to walk without crutches. Recognizing his nephew's musical talent, he recruited him to back his fiddling at local dances. "We started . . . at sundown," Monroe told NPR, "and the next morning at daylight, we were still playing music—all night long."[6]

Monroe inherited his father's work ethic. "I was raised in the old pioneer way," he explained in 1984, "and we worked hard. I still like to work. I keep horses on my farm . . . and I love to plow behind those horses. I'm not afraid to work, set a posthole, build a fence. . . . I can work hard in the field, lay right down . . . in the plowed ground, sleep a little bit, and go right ahead and work some more."[7]

By the age of eleven, Monroe was "working rather than going to school," said Danice Woodside. "He ran foxhounds and raised birds for cockfighting . . . he was loading railroad ties and hauling them by wagon to the Rosine train depot."[8]

Arnold Shultz (1886-1931), an African-American guitarist/fiddler who worked in the mines during the day, paid twelve-year-old Monroe five dollars a night to accompany him at square dances. Uncle Pen sometimes fiddled. "[Monroe] got the beat," said Pat Enright of the Nashville Bluegrass Band, "his timing, and to some extent his singing from blacks. He had blues notes in there."

Though he never recorded, Shultz left a lasting legacy. His bandmate Kennedy Jones, student Mose Rager, and Ike Everly, father of the Everly Brothers, spread his "pulling strings" thumbpicking style. "They influenced [Merle] Travis," said Kathy and Don Thomason, "who took the style to the rest of the world along with Chet Atkins."[9]

"[Shultz's] transitions between chords," explained Richard Smith, "were silky smooth. He also knew how to play in the sliding 'bottleneck' style . . . using a pocketknife to make the notes. The strap holding his guitar was not leather, just an old woven grass rope."[10]

"[There are] runs that I use in a lot of my music," Monroe told *Bluegrass Today*. "I don't say that I make them the same way that he could . . . he was powerful with it . . . he used a pick and could just run from one chord to another the prettiest you've ever heard. There's no guitar picker today that could do that."[11]

Joined by Charlie (1903-75) (vocals/guitar) and Birch (1901-82) (fiddle), Monroe debuted on radio in 1927. Their father's death, a few months later, left the seventeen-year-old an orphan (their mother had passed five years before). Leaving to seek their fortunes, Charlie and Birch briefly stopped in Detroit, where they worked at Briggs Motor Company. Continuing to East Chicago, IN, they secured jobs at the Sinclair Oil Refinery. Bill's sisters maintained the house for a while but left to join Birch and Charlie. Moving in with Uncle William, and then with Uncle Jack Monroe, the teenager found himself in a quandary when an outbreak of measles caused Uncle Jack's house to be quarantined. Uncle Pen invited him to "batch it" at his cabin. "He [did] the cooking for the two of us," Monroe remembered. "We had fatback, sorghum molasses, and hoecakes for breakfast, followed up with black-eyed peas with fatback, and corn bread and sorghum for dinner and supper . . . there were hard times, and money was scarce, but also there were good times. . . . I'd live them again."[12]

James Monroe purchased Uncle Pen's property in 1973 and presented it to his father as a birthday gift. He added a replica cabin in 2013.

Reuniting with Charlie and Birch in 1929, Monroe worked with his brothers at the oil refinery during the day and played music at night. The trio's first break came when *National Barn Dance* square-dance caller Tom Owens hired them as dancers. Returning to their music after two years, they hosted weekly shows for WAE (Hammond, IN) and WJKS (Gary, IN). Graduating to daily fifteen-minute broadcasts on WJKS, they added weekly appearances on the Saturday-night *Crazy Barn Dance* in 1934.

Wearied by the uncertainties of a musical career, Birch opted for millwork. Charlie and Bill continued as a duo. Hooking up with emcee Byron Parker, they transferred to WFBC/Greenville as the Kentucky Colonels. They became the Kentucky Songbirds in January 1936. Rejecting Victor's initial offer, the Monroe Brothers eventually signed with the Camden, NJ-based label. Their February 7, 1936, session yielded "Nine Pound Hammer," "Darling Corey," "Lonesome Valley," and their first hit, "What Would You Give in Exchange for Your Soul." During the next two years, they added twenty more tracks, including "Drifting Too Far from the Shore," "New

River Train," "You've Got to Walk That Lonesome Valley," "Will the Circle Be Unbroken," "Roll in My Sweet Baby's Arms," "Roll On Buddy," and "He Will Set Your Fields on Fire." "Bill's lightning mandolin and Charlie's distinctive guitar, including his signature G-run," said *Bluegrass Unlimited*, "created an aerodynamic sound that set them apart from other brother duos and their taut harmony singing revitalized the old mountain songs and gospel standards that made up their repertoire. Their stepped-up tempos and vocal dynamics foreshadowed the sound of bluegrass."[13]

There were problems, however. "They didn't get along," said Tracy Schwarz. "It's a wonder they were able to play together onstage."

Separating over "differences in artistic direction," in 1939, each brother formed a band of his own. Charlie's Kentucky Pardners would include mandolinists William Eugene "Red" Rector, Ira Louvin, and John Ray "Curly" Seckler. "Uncle Charlie kept to the style of the Monroe Brothers," recalled James Monroe, "but his later recordings added electric lead and steel guitar and he recorded with Hank Williams' Drifting Cowboys in 1950."

Forming the Kentuckians in Little Rock, Bill hosted a show on KARK for three months. Relocating to Atlanta, he placed an ad, in a newspaper, seeking musicians. The initial Blue Grass Boys included a lead vocalist/guitarist from Atlanta (Cleo Davis), a fiddler from Asheville (Art Wooten), and a bass player from Greenville (Amos Garin). "Bill was trying to follow the Monroe Brothers' style," claimed Davis, "with our extreme high harmony and smooth sound."[14]

Questioned about the Blue Grass Boys' name, Monroe told Davis, "I'm from Kentucky, you know, where the blue grass grows."[15]

Columbia Records' British-born producer, Art Satherley, signed Monroe in 1940. Thomas Edison's former secretary, Satherley worked with "race" musicians including Ma Rainey and Blind Lemon Jefferson and country artists such as Roy Acuff, Gene Autry, and Bob Wills. "[I'm] considered the daddy of it all," he boasted. "That's what they call me, the daddy of all recordings country: country black, country white."[16]

Satherley had deep respect for mountain music. "These so-called hillbillies," he said, "are tremendously sensitive people with deep emotions . . . the mountaineer is a realist. His songs deal with loneliness, misery, death, murder."[17]

With its 50,000-watt signal, Nashville's WSM reached most of the US and Canada. Arranging an audition, Monroe and his band impressed station owners and the Attica, IN-born "Solemn Old Judge," George Dewey Hay, host of the Saturday-night *Grand Ole Opry*. The Blue Grass Boys debuted on the show, in October 1939, with Jimmie Rodgers and George

Vaughn (Horton)'s "Mule Skinner Blues (Blue Yodel #8)," the A-side of their first single (paired with Clyde Moody's "Six White Horses"). Moody played mandolin on "Mule Skinner Blues"—Monroe's only recording with someone else on the eight-string (he played guitar). Ten years later, Horton wrote lyrics for Monroe's first Decca single, "New Mule Skinner Blues."

Monroe and the Blue Grass Boys cut their first records for Columbia affiliate Bluebird Records in 1940 and 1941 before an American Federation of Musicians recording ban. Once the ban lifted, in February 1945, they returned to the studio, promoted to Columbia's parent label. For the next half-decade, they would be one of its top artists. "Kentucky Waltz," "Footprints in the Snow," "Will You Be Loving Another Man," "Little Cabin On the Hill," and "Molly and Teabrooks" became classics. "Blue Moon of Kentucky" became the fifteenth state's official bluegrass song in 1988.

The Blue Grass Boys toured constantly. Sharing a tent show with *Opry* comics Tom "Jamup" Woods and "Honey" Wilds in 1942, Monroe launched his own tent show the following year. His musicians were under tremendous pressure. "You don't make a mistake on one of Bill Monroe's shows," said Davis, "especially on the road. . . . You must be nearly perfect. We weren't but we thought we were."[18]

Lake City, FL-born Robert Russell "Chubby" Wise was the only Blue Grass Boy to appear on all of Monroe's tracks on Columbia. "The fiddle bow fit my hand," he pointed out, "a lot better than them plough handles did."[19]

Wise (1915-96) grew up backing his father's fiddle on guitar and banjo. Moving to Jacksonville in 1930, and switching to the fiddle, he drove a cab during the day and played music at night. In 1938, he helped Craven County, NC-born fiddler Ervin Thomas Rouse (1917-81) compose "Orange Blossom Special." Monroe recorded it three years later. It would become one of bluegrass's most covered tunes. "The song belongs to everybody by now, I guess," Rouse said to Mother Maybelle Carter, "but it used to be my best number."[20]

"I gave my half to Ervin," Wise told the Associated Press, "but it didn't hurt my stature any . . . it got me a lot of jobs and, in a sense, a lot of money."[21]

Wise fiddled for Hank Williams, Red Foley, Ernest Tubb, Eddy Arnold, Merle Haggard, Frank "Hylo" Brown, Jimmy Martin, Mac Wiseman, Red Allen, Hazel Dickens & Alice Gerrard, and Larry Sparks. He co-wrote and played on Moody's 1949 million-selling country hit, "Shenandoah Waltz," while still employed by Monroe. Joining Hank Snow's Rainbow Ranch Boys in 1954, he accompanied the Canadian country singer for the next fifteen years. Snow produced the first of Wise's nineteen solo albums, *The Tennessee Fiddler* (1961).

As soon as he and clawhammer banjo player David "Stringbean" Akeman became Blue Grass Boys in 1943, Monticello, FL-born Howard Watts (1913-70) changed his name to "C. Cedric Rainwater" (soon dropping the first initial). Over the next five years, Watts' "superb timing, tone and 4/4 walking bass technique led many of his peers to regard him as the best acoustic bass player in the business."[22]

Jackson County, KY-born Akeman (1915-73) dressed in a long, red, checkered nightshirt and jeans (acquired from Little Jimmy Dickens) belted at his knees. As a Blue Grass Boy, he interspersed music with comic skits with bass player Willie Egbert "Cousin Wilbur" Westbrooks.

Sparta, TN-born Lester Raymond Flatt (1914-79) joined the Blue Grass Boys in March 1945. Picking him up at the Nashville bus station, Stringbean took him to play on the *Grand Ole Opry* without rehearsal. Flatt would sing lead on sixteen of Monroe's next nineteen singles and write "My Cabin in Caroline," "Come Back Darling," "Head Over Heels in Love with You," "I'm Gonna Sleep with One Eye Open," "God Loves His Children," and "Cabin on the Hill."

Shaped by singing hymns in church, Flatt's baritone defined bluegrass vocalizing. "Lester had wonderful intonation," said Mac Wiseman, "and he sang on key."

"Lester made a good singer with me," noted Monroe, "pretty fine."[23]

From the age of seven, Flatt played guitar in the "Carter Lick" style, which combined melody on the bass strings with rhythmic strumming on the treble strings. Maybelle Carter learned it from Lesley "Esley" Riddle (1905-80), the African-American guitarist who accompanied her brother-in-law and Carter Family bandmate, A. P. Carter, on song-collecting expeditions.

Debuting on the radio with Charlie Scott's Harmonizers in 1939, Flatt continued to work as a weaver until arthritis forced him to give it up in the early forties. Turning to music full time, he and his wife, Gladys (whom he married in 1934), relocated to Burlington, NC, where he briefly teamed with Moody. Following a stint with Jim Hall and the Crazy Mountaineers in early 1943, he joined Charlie Monroe as a mandolin player and tenor singer. The Kentucky Pardners' daily half-hour radio show (one of the first syndicated) distributed to seven stations via sixteen-inch discs and aired on *Noon Day Jamboree*. This freed them to play two shows a day in a filled-to-capacity 2,000-seat tent. They would record for RCA Victor in 1946, and Decca four years later, but Flatt, tired of singing backup and playing mandolin, had handed in his resignation and signed on with Charlie's younger brother in March 1945.

With the Blue Grass Boys continuing to evolve, Stringbean's clawhammer banjo picking "just didn't fit," said Flatt. "It would remind you of the old-time lick like Uncle Dave Macon played. It was a fine lick, and I love String, but it would really drag the rhythm down."[24]

Resigning in September 1945, Stringbean formed a comic duo with Lew Childe. Becoming a much-loved regular on *Hee Haw* (1969-71), he met a tragic end when intruders broke into his cabin and murdered him and his wife. Grandpa Jones discovered their bodies. Sam Bush memorialized them with "The Ballad of Stringbean and Estelle," written with Guy Clark and Verlon Thompson.

The arrival of Stringbean's replacement, in December 1945, would be a defining moment for bluegrass and the banjo. "Few players have changed the way we hear an instrument the way Earl Scruggs has," said Steve Martin, "putting him in a category with Miles Davis, Louis Armstrong, Chet Atkins, and Jimi Hendrix. His reach extends not only throughout America but to other countries."[25]

Hailing from Flint Hill, a small community in the heart of the Piedmont, near Shelby, NC, Earl Eugene Scruggs (1924-2012) was the youngest of farmer/bookkeeper George Elam Scruggs and the former Lula Ruppe's three sons and two daughters. They didn't own a radio until Earl was in his teens, but there was no shortage of music. George Scruggs (who died before Earl's eleventh birthday) was a fiddler and mandolin player. Lula played organ. Earl's brothers, Junius Emmett "Junie" and Horace, and sisters, Eula Mae and Ruby, played banjo and guitar. Junie's banjo featured on "Cripple Creek" and a medley of "Sally Goodin'" and "Sally Ann" on the Mike Seeger-produced *American Banjo Scruggs Style* (1956), acknowledged as the first bluegrass album.

Scruggs played clawhammer banjo from the age of four (and fingerpicked guitar). Remembering a "fuss" with his brother when he was ten, he told NPR, "I'd gone into a room by myself. . . . I had the banjo in there. . . . I was . . . pouting and, all of a sudden, I realized I was picking with three fingers. . . . That excited me to no end. I was playing a tune called 'Reuben.' . . . I went running out of the room and there was my brother. . . . I came out saying, 'I got it. I got it. I got it.'"[26]

Scruggs' three-finger roll would reinvent the banjo. "Here's where [the banjo] steps out of the band," said John Hartford, "and . . . becomes the lead instrument."[27]

Scruggs wasn't the first to play banjo with three fingers. Charlie Poole

(1892-1931) recorded in a "rolling" three-finger style in the mid-1920s. "A childhood accident while playing baseball left him with partially deformed fingers on his right hand."[28]

Between 1926 and 1931, Poole's North Carolina Ramblers, with brother-in-law Posey Rorer (fiddle) and Norman Woodlief (guitar), sold millions of records, including "Don't Let Your Deal Go Down," "Hesitation Blues," "If I Lose," and "Sweet Sunny South." "There are jazzy elements in some of Charlie Poole's music," said John Hartford.[29]

The Carolina Tar Heels' Doctor Coble "Doc" or "Dock" Walsh (1901-67) was the "Banjo King of the Carolinas." Monroe covered the Wilkes County, NC-born banjo player's "In the Pines" in 1940. Leadbelly recorded variations as "Where Did You Sleep Last Night" (1944) and "Black Girl." Kurt Cobain covered it with Nirvana on MTV's *Unplugged* and performed it with Courtney Love. Walsh and the Carolina Tar Heels introduced "My Home's Across the Blue Ridge Mountains" in 1929. Also known as "I'm Goin' Back to North Carolina," and collected in 1909, it was recorded by the Carter Family, Frank Proffitt, and Larry Richardson. Doc Watson, Clint Howard, and Fred Price included it on *Old Timey Concert* (1967), recorded at the Seattle Folklore Center.

Visiting his uncle Sidney Ruppe's house, at the age of six, Scruggs met Mack Woolbright (c. 1891-1960), a blind, SC-born banjo player who recorded with guitarist Charles Monroe Parker in the 1920s and penned "The Man Who Wrote 'Home Sweet Home' Never Was a Married Man." Scruggs also met Jesse Smith Hammett (1887-1930), a Cherokee County, SC-born banjo player who devised a three-finger technique after injury impeded his clawhammer playing. He taught the style to DeWitt "Snuffy" Jenkins (1908-90), who joined J. E. Mainer's Mountaineers in 1936. Scruggs heard Jenkins in Rutherford, NC.

There would be no denying Jenkins' impact on Don Wesley Reno (1926-84), the Buffalo, SC-born and Hayward County, NC-raised banjo/guitar player Scruggs replaced in the Morris Brothers in 1939. Scruggs' stint with Zeke and Wiley Morris, however, would be brief. Missing his widowed mother, he submitted his resignation, returned to Flint Hill, and took a job at the Lily Mills textile mill. He would not return to music until hooking up with Lost John Miller's Allied Kentuckians in 1945. He would play with the Knoxville-based group for only three months, but it would be long enough to catch the attention of the Blue Grass Boys' fiddler, Jim Shumate. When Monroe was seeking a replacement for Stringbean, Shumate remembered the twenty-two-year-old banjo player and recommended him. Summoned to an audition, Scruggs proved his mettle with "Sally Goodin'" and "Dear Old Dixie." He got the gig.

Scruggs' banjo would be bluegrass's most distinguishable sound, but Monroe would claim, "If it hadn't been for bluegrass, the five-string banjo would have never made it."[30]

"There wouldn't have been bluegrass," countered Tim Stafford of Blue Highway, "without Earl Scruggs."

"Monroe was the bandleader," explained Lance LeRoy, who managed Flatt after the breakup of Flatt & Scruggs, "and, as a Grand Ole Opry member, provided the forum."[31]

Despite being the father of Melissa Katherine (1936-90) and five-year-younger James (from his first marriage), Monroe kept his musicians constantly on the road. Paid sixty dollars a week, they performed three or four shows daily in the bandleader's tent and spent their mornings playing baseball against local teams (Monroe played shortstop). Touring six days a week, they hustled back to Nashville for the Saturday-night *Grand Ole Opry*. "We played in rain, we played in snow," recalled Scruggs. "We played where the power would go off and we would have to play by lantern light with no sound. We had two bad wrecks but nobody got hurt. . . . It seemed to make Bill stronger and it brought out the deep feeling and love he had for what he was doing."[32]

"[Monroe] wore them out," J. D. Crowe told me. "They weren't making any money. He probably didn't pay them half the time."

Conflicts rose over songwriting credit. Musicians felt slighted when Monroe published tunes under his name despite their input. "Blue Grass Breakdown" (on the flipside of the 1948 "Toy Heart" single) was a case in point. A banjo showcase, it was undeniably Scruggs' tune. The banjo player, understandably irked when Monroe took full credit, "changed the most noticeable chord," said Pete Wernick, "and made a hook out of an arpeggiated E minor chord; it was pretty different for country music of the 1940s."

Renaming it "Foggy Mountain Breakdown," Scruggs recorded it with Flatt and the Foggy Mountain Boys in 1940 and 1948.

Scruggs' decision to leave the Blue Grass Boys was more personal than professional. He was preparing to marry (Anne) Louise Certain, on April 18, 1948, two years after picking her out of the *Grand Ole Opry* audience. Returning to the Lily Mills textile mill, he had no intention to leave again.

Scruggs' departure set off ripples. Within weeks, Flatt and Rainwater left Monroe. Flatt phoned Scruggs, pleading with him to join their new band. Assured they would stay local, the banjo player reluctantly agreed.

Flatt & Scruggs' Foggy Mountain Boys rounded out with Shumate (fiddle), "Curly" Seckler (mandolin), and Molly O'Day's ex-bass player Malcolm "Mac" Wiseman (guitar and vocals). Wiseman would defect to the Blue Grass Boys within a few months. Benny Sims would replace Shumate in 1948, followed by other fiddlers including Chubby Wise, Art Wooten, Howdy Forrester, and Paul Warren. With alumni including Hylo Brown (bass, guitar), Jim Eanes (guitar), Everett Lilly (mandolin), and Earl Taylor (mandolin/harmonica), Flatt & Scruggs and the Foggy Mountain Boys remained together for twenty-one years.

Monroe refused to speak to his former employees for more than two decades. "Bill had a dressing room at the Ryman," remembered Del McCoury. "You'd come up steps, walk up a hallway, and go into this room. He let Ray Price and Hank Snow in there. I don't remember anybody else. Flatt & Scruggs had to tune up in the hallway. Bill wouldn't let them in his room."

"He didn't like the way they left them," said Monroe's son. "They were pretty close to my father's style of music. He trained them. Earl had the three-finger roll but my father brought him along. Lester was a good singer but Dad instilled in him the drive and timing of bluegrass music. Flatt & Scruggs had the power to come on the *Grand Ole Opry* but my father looked at them as a competitor. They had to come up with a sound that was different so they added a Dobro [resophonic guitar] player [Tellico Plains, TN-born Burkett Howard "Josh" or "Buck" Graves, 1927-2006]."

Monroe and Flatt reconciled in June 1971. "Josh and I got together," explained James, "and talked about getting Lester to come to Bean Blossom. [The day of the festival], they shook hands and my father said, 'Welcome.' That started their friendship again."

Monroe refused to speak to Scruggs for forty-five years. "When Earl was playing with his boys in the Earl Scruggs Revue," said James Monroe, "we did shows with them in Canada and the East Coast. My father didn't pay attention to Earl using electric instruments but he wouldn't go for it in his band. He wanted to feel respected."

Angered when Columbia signed the Stanley Brothers, in 1950, Monroe left when his contract expired and signed with Decca, remaining for twenty-three years and nine albums (not counting compilations), including his first, *Knee Deep in Bluegrass* (1958). The Blue Grass Boys' sixty-two Decca singles included "Uncle Pen," "Christmas Time's A'Comin'," "Raw Hide," "I'm Workin' On a Building," and the Monroe and Hank Williams-penned "I'm Blue, I'm Lonesome." The mandolinist released another three singles and eleven non-compilation albums, including *Father and Son* (1973) and *Together Again* (1978), with his son. *Bill Monroe and James Monroe: Special*

Memories (2008) released posthumously. "I did almost one hundred sides when I was a Blue Grass Boy," James Monroe said. "I played guitar on 'Jerusalem Ridge' and bass on 'Train 45.' I was on 'Blue Night,' 'Walls of Time,' 'Sally Goodin',' and 'Mother's Not Dead (She's Only Sleeping).' We never rehearsed much. We might go through a number once or twice before recording it but never the whole thing. There weren't many retakes. He'd knock it out of the park the first take. He didn't like to overdub; there was no polishing up his music."

The Blue Grass Boys frequently performed at what is now the Bill Monroe Memorial Park and Museum in Bean Blossom, IN. First coming to the fairgrounds as headliner of the Brown County Jamboree in 1951, Monroe bought the property by the end of the year. The eight-day Bean Blossom Bluegrass Festival, first held in June 1967, has become the longest-running bluegrass festival in the US. An annual Hall of Fame and Uncle Pen Days Festival launched on the site in September 1974. Hosting festivals in a dozen states, Monroe "kept musicians working," said his son, "but he didn't make much money. Sometimes, he went in the hole. You do a lot to keep your music going."

Playing his F-5 mandolin for the final time, on the *Grand Ole Opry*, on March 15, 1996, Monroe sustained a stroke a month later. "He spent a lot of time on his farm where he had horses and cattle," recalled his son, "but he wanted to go on the road. Everybody tried to get him to slow down; he didn't want to do that. He loved his fans and they loved him."

Returning from Bean Blossom, which he had run in his father's absence, James learned of the mandolinist's passing. "I saw him a week before," he recalled. "When I said, 'Daddy, I've got to go,' he looked away. He didn't want me to leave. That was the last time I saw him."

A memorial service at the Ryman Auditorium drew an overflowing attendance. "Everyone in bluegrass was there," said James, "along with Hank Williams, Jr., and Johnny Cash. Byron Berline came from OK. Fans came from all over the country. Emmylou Harris sang 'Wayfaring Stranger.' Ricky Skaggs and Marty Stuart sang 'Wicked Path of Sin.' Scottish bagpipers played 'Amazing Grace.' The audience followed as my father's casket was wheeled to the hearse. We went to the funeral home and got him ready to take back to Rosine. There was another service at the Methodist church, where he went all his life. The church filled with four or five hundred people and there were more outside. We put speakers outside so everyone could hear."

The Bill Monroe Foundation attempted to purchase Monroe's F-5 from his son for more than a million dollars in 2001 but was unable to come up with the money. Four years later, philanthropist Robert W. "Bob" McLean bought it and donated it to the Country Music Hall of Fame and Museum. McLean previously donated Mother Maybelle Carter's guitar.

Dozens of musicians followed Flatt and Scruggs as Blue Grass Boys. "I like the friendship of a man," Monroe told Radio McGill, Montreal, "but I don't think that I would've liked to have kept the same musicians for twenty-seven years . . . because his ideas would run out."[33]

He needn't have worried. Blue Grass Boys alumni including Flatt, Scruggs, Clyde Moody, Chubby Wise, Don Reno, Vassar Clements, Mac Wiseman, Jimmy Martin, Carter Stanley, Sonny Osborne, Bobby Hicks, Kenny Baker, Don Stover, Eddie Adcock, Buddy Spicher, Del McCoury, Bill Keith, Peter Rowan, Richard Greene, "Ranger" Doug Green, Byron Berline, and Roland White spread his music further. He taught them well.

Chapter 2

Foggy Mountain Breakdown

The inspiration for the fictitious Soggy Bottom Boys (*O Brother, Where Art Thou?*), Flatt & Scruggs and the Foggy Mountain Boys brought exuberance to bluegrass. Fans anticipated their TV shows as much as they did broadcasts of the *Grand Ole Opry*. Under the management, booking, and guidance of Scruggs' wife, Louise, they performed at colleges, headlined at Carnegie Hall, and twice set the stage of the Newport Folk Festival ablaze. Their theme song for *The Beverly Hillbillies* continues to air in repeats.

Revived in the Arthur Penn-directed *Bonnie and Clyde,* starring Warren Beatty and Faye Dunaway, Flatt & Scruggs' 1949 recording "Foggy Mountain Breakdown" received a Grammy in 1967. The Library of Congress added it to its recording registry. A 2001 version including Steve Martin (banjo), Vince Gill and Albert Lee (electric guitar), Paul Shaffer (piano), Leon Russell (organ), and Marty Stuart (mandolin) featured on *Earl Scruggs and Friends*. The album, which also included appearances by John Fogerty, Elton John, Sting, Johnny Cash, Don Henley, Travis Tritt, and Billy Bob Thornton, yielded a second Grammy for the banjo player. "*Bonnie and Clyde* and *The Beverly Hillbillies* broadened the scope of bluegrass and country music," Scruggs said in 1982, "more than anything I can put my finger on. Both were hits in so many countries."[1]

"Randy Lynn Rag," "Flint Hill Special," and "Flint Mountain Special" and instrumental albums *Foggy Mountain Banjo* (1961) and *Strictly Instrumental* with Doc Watson (1967) spotlighted Scruggs' banjo. Songs by Flatt, including "I'm Head Over Heels Over You," and "Don't This Road Look Rough and Rocky," mixed with traditional tunes such as "Roll in My Sweet Baby's Arms" and "Take Me in Your Lifeboat." Flatt & Scruggs covered the Morris Brothers' "Salty Dog Blues" but also tunes by Woody Guthrie, Johnny Cash, John Hartford, Tim Hardin, Donovan, and Buffy Sainte-Marie. They recorded Dylan songs including "Rainy Day Women #12 & 35" and "Like a Rolling Stone." Their albums included *Songs of the Famous Carter Family* (1961), recorded with Mother Maybelle Carter, and

Folksongs of Our Land (1962). The chasm between traditional bluegrass and progressive sounds, however, factored in the group's split by the end of the decade.

Flatt remained on a similar path with Lester Flatt & the Nashville Grass until his passing in 1979. Curly Seckler (1919-2017) led the band for another fifteen years. "Curly had a great sense of humor," said Penny Parsons, author of *Foggy Mountain Troubadour: The Life and Music of Curly Seckler* (2016). "It came across onstage and audiences loved him. The duets he did with Lester were amazing. He could anticipate when Lester took a long or short breath."

Continuing to push the limits, Scruggs formed the Earl Scruggs Revue with his sons Gary and Randy (youngest son Steve joined later). "There was quite a bit of picking at home," remembered Gary Scruggs (1949-). "Randy [1953-] and I jammed together, and when Dad was home, he'd join in. Steve [1958-92] began playing music after I moved out."

Scruggs' schedule kept him on the go. "When Flatt & Scruggs were performing the six-days-a-week Martha White-sponsored television shows live," said Gary, "I didn't see him much, just on Saturdays when they'd be in Nashville to do the six P.M. WSM-TV show and the *Grand Ole Opry*. The schedule was grueling. It was long before the interstate was completed. Travel was on two-lane blacktop roads and they were averaging 2,500 miles a week."

Even after Flatt & Scruggs began taping their show, the banjo player was "on the road more than at home," remembered his son. "They were no longer restricted to the live-TV circuit so they expanded their touring to all over the United States."

Scruggs was a true innovator. Robert Shelton of the *NY Times* wrote, "Earl Scruggs bears about the same relationship to the five-string banjo that Paganini does to the violin."[2]

"Dad stressed the importance of making the melody stand out among the flurry of notes he played in his Scruggs-style picking," said Gary. "I enjoy watching the TV shows; he looked relaxed and made it look easy. Banjo players talk about Dad's mastery of timing, tone, and taste."

During school vacations, the Scruggs brothers traveled with their father. "I enjoyed seeing band members interacting with one another," Gary recalled. "They were a very close-knit group."

In October 1955, the Scruggs family was heading to NC. Earl's brother, Horace, had called to inform him that their mother had had a serious stroke. "We were driving near Knoxville," remembered Gary, "when another car ran a stop sign or traffic light. Our car plowed into it. Randy and I had minor bruises but Mom and Dad sustained serious injuries. Dad broke both hips and was off the road for months. His injuries made it difficult for him to travel in a car, as Flatt & Scruggs had done for years, and led them to buy a used bus. They replaced the seats in the back with bunkbeds."

The accident also spurred the banjo player to learn to pilot a small airplane so he could fly to shows. "He was flying back to Nashville," said his son, "after an Earl Scruggs Revue concert, when he crashed. He suffered a broken left wrist, a broken left ankle, and a broken nose. The injuries caused him to be off the road for weeks but it didn't deter his love of flying. He continued to pilot a small twin-engine plane until the late 1990s, flying for pleasure and as a volunteer delivering blood on behalf of the Red Cross."

At the inaugural Newport Folk Festival in 1959, Hylo Brown and the Timberliners backed Scruggs. The banjo player returned with Flatt and the Foggy Mountain Boys a year later and in 1966. "One of Dad's last concerts was the 2011 Newport Folk Festival," said Gary. "I was there as part of his Family & Friends band. Pete Seeger sat in a chair on the side of the stage and listened."

Raised on a Grant, TN farm, about forty miles east of Nashville, Louise Scruggs (1927-2006) had incredible business savvy. "Bill Monroe wasn't as organized as Flatt & Scruggs," Del McCoury told me. "He wasn't a businessman. Someone walked up to him one time and asked, 'Can you tell me what bluegrass music is?' Bill thought for a minute and said, 'You've got to ask Louise Scruggs.'"

"Dad turned booking-agent duties over to Mom in 1955," noted Gary, "when the music business was exclusively a man's world. She gradually took on managerial duties. Along with Lester and Dad, she cofounded and ran the company that published Flatt & Scruggs material. She had input into song material and suggested concepts for several albums. When rock and roll was dominating the airwaves, Flatt & Scruggs remained busy, thanks to Mom. She marketed them as part of the folk-music movement."

The Beverly Hillbillies propelled them to superstardom, but when creator/producer Paul Henning first suggested that Flatt & Scruggs perform its theme song ("The Ballad of Jed Clampett"), "Mom immediately turned him down," recalled Gary. "She didn't like the connotation of the word 'hillbillies.' [Henning] didn't give up and talked her into viewing the pilot. He wanted her to see the Clampett family, especially Jed, portrayed in a respectful manner and as people who could compete in a sophisticated environment. After she viewed the pilot, with Dad and Lester, they accepted Henning's request. A singer from CA [Jerry Scoggins] sang the lyrics."

Debuting on CBS-TV in September 1962, *The Beverly Hillbillies* was an immediate hit. "It was Mom's idea to rerecord the song with Lester singing," said Gary. "Flatt & Scruggs' version became the first bluegrass record to reach number one on *Billboard*'s Hot Country Singles chart."

Flatt & Scruggs recorded the theme of *Beverly Hillbillies* spinoff *Petticoat Junction* and broke into country music's top ten with "Pearl, Pearl, Pearl," about the show's main character.

Recorded at Flatt & Scruggs' December 8, 1962, Carnegie Hall concert, a live thirteen-song sampling released shortly afterwards. The complete thirty-two tracks came out in 1998. "My mother was aware of the prestige of the booking," remembered Gary, "and wanted it documented. She called Don Law [head of Columbia's Nashville branch and executive producer of Flatt & Scruggs' records] and requested that Columbia record the concert. He answered by saying that he didn't know how it could be done. Mom responded, and I'm paraphrasing, 'Get engineers to bring a tape recorder and a few microphones and tape it.'"

Flatt & Scruggs played their final show on the *Grand Ole Opry* on Saturday, February 22, 1969. They announced their split on March 11, a few days before winning the "Best Country Performance, Duo or Group— Vocal or Instrumental" Grammy for their performance of "Foggy Mountain Breakdown" in *Bonnie and Clyde*. The Earl Scruggs Revue came together a few weeks later. "I was a sophomore at Vanderbilt and Randy was a sophomore in high school," said Gary. "Mom and Dad put a premium on education so it wasn't until 1971, after we graduated, that the Revue came into full-time existence."

The two oldest Scruggs brothers released two duo albums. *All the Way Home* came out in 1970. "It was largely covers of songs we liked," said Gary. "If I had to categorize our second album, *The Scruggs Brothers* [1972], some of it was country-rock and some what is now considered Americana. Dad played banjo on 'Hobo's Lullaby' and 'Trousdale Ferry Rag.'"

The Nitty Gritty Dirt Band covered "Randy Lynn Rag" on *Uncle Charlie & His Dog Teddy*. When they performed at Vanderbilt University, in 1970, Gary invited his parents to the concert. "I arranged for a meeting with the band prior to their performance," he recalled, "and we quickly became friends."

The Earl Scruggs Revue was booked for a week at Tulagi's music club, in Boulder, in June 1971. The Nitty Gritty Dirt Band's John McEuen attended every show. On the last night, McEuen brought his bandmate, Jeff Hanna. "We jammed late into the night at the motel," recalled Gary.

During the jam, McEuen, Hanna, and Scruggs discussed recording *Will the Circle Be Unbroken* (1972). "John's feet were off the floor for a while," remembered Hanna. "Earl said something like, 'If you guys would ever like to cut a track, I'd love to get in the studio with you.' We all filed that away as something that would be cool to do. John's brother, Bill, was our producer . . . he came up with this concept of doing a record with these people who were our heroes."[3]

"Dad was very helpful in reaching out to Roy Acuff, Mother Maybelle Carter, and Jimmy Martin," said Gary, "and inviting them to participate."

The triple album revised Scruggs' image. Airing on PBS in January 1971, *Earl Scruggs: His Family and Friends* also presented the banjo player "in a much different light," said Gary. "Guests including Bob Dylan, Joan Baez, and the Byrds helped to change the perception of Dad being just a country or bluegrass artist."

The ninety-minute documentary included a moog synthesizer playing "Foggy Mountain Breakdown" and a segment on the Revue's appearance at the November 15, 1969, Vietnam Moratorium, in Washington, DC, along with Arlo Guthrie, Pete Seeger, and Peter, Paul and Mary. "We were the only country-music band at the protest," remembered Gary, "and, as far as I know, the only Nashville act to voice opposition to that war."

Scruggs remained active until shortly before his passing from natural causes on March 28, 2012. "Béla Fleck, Sam Bush, Jerry Douglas, and I went to Earl's house in early 2012," said Pat Enright. "Earl was really sick. We spent a day with him playing music. As bad off as he was, his playing was still recognizable."

"During his last years," Gary recalled, "[Scruggs] remained friendly, modest, and sociable. My mother started a tradition of a combination birthday/picking party to celebrate his birthday in early January. After she passed, my cousin Grace Constant (whose mother was Dad's sister Ruby) and I continued that tradition. At Dad's last birthday picking party, there were 150 guests; he enjoyed seeing them all."

The banjo player's funeral service took place at the Ryman Auditorium, site of his wife's funeral in February 2006. "It was a fitting place," said Gary. "It was where Mom and Dad met. Eddie Stubbs officiated over the service and delivered the main eulogy. The Del McCoury Band, the Whites, Béla Fleck, Emmylou Harris, John McEuen, Marty Stuart, Vince Gill, and Patty Loveless performed. [Former Scruggs Revue member] Charlie Daniels spoke about what Dad meant to him. Pallbearers consisted of band and crew. WSM broadcast the service."

The Country Music Hall of Fame inducted Flatt and Scruggs in 1985. Six years later, the IBMA Bluegrass Hall of Fame inducted them, individually, with Monroe, as its first three inductees. The Country Music Hall of Fame held a Louise Scruggs Memorial Forum in 2007. The IBMA Hall of Fame inducted her in 2010.

Memorabilia pertaining to Scruggs and the Piedmont region displays at the Earl Scruggs Center: Music & Stories from the American South, in an "old courthouse in the middle of Shelby's town square," said Gary. "Dad was always willing to share his knowledge of music and the five-string banjo, and he took time to answer people's questions or show them how to play a banjo lick. His instructional book, *Earl Scruggs and the 5-String Banjo,* has been a valuable learning tool."

Gary's son with country singer Gail Davies, Earl's grandson, Christopher Alan "Chris" Davies-Scruggs (1982-), played guitar and sang for BR5-49 from 2002 to 2005. Since 2015, he's played bass for Marty Stuart's Fabulous Superlatives and led his own band, Chris Scruggs & the Stone Fox 5.

Chapter 3

Voice with a Heart

Crimora, VA-born Malcolm "Mac" Wiseman (1925-) has set the standard for bluegrass singing for more than six decades. In addition to dozens of solo bluegrass and country albums, the ex-Foggy Mountain Boy/Blue Grass Boy's discography includes recordings with the Osborne Brothers, clarinet/saxophone player Woody Herman, Doc Watson, Del McCoury, Johnny Cash, Merle Haggard, Charlie Daniels, and John Prine. "When I was young," Wiseman recalled, "radio was in its infancy. None of the stations paid salaries. They gave us airtime. They sold commercials to the local car dealers and businesses around town and kept all the revenue, but you had to get on the radio and build enough interest to draw a crowd when you played. You had to let people get familiar with your music."

Wiseman's "mom could read shape notes," he remembered, "and she played the old, pump organ at home and the piano for church services. My dad didn't play anything but we had one of the first hand-wound phonographs and one of the first radios in our community. I was but three or four years old. I fell in love with the old story-type songs.

"We moved to my mother's old home place when things got tough. My dad had to stand on lines to get work. Mom and I worked the sixty-five-acre farm, raising what we ate and drying it on the roof. In the winter, she sat in front of the radio, quilting. A program would come on and she would reach up, get her notebook, and jot down a verse or two of a song. A few days later, she would listen again and get the rest of it. She left me fourteen notebooks with songs in her handwriting. I treasure them very much."

Contracting polio at six months, Wiseman didn't walk until he was two. One leg was shorter than the other. "I wore shoes out on the side instead of the sole," he said. "I was thirteen when I reached my maximum growth. I went to Charlottesville to have a couple of corrective surgeries."

After studying broadcasting at Shenandoah Conservatory, Wiseman worked at WSVA in Harrisonburg, VA. "I did everything," he recalled, "from writing copy and operating the board to reading the news and weather. It was a skeleton crew because of the war, but I saw that the program director and station manager were driving Chevrolets and the hillbillies were driving Cadillacs. I figured I was in the wrong end of it."

Country music radio pioneer Oby Edgar "Buddy" Starcher took Wiseman under his wing. "I learned a lot from him," said Wiseman. "We were staunch friends up to his demise in 2001. He had a show on WSVA and he'd have me sing. If I were able to get back for my morning radio job, he'd ask me to play gigs with him and pay me five dollars a night."

Pike County, KY-born banjo player/vocalist Lois LaVerne "Molly O'Day" Williamson, leader of Wiseman's first professional band, "was the loveliest lady," he remembered, "a real country girl, the female Hank Williams."

When Bristol, TN's WCYB launched the six-day-a-week *Farm and Fun Time* in 1946, Wiseman signed on as one of its first acts, along with the Stanley Brothers and Curly King and the Tennessee Hilltoppers. Monroe was a frequent listener. "Bill would say to Earl [Scruggs], 'Wake me up when that Wiseman boy comes on,'" said Don Bryant of *Bluegrass Unlimited*. "Another time, according to Mac, Bill was making a guest spot on the Bristol station where Mac was working at the time and, in Lester [Flatt] and Earl's presence, said to Mac on the air, 'If you ever want to be on the *Opry*, let me know.'"[1]

Wiseman made plans after a few months to return to Crimora "to work in the produce business during the winter." Before leaving, he stopped at the WCYB studio. "I had already turned in my notice," he said. "Someone came over to me and introduced himself. It was Earl Scruggs. He had just left the Blue Grass Boys and wanted a job with me. I explained how I didn't think I could make money by playing music and he accepted that. Then, in the spring of 1948, he called again from Hickory, NC, where Jim Shumate lived. He wanted Shumate to play fiddle for him, but [Shumate] was working at a furniture store and wasn't going to leave until he knew that the Foggy Mountain Boys would fly."

Wiseman joined the Foggy Mountain Boys in Hickory but "we weren't doing well," he recalled, "just a show on a 5,000-watt radio station. I suggested we audition for WCYB, which we did. They hired us on the spot."

The arrangement ended after a few months. "Earl came to me before the noontime show," Wiseman recalled, "and said, 'Lester's talking about putting the boys on salary.' I told him, 'It's the wrong time of year to start paying a salary; it slows down in the winter,' and he said, 'It means you too.' I said, 'If it means me, take my notice right now.' They accepted it."

Before leaving, Wiseman participated in Flatt & Scruggs' first recording session. "We went to Knoxville to record at a radio station, WROL," he said, "and did 'We'll Meet Again Sweetheart,' 'My Cabin in Caroline,' and two gospel quartets, 'God Loves His Children' and 'I'm Going to Make Heaven My Home.'"

The Foggy Mountain Boys also recorded an audition tape to send to WWVA. "Lester did the emceeing," said Wiseman, "and I did the commercials. We finally heard back after I turned in my notice: 'We'd like to have the Foggy Mountain Boys but we've definitely got to have the feller who did the commercials.' They tried to get me to come back but I said, 'No, I can't do that.'"

Wiseman worked with Bill Carlisle and James & Martha (Carson) on Atlanta's WSB until "that show folded in the spring of 1949," he recalled, "and I called Monroe and asked if his invitation was still open. He said, 'Meet me in Alabama on Friday.'"

Spending eight months as a Blue Grass Boy, Wiseman "wasn't the greatest fan of Monroe's music," he recalled, "but I wanted to be on the *Opry*—hell or high water."

During his first show, Monroe asked Wiseman what he was going to sing. "The blood drained right out of me," Wiseman remembered. "I didn't know any of his songs except for a couple of tunes that Clyde Moody had sung. With the Foggy Mountain Boys, Lester sang any Monroe tunes we did. [Monroe] never criticized me and I learned his music very quickly."

Wiseman's first solo single, "'Tis Sweet to Be Remembered," released in 1951. "My music wasn't called bluegrass yet," he said. "It was just mountain music, hillbilly music. I didn't have a banjo in my band until just prior to going to the *Louisiana Hayride* in the mid-fifties. I used fiddle, mandolin, and [Merle] Travis-style guitar picking. Joe Medford came to me right out of high school. He played banjo like Scruggs so I hired him."

Scoring a top-ten hit with "The Ballad of Davy Crockett" in 1955, Wiseman followed with a country hit—"Jimmy Brown, the Newsboy"—in 1959. Based on an 1875 tune by Louisville-born William Shakespeare "WS" Hays, the Carter Family recorded it in 1931. Flatt & Scruggs covered it twenty years later. "[My record] couldn't knock the Browns out of first place," said Wiseman. "They had 'The Bells (Little Jimmy Brown)' and people were confused."

Behind the scenes, Wiseman was the first secretary-treasurer of the Country Music Association (CMA) in 1958. He was directing Dot Records' country-music division when he met Merle Travis. "There was a three-hour live television show, *Town Hall Party,*" Wiseman recalled. "Since I was working an office job, and didn't have to go on the road, I became a regular on that show every Saturday night, along with Johnny Bond, Joe Maphis, Tex Ritter, Fiddlin' Kate, and Merle. He and I had a thing going for a long time. He'd try to stump me with old songs. Finally, he gave up."

Wiseman, Travis, and "Fiddlin'" Red Herron collaborated on *The Clayton*

McMichen Story in 1982. The former Skillet Licker fiddler had been "on the radio every afternoon after I got home from school," remembered Wiseman. "I fell in love with his music, especially his ballads."

Enthused to have the Osborne Brothers accompanying him on *A Master at Work* (1966), Wiseman sang the first six songs by himself. "As we were leaving the studio," he recalled, "Bobby said, 'I'd be glad to sing with you.' The next six sides were duets. We did a double album together [*The Essential Bluegrass Album*] in 1979."

Wiseman's biggest hit was a 1960 cover of "One Mint Julep." Written by Rudy Toombs, it had been a top-two hit for R&B vocal group the Clovers in 1952. Wiseman scored a top-forty country hit with "(If I Had) Johnny's Cash and Charlie's Pride," by NY songwriter Cy Coben, in 1969.

Wiseman recorded several albums with Chubby Wise. "He played the longest bow," he recalled, "and could tear into a breakdown. We did an album [*Shares "Precious Memories,"* 2001] with 'Bashful Brother' Oswald [the Dobro player of Roy Acuff's Smoky Mountain Boys], not too long before [Oswald] passed."

Wiseman recorded *Del, Doc, and Mac* (1998) with Doc Watson and Del McCoury and joined Bobby Osborne and Jim Silvers for *The 3 Tenors of Bluegrass* (2000). "They were just good old boys," he said, "friends of mine. [Producer] Scott Rouse went to college in New England. When he came back to Nashville, he wanted to record uptown bluegrass, what he called 'groove grass.' Scruggs was on some of it. We went into the studio with the Osbornes, Doc, and Del. People likely laughed us out of town when they heard what we were doing but then they fell in love with it."

At Nashville's Land Between the Lakes, a band with "a fabulous fiddler" backed Wiseman. "Everything I vamped," he recalled, "she played melody to it. I commented to her that I enjoyed her work. Soon afterwards, I was in the middle of recording when my producer said, 'Woody Herman wants to do a country record and he wants you to do it with him.' That woman playing fiddle was his daughter."

Wiseman recorded *Standard Songs for Average People* (2007) with John Prine. "At Earl Scruggs' birthday party," Wiseman explained, "Fergie Ferguson, who runs Prine's Butcher Shoppe Recording Studio, told me, 'If you don't come down and see John, he'll kick your butt.' I called John and we got together at his studio. Fergie had the engineer play the backing track from one of John's songs and John and I sang it together. We looked at each other and said, 'We ought to do more of this.'"

Prine, Alison Krauss, Jim Lauderdale, Shawn Camp, Sierra Hull, and Ronnie Bowman appeared on Wiseman's *I Sang the Song: Life of the Voice with a Heart* (2017). "We cut ten new songs," he said, "my life story in song."

Chapter 4

Country Boy Rock and Roll

Monroe's first choice to replace Stringbean in 1945, Don Reno turned him down. "My uncle Harley joined the army," explained Reno's oldest son, Ronnie (1947-), "and Dad thought he should go with him. They could serve their time together. Of course, the first thing they did was separate them."

Discharged in 1947, Reno was the logical replacement for Scruggs a year later. "One night, as Monroe performed, Reno strapped on his banjo and walked right onto the stage. A surprised, but delighted Bill Monroe exclaimed, 'Where you been, boy? I've been looking for you.'"[1]

Reno played with the Blue Grass Boys for nearly a year and a half before Franklin County, VA-born Rudy Lyle (1930-85) replaced him in July 1949. He forged a longer-lasting bond with Asheville-born guitarist/vocalist Arthur Lee "Red" Smiley (1925-72). Meeting on the *Grand Ole Opry,* in 1950, when Smiley played with Tommy Magness's Tennessee Buddies, they recorded (with Magness on fiddle) a year later. They continued mixing sacred songs, Civil War-era songs, Cowboy Copas tunes, and lightning-fast instrumentals until Smiley's retirement in 1964. Reno would then team with Marion, VA-born George William "Bill" Harrell (1934-96), a mandolinist who had played with him and Smiley in the mid-fifties. Smiley rejoined his old partner in 1969 but succumbed to diabetes on January 2, 1972. Separating from Reno amidst personal conflicts, in 1977, Harrell recalled, "Promoters were hesitant about booking our different bands on the same day at a festival."[2]

Raised on a Clyde, NC farm, Reno played banjo from the age of five (his older brother had a band). "When Dad started," said Ronnie, "he played a lot like Earl Scruggs. They both idolized Snuffy Jenkins, and learned the three-finger roll from him, but Dad was also a guitar player and could play single-stringed music. He adapted that to the banjo. It sounded like he was using a flatpick but he was actually using a thumb pick and a finger pick."

Reno's guitar solo on "Country Boy Rock and Roll" (1956) was a bluegrass first. "I had an album [*Golden Guitar*] with [Reno] doing all this flatpicking," said Roland White. "Clarence [White] listened to that."

"[Reno] was the only one flatpicking a guitar at the time," said Alan Munde. "It was a more rural approach, kind of rough."

Playing banjo for Arthur "Guitar Boogie" Smith in 1940, Reno recorded with Woody Guthrie two years later. Reno played on Smith's "Feuding Banjos" (credited to the Rambler Trio) in 1955. When Eric Weissberg and Steve Mandell used their recording, in 1972, as the basis for "Dueling Banjos," on the soundtrack of *Deliverance*, Smith sued for copyright infringement. "He didn't disclose how much money he'd made from the movie lawsuit," reported the *Charlotte Observer*, "[but] Smith pointed to a picture of a forty-two-foot yacht on the wall of his office and noted Warner Bros. had bought the boat for him." Reno and Smith would reunite for *Feudin' Again* (1979).

Retreating to his Lynchburg, VA farm, Reno resurfaced, in the mid-seventies, with Frank Wakefield, Seattle-born David Nelson (1943-), Chubby Wise, and Pat Campbell as the Good Old Boys. He formed a band with his sons—Don Wayne, Dale, and Ronnie—by decade's end. After his death (October 16, 1984), they would continue as the Reno Brothers.

Bluegrass's "youngest old-timer," Ronnie Reno was seven years old when he joined his father and Smiley onstage on *Old Dominion Barn Dance* in 1954. "I was a young feller," he said, "but I just went up and started singing. My mom wouldn't let me go with them until she felt comfortable I'd be all right."

Reno joined his father's band in 1960. "Mandolin was the only instrument left," he recalled. "I had to play it to get in the band. I was so small; it fit me very well. Dad was a great mandolin player. He could play everything that Bill Monroe played; he started showing it to me. We had a fiddle player, Mack Magaha, who they called 'The Dancing Fiddle Player.' He worked for many years with Dad and Red and then played with Porter Wagoner. He knew old-time fiddle tunes and showed them to me."

Weathering the era of rock and roll, Reno & Smiley "had an hour-and-a-half morning TV show in Roanoke starting in 1957," said Ronnie. "We were able to stay busy while other bands were suffering, trying to find venues and reinventing themselves."

Reno & Smiley recorded "country tunes, mountain music, and traditional music" for Syd Nathan's King Records. The Stanley Brothers were also there but so were R&B acts such as Hank Ballard and James Brown. "King supplied jukeboxes at truck stops and restaurants," explained Ronnie, "and could get their music out."

After splitting from Smiley, in 1964, father and son started the Don Reno Band. Smiley continued the TV show for another five years. Between tours with his father, Ronnie played upright bass for Bobby and Sonny Osborne. "We were on our way to Detroit," he recalled, "when the bus broke down in Dayton. The Osbornes' father picked us up. We couldn't fit the bass in his car so I left it on the bus. There was a country band opening for us who had an electric bass player. I said, 'Sonny, do you want me to play electric bass?' After that, he and his brother fell in love with the electric bass. It was a bigger sound. They later added drums. We were competing with country acts."

Ronnie missed the November 1967 "Rocky Top" session. "The Osborne Brothers did it after Dad and I teamed with Bill Harrell," he said. "I came back a year later and that tune took us from small venues and nightclubs to concert stages. It made their career. It's become one of the biggest songs of all time."

The Osborne Brothers were the CMA's "Vocal Group of the Year" in 1973. Propelled by "Okie from Muskogee," Merle Haggard won "just about every other award." Haggard, known for straightahead country music, "admired Bill Monroe," said Ronnie, "and, of course, Monroe admired him."

The Osbornes opened for the Bakersfield superstar for three weeks, but Ronnie's thoughts began to drift. "When you're young," he said, "you want to do all these things. I had been with Bobby and Sonny for four and a half years and wanted to move on. I didn't have any intention of going with Merle but he heard that I left and called. The opportunity was too good not to take. I opened his shows for years. He was a force in helping me in the music industry."

Ronnie produced Haggard's *The Bluegrass Sessions* (2007) and his album with Wiseman, *Timeless* (2015). "I put all the players together," he said. "They were some of the greatest in Nashville—Carl Jackson, Marty Stuart. Sonya and Becky Isaacs sang harmonies. Their brother, Ben, played bass. Rob Ickes played Dobro. Merle loved bluegrass music and so did Conway Twitty. I taught Conway to yodel like Bill Monroe. He had a top-two country hit with my song, 'Boogie Grass Band' [1978]."

Ronnie continued to play bluegrass. "Merle didn't work during the summer," he explained, "because he liked to fish. It left the summer open for me. I'd go to festivals and do things with my father."

After Ronnie left Haggard in 1981, "Dad, my two brothers, and I started doing two tours a year," he said, "one in the spring and another in the fall. We'd work our way across the country, spend a week or so in CA, and work our way back. My father only lived three years after I left Merle but we did quite a few things together. Dad never took a backseat with his playing. Years of traveling, smoking, and eating bad affected his voice but not his picking. His playing was superb to the day he passed."

The Reno Brothers stayed together for sixteen years. "Dad asked me to look after the boys when he got sick," said Ronnie. "There's quite a span between my brothers and me—fourteen years between Dale and me, and sixteen years between Don Wayne and me. We have different mothers. We had tight brother harmonies but they wanted to expand their music. They got together with Hayseed Dixie for twelve years—it was wild—but the art form was incredible."

Ronnie has hosted *Reno's Old Time Music Festival* on the RFD/Family Network since April 2012. "We've done over two hundred shows," he said, "with amazing guests like Bill Monroe, Ralph Stanley, the Osborne Brothers, Jim & Jesse, and newer acts like the Lonesome River Band and IIIrd Tyme Out."

Chapter 5

Rain and Snow

The lead singer/guitarist for the Blue Grass Boys from 1963 to 1964, Franklin Delano "Del" McCoury (1939-) was the IBMA's "Male Vocalist of the Year" in 1991, '92, and '93. The Del McCoury Band, with his sons—Ronnie (1967-) and Robin Floyd "Rob" (1971-)—was "Entertainer of the Year" from 1994 to 1997. Ronnie was "Mandolin Player of the Year" eight straight years while Ashland, KY-born Jason Carter (1973-), who joined in 1992, is a three-time "Fiddle Player of the Year." Nominated for ten Grammys, McCoury scored "Best Bluegrass Album" awards for *The Company We Keep* (2006) and *The Streets of Baltimore* (2013).

Del and Dawg: Live (2016) reunited McCoury with David "Dawg" Grisman (1945-), the Hackensack, NJ-born son of a trombonist. Playing piano from the age of seven, Grisman had temporarily withdrawn from music after his father's death when he was ten. He acquired a mandolin at sixteen and became a regular at the Sunday-afternoon picking sessions in Greenwich Village's Washington Square Park.

Grisman came under the mentorship of Ralph Rinzler (1934-94), the NJ-born son of a Russian-Jewish doctor. Graduating from Swarthmore College in 1956, Rinzler spent seven years studying with traditional Southeastern musicians. His middle-school art teacher had been Grisman's mother. Two years old when they met, Grisman "learned so much from him." He told *No Depression,* "He lived two blocks away from me. Ralph [would] come home from work late and we'd go over there at around 10:30 at night. He turned us on to all kinds of music, playing tapes and playing music with us. At midnight, without fail, the phone would ring. It would wake up Ralph's dad, who was a doctor, and he would get mad, and I'd have to go home."[1]

Between classes at NY University, in 1963, Grisman played with the Even Dozen Jug Band. The group recorded only one album but its members would make history. Leader of the Lovin' Spoonful in the sixties, John Sebastian scored solo success in the seventies. He reunited with Grisman

David Grisman, 2016

and recorded a duo album, *Satisfied* (2007). Maria Muldaur (D'Amato) joined Jim Kweskin's Jug Band, which included her then-husband Geoff Muldaur, and later became a respected, roots-oriented soloist. Steve Katz became a founding member of the Blues Project and Blood, Sweat & Tears. Stefan Grossman broke new ground with his blues/ragtime guitar playing, while Joshua Rifkin gained fame by rearranging Scott Joplin ragtime classics.

Recording a Red Allen jam session at Frank Wakefield's Hyattsville, MD home on April 11, 1963 (and releasing it thirty-one years later as *The Kitchen Tapes*), Grisman joined Allen's Kentuckians in 1966. He had already recorded the jazz-meets-bluegrass *Early Dawg* (1964) with Del (guitar) and Jerry (bass) McCoury and Bill Keith (banjo). Jerry Garcia, whom Grisman met at a Monroe concert in Everson, PA's Sunset Park, gave him the name "Dawg." "I played with David and my brother at a college in Troy, NY fifty years ago," said Del McCoury in November 2016. "The banjo player was Winnie Winston. Chris Warner replaced Winnie when we played at Carlton Haney's bluegrass festival. We weren't there the first year [1965] but we came the second. We weren't booked but Ralph Rinzler was emceeing and I knew him. I asked if we could play and he said, 'I'll put you on last.' We played the Birchmere Hotel the next night.

Del McCoury, 2016

"David was mischievous when we met. Ralph had the Blue Grass Boys stay at his house. David's parents were away on vacation. My brother, Jerry, was with me but he didn't usually travel with us. He's three years younger so he would have been fifteen. It was hard to wake him one morning; we'd been up almost all night. David threw a cherry bomb under his bed.

"I didn't know David played until he and my brother were playing with Red Allen. He asked Jerry, after I quit Bill [Monroe], if I'd play with him. He was already a great mandolin player."

Grisman consistently expanded musical possibilities. "I enjoy classical music, Latin, folk, and ethnic music too," he told one interviewer. " . . . I even wrote a string quartet piece and did commercial music. . . . Bluegrass music has been perfected and you can't play better than Bill Monroe, Flatt & Scruggs, and The Stanley Brothers."[2]

He continued to *No Depression,* "It's been a lifetime of listening . . . drawing on all these influences . . . figuring out what Bill Monroe played, what Jesse McReynolds played, learning a Billy Strayhorn tune, a Django Reinhardt tune, learning a Django Reinhardt tune from Stephane Grappelli, learning a Django Reinhardt tune from Svend Asmussen, or whatever other situation you find yourself in."

York, PA-born McCoury grew up listening to the *Grand Ole Opry* and the *Old Dominion Barn Dance.* "We got our bluegrass that way," he said, "from the radio."

McCoury's nine-year-older brother, Grover Cleveland ("G.C."), taught him to play guitar when he was nine. "G.C. brought home a record by Flatt & Scruggs in 1950," he remembered. "When I heard 'Roll in My Sweet Baby's Arms,' I decided to take up the banjo."

Keith Daniels played an essential role in the Capitol District's bluegrass scene. "[Daniels] owned a restaurant on the outskirts of Washington, DC," McCoury recalled, "and played with the Stevens Brothers on a Chambersburg radio station. He got me to join that band but before long, he said, 'Let's quit. I'll get us another band.' He hired a bassist, a guitarist, and a Dobro player and put together the Blue Ridge Ramblers. He could play anything—guitar, banjo, fiddle, and mandolin—but he was also a good salesperson. We played on the *Old Dominion Barn Dance*. Don Owens had a show on Richmond's channel 5 with the Bluegrass Champs [the Stoneman Family]. Keith got us on there as guests."

Musicians including John Duffey, Charlie Waller, William Hundley "Bill" Emerson, Jr., and Eros, LA-born Bernarr Graham "Buzz Busby" Busbice (1933-2003) gathered in the basement of Daniels' restaurant to jam. "That's where a lot of us met," said McCoury. "Charlie asked me, 'Do you know the first three-finger banjo picker I played with?' It was Keith Daniels—my old boss. This was in the early fifties, before the Country Gentlemen. Charlie had come up from LA and was playing with Buzz. Don Stover played in that band, along with Bill Harrell.

"The rival band in Baltimore was Earl Taylor and the Stony Mountain Boys. I bought my first good banjo from Walt Helmsley. They were playing seven nights a week with a matinee on Sunday. Earl told me one night he saw someone at a table for two. He knew everybody who came in the bar but this person was a stranger. After finishing, he was packing up. He put his mandolin in its case, turned around, and this person was standing there with his hand held out. He said, 'My name is Alan Lomax and I'm going to put you in Carnegie Hall.' Earl said, 'I've heard that story before.' Promoters will promise everything but he did it."

McCoury first played with Monroe, in February 1963, when the mandolinist traveled only with bassist Bessie Lee Mauldin and fiddler Kenny Baker. "I was playing with Jack Cook at the Chapel Café in Baltimore," he remembered, "when someone walked in, wearing a big white hat. I said, 'That looks like Bill Monroe but he wouldn't be in this place,' but sure enough, it was. He came to talk to Jack about going to NY. Jack said, 'Have you got a banjo player?' When Bill said no, he said, 'We'll take Del with us.'"

The situation worked well. Following the NY show, Monroe offered McCoury a job. He turned it down. "I liked playing with Jack," he explained, "so I didn't accept right away."

McCoury waited a month before going to Nashville to see Monroe. "I got a room at the Clarkson Hotel," he remembered, "and called him. He said, 'I'll come in the morning.' I waited in the lobby until he came. Bill Keith came walking in, too. Monroe took both of us to a restaurant and bought us breakfast. He didn't talk a whole lot. We went next door to the National Life and Health Insurance building and took an elevator to a floor where he had a room. He settled for me on guitar and Keith [who took the name Brad] on banjo. I had never heard anyone play like him. He had a style of his own. He played Scruggs style, which is what I played, but Don Stover also influenced him."

McCoury "hadn't gone to Nashville to play guitar, but I was 700 miles from home," he said. "I wound up lasting longer than Keith did. He quit in the summer, in the middle of a tour, and went back to Boston. Monroe asked if I knew any banjo players and I said, 'I don't know a soul here but I know a guy in York County [Steve Arkin].' He said, 'Let's call him,' so we went to a phone booth. I dialed the number and let Bill talk. Afterwards, he walked out of the phone booth and we started walking up the street. 'What'd he say, Bill?' 'He'll be here in the morning.' Then, Kenny Baker quit. Bill had problems keeping musicians."

During a week off the road, McCoury returned home to PA. Before he left, Monroe instructed him to keep his eyes open for a fiddle player. McCoury went to see Cook's band at "the same little old bar." "Billy Baker was playing fiddle," he remembered. "I told him Monroe needed a fiddle player and he said, 'I'll go back with you.'"

McCoury became a member of the *Grand Ole Opry* in 2003. "The *Opry* means a lot to me," he said. "I listened to it with my dad and my brothers every Saturday night before we got a TV in 1948."

On his first *Opry* appearance, McCoury sang but didn't play a note. "I wasn't in the union yet," he said. "Monroe got Keith in a day after we got there because he had tunes he wanted to record but I wasn't on the recording. He got Benny Williams to play guitar. When we played on the *Opry*, Bill said that I couldn't play the guitar. It seemed odd. I didn't know what to do with my hands. The next week, he took me to the union hall and signed me up."

Occasionally playing the Ash Grove, in L.A., for a week or two, McCoury met the Golden State Boys. "Hal Poindexter was the leader, guitar player, and lead singer," he said. "When they found out I played banjo, they offered me a job. I said, 'No, I'm satisfied with Bill.'"

The Blue Grass Boys traveled in a 1959 Oldsmobile station wagon. "That car was only four years old," said McCoury, "but it had 350,000 miles on it. My spot was between Bill and Kenny Baker. They had seniority so they sat by the window. The car had a hump in the middle. I'd cross my legs and put my head in my lap. I slept as if I was in a big featherbed. I couldn't do that today."

McCoury and Baker stayed at the Dillards' house for a week. "They told us that they were down to one can of Campbell's soup when they got that job with Andy Griffith," said McCoury. "I got to be great friends with them; they were so wild. Three of them were living in Topanga Canyon. The bass player [Mitch Jayne] was married so we didn't get to see him much. Every night, after we played at the Ash Grove, they'd pick Kenny and me up in a '56 Cadillac and take us to their house, where we'd party for the rest of the night. We never got any sleep. Other musicians would come—the White boys and the Gosdins liked Kenny Baker's fiddling—and we'd play all night. Monroe told me, one night, before I left the bar, 'You'd better get some sleep.' I wondered, 'How does he know we're not sleeping?' I was probably forgetting words of songs."

The first night at the Ash Grove, McCoury met Doc Watson. "Rinzler booked him to open our shows," he recalled. "He was blind but he came by himself. He and Bill sang some Monroe Brothers numbers together. He asked me to play rhythm guitar when he did his set. I said, 'I don't know what you're going to do.' 'I just play old fiddle tunes on the guitar.' I said, 'Okay, I'll give it a try.'"

McCoury told Baker about the Golden State Boys' invitation. "[Baker] said, 'Let's go,'" he remembered. "I said no, but he kept on me and finally talked me into it. I called Ray Gosdin and said, 'I'm thinking of coming but I have a fiddle player who wants to come too.' He said, 'I'll call you back in an hour.' When he called, he said, 'Bring him along.' I said, 'There's one more thing I've got to do—get married.' I hadn't told him about that before, but if I didn't do it, I was going to lose her. Within a week, I quit Bill, Jean and I got married, and I was on the West Coast. Everything was happening at once. We ran into a banjo player that Billy [Baker] knew, Steve Stephenson. Billy said, 'Go back to guitar. We'll get Steve to play banjo, find a bass player, and get a TV show [*The Worthington Dodge Show*].' His mind was working all the time."

The Golden State Boys hosted a Sunday-afternoon show in Huntington Park. "Everybody played on it," remembered McCoury, "people like Merle Haggard and Buck Owens, but my wife got terribly homesick. She'd get on the phone with her dad and cry. She had never been away. It never bothered me; I could be at home anywhere."

Shortly after returning East, McCoury received a call from Rinzler. "Come to Philadelphia," Rinzler instructed him. "The Greenbriar Boys are booked for two weeks and John Herald's alone."

"A windshield had dropped on Frank Wakefield's left hand," explained McCoury, "and broken all the bones. Bob Yellin had been in a car wreck and his lung had collapsed. Ralph was going to play mandolin and he wanted me to play guitar and sing."

After filling in with the Greenbriar Boys, McCoury reunited with Billy Baker and formed the Shady Valley Boys. "He moved thirty minutes from me," he said. "We played clubs around town."

When the group disbanded, McCoury put the Dixie Pals together. "I'll tell you about that name," he began. "We were playing in a club and someone said, 'What's the name of this band?' I didn't say anything because he was talking to my fiddle player. Then he said, 'You're the Dixie Pals.' I said, 'We are?' I hadn't thought of a name—we were just playing for fun—but it stuck. It stayed with me until Ronnie came in and the boys said, 'We should call it "The Del McCoury Band."' I was never a stickler about a name."

The new name wasn't the only change. "I loved the banjo," said McCoury, "but it was hard to find a good rhythm-guitar player. I could keep them tighter if I played guitar because they could follow my rhythm. I didn't brag on myself but I knew I had it. The most important part of music is timing."

Raising a family, McCoury "needed a steady paycheck," he said. "You couldn't make a lot of money playing clubs so I worked at my father-in-law's sawmill and then got a job with the logging operation owned by my wife's uncle. I learned everything regarding logging—cutting trees down, sawing on what they call the 'yard,' measuring logs, loading and unloading trucks, sharpening chainsaws, whatever came along. I did it until the kids got out of high school. All that time, I kept playing bluegrass festivals and recording. I lost a lot of sleep."

McCoury's sons played an increasing role in his music. "My band played in NY when the kids had Christmas vacation in 1979," recalled McCoury. "Monroe and the Lewis Family were on the show. I brought Ronnie. [Monroe] took a liking to him. I remember him taking his hat off and putting it on Ronnie. He laid his mandolin in his lap and said, 'Play me one.' Of course, Ronnie didn't know a thing about a mandolin yet; he was only twelve. I kept a mandolin in the luggage rack of my bus. When we were on the road, it was easy to take down and play. It needed repairs so Dick Smith, who played banjo, said, 'Let me take it home; I'll work on it.' I said, 'Okay, but you don't have to be in a hurry.' It wasn't long before Ronnie said, 'When are you going to get that mandolin back?' He kept on

Dick to get it fixed. Once we got it back, he never laid it down."

"When I was nine," Ronnie recalled, "I saw Marty Stuart. He was this young mandolinist—about seventeen—surrounded by all these older guys in a bluegrass band, Lester Flatt and Nashville Grass. I thought he was cool, and I thought if he could do it, maybe I could do it. That same year Bill Monroe came to our house, which got me thinking about playing mandolin."[3]

By the summer of 1980, McCoury, his oldest son, and Smith were playing with fiddler Sonny Miller. "Ronnie could play rhythm," McCoury said, "but I warned him, 'Don't try to play breaks.' As we rode along, Dick and Sonny showed Ronnie stuff. By the end of summer, he was taking breaks and playing instrumentals. He wasn't playing a good mandolin but he was getting a sound out of it. They have it in a case in the Ryman Auditorium."

McCoury's son Rob "started playing before Ronnie," he said. "He was playing banjo when he was nine. He was interested in that three-finger roll. After my brother quit, Rob played bass. When my banjo player [Paul Silvius] went back to Boston, I told Rob he was going to play banjo. He dreaded it; he was comfortable playing bass. He stepped right up, though, and learned it. It didn't take him long."

Recording *The McCoury Brothers* (1995), McCoury's sons took their own approach. "It gives us an outlet to try something different," said Ronnie, "sing different songs, and perform with different people . . . it allows us to be more like a jam band."

McCoury befriended Sam Bush early on. "I like what he does but I couldn't picture myself doing anything like it," he said. "He told me that I was the one who got him singing. We were playing Carlton Haney's festival. Sam was booked with his band [the Bluegrass Alliance]. He came to where I was jamming and I said, 'Play one with us.' He said, 'I can't; I mashed my finger in a car door'—one of his picking fingers. He couldn't play the mandolin. I said, 'You can sing, can't you?' and he said, 'I'll try.' That was the first time he sang a note in his life, he told me.

"It's the same with [Grisman]. He has no confidence in his singing. He said, 'If I sing something wrong, let me know. I know I'm not a good singer.' I said, 'No, man. I like singing tenor to your lead. Keep doing what you're doing.' David's a great showman. He's written some great melodies. He can direct a band with his hair. Of course, he doesn't have as much as he used to. We get along good but he and Sam don't—them both being mandolin players. They talk but they can't be together too long."

After his sons finished high school, McCoury and his wife "didn't owe anybody anything," he said. "Ricky Skaggs and Sharon White told me, 'Del, move to Nashville,' so we started thinking about it. We were in good enough shape that we could keep our house in PA. It's lonesome but we still have it. We looked for a house in Nashville. We thought that, if things didn't work out, we could sell it. We were there for ten years before Ricky told me his house was for sale. I didn't want to move again but Jean and I went to look at it and decided to buy it. Then, we had four houses."

McCoury's tour de force remains "Rain and Snow," a traditional murder ballad included in *English Folk Songs from the Southern Appalachians* (1917) and covered by the Grateful Dead on their first album. "I got it from Dick Staber, who played mandolin for me," McCoury said. "The version I heard had Peter Rowan singing. He hadn't recorded it yet. Dick and I worked on it, but by the time I recorded it, in late '71, I had another mandolin player—Donnie Eldreth."

McCoury's repertoire includes the Lovin' Spoonful's "Nashville Cats," by John Sebastian. "The only other people to cover it were Flatt & Scruggs," he said. "Jerry Douglas was producing me in the studio. I said, 'Jerry, I'd like to do 'Nashville Cats.' I didn't know all the words but I knew enough to sing it for him. He said, 'Let's try it.' When we played in Woodstock, John Sebastian came to the show. I asked if he'd sing it with us and he said, 'No, but I'll play it with you.'"

Rounder Records' Ken Irwin phoned Steve Earle, in 1998, seeking songs McCoury could record. Earle sent "If You Need a Fool." "It needed another verse," recalled McCoury, "so Steve wrote another verse. We put it on *Blue Side of Town.*"

McCoury heard Earle's "Copperhead Road" on the radio but he still "didn't know who he was" when they played together at the Station Inn. "He asked us to back him up," he remembered. "Afterwards, he said, 'Would you be interested in doing a record?' I said, 'I guess we would.' 'Great, I'll write some songs.' I thought it'd be at least a year away and forgot all about it. He called within a month and said, 'I've got the songs.' He had gone to Ireland and written. We went to a studio and recorded *The Mountain* [1999] and then toured—thirty days in the U.S. and thirty days in Europe. When we performed on *The Tonight Show*, we went from his 'I Still Carry You Around' into 'Nashville Cats.' The place went wild."

In 2000, the Del McCoury Band participated in a *Grand Ole Opry* package show and joined *O Brother, Where Art Thou?* soundtrack artists for the *Down from the Mountain* tour. "T Bone Burnett wanted me to sing in the movie," he recalled, "but I was overseas with Steve Earle and couldn't do it. We did the *Down from the Mountain* tour with John Hartford, Ricky Skaggs and his band, his wife, Sharon White, Alison Krauss and Union Station, Emmylou Harris, David Rawlings and Gillian Welch, Chris Thomas King and Colin Linden, and the Fairfield Four. Ralph Stanley was the 'biggie.'

Alison sang with him. Ralph sang 'Amazing Grace' and the whole troupe sang behind him. Vince Gill and Patty Loveless did the *Grand Ole Opry* tour with us. Eddie Stubbs emceed."   .

Appearing semiregularly at Roy and Rebecca Carter's High Sierra Music Festival, McCoury gave little thought to hosting a festival of his own. "I didn't want the headache," he remembered, "but my manager, Stan Strickland, said, 'Let me call Roy Carter and have him come to the East Coast. We'll see if we could find a good location.' By the time he flew in, Roy had a few places in mind. The second was the Allegany Fairgrounds in Cumberland, MD. When we got there, I said, 'I don't want to go any further.' It's a very beautiful site. The Potomac River circles the fairground. Right across the river, you could see WV. We thought we'd lose money the first year [2006] but we didn't lose much. We had country bands but they didn't draw the way the jam bands did. The second year, we made a profit. We've kept growing since."

Richard Thompson's "1952 Vincent Black Lightning" has become a staple of McCoury's shows. "It's a modern folk song," he said. "Ronnie played a tape of it for me."

The Del McCoury Band shared the bill with Thompson at the 2009 Newport Folk Festival. "I didn't want to do '1952 Vincent Black Lightning,'" said McCoury, "but the crowd kept requesting it. Richard told me he liked our version."

Woody Guthrie's daughter Nora produced a tribute to her father, in Tulsa, in 2013. McCoury sang "So Long, It's Been Good to Know You" and "Philadelphia Lawyer." "Nora told me her father would have loved to have had a band like mine," he said, "but couldn't afford it. That was a great compliment. She asked if I'd be interested in writing melodies to her dad's lyrics. I said, 'I sure would.' She sent me twenty-six songs, some in Woody's handwriting. It's amazing how much he wrote. He must have written about everything he saw or heard." (*Del and Woody* released in 2016.)

McCoury's sons alternate shows with him and their own Traveling McCourys. "My manager and agent set my dates first," said McCoury. "[Grisman] is with my agent, Crossover Touring, now. They book his sextet, his bluegrass band, and Del and Dawg. David and I have fun. We tell stories onstage but the best ones we can't tell in public."

Chapter 6

Panama Red

A Blue Grass Boy from 1965 to 1967, Wayland, MA-born Peter Rowan (1942-) continues to deliver brilliant songwriting, earthshaking tenor vocals, and plaintive cowboy-style yodeling. Bluegrass is only one hue in the oldest of three brothers' palette. Rock and roll, reggae, country music, American Indian chanting, folk balladry, and Hawaiian slack key are as much a part of his musical lexicon. He played psychedelic rock, with David Grisman, in Boston-based Earth Opera in 1967. He joined Richard Greene, Andy Kulberg, and Roy Blumenfeld in Seatrain two years later and was a founding member of Old and In the Way with Grisman and Jerry Garcia a year after that. In addition to recording with his brothers Chris and Lorin, he collaborated with Jerry Douglas, Tony Rice, Jim Rooney, Bill Keith, and Steve Earle, along with Norteño accordionist Flaco Jimenez, the Nashville Bluegrass Band, Northern Lights, and Czech bluegrass band Druha Trava. His own bands have included Free Mexican Air Force, Crucial Country, the Peter Rowan Bluegrass Band, and Twang an' Groove.

Three years after his Buddhism-meets-bluegrass *Dharma Blues* (2014), Rowan celebrated the sounds of the fiftieth state with *My Aloha* (2017). "Music works," he told me, "when it makes my heart feel big."

Premiering *Dharma Blues* at Humboldt State College, Rowan "wasn't sure people would get it," he said, "but they went wild. Musically, it has a bluesy drone. Many of the songs existed in other forms. They wrote themselves as I was traveling through India and Japan, every two or three years, studying with lamas. *Dharma Blues* was a long journey but people wanted to hear what it said.

"You don't usually hear lead banjo with a trap drum set," pointed out Jody Stecher, who played fretless banjo and Indian bass sitar, "as you do on 'Raven' [sung by Rowan and Gillian Welch] or Jack Casady's electric bass and bass balalaika. It was marvelous to have no conflict between new and old."

"[*Dharma Blues*] had the feeling and inspiration," explained Rowan, "and yet I was supposed to be Panama Red, a fake historical figure. It's a fun character to portray. It's influenced my stage manner and [the way] I approach an audience. John Hartford used to say, 'Man, you look like you're trying out for a Hollywood Western, like you just walked on the lot.' I duded myself up in the context of my love of the Southwest, the authentic American, Spanish-American, American Indian history. Those influences have been with me since I was a child. My journeys through the Southwest yielded songs like 'Midnight Moonlight' and 'The Land of the Navajo.' 'Panama Red' was the preparation to go on that journey."

Rowan grew up "square dancing on Friday nights and ballroom dancing on Saturdays," he recalled. "We danced to quartets—piano, sax, bass, and drums."

A *Life* magazine cover of Elvis Presley with a guitar slung over his shoulder "changed everything," Rowan said. "My brothers and I had been playing ukuleles. When we saw that picture, we went out and tried making straps out of dog leashes so we could hang those ukes from our bodies. Very quickly, we formed this band, the Cupids, and hung guitars from us—this was the way to go.

"I went to a show at Mechanics Hall in Worcester. . . . Joe Smith introduced the G-Clefs, the Cadillacs, the Johnny Burnette Quartet, Jimmy Bowen, and Buddy Knox. I was seeing the future. Chuck Berry walked onstage, with his beautiful, blond Gibson F-hole guitar, wearing a green tuxedo and a black string tie. He shrugged his shoulder, looked at us, said, 'This is my foolishness suit,' and burst into 'School Days.' It was all over for me."

Rowan wrote songs before playing bluegrass. "My flexibility and enjoyment of the artistic world," he said, "may be my downfall in the commercial sense but I let a song take me where it wants to go. If it wants to go to Jamaica, I go to Jamaica. Writing songs is about turning things down, honing the vast idea to something more succinct. Bill Monroe was a great songwriter. I wrote 'The Walls of Time' with him. In bluegrass, there's the hot instrumental side and the songwriting side. Both camps, in the best situations, feed off each other and admire each other. When Garcia put music to [Robert] Hunter's words, there was something bigger than either one of them could do alone."

Rowan made his first foray to Boston's Hillbilly Ranch at seventeen. "A friend had a band, Bob French and the Rainbow Boys," he remembered, "and he hired me to play mandolin. Joe Val introduced me to bluegrass's country-music side. Bob Siggins, Jim Rooney, and Bill Keith drew me to the Harvard Square folk-music side. I played more with country musicians than I did with college bluegrass players. A country audience isn't like a folk audience—all ears listening. A country audience is having a good time. They're drinking and they're talking. To reach them with your voice, you have to come from a different place than a pristine performance of the song. . . . There was a way to relate to the college kids but I needed resistance to focus and grab the audience."

Everett, MA-born mandolin player, high tenor singer, and typewriter repair tech Joseph "Joe Val" Valiante (1926-85) mentored Rowan. "Bob Emery and I would pick Joe up around 5:30," Rowan recalled, "after he had supper. We would wait outside in the station wagon and his wife, Thelma, would tell him, 'Your hillbilly friends are here.' We'd drive back to the old farm where I grew up, put up by the Irish Rowans when they came over in the 1890s, and we'd pick all night."

Rowan filled in for John Cooke on a Charles River Valley Boys tour and played mandolin with Keith & Rooney. "That's how I got with Bill Monroe," he said. "Keith left because Monroe was playing *Hootenanny*, a TV show that blackballed Pete Seeger. Del McCoury left after that. A year or so later, I was on the scene. Rinzler brought Monroe to New England to play a fiddle contest, and a concert at Jordan Hall on Doc Watson's birthday, and I played with him. We played a fiddle contest in VT but

Peter Rowan, 1985

Ralph wanted a show that could hit urban audiences in mainstream halls. I wasn't in the band yet but I went to Nashville so Monroe could try me out in his world. I played with him once in '63. By Thanksgiving 1964, I was in the band. Bill had another person he had been working with for a long time. He had to make a decision. I was bumping someone out of his job [Sandy Rothman] but Bill saw that I was eager to progress in music and not just have a gig. He liked that. He saw a bit of himself in me. We had a different kind of relationship than just professional. By 1965, we were on the road but we had already been playing around Nashville. There were two years of him seasoning us before we went into the studio."

Writing songs in Nashville, Rowan received advice from country-music superstar Porter Wagoner. "He listened to them," he recalled, "and said, 'Pete, those are mighty smart songs, but the country audience isn't mighty smart. Your songs are too complicated.'"

Hoping to connect with "the younger generation," Rowan left the Blue Grass Boys and returned East. "I was only twenty-four when I formed Earth Opera with Grisman," he said. "We had a musical connection before he decided to go full steam into jazz [Grisman produced an album by Rowan's brothers, Chris and Lorin, in 1971]. David's a very sympathetic player and he went with whatever I was coming up with, which was a ballad version of bluegrass. Our vision was a mando-cello and a guitar. Our model was the Incredible String Band. Simon & Garfunkel's manager wanted to sign us and orchestrated our demo. Years later, when I heard that demo, I almost ate my hat because it's superb. It has very clear, beautiful singing, and David's wonderful playing, but we thought, 'No, we have a band in a flooded basement in Cambridge and we've got to get back and rehearse.' We left NY and put Earth Opera together."

"It had bluegrass feeling in it," Rowan told *No Depression,* "but we were playing it all in what was legato, arpeggio chords, rather than strummed chords, so that every note would ring out in a chord, rather than just the rhythm part."

Rowan embraced the excesses of rock and roll. "I was in a weird frame of mind during those years," he recalled. "'The Great American Eagle Tragedy' became an FM hit and Earth Opera toured with Jim Morrison and the Doors. I started doing wild things onstage. If there was an American flag, I'd wave it over my head and do rock-star theatrics. I'd be down on my knees, putting my head in the bass drum, singing into the bass drum mic. It was pathetic. I wanted everything to be intuitive. That's not good for a leader. I was coming from Bill Monroe, where everything was intuitive but you had everything on stringed instruments. When you add bass and drums, intuition comes at a different point in the music."

Rowan reconnected with Grisman and Greene in Old and In the Way. Jerry Garcia played banjo. "When Jerry and I met," Greene remembered, "he was a bluegrass fanatic. He traveled the country, watching Bill Monroe play in barns. After the Grateful Dead started, he was still playing bluegrass. He had this double life. He and Grisman were both living in Marin County. They started jamming on bluegrass tunes and the band fell together."

"I didn't idolize Jerry Garcia," said Rowan. "I didn't even know much about the Grateful Dead. Grisman played me one song I had in common with them—'Cold Rain and Snow'—but looking at it from more of a perspective, I always felt like I was a kid, not an ingénue but someone with potential. Jerry Garcia wasn't somebody with potential. He was delivering 100 percent all the time."

"We had a lot of fun," said Grisman, "playing the bluegrass music we loved."[1]

"Audiences were huge," remembered Greene. "We sold out clubs, with lines around the block, just because Jerry was playing banjo."

"Bluegrass is like chamber music," Garcia told *Relix,* "it's very quiet, and if the audience got at all enthusiastic during the tune and started clapping . . . it would drown out the band, we couldn't hear each other."[2]

After a few months, Greene dropped out. John Hartford briefly replaced him before the Kissimmee, FL-raised Vassar Carlton Clements (1928-2005) took over on fiddle. "[Music] was God's gift," said the "Father of Hillbilly Jazz" to the *NY Times,* "something born in me. I was too dumb to learn it any other way." He said that he listened to the *Grand Ole Opry* and would "pick it up one note at a time." He explained, "I was young with plenty of time and I didn't give up. . . . I don't read music. I play what I hear."[3]

"[Clements] played the maximum of mind-blowing but beautifully tasty stuff," remembered Garcia, "and the music had enough interesting kinds of new changes and new things happening—Pete's good songs for example—so that [he] had a chance to blow with a lot of range. More than he does normally. That was neat."[4]

Chapter 7

Blue Rondo

Classical technique, spontaneity, and a love of bluegrass combined through Beverly Hills-born Richard Greene's fiddling. "He's already smart and hard enough to get along with," Bill Monroe told a University of Wisconsin audience. "We'll never handle him now."[1]

Commissioned by UCLA's Herb Alpert School of Music to compose a piece for violin and symphony orchestra ["What If Mozart Played with Bill Monroe?"], in 1999, Greene said, "Mozart was far more adventurous and went to more places than the I-IV-V of bluegrass."

Greene took his first fiddle lesson with Mike Seeger but played "as close to Scotty Stoneman as I could," he said. "Scotty's fiddling went straight to my heart. His playing came from nonphysical places. The index finger on his left hand was permanently damaged [he played with three fingers] and he grabbed the bow [with his right hand] like an axe handle. There was a hole in his violin; you could put a magazine through it. His physiology and equipment were completely flawed but it didn't matter. Music came out of that system in the most unbelievable way. He had a different approach to bluegrass. He treated it like a jazz idiom, playing figures that crossed the line. In bluegrass, you get one solo in a song, if you're lucky. He didn't pay attention to that. He played solo after solo until he was done."

The only Southerner in the NY-based Greenbriar Boys, mandolinist Frank Wakefield, who replaced Rinzler, "was the analog to Stoneman's digital," recalled Greene (1942-). "They both had their own style within the context of bluegrass. There were only six or seven bluegrass bands at that time. The first one to come to CA was the Greenbriar Boys. I wanted to play bluegrass so I walked up to them during their sound check and said, 'Hey, do you need a fiddle player?' They said, 'No, but we need a bass player.' I said, 'Fine, as long as you let me play fiddle on a few tunes.'"

Greene drove cross-country, in his '57 Chevy, with a bass between the two front seats. "I was driving with my right hand," he said, "and learning fingering with my left. By the time I arrived in NY, I could play. It's an easy pattern—I-IV-V—with very simple noting. The biggest part of bluegrass bass playing is muscularity."

Greene's bass-playing days would be short-lived. Returning to the West Coast, he fiddled for the Kentucky Colonels but "they hired Scotty Stoneman after a few times."

In February 1966, Bill Monroe "needed a fiddler with six hours' notice for a show in Montreal," Greene remembered. "I met him on the stage. I had never seen him in person. I asked the guitar player [Rowan] which one was Monroe."

The Blue Grass Boys' Northerners, Greene and Rowan shared a room on the road. "We built a good friendship," Greene said, "and it's lasted decades. He could flatpick, connecting runs between chords as well as anyone. We were total pot smokers. Bill didn't like that and we had to hide it. We had this secret club of two. We were serious about the music but we were stoned much of the time. I was a chain pot smoker for forty years but I quit and it wasn't a problem."

Greene's first weeks with Monroe were "horrible," he remembered. "I was good enough to join the Blue Grass Boys but I sped up a lot. Monroe asked me to play rhythm without background licks for the next several months. I played lead only on my solos, a very restrictive assignment from the master of bluegrass. Of course, I loved it. I loved everything he said; I worshipped him. That process led to a bowing technique, 'the chop,' that fixed my playing."

Recording "Blue Night," Greene devised a new fiddling technique—double-stop unison. "I played the same note on two adjacent strings," he explained, "a fifth apart. It's quite a stretch. No one had done it before. Monroe was very proud and he'd give audiences a little talk about what I had done."

Diminishing finances, however, left Greene frustrated. "Most of the time, we only had two shows a week," he said, "Friday night at the *Opry* and a Saturday matinee. Each would pay thirty-five dollars. That was our income. Peter was our booking agent but he wasn't systematic about what he was doing. One time, we went to the wrong state—the same town name—driving all night in this decrepit bus. We got there, no gig."

Leaving the Blue Grass Boys in March 1967, Greene returned to Boston and joined Jim Kweskin's Jug Band, finding them "interesting musically and in every other way." The band included Bill Keith, Fritz Richmond, and Geoff and Maria Muldaur. "My albums with Monroe [*Bluegrass Time*] and the Jug Band [*Garden of Joy*] have some of my best playing," he said. "I look back and don't know how I did it."

Seatrain was a merging of ex-Blue Grass Boys (Greene and Rowan) and the Blues Project's former rhythm section (Andy Kulberg and Roy Blumenfeld). "Lloyd Baskin was a pop singer and keyboards player," said Greene. "Peter Rowan wasn't in at the beginning but I brought him in. It was very improvisatory. When I played, I was completely free. I was a jazz fanatic and went outside the boundaries. It worked in a way that would never happen again. Our first album, *Planned Obsolescence*, was the Blues Project fulfilling their contract. The next was the A&M record [*Seatrain*], which had some good moments but overall wasn't great. The next two [*Seatrain* and *The Marblehead Messenger*] were on Capitol and produced by the Beatles' producer George Martin. The first had 'Orange Blossom Special.' The band flew to London; there was a lot of money behind us. We were in George Martin's AIR Studios and had already done a few tracks. He asked, 'What about this "Orange Blossom Special"?' It was on the demo we sent him. We went into the studio and played it for him, just showing him how it went. The tape was rolling and that became the take on the album. That's how you make the best music; you don't think about it.

"It wasn't always friendly within the band, especially when we were trying to climb the ladder to commercial success. If you're a bluegrass band, there's not much to fight about, but commercial music opens the doors to all kinds of ideas. Peter hated being commercial. It upset his sensibilities. Andy Kulberg and I were dying to be rock stars. I had a huge ego and thought the definition of success was millions of fans screaming at you. After a year, the gigs got fewer and it became a struggle. They did one more album without me and that was it."

Greene recruited Rowan, Grisman, Keith, and Clarence White for what became Muleskinner in 1973. "Richard invited us all to play on KCET with Monroe . . . ," recalled Rowan in his liner notes of their 1974 album, "as a sort of a *Father of Bluegrass and His Sons* show. Well, [Monroe's] bus broke down in Stockton and we had to do the show on our own. . . . Clarence's gentle soul was our unifying force, holding our music together; we had all the time in the world and no idea how quickly things would change."

White's tragic death ended Muleskinner but Greene and Grisman continued to play together, hooking up with Taj Mahal in the Great American Music Band (or the Great American String Band). "Taj and I became friends at a Kentucky Colonels concert," Greene said. "It was a serious acoustic quintet—two guitars, mandolin, bass, and fiddle. Jerry Garcia played with us once in a while. We toured with Maria Muldaur. It was the first time improvised music was played on bluegrass instruments by musicians paying homage to bluegrass but not playing bluegrass but original compositions."

The Richard Greene Quartet and the Grass Is Greener included players such as Tony Trischka, Chris Thile, Butch Baldassari, Buell Neidlinger, and Lamar Grier's son David. "Tony can play traditionally," Greene said, "but he goes way outside when he wants. We toured Japan with Peter Rowan's Red Hot Pickers [with Andy Statman and Roger Mason] in 1979 and released two albums in Japan on Nippon-Columbia. David picked up the mantle from Clarence White and took guitar flatpicking to a whole other level. He's a total improviser; he never plays the same thing twice. I did four albums with Tony Rice. He worked things out in advance. Grier just starts playing."

Appearing with a reunited Jug Band (sans Kweskin) at the 1987 Newport Folk Festival, Greene "had the flu," he recalled, "and could hardly move." His last shows came during the Jug Band's 2003 Japanese tour. "I loved playing in that band," he said. "Keith was still there, but I contracted a bacterial heart disease. The cure was six weeks of antibiotics, pumped directly into a vein. There were severe side effects; I couldn't move. They had other dates booked. Tearfully, I had to turn them down. It led to me no longer playing music."

Since then, Greene has participated in only "two or three recording sessions under very special circumstances," he said. "I did it for fifty-three years without stopping, but I had hand problems throughout my career. To play my first note with a good sound, I'd have to practice for forty-five minutes. I've moved my skills into photography. Both art forms involve arranging elements in a composition.

"A couple of months ago, I owed a favor to a friend in Seattle. I drove to her festival and presented a seminar on the 'chop.' I had to practice. At the seminar, Darol Anger told me that Grisman lived in Port Townsend [about two hours north]. I called him and my wife and I went to visit. We were sitting around, drinking wine, with him and his genius bass-player son, Sam, and he kept saying, 'Get your fiddle; let's do some playing.' I realized that a window was open that would afterwards close forever. I went to the car and got my fiddle. The three of us jammed for hours. I don't touch the fiddle anymore but once in a while I have a dream that I'm playing a solo. That feels good."

Chapter 8

Double Stop

Replacing Greene as a Blue Grass Boy in March 1967, Byron Berline (1944-) was already attracting attention with his broad-stroked fiddling and mandolin playing. Making his recording debut on the Dillards' *Pickin' and Fiddlin'* (1965), he won the National Oldtime Fiddler's Contest, in Weiser, ID, in 1965, 1967, and 1970. "I learned my first tune on the fiddle," he said, "when I was five."

Born in Caldwell, KS as the youngest of fiddler Lue Berline's five children, Berline grew up on a Norman, OK farm. "Everybody played something," he remembered. "My mother played piano. My dad played fiddle, banjo, and mandolin. My sisters played piano and band instruments. One of my older brothers played banjo and guitar. Besides playing in the living room, we'd go to fiddle contests, schools, PTA meetings, anyplace we could play old-time fiddle music and things that people would dance to—square-dance tunes, jigs, or waltzes."

"Lue was a crusty old son of a bitch," recalled Jim Rooney. "He had a gravel voice and about every word was 'godd---.' . . . Monroe really like Byron's fiddling and he liked Byron's old man a lot, too."[1]

The younger Berline's fiddling retained its old-time feel. "I loved Texas fiddlers like Benny Thomasson, Major Franklin, and Johnny Gimble," he said, "and bluegrass fiddlers like Benny Martin and Kenny Baker. Vassar Clements was a good friend. My dad enjoyed Bob Wills. There wasn't any fiddler that I copied—more my dad than anybody—but I listened to everything I could. [Rock and roll] didn't grab me as it did other kids. If it didn't have a fiddle, I didn't want to listen to it. When the Beatles and the Byrds came out, I enjoyed their music but I never thought I'd get involved in it."

Berline met the Dillards on November 22, 1963, the day of Pres. John F. Kennedy's assassination. "They came to UO [University of Oklahoma]," he said, "where I was attending school. I didn't think they were going to go ahead with the show but I'm glad they did. I had never seen a bluegrass band like them."

Word of the teenager's prizewinning fiddling passed to the Dillard brothers. "After the show, I went backstage and we jammed," recalled Berline. "They invited me to play with them at the Oklahoma City Folk Music Club. Then, they decided to do an album with me in the summer. They were professionals. When the musicians that you're playing with know what they're doing, you can excel. I noticed that with them right away."

Performing with his father at the Newport Folk Festival in 1965, Berline met Monroe. "Tex Logan was a good friend of Bill's," he recalled, "and he introduced us. I jammed with him onstage and he was very complimentary to me. He told me, 'I'd like you to play with me.'"

Studying for a physical-education degree, and competing in football, javelin, shotput, and discus throwing, Berline turned down the offer. After graduating in January 1967, he reapplied. "I joined the Blue Grass Boys in March," he remembered. "Lamar Grier was on banjo. James Monroe was on bass. We didn't have a guitar player. Peter Rowan had just left. Eventually, we signed Roland White to play guitar."

Debuting on the *Grand Ole Opry*, Berline spent seven months with Monroe before receiving his draft notice. Participating in a three-hour recording session on August 23, 1967, he featured on "Virginia Darling," "Sally Goodin," and "The Gold Rush," an instrumental he wrote with Monroe. "He had the idea," Berline said. "I wrote a third part but I didn't get any credit. That was okay. I didn't care. I was glad to be playing with him. It wasn't too fast or flashy but mandolinists, guitarists, and banjo players love to play that tune."

Discharged from the army in 1968, Berline hooked up with Doug Dillard and the Byrds' former lead singer Harold Eugene "Gene" Clark's Dillard-Clark Expedition. After playing with Poor Richard's Almanac during a break from graduate studies in January 1969, he reunited with Dillard after graduation.

During a private Kentucky Colonels reunion, at Clarence White's Topanga Canyon home, on July 12, 1971, Berline discussed forming a band with bassist Roger Bush. "Roger and I had just left Doug Dillard," he said, "but we wanted to keep going. We were playing Vegas dates with Kay Starr and needed a banjo player—Herb Pedersen sat in with us for a while—and a guitar player/tenor singer so we got Kenny Wertz. He was friends with Chris Hillman. They played together in the Scottsville Squirrel Barkers."

The Flying Burrito Brothers had a European tour scheduled but the group was in tatters. Berline and Wertz put a band together to fulfill their engagements. "Chris Hillman and Al Perkins had left to play with Stephen Stills' Manassas," he explained. "Rick Roberts was hanging around so he played guitar. We got Alan Munde to play banjo and guitar."

"Byron and I had gone to fiddle contests," recalled Munde. "I backed him on guitar but I played banjo when I jammed in the fields, trying to keep up with fiddle players. I was playing in the Keith style, which was relatively new."

Munde was ready for a change. He had been playing with Jimmy Martin for two years but "wasn't making any money," he said. "My car was old and falling apart. I was broke. I had to do something else. I have a bachelor's in education so I thought about going into teaching." Munde would teach banjo and the history of bluegrass at South Plains College, near Lubbock, from 1986 until 2007.

James Henry "Jimmy" Martin (1927-2005) was truly something. Raised on his parents' hog farm, in Sneedville, TN, he bought his first guitar at the age of ten with money raised by selling hides from possums he hunted. "I wanted to play and sing on the radio," he told *No Depression*, "and be an entertainer."[2]

Though he grew up without electricity, Martin "had a battery radio, a little old Philco," he recalled. "Roy Acuff, Bill Monroe, and Uncle Dave Macon, they were my favorites—and DeFord Bailey. . . . I went around burning brush piles or hoeing corn, singing 'Wabash Cannonball,' 'Great Speckled Bird,' 'Blue Moon of Kentucky,' or 'Wicked Path of Sin.' They'd tell me, 'Go on to bed; we have to get up and work tomorrow' or 'Go to church.' I'd tell my mother, 'You all just run me to bed; one of these times you're going to turn that radio on, and I hope before I die I get to sing with Bill Monroe.'"[3]

Fired from a factory job for singing while he worked, in 1948, Martin took a bus to Nashville. Maneuvering his way to the dressing room at the *Grand Ole Opry*, he introduced himself to Monroe and began to sing. He impressed the bandleader with his pure vocals and would replace Wiseman in December 1949. Appearing on forty-six tracks over the next five years, he sang lead on "Uncle Pen," "I'm Blue, I'm Lonesome," and "The Little Girl and the Dreadful Snake." "Jimmy's temperature is higher than the rest of ours," said Jeff Hanna. "He's a wild man in the best sense of the term, and he's the only one who brought the fire of rockabilly music to bluegrass."[4]

Resigning from Martin's Sunny Mountain Boys, in January 1972, Munde boarded a plane, in Oklahoma City, with Berline. Connecting with Bush, Roberts, Perkins, and Eric Dalton, they continued to Holland to play their first gig. "I hadn't rehearsed with them," remembered Munde. "I turned off the volume of my guitar. As I got to know the songs, I turned up louder and louder."

Recorded during the tour, *Last of the Red Hot Burritos* included a three-tune bluegrass mini set. "I looked for that album for years," said Michael

Cleveland. "I was obsessive about 'Orange Blossom Special' and collected recordings of it. I knew there was a version on that album with Byron Berline playing fiddle. I finally found a used cassette copy. It was country-rock aimed at a rock-and-roll audience but when they started playing bluegrass, the crowd went nuts."

Turning their focus to Country Gazette, Berline, Wertz, Munde, and Roger Bush released *Traitor in Our Midst* in late 1972. United Artists promoted it heavily. "They were flush with money," said Munde. "They had just had a big hit with Don McLean's 'American Pie.'"

Roland White replaced Wertz after Country Gazette's second album. "When I was working with Jimmy Martin," said Munde, "Roland was playing with Lester Flatt. Bluegrassers would go to Bobby Green's Dusty Roads Tavern on Thursday nights and jam. Roland was part of that."

The lines between bluegrass, country music, and rock were blurring. The Monkees' Michael Nesmith was playing with the First National Band. Rick Nelson had the Stone Canyon Band. The Eagles, Poco, and Loggins & Messina were getting off the ground. Gram Parsons was singing with Emmylou Harris. The Nitty Gritty Dirt Band was recording with bluegrass and country-music legends. Jerry Garcia was playing pedal steel on Crosby, Stills, Nash & Young's "Teach Your Children" and banjo in Old and In the Way.

Berline recorded with the Rolling Stones, Bob Dylan, Elton John, Willie Nelson, Doc Watson, Rod Stewart, the Band, Vince Gill, and John Denver. Delivering his two-week notice to Country Gazette, he wasn't band-less for long. "I got together with Dan Crary and John Hickman," he said, "and had a jam at my house. We got Alan Wald, a guitar player who lives by the beach, and Jack Skinner, who's a bass player and singer-songwriter. We went to Jack's apartment studio and recorded as Sundance. Dan plays fiddle tunes note for note. Hickman is one of the top banjo players around. He's very melodic but he can also be subtle."

Berline, Crary, and Hickman "enjoyed playing as a trio so much that we kept doing it for eleven years," Berline remembered. "Eventually, we hired Steve Spurgin [bass/vocals] and recorded *Now They Are Four* [1989]. We wanted to beef it up even more so I talked everybody into hiring John Moore around 1990. He fit the bill perfectly, playing mandolin, guitar, and singing."

As California, the quintet was the IBMA's "Instrumental Group of the Year" in 1992, 1993, and 1994, ending their reign only after Berline moved to Guthrie, OK (his wife's hometown) in 1995. "I had started collecting instruments," Berline explained, "and needed a place where I could start selling them. We found a building with an upstairs concert hall. I have the fiddle shop downstairs. John Hickman worked as a luthier but his health forced him to retire."

Since 2002, Berline has played an 1880 George Gemunder fiddle. "It fits me well," he said. "I have every stringed instrument that you could think of. I have a few prewar instruments, three to four hundred fiddles. Someone told me, 'It gets into you like a rusty fishhook.' He's right. Once it gets into you, it's hard to quit."

Munde continued to lead County Gazette until the late eighties. "I wanted to play like Earl Scruggs and Doug Dillard," said the Norman, OK-born banjo player. "When I started with Jimmy Martin, I did it the way he wanted me to do it—he was the boss and he had the record deal—but, as an artistic person, I wanted to do things differently."

Munde (1946-) grew up listening to his parents' collection of 78s. "I remember a Strauss waltz and a musical or two," he said. "My father was from Providence and he enjoyed the accordion. My older brother, Mike, and my younger sister studied it because of his interest, but for me, it was the guitar. When Mike came home from the navy, in the late fifties, he had a guitar and a record on how to play it. He left it behind when he went off to college and I started playing. This was during the folk-music boom. I heard a banjo and really liked the sound. I worked and earned enough money to buy one. I started to search out people who knew how to play. It was difficult but I eventually found people who played music that fit a banjo."

Munde received Flatt & Scruggs' *Foggy Mountain Banjo* (1961) from a friend for Christmas. "That lit my fire," he said. "I loved the crackly, energetic, consistent rhythm and the tone. I knew it was a human doing it but I couldn't imagine how. There was an artistic rendering of Lester Flatt and Earl Scruggs on the cover. It showed them with fingerpicks. I had a sense of that. I knew you used your thumb, index, and middle finger, but how you orchestrated each note I had no idea. I didn't know they organized into patterns of eight. I searched out somebody who knew how to do it and he showed it to me. That's all it took; I had already played guitar for a year and knew about chords and melodies. Playing with other people was the learning process of the day."

Munde spent his spare time hanging out in a local music store. "Musicians would drift through, trying out guitars or banjos," he said, "and I'd listen to them. Mance Lipscomb came in one time. He sat for an hour or more and played."

Forming a band with "musicians my age—seventeen or so," Munde frequented an open mic at UO. "Byron was a student," he recalled, "and he heard us play. He remembered me when I ran into him at the music store and we played together. He took me along when he went to pick with banjo player Eddie Shelton in Oklahoma City. Eddie was twenty years older than I was. He was a huge help to me and taught me a lot. He knew musicians in Dallas [Mitchell Land, Louis "Bosco" Land, and Harless "Tootie" Williams, the Stone Mountain Boys], where he was originally from. They'd come up for a weekend and pick. Occasionally, I'd play a tune with them, but mostly I soaked up the sound and watched their hands."

Jamming at the Mountain View Folk Festival, in 1978, Munde caught Courtney Johnson's attention. When he got back to KY, Johnson raved to Wayne Taylor and Sam Bush about a banjo player who played fiddle tunes in the style of Bill Keith. "We made plans to meet at a fiddle contest near Kansas City," remembered Munde. "I went with Byron's dad. Sam Bush was only sixteen but he was already a spectacular player. He liked rock and roll and Jean-Luc Ponty's end of the jazz world. He took the technique and virtuosity of fiddle and mandolin playing and transferred it to his other interests. When I got out of college, our idea was to have this band, Poor Richard's Almanac. Wayne lived in Hopkinsville, KY so I moved there in January 1969. Almost immediately, I got my draft notice. Before I went for my physical, we recorded on a home reel-to-reel. The sound was lame but the music was interesting. The Dillards recorded 'Duelin' Banjos'; we did it as 'Fussin' Banjo.' We did another Dillards tune that we called 'Little Joseph.' They called it 'Old Joseph.' It's 'Old Joe Clark' with funny tuning on the mandolin."

Meanwhile, the military turned Munde down. "My blood pressure was too high," he said. "I remember seeing two spaces on the form and watching the navy doctor circle physically unfit. This was 1969; the Vietnam War was raging. If I had gone, you'd be speaking with a dead man. I never would have made it. I was thankful but I've suffered for it. I've had open-heart surgery."

Recording with electric guitarist Harlow Wilcox and the Okies, Munde scored a hit with "Groovy Grubworm," selling close to a million copies. When Wilcox relocated to Nashville, in October 1969, Munde tagged along. "I went to the DJ convention with some friends from Norman," he said, "and Wayne Taylor told me about a gathering at the Noel Hotel in downtown Nashville. We hung out there with him and Sam Bush, playing all weekend."

During the jam session, "Jim & Jesse's banjo player, Al Osteen, told me that Jimmy Martin's banjo player was leaving," said Munde. "If I were interested, he'd introduce me. Jimmy came into the hotel later and I played a tune or two for him. He came back the next night. Doyle Lawson was in Jimmy's band. I had met him in KY and we had picked a little. He remembered and told Jimmy that, if he hired me, he'd work with me to play in his style."

Hailing from Ford Town, TN, Lawson (1944-) played mandolin from the age of eleven. "Mr. Bill [Monroe] was my inspiration," he said. "He came on the *Opry* and grabbed me. I was no more than five years old. My mother told me who it was and about the instrument that he was playing and I said, 'That's what I'm going to do when I grow up.'"

Lawson's father sang in a gospel quartet. One of its members had a mandolin. "I asked if I could borrow it," Lawson remembered. "I wanted to learn to play. He did, I did, and here we are all these years later and I'm still at it."

Attending a church revival, where his father's quartet was singing, Lawson "went to the car when it started raining," he remembered, "and I used the rain as an excuse to sit in the car and play the mandolin. I couldn't use more than one or two fingers but I figured out a melody. I was proud of myself. When my dad came out of the church and I showed him, he said, 'That's all well and good but, next time, you'd better be inside the church.' He made his point; there were other things as important if not more. My father's quartet didn't sing for money. Sometimes, a church took up a collection. At best, it paid for the gas, but that's not what it was about—they loved to sing and they believed what they were singing. At a regular church meeting, we had the congregation singing from the hymnbooks, songs like 'When the Call Is Up Yonder' and 'Rock of Ages,' songs that have been around for ages and ages."

On the third day of February 1963, eighteen-year-old Lawson hooked up with Jimmy Martin in Nashville. "We met when I was fourteen," he said. "He was from the same county I was living in. My dad had come from Hancock County. In 1957, he bought a mountain farm and moved us back there. Jimmy Martin's brother-in-law lived on the farm next to ours. He took an interest in me and introduced us. Over the next three years or so, whenever Jimmy was visiting, he'd pick with me. When he found out that I picked up a banjo, he told his brother-in-law that I should stick with it; he might need me someday. Little did I know, four years later, I'd get the call. I hopped on a bus and got to Nashville about three in the morning. I called his house and they said, 'He's not here but he knows you're on your way. As soon as he comes, I'll tell him to get you.'"

Waiting for what seemed like an eternity, Lawson "started thinking that if he didn't show up, I didn't know what I was going to do," he remembered. "I didn't have the bus fare to get back home."

He needn't have worried. Martin arrived and things worked out.

Firmly entrenched in the Sunny Mountain Boys by Munde's arrival, Lawson's proposal was accepted. Munde went home to pick up his 1961 Buick, banjo, guitar, and clothes. Withdrawing $350 from his savings, he returned to Music City and reconnected with Martin, with whom he would play from October 1969 until October 1971. "At the first show in Hamilton, OH," he recalled, "we just went out and played. I rehearsed a little with Doyle on the bus. During the show, Jimmy was playing a slow song. I started to do a Scruggs-style roll. Immediately, he turned around and said, 'Don't do that.' After the show, he told me, 'I'm not angry but that's not part of my music; that's Flatt & Scruggs' music. It doesn't fit my timing.' [Martin] was clear about what he wanted the banjo to be—a harmonic strummer. It was simple conceptually but difficult to perform exactly. Jimmy played guitar and had a strong sense of rhythm. He wanted you to match that. It's not apparent in the music but he had what he called 'lazy notes' and 'quick notes.' We would sit and play and he'd ask me, 'What would you play as a solo?' and I'd play whatever I thought of doing. He'd say, 'That's good but why don't you try this?' and he'd hum to me. Everything about his music was highly organized. When he was with Monroe, one of his disappointments was that the band was never solid. Musicians would come and go. They wouldn't rehearse. He'd play on the *Grand Ole Opry* and see Hank Williams' Drifting Cowboys and Ernest Tubb's band and they were sharp, tight, and well organized. That's what he wanted to bring to bluegrass. When he did a lick, he wanted you to do the lick that went with it. We never rehearsed much, unless we were going to record, but I practiced hard; we had to play the same way, every time. He was prickly and rough; many people didn't like him. He drank too much, and did things he shouldn't have, but he was professional when it came to music."

Munde joined Roland White, Sam Bush, Curtis Burch, and John Cowan to record *Together Again for the First Time* (1977). "It never made the splash it should have," he said. "Sam can play anything but he worked hard to replicate the things I did on the banjo on the mandolin. It really was different."

Chapter 9

Man of Constant Sorrow

Between 1946 and 1966, Coeburn, VA-born Carter and Ralph Stanley and their Clinch Mountain Boys challenged Monroe and Flatt & Scruggs for supremacy of the bluegrass world. Their nearly 350 tracks included "Mountain Dew," "Little Maggie," "Little Birdie," "How Mountain Girls Can Love," "Stone Walls and Steel Bars," "Man of Constant Sorrow," and "Rank Strangers." "It was another stream," said Tim Stafford (Blue Highway), "its own stream."

A heavy drinker, Carter Stanley (1925-66) died of cirrhosis of the liver at forty-one. "Carter was the king of the Stanley Brothers," said Sam Bush. "Ralph only sang lead on a couple of songs.'"

Carter's passing marked a new beginning for Ralph (1927-2016), who switched to clawhammer after his death. Accompanied by top musicians, including Ricky Skaggs, Keith Whitley, Larry Sparks, Charlie Sizemore, Ron Thomason, and Ralph Stanley II ("Two"), the tenor-voiced banjo player toured extensively, recorded prolifically, and preserved mountain traditions. "I was aiming to establish my own sound," he explained in his autobiography, "which was more old-time mountain-style than Carter was really comfortable with."[1]

Receiving an honorary doctorate of music from Lincoln Memorial University in TN, in 1976, Stanley proudly affixed the title "Doctor" to his name. "The way Dad played banjo was unbelievable," said Stanley II. "He and Earl had the drive. When they played a roll, it was like a machinegun going off. Earl played a flathead banjo but Dad went to an arch-top. It had a brighter tone, a crisper sound. Dad played the melody notes, what he was singing. He never played anything so fancy that it went over people's heads."

Joining the Stanley Brothers in 1952, Valdese, NC-born bassist/guitarist George Shuffler (1925-2014) added to their signature sound. Shuffler's crosspicking, developed after guitarist Curley Lambert's 1961 departure reduced the group to a trio, allowed him to maintain rhythm on the guitar while playing melody. Alternating between his bass and the guitar slung

Ralph Stanley, 1997

across his back, he pioneered "the concept that when a fiddle player takes his part [solo], and a banjo player takes his part, the guitar player could also take his part."[2]

"I tried Merle Travis-style guitar and Mother Maybelle Carter-style guitar," said Shuffler in 2007, "but single-string leads just were not getting it." Carter disliked his "two notes down, one up, crossing over strings" approach, Shuffler recalled, but "after it started selling, I could not do it enough to satisfy him."[3]

Shuffler's brother Ron (1945-) played bass with David Peterson & 1946, Dale Ann Bradley, and Michael Cleveland & Flamekeeper. "I'm the youngest of six boys and three girls," he told me. "George was the second child and twenty years my senior. Dad played clawhammer banjo and Mom sang in the church choir. The girls learned to play piano and all the boys learned multiple instruments. George was the first. My dad got him a cheap guitar. A man across the creek showed him basic chords. His interest in music grew and grew. Dad finally got him a Gibson J-45, which the family still has. He played that guitar on recordings with the Stanley Brothers."

George Shuffler's childhood home reverberated with music. "Jim Shumate lived in Hickory, twenty minutes from Valdese," his brother remembered. "The Stanley Brothers' fiddler, Chubby Anthony, lived about thirty miles away. Pee Wee Lambert and Tiny Davis lived in Shelby. Pee Wee played mandolin for the Stanley Brothers and Tiny played banjo for Monroe. We lived on a small farm but the door was always open for musicians. No one said a word if we played until the wee hours. My parents would sleep in the back bedroom, get up at the crack of dawn, start milking cows and going about their day. It was amazing, the tolerance they had."

George Shuffler's Melody Mountain Boys included his twelve-year-old brother John (bass) and Lester Woodie (fiddle). They would all play with the Stanley Brothers. George would be the first. By then, he had appeared on the radio with Danny & Charlie Bailey and with Jim & Jesse and worked with a blackface comedy team, Mustard and Gravy. Hooking up with the Stanleys in 1951, he went home after a few months. "They called him [George] back to record," said his brother, "and talked him into going back on the road. He would spend sixteen years with them."

Although he stayed with Ralph Stanley for only a few months after Carter's death, Shuffler's influence would be apparent in guitarists Larry Sparks, Keith Whitley, Renfro Proffitt, Danky Marshall, Junior Blackenship, Hank Smith, and James Alan Shelton.

Joining Don Reno & Bill Harrell and the Tennessee Cut-Ups as a bass player, Shuffler shifted to guitar when Ronnie Reno left for the Osborne Brothers. Jerry McCoury took over on bass. Singing gospel music with a family group the last years of his life, Shuffler passed away five days before his eighty-ninth birthday.

Keith Whitley (1955-89) met Cordell, KY-born mandolin/fiddle player Rickie Lee "Ricky" Skaggs (1954-) at a high-school fiddlers' convention in 1969. The Ashland, KY-born and Sandy Hook-raised guitarist/baritone singer was playing in a band with his brother Dwight on banjo. Skaggs, who was playing with his father, Hobert, had already staked his claim as a future superstar. Playing "Ruby, Are You Mad at Your Man" for Monroe at the age of six, he appeared on Flatt and Scruggs' TV show the following year. When the teenagers harmonized backstage, it was magic. Skaggs joined Whitley's band.

Stanley's opening act at a show in 1971, Skaggs and Whitley extended their set when the headliner was late. After he arrived, and heard them singing Stanley Brothers songs, he hired both seventeen-year-olds. "Keith and Ricky were fine young men," he told the *Chicago Tribune*. "They had talent. . . . I've always told my band to be down-to-earth and friendly with people . . . never ignore anybody because everybody's equal and everybody pays the same price to get in to see you."[4]

"We sang a lot as we were driving," recalled Skaggs, "to help keep Ralph awake when he was driving at two or three o'clock in the morning. He'd say, 'All right, boys, let's sing some.' That was it; we'd wake up and sing . . . that's how we worked up songs on the road and that's the way life was with the Stanley Brothers."[5]

Skaggs departed for the Country Gentlemen in 1974 but Whitley continued to sing with Stanley for more than a decade. Setting out on his own, in 1984 he moved to Nashville and scored chart-topping solo country hits with "Don't Close Your Eyes," "I'm No Stranger to the Rain," and the title track of his album, *When You Say Nothing at All* (later a hit for Alison Krauss). Struggling with alcoholism, he surrendered to his demons on May 9, 1989, at the age of thirty-three.

Don Rigsby (1968-) met Stanley on his sixth birthday. "My family had been through a lot of trauma," recalled the Isonville, KY-born mandolinist. "Dad had been injured in an industrial accident, in 1971, and we nearly lost him. There was so much negativity that anything positive stood out. Keith Whitley lived seven miles from us and came to see Dad while he was hurt. After he got back on his feet, Dad went to a flea market and bought

Ricky Skaggs, 1996

Ralph Stanley's *Let Me Rest on a Peaceful Mountain.* It opened with Ralph's recitation about Carter, 'Hills of Home.' His voice enthralled me; it was so gentle. He was coming to the Paramount Art Center and my dad found out about it. For my birthday, he and my mom took me to the show."

Before the concert, Rigsby's father "snuck around to the backstage" and spoke with Whitley. "Mom and I were sitting in the audience," Rigsby recalled, "when Keith walked up and said, 'Is this the young feller who wants to meet Ralph Stanley?' I was speechless. I tipped my head and he said, 'C'mon.' I looked at my mom and dad and they gave me the okay. Keith picked me up, put me on his shoulders, and carried me backstage. The dressing room wasn't anything fancy. There was a single lightbulb hanging from a fixture. Keith set me down and told Ralph that it was my birthday. Ralph shook my hand and asked me what I wanted for my birthday. I told him I'd come to see him for my present. He said, 'Do you have any songs you want to hear?' I told him 'Hills of Home' and 'Little Maggie.' He did them in the show and dedicated them to me."

Columbus, OH-born Ron Thomason (1944-) played with Stanley in the early seventies. A self-deprecating humorist, mandolin player, drawl-heavy singer, and champion horse breeder, he's released a dozen albums with Dry Branch Fire Squad and hosted the Grey Fox Bluegrass Festival (and its predecessor, Winterhawk) since 1984. Thomason caught the bluegrass bug at the age of five. "I remember being in my father's Chevy truck," he said, "when the Stanley Brothers' 'How Mountain Girls Can Love' came on the radio and changed my life."

Thomason was attending Ohio University when Stanley performed at the school. "I went backstage and spoke to him," he recalled. "He had Larry Sparks, Melvin Goins, and Curly Ray Cline with him. Soon afterwards, I went to hear them at a knife-and-gun place in Columbus. After Ralph's set, we were in the dressing room and he said, 'Can anybody help me?' I said, 'I will' and I did. We didn't see each other for a couple of weeks but he gave me a call and I went to help him again. He said, 'If you're not doing anything, why don't you throw your stuff on the bus?' I said, 'I've got a job but if you give me time to quit, I'll go with you,' which is what I did."

The Clinch Mountain Boys were the first bluegrass group to sing a cappella gospel songs. "That split the atom," said Thomason. "I heard Monroe singing a cappella backstage at Bean Blossom—duets, trios, and quartets—but he never did it on records or during performances. He considered it not bluegrass."

Opening for Jerry Lee Lewis, the Clinch Mountain Boys received a case of Scotch backstage, accompanied by a note saying they could keep it if they send their bass player to Lewis's dressing room. That bass player was George

Shuffler. "We became lifelong friends," said Thomason. "I presided over his funeral. I've never admired a man more. We had so much in common. He was a horseman and I wanted to be a horseman; I had a horse."

Shuffler left in the middle of Thomason's tenure with Stanley. "It was around the time that Ralph married Jimmi," Thomason said. "He'd drive a couple hundred miles to play for $250. That's how hard times were. Ralph and I were the only two who could drive the bus. He brought Jimmi along so that left most of the driving to me. I was young and healthy—I'd been an athlete all through high school and college—so I didn't mind. Ralph appreciated it. I stayed longer than I would have otherwise. I played with him, without missing a gig, for only six to eight months, maybe a year. I wanted to do different things. I made a record of my own and played with some local bands."

Thomason continued to get calls from Stanley. "He needed me to drive the bus," he explained, "so I drove for him for another eight months."

The situation exploded in Middletown, OH. "When I got there, Ricky Skaggs was playing mandolin," Thomason recalled. "Ralph told Ricky, 'Ron will play mandolin when he's around.' It was awkward. It was the last time I agreed to go."

After working with Stanley, Thomason was unsure of his future as a musician. "I was obviously not going to be playing at that level," he noted, "but a person who had a bar, the Crying Cowboy Saloon, talked to me and said, 'Would you put a group together and play Thursday nights?' I don't like owing money. I've paid for every house, farm, even horses, in cash, but I still owed money for college. I was teaching school and then working in a factory—sixteen hours a day. I called a few musicians and we went to play."

Thomason and the Dry Branch Fire Squad stayed at the Crying Cowboy Saloon for a month. "Ralph came in one night," he recalled. "We were his warmup band. George was back with him. Ralph would have never had his bluegrass festival if I hadn't suggested it to him. He had the right location. I knew someone who could print the tickets, someone who could do sound. I told him, 'All it'll take is getting your friends to come over and play.'"

The following year, Stanley booked Dry Branch Fire Squad for his festival. Monroe heard them and hired them for Bean Blossom. "We were off to the races," remembered Thomason. "Pete Kuykendall saw us at Bean Blossom and hired us to play his Indian Springs Festival. Nancy Talbott got us to the Berkshire Mountains Bluegrass Festival."

Launched in 1976, the Berkshire Mountains Bluegrass Festival attracted top acts to the Rothvoss farm in Ancramdale, NY, but Talbott was "never successful enough to pay all her bills," said Thomason. "She borrowed money from the person who ended up my partner, Mary Doub. I got a call late one night. It was Mary. My wife at the time and Mary's husband had done business together—selling catamarans. Mary's father controlled the garbage business in Baltimore and they own a camp in the Adirondacks, next to the Vanderbilt Camp, and a huge compound in Owings Mills. She asked me if I wanted to have a bluegrass festival. I told her I didn't know anything about festivals but she said, 'You don't need to; we'll hire the work out.' She wanted the Seldom Scene to be the key act and knew I was friends with John Duffey. I said, 'I can do that.' Then she said, 'Let's be partners.' We were off to the races."

Launching the Winterhawk Bluegrass Festival in 1984, Thomason and his partners "did all the mailings by hand—the four of us—for six years," he recalled. "Everything that had anything to do with the festival, we did ourselves. Eventually it got to where we didn't want to do it anymore and hired a staff."

After the festival turned its first profit, Thomason considered ways to spend the proceeds. "By then, we had a successful horse business," he said. "The money wasn't going to change our lives. My ex-wife said, 'Why don't we give students a leg up?' I talked to Mary and we set up a scholarship. Even in our darkest days, after we moved the festival [renamed the Grey Fox Bluegrass Festival in 2000] to the farm in Oak Hill, NY, in 2008, we kept giving those scholarships."

Teaching math and English on all levels, and remedial English at Wright State University in OH, for thirty years, Thomason came home one day, in 1999, and spoke with his ex-wife. "We had been training horses for twenty years," he said. "We had a horse nominated for the 1996 Olympics and a two-time Canadian national champion. My ex-wife said, 'We're paying people ten times as much as what you make teaching for what you know how to do.' I got the message.

"We had Winterhawk, and we were doing well, but I didn't want to give up teaching. It was like being a minister, a calling. The Ohio State Senate honored me twice as a 'Teacher of the Year.' I wept when I quit but I left at the right time. I have a beautiful ranch bordering the San Isabel Wilderness on Eagle Peak Mountain, about eighteen miles from Westcliffe, CO, but the greatest reward is when my students come to see me."

Before inheriting leadership of the Clinch Mountain Boys, Ralph Stanley II shared a "Best Bluegrass Album" Grammy with his father and Jim Lauderdale for *Lost in the Lonesome Pines* (2002). His solo *Stanley Blues* was its competition. "I wouldn't have felt right winning against them," he said.

Stanley II (1978-) had been encouraged to follow in his father's footsteps. "Dad had a personalized Stanley-tone banjo made for me," he recalled. "He showed me the basic roll but it didn't feel right to me. A guitar seemed more natural. I wanted to play lead for my dad, do something different to complement him. I played in the crosspicking style but I took from all the players and made my own way of doing it. I wanted to sing lead and do what my uncle Carter did."

Born in the same hospital where his uncle died twelve years before, Stanley II "never met him," he said, "but I feel like I know him from the records. The Stanley Brothers' music hit me when I was small. I was fortunate to have access to it and hear it all the time."

Traveling with his father during school breaks from the age of twelve, Stanley II's first "official" show came on August 8, 1995. "I was so nervous," he remembered. "I was young and my voice was changing. Later on, I asked my father why he had been patient with me. He said, 'Well, I knew you were going to get it and your rhythm-guitar playing was the best I'd had in years.'"

Stanley II shunned special treatment. "We didn't treat it as though I had an advantage," he said. "Dad and I were always straight up with each other and he respected me for that."

At the age of seventy-two, Stanley's career lifted to a height he and his brother never imagined. His unaccompanied "Oh Death" on the *O Brother, Where Art Thou?* soundtrack scored a Grammy for "Best Country Music Performance—Male." "*O Brother, Where Art Thou?* was the best thing that ever happened to Dad," said Stanley II, "but his music is what led to it needing to be made. It was a blessing from above, the 'break' he had been hoping to get. He deserved every bit of it."

Stanley and the Clinch Mountain Boys headlined large theaters and appeared at major festivals. "Tom Petty was scared to shake Dad's hand," said Stanley II. "He asked me to walk over with him to meet him. At McCabe's Guitar Shop, we kicked off with 'Little Maggie' and he went wild. He stood up and started hollering. He loved every minute of it."

As the end came into focus, Stanley sent word to his son. "He wanted me to carry the band's name," said Stanley II. "That was a sad day but it made me feel good, too."

Stanley's June 28, 2016, funeral took place at the site of his music festival. "It's where my dad and Uncle Carter grew up," said Stanley II, "and where they're buried. It's only fifteen minutes from their museum. We have a trolley that goes to it."

Chapter 10

Air Mail Special

Together with the Virginia Boys' Carl Jackson, Vassar Clements, Jimmy Buchanan, Glen Duncan, and Allen Shelton, Jim McReynolds (1927-2002) and his younger brother, mandolinist/lead singer Jesse (1929-), brought a new dimension to bluegrass. "[When] you see people singing along with you," McReynolds told *No Depression* in 2000, "it just gives you a good feeling . . . they're really your fans."[1]

Grand Ole Opry members since March 2, 1964, Jim & Jesse commemorated a half-century together in 2002. It would be their final celebration. Diagnosed with cancer, Jesse successfully battled it. Jim wouldn't be so fortunate, succumbing to throat cancer on New Year's Eve 2002.

Jim's younger brother remained active. His fourth solo album, *Jesse & Friends: Songs of the Grateful Dead* (2010), was one more milestone in a lifetime of many. "My wife has always been a Grateful Dead fan," the eighty-seven-year-old mandolinist told me. "I hadn't listened much to them—I was strictly bluegrass and country—but she played me something and I recognized it—'Black Muddy River.' It's a simple tune. I said, 'I could do that.' Recording engineer Steve Thomas helped me pick out more tunes. It took five years to finish."

Growing up less than ten miles from the Stanley birthplace, in Carfax, VA, the McReynolds brothers were immersed in music. "Dad [Claude] played fiddle," remembered Jesse. "Our grandfather [Charles McReynolds] was a fiddler. He recorded during the 1927 Bristol Sessions with the Bull Mountain Moonshiners [with uncle Bill on guitar]. About three years ago, I recut my grandfather's 'Johnny Goodwin' and 'The Girl I Left Behind' with Carl Jackson for *Orthophonic Joy: The Bristol Sessions Revisited*. I played my grandfather's fiddle. It's close to two hundred years old. I'm working on another project with it. Fifty-six other fiddle players are playing with me."

The brothers' mother, Savannah, "played guitar enough to show me some chords," recalled Jesse. "Live music was our entertainment. People came to our house every weekend. We'd sit on the porch, or in the living

Jesse McReynolds, 2014

room, and play music and buck-dance. There were banjos and guitars but everyone in my family wanted to play the fiddle because of my grandfather. My brother-in-law, who married my older sister, loaned us a mandolin. I learned to play it a little."

Epic Records producer Billy Sherrill conceived Jim & Jesse's bluegrass tribute to Chuck Berry, *Berry Pickin' in the Country* (1965). "We did a lot of rehearsing for it," remembered Jesse. "When we went into the studio to record, there were no overdubs. It went direct to tape. Chuck Berry wrote the liner notes."

McReynolds' mandolin featured on a song ("Runnin' Blue") on the Doors' *Soft Parade* (1969). "I overdubbed my part," he recalled. "I had heard of the Doors but I didn't know Jim Morrison. I got a lot of publicity for it and it put me into a different field. People started asking me to do sessions in Nashville with rock-and-roll groups. I didn't even know who they were; I wasn't a big rock-and-roll fan."

McReynolds specialized in "split-string" playing, picking only one of the mandolin's doubled strings at a time. Hearing Scruggs' banjo rolls on a radio broadcast of the *Grand Ole Opry*, he adapted the technique to mandolin. "I didn't know he was playing with fingerpicks," he said. "I did it the hard way with a straight pick. Somebody called it 'crosspicking.' We featured it on our first single, 'Are You Missing Me,' in September 1952."

Favoring rhythm over hot guitar picking, Jim was "more business oriented than musical," recalled Jesse. "When we moved to Nashville, we married two sisters. Jim and his wife took care of the booking and business. I just wanted to play music."

While his older brother served in the army (1945-47), Jesse played guitar for a band on a Norton, NC radio station. Discharged after two years, Jim bought a mandolin. "He played it when we started," said Jesse, "but I was more interested in the mandolin than he was. We switched instruments and started doing shows as the McReynolds Brothers and the Cumberland Mountain Boys. We recorded ten tracks with Larry Roll, in 1951, as the Virginia Trio."

Signing with Capitol Records, in 1952, Jim & Jesse formed the Virginia Boys. Later that year, Jesse began a two-year stint in the military.

Vassar Clements replaced Chubby Wise in the Blue Grass Boys for a few months in 1949 and returned in 1955, 1961-62, and 1967, but he was working at a paper mill when Jim & Jesse ran into him in Valdosta, GA around 1957. "He came to one of our shows," Jesse remembered, "and came backstage. We played together. He had his own style, which I

Vassar Clements, 2001

admired. We got him to leave the paper mill and start working with us."

Jim & Jesse and the Virginia Boys with Clements appeared at the first Newport Folk Festival in 1959. "That's where Bill Monroe got the idea for a bluegrass festival," said Jesse. "He started Bean Blossom but his first festival was in Roanoke. At one time, he had festivals all over the country. We worked with him quite a bit. I remember the first time we met. Jim and I were two country boys from the hills of VA. We stood back while everybody met him. He finally shook hands with us and we went our way. Bill told someone, 'Those McReynolds boys sure are hard to get acquainted with.' After we started playing shows with him, he got to be friends with Jim. I don't think he could ever figure me out but he complimented my mandolin playing."

The brothers moved to Nashville in 1958. "Martha White got us on the *Grand Ole Opry* in 1961," said Jesse, "but they got Tennessee Ernie Ford to do their commercials. We had to depend on the road, opening shows for country artists. Promoters would ask if we had records on the charts. Country radio wasn't playing bluegrass so we went into the studio, in 1967, and did a country album, *Diesel on My Tail*. It was the opposite of bluegrass but the title track was the most popular song we ever did [breaking into country music's top twenty]. We had to get on country shows and you could not do that with a bluegrass band. Unless you had a record on the charts, you were nothing."

Contracting throat cancer in the mid-nineties, Jim no longer sang. Despite being on medication, he continued to drive and almost wrecked the bus a couple of times. "We finally got him to quit," said Jesse. "He stayed with us as long as he was able.

"When he got sick and went into the hospital, the boys in the band took his place singing. After he passed, I picked up the best musicians I could. My son, Keith, has been traveling with us since the late seventies, playing bass. It ended up with three of my grandchildren in the band."

McReynolds remained at the cutting edge, doing things such as the Grateful Dead album. "If it had still been Jim & Jesse," he said, "I never would have done that, but I want to do things that no one has done. I asked Sho-Bud to make a new instrument for me. It's part Dobro, part mandolin, and it tunes like a mandola [C, G, D, A]. We call it a 'mandolobro.'

"I don't have an urge to go back to traveling but I'm still doing the *Grand Ole Opry*. I try to stay within six hundred miles of Nashville."

Chapter 11

Rocky Top

More than two and a half decades after Monroe's first recordings, Bobby and Sonny Osborne so drastically reshaped bluegrass that many consider them the last of the pioneering first generation. Adding electric instruments, pedal steel guitars, and drums to hard-driving, straight-ahead bluegrass, the Hyden, KY-born and Dayton, OH-raised sons of a schoolteacher/grocer bridged the traditions with the experimentation that was to come. "Newgrass would have been much different without the Osborne Brothers," said Laurie Lewis. "Sonny was low tuning his banjo before John Hartford. Even now, Bobby's wide open to new things."

Sonny Osborne (1937-) retired in 2004, but his six-year-older brother continued to plow new ground with his high tenor vocals and pace-setting mandolin playing. Bobby Osborne was performing at the Ryman Auditorium with Mac Wiseman and Jesse McReynolds, as Masters of Bluegrass, in July 2016, when Sonny made a guest appearance with Rhonda Vincent & the Rage. Singing several songs together, the brothers reunited for the first time in eleven years. Five months later, Bobby (1931-) recalled humble roots. "It was four miles across the mountains to civilization," he said. "All we had to get around was a mule and a horse or walk. There were no streetlights, no roads, and no cars. People had wagons but they'd run them through the creek to keep from digging out a hillside for a road.

"What you ate in the winter, you raised in the summer. Everyone had a horse, a hog, and a cow. The horse was your transportation, the cow your milk and butter, and the hog your meat. It was hard living.

"Everybody went to church and Sunday school. The church sent a woman from NJ, Elizabeth Loggavel, who did wonders for the Thousand Sticks area. Dad was a schoolteacher and his two brothers taught.

"Of course, where I'm from, coal is the biggest thing. No one had electricity. We had kerosene lamps; we called it 'coal oil.' People went to bed early because they had no lights in their house. Bathrooms were outdoors; there was no running water. You had to get your water from a well.

"When Saturday night came along, we'd listen to the *Grand Ole Opry*. People who didn't have a radio would go to somebody's house that did. There was always somebody playing banjo, guitar, and fiddle. Up and down the creek, people had to have entertainment. Whoever had the biggest house, on Saturday night, they'd have a square dance. People would dance until midnight and use flashlights and lanterns to go home. That's why they called it 'hillbilly music.' There were hillbillies in them mountains, you know."

Music ran through Osborne's veins. "When a baby is born," he said, "no one knows what it's going to become, but if it has music inside from hundreds of years ago, it's liable to come out. That's what happened to me. Every one of my mom's brothers played guitar. My dad played. I heard it from both sides of my family. My brother and sister did too. The three of us played together."

Jimmie Rodgers and Ernest Tubb were early influences. "[Rodgers] was the first person to play guitar and sing," said Osborne. "That's why they call him the 'Father of Country Music.' People tried to imitate him, including my dad. He taught me the guitar when I was ten. I wanted to sing like Ernest Tubb and I learned his songs. When I was sixteen, my voice changed to where it's at now. I still sang his songs but in a higher key. When I saw him onstage, I made up my mind that was what I wanted to do. I finally met him and we played shows together after my brother and I came to the *Opry*."

Borrowing money in 1941, Osborne's father, who had been teaching, traveled to Dayton in search of better-paying employment. "The first place he stopped was National Cash Register," said his son. "He put in an application, got a job, and worked there until he retired. He brought the family up to Dayton. I was ten but it was my first time in a car."

Osborne found a thriving music scene in the Buckeye State's fourth-largest city. "Every time I turned around, there would be someone who could play better than me," he said. "I'd learn from him. Whenever Monroe or Flatt & Scruggs came, I'd go and study how they talked, the clothes they wore."

"Cousin" Ezra Cline and future Monroe/Flatt & Scruggs fiddler Curly Ray Cline formed the Lonesome Pine Fiddlers in 1938. Together with Jimmy Martin, recently separated from Monroe, Osborne joined on guitar the summer after his sophomore year of high school. "This was before I even saw a mandolin," he said. "I didn't even know what one looked like. When it came time to go back to school, I was making money by playing music. I didn't like school anyway so I quit. I stayed and worked with them for three years."

The Lonesome Pine Fiddlers recorded Osborne's "Pain in My Heart," written with Melvin Goins and Paul Williams. Flatt & Scruggs covered it in 1949. The Osborne Brothers would start a booking agency with Flatt after his separation from Scruggs in 1969. Martin and Osborne would leave the Lonesome Pine Fiddlers and, joined by Charlie and Curly Ray Cline, hook up with Little Robert Van Winkle.

In July 1951, Ralph Stanley was in a serious auto accident. While he recuperated, Carter joined the Blue Grass Boys. Osborne phoned Martin and persuaded him to join him as the Stanley Brothers' replacement on WCYB. The partnership wouldn't last. "When Ralph got well in October," said Osborne, "Carter quit Monroe and the station let us go. Jimmy went back to Knoxville. Pee Wee Lambert had been playing mandolin, and singing the high part, but the Stanley Brothers asked me to take his place. I did it for three months before getting drafted into the marines and going to Korea. I planned to go back with the Stanley Brothers afterwards, but while I was gone, Sonny learned the banjo."

Martin hired both brothers, recording six sides for RCA. "Earl Scruggs took the banjo to a new level," said Osborne, "but Sonny took it even further. He could play in Earl's style but he liked the Beatles and wild guitar playing. He transferred that to the banjo and worked it into a style of his own. It fit what we were doing."

Osborne based his mandolin playing on fiddling. "The fiddle has four strings," he explained. "The mandolin has eight but they're tuned in unison so you have a pair of first strings, a pair of second strings, and so on. They note the same as a fiddle. They don't sound the same because of the bow—you put rosin on a bow that comes out of trees growing in the wilderness—and you use a flat pick to play mandolin."

In 1955, the Osborne Brothers visited a DJ in Pigeon Roost, about twenty-five miles from Hyden. "We didn't know anything about him," Osborne recalled, "but he said, 'If you record a tape, and pay my train fare to Nashville, I might be able to do you some good.' We didn't know many songs but 'Ruby, Are You Mad' was one of them. Sonny and another banjo player put it on tape. The DJ got with the right people and played it for them. MGM wanted to put it out. He came back and told us the news."

Osborne first heard "Ruby" as a youngster. "My grandmother and my mom's sister lived in Hyden," he recalled. "I'd go over and stay with Aunt Gladys. Her brother had a restaurant downtown. Cousin Emmy and Her Kinfolk had 'Ruby' on the jukebox. That record [released in 1946] played daylight to dark."

The Osbornes planned to feature two banjo players on their recording, but the second banjo player (Noah Crase) disappeared a month before the

July 1, 1956, session. "My brother lent me his spare banjo," remembered Osborne, "and gave me a set of picks. There was nobody else around who played banjo. I got busy and learned how to play it. We went to Nashville and recorded. I ended up playing banjo on 'Ruby,' 'Down in the Willow Garden,' 'Ho Honey Ho,' and 'Della Mae.'"

The Osbornes and Harley "Red" Allen (1930-93) teamed in 1956. The Hazard, KY-born guitarist/tenor singer "had the Kentuckians," remembered Osborne, "and Sonny and I had the original Sunny Mountain Boys. We got a job in a club where they sold alcohol. Our singer didn't want to play a place like that and went back to TN. Red came and sang the low tenor part. Whatever we were doing, he fit like a glove."

Appearing on WWVA's *Wheeling Jamboree,* in 1958, the Osborne Brothers heard Dusty Owens' "Once More." "We ain't never heard anything like that," Osborne told *Bluegrass Unlimited,* "so we just sat in the car and sung it over and over and over again, so we wouldn't forget it."[1]

Recording Owens' ballad, they developed an "inverted stacked harmony" with Bobby singing a high lead line, Sonny baritone, and Allen tenor. MGM resisted its release but "Once More" became a top-sixteen crossover hit.

The Osborne Brothers continued to break new ground. They became the first bluegrass band to perform at a college (Antioch College, Yellow Springs, OH), on May 14, 1960. "People who went to college were what we called 'high falutin'," said Osborne. "They were well educated, more than people like us. We didn't get to go to school. We never thought about college, but a folklore professor, Neil Rosenberg, recognized that college kids were beginning to like bluegrass and he got the idea to bring us to Antioch College. We didn't think of it as anything but a place to play. We went thinking they wanted country songs so that's what we did. It was no problem. Then Neil told us to go back out and play 'Little Maggie' and 'Pretty Polly.' He said, 'I know this crowd likes that kind of music.' We played Stanley Brothers songs, Bill Monroe songs, and Flatt & Scruggs songs and that crowd went crazy.

"Folk music and bluegrass kept coming together. We took [John Denver's] 'Take Me Home, Country Roads,' and [the Eagles'] 'Midnight Flyer,' and turned them into bluegrass."

The Osborne Brothers appeared on jazz vibraphonist Gary Burton's *Firebird* (1966). "He had the best musicians in town," recalled Osborne, "but he showed everybody exactly what he wanted them to play. Imagine telling Buddy Emmons how to play steel guitar. When he came to me, he said, 'I'm not familiar with that thing you're playing. What is it?' I said, 'It's a mandolin.' He looked at me and said, 'Do whatever you want with it.'"

By the late nineties, Sonny "was burnt out," said his brother. "He wanted to quit five years before he did. He wanted me to quit with him but I couldn't. Music was something I was born to do. It was tough without him. He was as much the Osborne Brothers as I am."

Rocky Top X-Press includes Osborne's three sons. "Wynn plays banjo," he said. "My oldest son, Bobby, Jr., plays snare drum and my youngest son, Robby, plays guitar and bass."

Osborne celebrated his fifty-third year at the *Grand Ole Opry* in 2016. "There're standing-room-only crowds every Friday and Saturday night," he said. "I couldn't turn it loose."

Original (2017) was Osborne's first album in eight years and his first Grammy-nominated release. In addition to an updating of the Osborne Brothers' "Pathway of Teardrops," it included covers of Eddy Arnold's "Make the World Go Away," Elvis Presley's "Don't Be Cruel," and "They Call the Wind Maria," from *Paint Your Wagon*. Debuting at the top of the bluegrass charts, its first single (a cover of the Bee Gees' "I've Gotta Get a Message to You") featured Sierra Hull (mandolin), Stuart Duncan (fiddle), Alison Brown (banjo), Rob Ickes (Dobro), Trey Hensley (lead guitar), Todd Phillips (bass), and Kenny Malone (percussion). Vince Gill, Sam Bush, Claire Lynch, Michael Cleveland, and the McCoury brothers also appeared on the album. Producer Brown met Osborne while working on Peter Rowan's *The Old School* (2013). "He made the comment that he didn't think he would ever get to make another record," she told *Billboard*. "That just struck me as something that I really didn't want to see happen. He needed to make another record."[2]

Chapter 12

The New South

Jimmy Martin's banjo player from 1956 to 1960, James Dee "J. D." Crowe continued to attract monumental musicians to his own bands—the Kentucky Mountain Boys and J. D. Crowe & the New South. "Everyone wanted to play with him," said Béla Fleck, "and be bestowed with the J. D. Crowe diploma."

Like Bobby Osborne, the Lexington, KY-born banjo player's earliest influence was Ernest Tubb. "He made me want to play electric guitar," Crowe remembered. "I didn't get my first banjo until I was thirteen. I got it because I saw Flatt & Scruggs at *Kentucky Mountain Barn Dance*. I was in awe of all of it, especially Earl's banjo playing. The banjo had been a comedic instrument. Humor went with Grandpa Jones, Stringbean, and Uncle Dave Macon. I liked watching people play it but I didn't care to hear it on the radio or a record. It didn't appeal to me. Earl was different."

Crowe (1937-) debuted on a Saturday-night radio show hosted by Homer Harris & Stardust in 1954. "The station had an amateur contest," he said. "I entered and won. The prize was to be a guest on the show. The Saturday night that I was on, Jimmy Martin was listening to his car radio on his way to Middletown, OH. He had just left Bill Monroe. He was driving through Lexington and heard me. He called the station, wanting to know who was playing the banjo. My dad talked to him."

Martin made an unexpected appearance at the station. "It was the first time I saw him," said Crowe, "but I knew who he was and that he had played with Monroe. After he got to OH, Smokey Ward hired him to play on his daily hour-and-a-half show. That's when he called, wanting me to pick with him. He even drove back [about two hours] to get me. He cleared it with my parents and I went with him. I stayed for a few months and then went back to school. That's when he teamed up with the Osborne Brothers. I met them at the radio station. They came down to do a guest slot."

Crowe spent his 1955 summer break with Mac Wiseman. "It was much different from what I had been doing," he said. "We traveled a lot. Mac starred on the WRVA *Old Dominion Barn Dance*. That's where I met Don Reno and Red Smiley."

Separating from the Osborne Brothers, Martin reformed the Sunny Mountain Boys in late 1956. When the banjo player didn't work out, he called Crowe. "He was living in Detroit," Crowe recalled. "I stayed with him for five years and recorded thirty-three sides for Decca."

In late 1957, Crowe and Martin headed to Shreveport and KWKH's *Louisiana Hayride*. Three years later, they moved to WWVA in Wheeling, WV, home of the original *Jamboree*. "They held it in a huge auditorium," remembered Crowe, "and had big crowds every Saturday night."

Martin would "be on the road for thirty days," added Doyle Lawson, "come home for seventeen or eighteen, and go out again. These days, touring is reserved for the weekends, but in those days, you worked every day."

Crowe stayed with Martin until 1961, but he "was tired and the money just wasn't enough," he recalled. "I figured it'd be best to go home to Lexington."

Securing an eight-to-five day job, Crowe played two or three nights a week with Bob and Charlie Joslin. "We met when we were kids," he said. "I'd heard that they were playing at a club so I went to see them. Afterwards, we got together as the Kentucky Mountain Boys and started playing nightclubs. It took off and we had a lot of success. We played what we wanted to play. I was tired of playing the same style all the time and wanted more variety. We did country songs and converted a variety of things to bluegrass."

"People wanted to see us play," said Lawson, "but we needed something that was our own. We couldn't just do Flatt & Scruggs, Monroe, and Jimmy Martin tunes. J. D. and I discovered that we could take a song from any genre. I thought of a song I had done as a kid with two cousins, Roy Hamilton's 'You Can Have Her.' I suggested it to J. D. and he said, 'Let's do it.' Crowe, like me, was a big fan of fifties rock."

Transforming rock, pop, and country hits into bluegrass "was pragmatic," explained Fleck. "They had gigs for weeks in the same place. If they did the same songs every night, and just stuck to traditional bluegrass, people would get tired and stop coming. They played songs people knew and it worked well."

The Kentucky Mountain Boys were playing at Martin's Tavern, in Lexington, on a hot summer night in July 1964. Driving by with his car windows open, ex-Blue Grass Boy Bobby Slone heard their music. "People had been telling him to listen to us," recalled Crowe, "but he hadn't been able to find where we were playing. When he stopped in, someone came up to me and said, 'There's a left-handed fiddler here. You ought to get him up and let him play,' so I did. We'd stay together until 1988. I still miss him [Slone died from rectal cancer on August 12, 2013]. He wasn't a bluegrass player, more of a country or Western swing fiddler, but he did all right. He was also a good upright-bass player."

After Red Allen left in early 1966, Crowe tried a few replacements. "I had Red's son, Harley, for a week," he remembered, "about all I could take of him. I liked him but he liked the bottle too much. Then, I hired Glen Lawson, then Jimmy Gaudreau. That's when Doyle Lawson came in. The sound changed but that was fine. I wanted to do something different. We rehearsed and I got them in shape."

Lawson remained with the Kentucky Mountain Boys until August 1971 with the exception of six months. "We had to work day jobs," he said, "and play music at night."

"We were playing three nights a week at Martin's Tavern," remembered Crowe, "and it was always packed. You couldn't fit in another person. The owner of Holiday Inn came down and introduced himself. He asked me if I'd like to work in the hotel's Red Slipper Lounge. It went in one ear and out the other. I'd heard a lot of bull crap. I said, 'Sure, I would' and didn't think any more about it. He came back the next week and told me, 'We'd like to have you.' We went on a trial basis, starting with three nights a week. The first night was packed. After two weeks, he called me to his office and said, 'We want to sign a contract for a year.'"

The Kentucky Mountain Boys played five nights a week at the Holiday Inn for the next seven years. "It was seasonal," said Crowe. "We'd leave at the end of April and not come back until Labor Day. During our break, we played concerts and festivals. Then, we'd come back and do another eight months. It worked out well. During the winter, there weren't many places to play. We had a class-A job. We didn't have to worry about being shot or stabbed. Once in a while, people would get a little rowdy but that was okay; that's what we wanted."

"We had a steady gig at the Holiday Inn," added Lawson, "and recorded an album to sell there. Dave Freeman had a mail-order music company, County Sales. He got hold of the record and distributed it. It spread."

By 1971, Lawson was yearning for a change. The Country Gentlemen needed a tenor singer and mandolin player. "It was his chance," said Crowe, "and he wanted to try it. I told him, 'You'll probably starve to death, but if that's what you want to do, have a go at it.'"

Larry Prentis Rice (1949-2006) replaced Lawson. "Bobby knew him from CA," said Crowe. "He jumped at the chance. I hired his brother, Tony, to play guitar. He had been with the Bluegrass Alliance. They had a different kind of rhythm but it wouldn't fit with the New South. He had to change but I knew he could do it. He didn't sound like anybody else. He didn't have a great singing voice but he had great timing in his vocals, the way he would space his words, and that's what I liked."

The second of four brothers, Danville, VA-born David Anthony "Tony" Rice (1951-) moved to L.A. at the age of two. Acquiring his passion for music from his father, Herbert Hoover Rice, a mandolin/guitar player and founding member of the Golden State Boys, he appeared on the *Town Hall Party* radio show at the age of nine. The Kentucky Colonels were also on the show and Rice heard Clarence White for the first time. "[Out] of my inability to play like Clarence White," Rice said, "came my own identity as a separate musician . . . with the exception of, you know, a few things like rhythm style and some of the techniques he used."[1]

By his twelfth birthday, Tony and Larry (who would join the Golden State Boys) had a band. Rice moved East in 1965. Six years later, he met Sam Bush and Bluegrass Alliance at Carlton Haney's festival. Recruited into the band, he left after a few months and reunited with his brother in the New South.

Reaching for a mainstream audience, Crowe added a drummer and electric bassist for *Bluegrass Evolution* (1973). "Some people liked it," he said, "some even loved it, but others didn't. I didn't care. I was doing what I wanted to do. That's how new things are found.

"Larry, Tony, Bobby, and I stayed together for a while but Larry had a drinking problem. I told him he could either straighten up or leave and he decided to leave. Sam Bush subbed for a couple of weeks. He was only seventeen. I had to sneak him into the club. I called Ricky Skaggs and got him to play mandolin and sing tenor. Then, I hired Jerry Douglas to play Dobro. They were leaving the Country Gentlemen. That was the classic New South—Bobby, Tony, Ricky, Jerry, and me."

Returning to an acoustic format, the J. D. Crowe & the New South's self-titled 1975 album (Rounder 0044) was a cornerstone of progressive bluegrass. "I remember J. D. Crowe tearing my face off with his banjo," said Dan Tyminski, "but when I listen now, I gravitate towards Tony's guitar playing. I've never been a fan of any banjo player who wasn't playing with an awesome guitar player."

J. D. Crowe and the New South toured Japan for ten days, in 1975, starting in Tokyo and playing eight concerts. "Every show sold out," recalled Crowe, "800- to 2,000-seat concert halls."

"We took the bluegrass world by storm," Douglas added, "and saw how popular our music was in a completely different culture."

It would be the classic lineup's last hurrah. "I knew they were going to leave," said Crowe. "Tony was tired after being with me for five years. If you keep someone that long, you've gotten the best out of him."

"Tony was taking what he felt was a step up in his musicality," remembered Douglas. "David Grisman was premiering this new kind of music and Tony was an important part of it. Ricky and I were finally going to have the band we wanted [Boone Creek] but it didn't last long. He left for Emmylou Harris and I joined up with the Whites. We mostly did old country songs but it was sparser than other bands I'd played with. There was no banjo, less competition for backup behind the vocals. The Whites were great singers and I learned about playing behind a singer. I had such a great time with them; it was family."

"If I hadn't left," Rice said, "it wouldn't have stayed together much longer anyway, I don't think. Ricky had a real staunch traditional side, even back then, and he wouldn't have hung around . . . it's almost like it was so good, it was doomed to burn itself out real quick."[2]

Rice's albums with the David Grisman Quintet (DGQ) influenced bluegrass and jazz. Their self-titled debut (1977) included Rice's "Swing 51." Reaching number fourteen on *Billboard*'s jazz chart, *Hot Dawg* (1978) included Rice's "Neon Time" and "Devlin"; six Grisman originals including "16/16"; "Dawgology," written with Richard Greene; and Django Reinhardt and Stephane Grappelli's "Minor Swing," featuring Grappelli on violin. "Grisman had prepared chord charts," Rice recalled. "We went to the studio, looked at a chart, played a few minutes and . . . recorded it."[3]

Rice left the quintet before a 1978 tour with Grappelli. "Musically, my heart was not in it," he told the *NY Times*.

Grisman appeared on Rice's solo albums *Acoustics* (1977) and the jazz-inspired *Manzanita* (1979), which also included Bush, Skaggs, Douglas, and DGQ members Darol Anger and Todd Phillips. Reuniting in 1993, Rice and Grisman recorded *The Pizza Tapes*, with Jerry Garcia, and the experimental *Tone Poems* a year later.

The Tony Rice Unit with Wyatt Rice (second guitar), Jimmy Gaudreau (mandolin), and the Simpkins brothers—Rickie (fiddle) and Ronnie (bass)—emphasized the bluegrass/jazz connection. *Mar West* (1980) included Miles Davis's "Nardis" while *Backwaters* (1982) featured "On Green Dolphin Street" and a John Coltrane-inspired "My Favorite Things." "If we have guitar, mandolin and fiddle," Rice said, "there's no rule that we have to play bluegrass music."[4]

Joining Rice, Grisman, bassist Mark Schatz, and Alison Krauss as the Rounder All-Star Bluegrass Band, in 1988, Crowe appeared on PBS's *Lonesome Pine Special*. "Alison wasn't yet eighteen years old," he recalled. "She had just won the Kentucky Fried Chicken band contest in Louisville."

In addition to recording a dozen solo albums, Rice collaborated with Ricky Skaggs (*Skaggs & Rice*, 1980) and Norman Blake (*Blake & Rice*,

Tony Rice, 2000

1987; *Norman Blake and Tony Rice 2*, 1990). He recorded two albums—*The Rice Brothers* (1989) and *The Rice Brothers 2* (1994)—with Larry, Wyatt, and Ron. He and Larry joined Chris Hillman and Herb Pedersen for *Out of the Woodwork* (1997), *Rice, Rice, Hillman & Pedersen* (1999), and *Runnin' Wild* (2001). Moving to CA in 1980, he owed Rounder Records a bluegrass album. "They paid him upfront," said Crowe, "but he hadn't recorded it. Finally, they told him they wanted the album. He called me; I had played on his first solo album. We needed a tenor singer and I immediately thought of Doyle. We got Bobby Hicks [fiddle] and Todd Phillips [bass]. The Bluegrass Album Band did its first two albums without Dobro and then brought Jerry Douglas in for the third. He stayed until we broke up in 1996."

Muscle tension dysphonia reduced Rice's voice to a whisper; he last sang in public at the 1994 Gettysburg Bluegrass Festival. Although he took a non-singing, co-leader role in a quartet with Peter Rowan, lateral epicondylitis (tennis elbow) and arthritis made it painful to play guitar and forced his retirement. "I certainly hope to have things in my life more stable again," he told the *NY Times* in February 2014, "where I can start to concentrate on being on the road, with my friends and my musicians, playing good music. It's a work in progress. It just happens to be going a hell of a lot slower than I wish it would."[5]

After years of hitting it hard, Crowe "wanted to get away from music" and took a break in the early nineties. "I spent a lot of time playing golf," he said. "I figured I'd get back to music when I wanted, when the time was right, and when I ran into good talent—people like Richard Bennett [lead vocals/guitar], Don Rigsby [mandolin], Phil Leadbetter [Dobro], and Curt Chapman [bass]."

Releasing the Grammy-nominated *Flashback* (1994), this edition of the New South was as impressive as any Crowe assembled. Tony Rice-influenced Bennett played with Flatt & Scruggs fiddler Benny Sims at fifteen. In addition to five solo albums, he recorded three albums with Jimmy Gaudreau and Mike Auldridge and joined Bobby Osborne's Bluegrass Express in 2004.

Working with Crowe was "a pilgrimage," said Rigsby. "I was a disciple of Ricky Skaggs and followed his path as much as I could."

Rigsby felt a strong connection with Ralph Stanley. "The Baptist Church played a big role in Ralph's life," he said, "and that's the church I attend. The doctrine affects your soul from top to bottom. He ran from it but in the end, he bowed to the will of God. He said that he was put here to sing but I think God put him here as a gift to all the people who experienced his magic. He was God's gift to me. Losing him in close proximity to losing my dad was hard. I felt like I was losing another dad."

Magoffin County, KY-born guitarist/singer Charlie Sizemore (1960-) provided Rigsby's first break. Replacing Whitley in 1976, the son and grandson of banjo players had remained with the Clinch Mountain Boys for a dozen albums. "I met Charlie when he was singing for Ralph," recalled Rigsby, "and worked with him for three years while we were going to college. He was studying government at the University of Kentucky and I was at Morehead State studying journalism. He went on to the Nashville School of Law, passed the bar, and became an attorney."

Rigsby turned banjo player/bandleader Sammy Shelor down three times before agreeing to join the Lonesome River Band in 1992. "The first time I was in college," he remembered, "and thought I should finish. The second time, Dan [Tyminski] was going to play banjo and I was going to play mandolin, which would have been interesting. The third time was after Dan left. He had made such a big impact that people needed a buffer to get used to the idea that it wasn't going to be the same. The next time, Dan had been gone a while, so I said yes.

"We were quite successful. Kenny Smith [guitar/vocals] came onboard and we saw the world. We were on television and played big festivals. I brought more of a mountain sound. Dan was a refined singer but I was more influenced by the Stanley school."

Rigsby became a member of Longview in 1996. "It was Ken Irwin's present to himself for Rounder's twenty-fifth anniversary," he recalled. "He put people together to sing at a festival in NC. James King and I sang with Dudley Connell. Ronnie Simpkins played bass. Ron Stewart played fiddle. We recorded live and it sounded so good. Ken and I had been discussing me producing a record so we started putting it together. I thought of Glen Duncan [fiddle] and Joe Mullins [banjo]. Marshall Wilborn [bass] was obviously a good choice. When we recorded the album, we did a show at Longview Farm. It was so good, we kept making records and playing shows."

Along with the Lonesome River Band's Kenny Smith and Ronnie Bowman, Rigsby sang "Southern Streamline" and "Rambunctious Boy" on John Fogerty's Grammy-winning *Blue Moon Swamp* (1997). "Whitesnake tried to do it," Rigsby said, "but they didn't work out. Jerry Douglas recommended us. Kenny, Ronnie, and I flew to L.A. and spent three or four days recording. We sang each song fifty times. There was a note in one song that I only got right twice . . . but I got it right."

Leaving the Lonesome River Band in 2001, Rigsby became director of KY's Center for Traditional Music at Morehead State. "It was a good opportunity," he said, "to make sure bluegrass was not only preserved but advanced forward."

Appearing (with Bowman) on Alan Jackson's *Bluegrass Album* (2013), Rigsby performed with the country-music superstar at Carnegie Hall and on *The David Letterman Show*. "We got resistance from the fringes," he recalled, "who said that [Jackson] was a country artist, and had no right to make a bluegrass record, but that's all he listens to. We only did a handful of shows. He didn't come to take bluegrass money. He didn't need it."

Rigsby divides his time between Flashback and the Band of Ruhks, a group he conceived with Bowman and Smith after a 2010 Lonesome River Band reunion. They released a self-titled album in 2015. Rigsby collaborated with San Francisco-based David Thom on *New Territory* the following year. "We were thinking of things we could do," said Rigsby, "that were out of the box."

Phil Leadbetter (1962-) left music, in the late seventies, to attend nursing school. After working as a nurse for a decade, the Knoxville-born Dobro player hooked up with Grandpa Jones and Vern Gosdin. He recorded two albums with Crowe & the New South, formed Wildfire and Grasstowne, and played with Buck White and the Whites. Diagnosed with

Hodgkin's lymphoma (a cancer of the blood) in 2009, he endured three years of intense treatment. Three months after stem-cell treatment in early 2012, he teamed with Dale Ann Bradley. Three years later, he reunited with the musicians who had recorded J. D. Crowe & the New South's *Flashback* nearly a quarter of a century before. They released three singles as Flashback (without Crowe), in 2016, and an album the following year. Banjo player/baritone singer Stuart Wynd joined Rigsby, Bennett, and Leadbetter after the album's completion.

Leadbetter's son, Matt, played Dobro for the Lonesome River Band, Blue Moon Rising, and Valerie Smith & Liberty Pike. He joined Dale Ann Bradley in early 2017.

Doyle Lawson and Quicksilver's eighteen IBMA Awards, between 1990 and 2012, included seven for "Vocal Group of the Year" and seven for "Gospel Performance of the Year." The IBMA Hall of Fame inducted Lawson in 2012. "Bluegrass is the most honest, emotionally sincere music there is," he said. "I might be a little biased but I've played it all my life, pretty much."

Doyle Lawson, 2010

Lawson's friendship with Crowe continues. "J. D. is still as close to me as a brother would be," he said. "We've never quit picking."

Five months before his eightieth birthday, Crowe was content with retirement. "I'm not playing much," he said. "I don't have the desire. I did it for sixty years. That's enough. When you've played with the best, where do you go from there?"

Chapter 13

Docabilly

Fiddle tunes, blues, pop, folk, Western swing, New Orleans/Django Reinhardt-style jazz, rockabilly, country music, gospel, and Carter Family/ Jimmie Rodgers songs transformed with the guitar, banjo, and harmonica playing and warm baritone vocals of Arthel Lane "Doc" Watson (1923-2012). Guy Clark compared Watson's playing to Michelangelo's *David* and Da Vinci's *Mona Lisa*. Sam Bush memorialized him with "Doc Watson Morning." A Grammy recipient in 1973, 1974, 1979, 1986, 1990, 2002, and 2006, Watson received the Lifetime Achievement Award in 2004. "Doc was an extremely intelligent man," said David Holt, "and he had far-ranging thoughts. He was full of passion. He was complicated, not an old man sitting on a porch. I've known musicians who play faster, with more notes, but Doc was the most musical. Sam Bush told me that it's timing, tone, and taste. Doc had all three."

"Doc was always just Doc," remembered T. Michael Coleman, Watson's bassist from 1972 to 1987, "no pretense, no inflated ego, and no set list. He invited the audience into his living room and they felt right at home."[1]

"People thought of Doc as the grandfather who played folksongs," said Watson's longtime guitarist Jack Lawrence, "but all through the 1940s and '50s, he was playing whatever was on the radio: country hits and pop songs. *Docabilly* [1995] took him back to where he came from. He loved the Everly Brothers and songs like 'Shake, Rattle, and Roll.'"

Raised with five brothers (Russeau, Arnold, Ottis, Linney, and David) and three sisters (Ethel, Ruby, and Jewel) in a three-room house near Deep Gap, NC, an unincorporated Watauga County community named after the natural gap at the Blue Ridge Mountains' Fire Scale Mountain, Watson had music in his blood. His father, General Dixon Watson (1892-1949), a day laborer/farmer, played banjo. His mother, the former Annie Greene (1895-1985), sang at the Baptist church. Older brother Arnold played harmonica and five-string banjo; younger brother David played fiddle.

Losing his sight to a congenital vascular disorder before his first

Doc Watson, 1999

birthday, Watson found his path through music. He spent hours listening to the wind-up phonograph and jazz, blues, and country discs his father purchased with money earned at a mill. The collection grew as General Watson bartered with neighbors for their old records.

Playing harmonica at five, Watson acquired his first banjo, built by his father using the skin of his grandmother's ailing cat, at eleven. A schoolmate at the School for the Blind in Raleigh showed him a few chords on the guitar. "One of my cousins had a guitar," Watson said to me in 1988. "My father told me that, if I could learn to play a song, he'd take me downtown to get a guitar."

Cutting dead chestnut trees and selling the wood to a tannery, Watson raised enough money to buy a ten-dollar Stella guitar and Nick Lucas instruction book. Shortly afterwards, a music storeowner helped him to acquire his first good instrument—a Martin D-18—at cost (ninety dollars) with payments of five dollars a month. Busking with his older brother Linney, at a fruit stand, Watson paid for the instrument months ahead of schedule.

Watson and a band were playing a show in a Lenoir furniture store, broadcast by WHKY/Hickory in 1941, when the announcer mentioned that Arthel was an unusual name for a musician. An audience member yelled, "Call him Doc," presumably referring to Sherlock Holmes' Doctor Watson, and the name stuck.

Marrying the former Rosa Lee Carlton (1931-2012), his fifteen-year-old third cousin, in 1947, Watson deepened his ties to music. A guitar player and songwriter, Carlton penned "Your Lone Journey" with her husband. Emmylou Harris, John Hartford, David Grisman, and Robert Plant & Alison Krauss covered it.

Rosa Lee's father, Gaither Carlton (1901-72), had played fiddle and banjo, in the 1920s, for Al Hopkins & the Hillbillies and Clarence "Tom" Ashley. Born Clarence Earl McCurry, Ashley (1895-1967) joined a medicine show at the age of sixteen. Recording solo, and with the Blue Ridge Entertainers and Carolina Tar Heels (featuring three-finger banjo player Dock Walsh), Ashley introduced "Rising Sun Blues" ("House of the Rising Sun"), "Little Sadie," "Dark Holler," "Greenback Dollar," "John Hardy," "House Carpenter," and "Coo Coo Bird." Jerry Garcia credited him for influencing his banjo playing. Leaving music during the Great Depression, Ashley worked in WV coalmines before starting a trucking company. He appeared with the Stanley Brothers as a comedian, not a musician. Attending the Union Grove Old Time Fiddlers Convention in 1960, he hadn't played banjo professionally for two decades. Nevertheless, he was demonstrating one of his old tunes during a parking-lot jam when Rinzler heard him and invited him to record. The following Labor Day weekend, Rinzler set up recording equipment in Ashley's living room. Invited as an accompanist, Carlton brought his son-in-law to play banjo and guitar. Watson had played in Jack Williams' country-swing band, the Country Gentlemen, in Johnson City, since 1953. Playing in a band without a fiddle, he had found a way to compensate on his Les Paul electric guitar (Rinzler had him switch to a borrowed acoustic). "Doc learned to play fiddle tunes on electric guitar," said Lawrence, "because he heard Grady Martin and Hank Garland doing it. He showed me licks he got from Smitty Smith, who played with Ernest Tubb in the forties."

"I started off playing with a thumb lead," Watson told *Frets*, "Maybelle Carter style. . . . When I began to listen to Jimmie Rodgers, I figured out there was something being done there besides the thumb and finger, so I got a pick and started working on it."[2]

"If the picker's personality isn't expressed in the picking technique," he continued to *Guitar Player*, "there's something missing."[3]

Folkways released *Old Time Music at Clarence Ashley's* in January 1961. Ashley's band with Clint Howard (guitar/vocals) and Fred Price (fiddle), along with Watson, made its NY debut a month later in a sold-out 450-seat auditorium at Greenwich Village's P.S. 41. In his *NY Times* review, Robert Shelton pointed to Watson's superb instrumental skill.

Watson's relationship with Rinzler continued to grow. When the band traveled to the University of Chicago and the Ash Grove in L.A., he shared "driving duties," keeping Rinzler awake with his endless repertoire. Encouraging him to stick with acoustic music, Rinzler assured him that performing on the folk circuit would enable him to support his family. Watson agreed to try it. Becoming his manager, Rinzler arranged a tour with Monroe of colleges, folk-music coffeehouses, and NY's Town Hall. "Ralph's the key to me being on the road," Watson said. "He did the discovering. Ralph's a very modest fellow but, without him, I couldn't have done it."

"My main motive," Watson said during a 2012 press conference, "was to earn a living for a sweet little woman and two children."[4]

Helping him to assemble a repertoire of Child Ballads, songs from Cecil Sharp's collection of Appalachian folk music, old blues, and tunes from Watson's family, Rinzler reinvented the guitarist as a lovable folk icon. Recording with Viper, KY-born folksinger Jean Ritchie (1922-2015) at Folk City in 1963, Watson released his self-titled solo debut the following year. "The first three years, Doc didn't own an acoustic guitar," said Lawrence. "He could have traded his Les Paul for an acoustic but he didn't. He kept it until he died."

Watson finally bought a 1945 Martin D-18 acoustic guitar from Mark's Stringed Instruments in NY in 1963. "I used that guitar on *Arthel's Guitar* [2013]," said Lawrence. "Doc gave it to me in the eighties. I grew up listening to that guitar on records."

Watson wasn't the first bluegrass guitarist to flatpick. Bill Napier's mandolin-like flatpicking featured on the Stanley Brothers' "Mountain Dew" (1957), and George Shuffler flatpicked in a similar style, but the technique went back further. "When Bill Monroe recorded 'Muleskinner Blues,'" said Lawrence, "he kicked it off with a flatpicked guitar solo."

Traveling by himself by bus at first, Watson wouldn't be alone for long. Phoning from the road, he learned that his wife had taught their son, Eddy Merle Watson (1949-85), named after country singer Eddy Arnold and guitarist Merle Travis, a few chords on the guitar and the teenager had run with it. Within a year, the fifteen-year-old was touring the country with his father. They would work together for a quarter of a century. "Merle was a great blues and slide guitar player," said T. Michael Coleman, "and an unbelievable finger-style player. He learned it from Mississippi John Hurt."

The Grateful Dead's original soundman and clandestine chemist, Owsley Stanley, released a seven-CD set—*Bear's Sonic Journals/Doc & Merle Watson: Never the Same Way Once—Live at the Boarding House—May 1974* (2017). "We were like a freight train," recalled Coleman. "There was a lot of power for three people, a lot of drive and syncopation."

Hailing from a small cotton-mill town, Mayodan, NC, near Greensboro,

Coleman (1951-) played with rock bands throughout junior high and high school. "We played every Saturday night in Stoneville, NC," he said. "My father and the drummer's father put on dances. It was a place where kids could go and stay out of trouble."

Heading to Appalachian State University, in Boone, NC, Coleman wasn't sure he would play again. "I was in tears," he remembered, "riding back from my last performance before college. Boone is in the vortex of America's traditional music. I remember going into a music store and seeing a poster of Doc Watson. I said, 'Who's that?' I soon found out."

By then, Coleman was "playing rocked-up folk music with a band in the mountains," he recalled. "Mumford and Sons is what we were doing back then. We were before our time. Joe Smothers and Clay Buckner [Red Clay Ramblers] was in that band. Merle liked us and we opened for him and Doc many times. About a week after we disbanded, Merle cornered me in a hardware store and said, 'Do you want to play with me and Daddy?' I said, 'I'd love to.' He said, 'Come down to the house and we'll see if it works out.' I went to Deep Gap, ten miles from Boone, and we played 'T for Texas.' That was the last time we rehearsed for fifteen years. I sat in the middle because Doc's repertoire was so vast, there was no way I could learn all the tunes. I had to watch their hands. They were riding the wave of *Will the Circle Be Unbroken* and wanted a larger sound."

Merle was conflicted about touring. "He was more of a homebody," said Coleman, "than he was a traveler. He handled all the business, all the road prep, and all the advance work. That was a lot to take on. When I came on the road, it relieved a lot of pressure."

Beginning in 1983, Merle increasingly asked Jack Lawrence to replace him on the road. Lawrence (1953-) would accompany Watson for twenty-seven years. "Doc wasn't a songwriter," recalled the Charlotte, NC-raised guitarist, "but he had a knack for finding material that he could make his own. He was a big fan of the Moody Blues' *Days of Future Passed*. He was always talking about 'Nights in White Satin' so I said, 'We ought to do it.' It became part of our show and we got tons of requests for it."

Lawrence was fifteen or sixteen when he met Watson at Union Grove. "I asked him how he grasped his flatpick," he remembered. "To my surprise, it was exactly the way I had been doing it. I was aware of bluegrass from the time I was five or six. My dad was a TV technician and we had an antenna on an extremely tall mast. We could pick up Flatt & Scruggs' TV show twice every Saturday. The Lewis Family had a show out of Augusta, GA. Reno & Smiley had a show out of Roanoke. On the radio, WLOS, in Asheville, had a bluegrass show with Hubert and Pee Wee Davis and the Jones Brothers."

With his father moonlighting as a music-hall sound technician, Lawrence "grew up backstage among first-generation players," he recalled, "and I immersed in it. When I was four, I found my dad's Martin guitar under his bed. I never had a chance."

Seeing Flatt & Scruggs in concert "showed me anything could happen when you're onstage," said Lawrence. "After they were introduced, they came charging out, not saying a word, and went into their first song. It was very powerful but one of Earl's fingerpicks came off and flew into the first row. It stopped everything. They joked about it while someone retrieved Earl's pick, gave it back to him, and the show proceeded."

Encountering George Shuffler at the music hall, Lawrence "was influenced by his guitar playing," he said, "and I got to be friends with his brothers. I still keep in touch with his widow. His brother Ron played bass on my last record."

By the age of twelve, Lawrence was regularly accompanying fiddlers. "My first professional bluegrass band," he said, "was Carl Story and His Rambling Mountaineers. They were as old-school bluegrass as you could get. They had a TV show in Charlotte and I played on that show. They started taking me out with them during the summer."

Rock and roll was taboo in Lawrence's childhood home. There, it was strictly country music and bluegrass. "I started listening to other music on a transistor radio when I was thirteen," he said. "I was certainly aware of the Beatles and Elvis Presley and I saw a connection with bluegrass. Listen to Bill Monroe's pre-Flatt & Scruggs stuff like 'Rocky Road Blues' and then listen to Chuck Berry's guitar style; it comes from Monroe's heavy, downstroke, bluesy mandolin."

After graduating from high school, Lawrence and banjo player Terry Baucom teamed at the Land of Oz amusement park. Baucom would become a founding member of Boone Creek and play with Doyle Lawson & Quicksilver and IIIrd Tyme Out.

Attending Carlton Haney's bluegrass festival in Camp Springs Park, outside Reidsville, NC, in 1965 (the first such multiday event), Lawrence noticed "a tremendous shift in band personnel," he said. "I'd never seen anything like it. Tony Rice left the Bluegrass Alliance and Jimmy Gaudreau left the Country Gentlemen to start II Generation [Second Generation] with Eddie Adcock. Tony was supposed to go with them but he decided to go with J. D. Crowe instead."

At Camp Springs Park, Lawrence was one of many guitarists hoping to audition for the Bluegrass Alliance. "All these guitar players were lining up," he said, "and none of us knew they had already hired Curtis Burch. When I figured it out, I felt bad for Curtis."

Lawrence hooked up with Adcock and Gaudreau in Washington, DC, but it didn't work out and he left after a week. "I had a job offer from the New Deal String Band so I took that. A few months later, I saw II Generation and New Grass Revival at Carlton's festival in Lakeland, FL. New Grass Revival had just split from [Bluegrass Alliance leader/fiddler] Lonnie Peerce. In the beginning of December, I got a call from Lonnie. He talked me into joining the Bluegrass Alliance. I was there for not quite a year but I realized I had made a mistake and went back to the New Deal String Band."

Lawrence had worked on the Raleigh-based New Deal String Band's instruments as a technician, and seen them at Union Grove, but "they seemed on the scary side," he remembered. "They were hippies and did weird material. They were playing bluegrass but they weren't playing songs associated with bluegrass. It was almost rock and roll. Sam Bush gives the New Deal String Band credit for inspiring him to go off on the newgrass thing but we never made any money. They recorded *Bluegrass* [1969] before I joined but they never recorded anything else."

Members of the New Deal String Band introduced Lawrence to Clarence White's guitar playing. "You could definitely hear Doc's influence," he said. "Clarence had a twisted sense of timing and did quirky things like Django Reinhardt and Joe Maphis licks but I could hear where he was coming from."

Hearing White mention Reinhardt as one of his major influences, Lawrence became fascinated with the French Gypsy guitarist. "The New Deal String Band had Django's records with Stephane Grappelli," said Lawrence, "and they covered 'After You're Gone' and 'Lady Be Good.'"

After five years with bluegrass bands, Lawrence "switched to electric guitar so I could earn a living," he recalled. "I didn't use a capo and forced myself to play in different keys and positions. I ended up with an electric country-rock band with guitarist/vocalist Joe Smothers [later a member of Doc and Merle Watson's Frosty Morn]. We did well for a few years until, like many bands, inner turmoil killed it. I went back to playing bluegrass with Terry Baucom [ex-New Deal String Band guitarist/vocalist], Leroy Savage, and Tony Williamson, who's a great mandolin player. We could have done well but it was hard to keep together. Terry got an offer from Doyle Lawson and we lost interest after he left."

Starting an acoustic guitar duo around 1979, Lawrence and Smothers "wrote tunes and traveled extensively for four years." Smothers introduced him to Merle Watson. "Merle would sit in, playing slide guitar," Lawrence said. "Joe and I opened shows for Doc and Merle. We never played together but Doc complimented my playing."

Hearing that he had split from Smothers, Merle phoned Lawrence, in

1983, and asked, "What are you doing tomorrow?" "I was going to mow the grass," remembered Lawrence. "I'll leave a ticket for you at the airport," continued Watson. "Meet up with Doc and go to Chicago for the gig. I don't want to go."

Lawrence "did the sound check, had dinner, and played the show without rehearsal," he recalled. "Doc mentioned songs he wanted to do and it worked out. The first year, I did half the gigs. The second year, I did 98 percent. Merle had been playing with his father for almost twenty years and was tired of the road. He loved doing construction, driving heavy equipment, and moving dirt with bulldozers. He didn't know whether he wanted to be a contractor, put a band together, or take a break. Those questions will never be answered."

"Merle had a foreshadowing of his death," said Coleman. "After our last show, he and Doc drove me to the airport to go back to Nashville, where I was living. Merle was telling him that he had to go on."

In the early hours of October 23, 1985, a few days before *Frets* named him Fingerpicking Guitarist of the Year in folk, blues, and country music, Merle Watson "injured himself while cutting wood on a table saw at his

Merle Watson, 1985

home," reported the *L.A. Times*, "and drove [his] tractor to a nearby house for treatment."[5]

"On the way back down the steep incline of the couple's drive," continued Charlie Downey, "the tractor brakes locked, leading it over a high embankment. Merle was thrown off the large tractor which then landed on him, killing him instantly."[6]

"I got a phone call," remembered Coleman. "I don't remember who it was but they told me Merle had died. I immediately called Doc and said, 'I'm on my way.' Someone related to me later that Doc was very upset. People had questions about what he was going to do. He said, 'Don't worry; Michael is on his way.' That shows how close we were."

Around 5:00 A.M., Lawrence got a call from T. Michael Coleman. Doc phoned three hours later. "He was devastated," Lawrence remembered. "The day after Merle's accident, we were supposed to go out for a two-week tour. Doc was calling to tell me that he might have to cancel. He didn't know what he was going to do. Of course, I understood. He asked me to come up to his house. He needed me whether there was anything I could do or not. I went up straight away. He met me on the front porch, gave me a big hug, and cried on my shoulder. I told him, 'I'm here for you.'"

"It wasn't easy being Doc's son," said Holt. "Doc was such a powerful personality. Merle shone with his fingerpicking. He applied that to his slide playing and came up with something new. Merle was Doc's partner, career guide, eyes, and son. He lost all those things."

"A lot of musicians came to Merle's funeral," said Coleman, "but it wasn't very musical. The church minister handled it. Rosa Lee was so distraught there was a cousin watching Doc. After the ceremony, I walked up to Doc and said, 'Come with me.' I took Doc to the casket. He lay his head on the casket and talked to Merle while crying and saying things like 'I'll see you soon.' Musicians gathered around the casket and sang Merle's favorite song, 'Midnight Rider,' by Gregg Allman. That's the way we said goodbye."

A couple of days after the funeral, Watson phoned Lawrence again. "He had decided to do the second week of the tour," recalled Lawrence. "We were all in a haze. We had lost someone close. Doc had a dream where he was in a desert and couldn't find his way. He felt Merle touch his arm and say, 'Follow me, Dad. Everything is going to be okay.' He got up that morning and called [booking agent] Mitch Greenhill. Then, he called me. Within three days of burying Merle, we were back on the road."

"I thought Doc would never go on the road again," said Coleman. "I was very surprised when, in a couple of weeks, he said he was ready. He felt closer to Merle when he was on the stage. The first place we played was the Great American Music Hall in San Francisco. Jack, Doc, and I walked out onstage. People stood up and applauded. Everybody was crying. They knew how hard it was for us."

Working on a solo album when Merle died, Lawrence left it uncompleted. Two tunes were included on *About Time* (1997), along with tracks recorded with Doc. Sam Bush, Jerry Douglas, and the Del McCoury Band played on Lawrence's next album, *I Don't Need the Whiskey Anymore* (2002), and Curtis Burch played Dobro on *Arthel's Guitar*. "The title track was an instrumental I wrote," said Lawrence. "It's very Doc-like."

Leaving Watson after fifteen years, Coleman signed on with the Seldom Scene in 1986. "It was difficult to leave Doc," he said, "but he had rumbled for quite a while that he was going to retire, which he did not do. I wanted to be ahead of the curve. I had two small children at home and had to think about the future."

MerleFest (Merle Watson Memorial Festival) launched in 1988. "Since Steve Johnson became artist relations director in 2013," said Lawrence, "it's gone back to being mostly acoustic. Steve has a grasp of the festival's history. Five of us have played every MerleFest—Sam Bush, Jerry Douglas, Peter Rowan, my friend Joe Smothers, and me. We performed together, in 2015, and it was wall to wall, standing room only."

Merle's son, Richard, began touring with his grandfather in the late eighties. "Doc said that he would never take Richard on the road," recalled Lawrence, "but I got an itinerary from our travel agent with three tickets instead of two. At the end of the tour, I got my paycheck and found out he had brought Richard in as a full partner. Doc and I made a deal, in 1990, to take expenses off and split the rest evenly. It was at a time when he had decided to retire. We played out the rest of the calendar and didn't do anything for three months. Then, he called. He was antsy. After getting off the road, I had become involved with a guitar store doing repairs. I was home every night. I didn't make a lot of money with Doc. It was hard to support my family. The first time he called, I was lukewarm about the idea. He called back, thirty or forty minutes later, and offered me that deal as an equal partner. When he brought Richard in without discussion, I was upset. Now I had two Watsons to take care of and I was making more than 15 percent less to do it."

"Doc trusted Richard to make decisions that had to do with the family," said Holt, "and he was Doc's eyes on the road."

"I'm proud of him . . . ," Watson told the *Wilkes Journal-Patriot*. "He's got a wonderful personality, just like his dad had . . . he's a fine musician and he's finally got over stage fright. He has a lot of Merle's attributes."[7]

Richard Watson would suffer a fatal heart attack in June 2015.

Lawrence played his last full show with Doc in Johnson City, in

December 2011. "Merle played this annual show before me," he said, "and I did twenty-six of them. It had been close to a year since I'd played with Doc. I couldn't believe how much he had slipped. The audience was sobbing. He shouldn't have been on the road. At MerleFest 2012, his last year, he played in a key different from the rest of the band. John Cowan and I were in the wings crying. When they called me out, and I sat beside him, he asked me what we were going to play and I said, 'I Know What It Means to Be Lonesome,' a song he and I played late in our relationship. I touched his arm and he sat up straight, said, 'Key of D,' and put his capo on the second fret. When I left the stage, he slipped again. Our musical relationship was so tight he could pull it back when I was there."

Experiencing complications during colon-cancer surgery, Watson died on May 29, 2012. Nearly four hundred people attended his June 3 funeral at the Laurel Springs Baptist Church. "Just in case there's jamming at the Pearly Gates," said Holt, "I purchased an 'A' Hohner Special and put it in his pocket."

Holt (1946-) met Watson nearly three decades before. "I hosted a show on TNN [The Nashville Network], *Fire on the Mountain*," he said, "and Doc and Merle were guests in 1984. We played together and the rhythm we hooked into was powerful. The next year, I asked them to record *Reel and Rock* with me. Shortly after we finished it, Merle died. I stayed in touch with Doc and we did a few gigs. Then, I asked him to do *Grandfather's Greatest Hits* [1991]. Chet Atkins, Duane Eddy, Sam Bush, and Jerry Douglas played with us."

Holt and Watson bonded after Holt's daughter died in a car accident. "Doc was more than sympathetic," he said. "He was one of the first people to come to my house. He came that evening. Losing a child cemented us in a way that couldn't have happened any other way. It was something we both understood."

In 1998, a NC public-TV station asked Watson and Holt to play a concert as a fundraiser. "It was a huge success," recalled Holt, "and Doc's agent started booking us. We won a Grammy for the three-CD set I produced, *Legacy*. He spoke his life story and we played songs important to him. We started playing together—hundreds of jobs over the next fourteen years."

Born in North Garland, TX, not far from Dallas, Holt recalled the day he fell in love with roots music. "We were coming back from the store," he remembered. "My brother and I were mad at my mom. She wouldn't buy us the Ovaltine with the Captain America decoder ring and we were giving her grief. She pulled the car to the side of the road and said, 'Get out!' She grabbed us by the ears, marched us up to the work-crew supervisor, and said, 'I've got these two little boys who have never worked a day in their lives.' The supervisor gave us each a cotton sack at least ten feet long, showed us how to pick the cotton, and let us go. The inside of a cotton plant is soft but everything around it is full of stickers. My hands were bleeding. I looked at my mom, hoping she would save us, but she just gave me this look. The supervisor could see that we were over our heads. He snuck behind us and, in a low voice, started to sing, 'There's a long, wide road in Heaven I know.' From all around us came these beautiful black voices singing 'Don't leave me behind.' It was gorgeous. We stopped crying and started picking cotton. I picked an eighth of a bag of cotton that day. My mother didn't know that putting me in the center of that cotton field would make me a professional musician but it did."

Moving to Southern CA in his midteens, Holt became an avid viewer of *Hee Haw*. "My mother would say, 'Don't listen to that old *Hee Haw* show; that's a stupid show,'" he remembered. "I'd say, 'No, Mom, these guys are really great.'"

Holt made his debut appearance on *Hee Haw* in 1980. "They started having me more and more regularly," he said, "until I opened the second half with a song everybody—Roy Clark, Grandpa Jones, and Roy Acuff—could sing. I never did barnyard jokes and always wore a white suit or something snappy. Grandpa Jones and I became good friends. He was a wonderfully funny man. He wasn't a comedian, just someone who said funny things."

Practicing slide guitar, guitar fingerpicking, and old-time banjo daily, Holt also plays harmonica, mouth bow, bones, spoons, and "all these crazy instruments," he noted. "I don't use them as a novelty but as musically as possible. I play them so people stay with me for an hour-and-a-half concert."

Banjo remains Holt's instrument of choice. "I fell in love with the sound of the banjo," he said, "so I went to see Ralph Stanley. I had been listening to his records. I loved his clawhammer playing. It was very rhythmic. What he played on tunes like 'Rocky Island' or 'Bound to Ride' fired me up. There were only a few people at the concert. I went up and talked to him after the show. He told me that, where he lived, there were many musicians. I decided to travel, with a friend, from GA to WV, through the Appalachians, stopping at fiddlers conventions and meeting people who played banjo."

Holt made an onscreen appearance in *O Brother, Where Art Thou?* "Joel Coen wanted me to play fiddle on 'Indian War Whoop,'" he said. "I play the fiddle a little but I worked hard for a month. I flew out to Hollywood [and went] to the backlots of Warner Brothers with [mandolin player] Ed Schnatterly. The Coen brothers looked at me and said, 'You look too normal to be a fiddle player. Let him play fiddle; you play the mandolin.' We switched instruments.

"In our scene, 'Baby Face' Nelson is being led to the electric chair and we're leading this big crowd with torches. George Clooney, Holly Hunter, and John Turturro say their lines, look over, and see a parade coming down the road. The camera cuts to us leading the parade. Ed and I tried doing it straight but they said, 'That's great but could pretend you're crazy and drunk?' We started making faces and dancing while we played. We were thinking they were never going to use it—it was so ridiculous—but when the movie came out, that was the scene used. A friend in England saw it and emailed me, 'You've got your fifteen minutes of fame. That's the good news. The bad news is they billed you as 'The Village Idiot.'"

Episodes of *Riverwalk Jazz*, which Holt hosted for twenty-five years, are located in the Stanford University Library and archived online. "It allowed me to share some of my favorite music," he said, "vintage and classic jazz. I had a thrill meeting black jazz musicians from the same era I was studying about mountain music—the 1920s, '30s, and '40s."

PBS has been airing *David Holt's State of Music*. "We just finished shooting eight half-hour episodes," he said.

Chapter 14

Old-Time Revival

Pete Seeger's fourteen-year-younger half-brother, Mike (1933-2009), became a devotee of old-time music while perusing the Library of Congress's Archive of American Folksong and listening to discs from the 1920s and '30s. The son of folklorist Charles Louis Seeger and composer Ruth Crawford Seeger, Mike and his three younger sisters grew up in a home where Woody Guthrie, Leadbelly, and John Jacob Niles were regular visitors. Elizabeth Cotton was the younger children's nanny. Mike taught himself to play autoharp, banjo, fiddle, harmonica, Dobro, and guitar and sing Sacred Harp.

On May 25, 1958, WASH's John Dildine hosted an on-air picking session. Besides Mike, guests included Tom Paley (1928-2017), a NY-born guitar/banjo/fiddle player who cut his first album, *Folksongs of the Southern Appalachian Mountains,* in 1953, and Queens, NY-born banjo player/guitarist John Cohen (1932-). Cohen—a friend of Jack Kerouac, Allen Ginsberg, David Amram, and later Bob Dylan, and the inspiration for the Grateful Dead's "Uncle John's Band"—was a true renaissance man. Possessing an encyclopedic knowledge of traditional music, he was a skilled photographer, filmmaker, and producer of *High Lonesome Sound: Mountain Music of KY* (1962). "I heard Tom Paley at a wingding," Cohen remembered. "He was a graduate student in the math department when I was at Yale. We found each other and started playing together. I organized hoots and we became the mainstays. I went to South America as part of my master's degree. Tom was assistant teaching in MD when he came across Mike Seeger. I'd met Mike at Pete's house but I didn't really know him. I was at Tom's house making copies of old 78s when John Dildine asked if we'd appear on his show. 'By the way,' he said, 'Mike Seeger would like to join you.' We met on our way to the radio station. We barely played before going on the air—the first performance of the New Lost City Ramblers. We did solos, duets, and trios."

Excited by the results, Cohen phoned Folkways Records. "Moe Asch didn't even ask us to audition," he recalled. "Mike had already done projects for him. He had to overcome the image of being Pete's half-brother and be his own person. Peggy Seeger played Pete's songs and continued in his tradition with political songs but Mike had a different mission, which merged very well with Tom's and mine."

As a guitarist, Cohen took a unique approach to old-time music. "There were hundreds of flatpickers in country music," he said, "but I made it more evident than it had been on old-time records. I was partly inspired by the crazy stuff that Riley Puckett did with the Skillet Lickers."

Attending summer camp as a youngster, Cohen met Waddy Wachtel, a counselor who "had been to KY with Margot Mayo [leader of the American Square Dance Group] and learned to play banjo in the old-time, down-picking style." Another counselor had an album with tracks by Uncle Dave Macon and the Carter Family and an album by Woody Guthrie. "Woody started with hillbilly bands," said Cohen, "and he based songs and melodies on old records. Pete traveled with Woody and loved this music too. On an early album, he did 'Muleskinner,' with Sonny Terry on harmonica, and took a banjo break. I asked him, 'Pete, where'd you get the idea?' He told me, 'From Bill Monroe records.'"

Harry West (1927-2014), a VA-born mandolinist living in NY, and guitarist Artie Rose occasionally played with Paley. "They didn't play concerts," said Cohen, "but they did some nice sessions. My brother was in the Shanty Boys with Roger Sprung. They played old-time music, folksongs, and summer-camp songs, but the New Lost City Ramblers was the only band with a fiddle, mandolin, and an autoharp. We played sounds that weren't part of the folksong revival, which followed Pete's guitar and banjo. It was quite a change."

Finding material was no problem. "Harry Smith's *Anthology of American Folk Music* came out in 1952," said Cohen. "Before that, I was collecting old 78s. Tom had a big collection. Mike's mother transcribed Library of Congress tapes. Our second concert was in Philadelphia. Someone I didn't know [Gene Earl] came to me after the show and said, 'I collect records. Would you like to come over and listen to them?' He didn't know anything about folk music—he was just a record collector—but I started going to his house in NJ on my motor scooter and bringing a tape recorder. I could record anything I wanted; there were 10,000 records. I had no idea of what they were or who any of the artists were. It was a wonderful challenge. Mike started doing the same thing with Dick Spottswood and other collectors. They let us have access to their records because we were promoting the music they collected and loved. It was a two-way street."

Mike Seeger produced *Mountain Music Bluegrass Style* in 1958. "It was the first time 'bluegrass' was used to describe the music," remembered Cohen. "The title was originally very academic, something like *Southern Appalachian Music Played in the Style of Bluegrass*. I changed it."

One night, Seeger told Cohen, "Come with me; I have to record a bluegrass fiddler—Tex Logan." "We crowded into this little studio," remembered Cohen. "Mike was playing banjo. I backed them on guitar. [Logan] did some of the farthest-out, wildest, old-time bluegrass fiddling you've ever heard. I didn't know how to accompany him. I was unfamiliar with Lester Flatt's runs and the whole bluegrass tradition. I was winging it. Nobody noticed, but a year or two later, Bill Keith asked me, 'Were you playing on the Tex Logan recordings?' I said, 'Yeah.' He said, 'I noticed.'"

Seeger's and Cohen's fascination with field recordings "went off the deep end and we did several albums about ballad singing," Cohen recalled. "Mike did a series on early Nashville people like the McGee Brothers. He produced Elizabeth Cotton and pursued Lesley Riddle."

The New Lost City Ramblers played the first Newport Folk Festival in 1959. "We made our first record in September 1958," recalled Cohen, "and it came out at the beginning of '59. It sold 200 copies but it got around the country. We were very happy to be at the festival; we had done only two concerts before. We were the only ones playing old-time music. We came dressed just as we were. We were young, un-slick, and unprofessional but the press included us in magazine articles about the festival."

Cohen traveled to KY later that year. "The Ramblers were working on a project about the songs of the depression," he said, "and learning old songs from records. I had never experienced a depression even though I was born during the depression. I decided to go to KY, where there was a depression, but I didn't go looking for the poverty. I went for the music, which was terrific and powerful. I was interested in banjo playing so I didn't pursue fiddlers. Jean Ritchie had been there. Merle Travis had gotten songs from there. There were great recordings at the Library of Congress that Alan Lomax made in 1939. They were in the back of my mind but I had no names, no connections. I started out working with the United Mine Workers. They took me to someone who was very hesitant to play but, because it was the union, he had to do it. It was the same with 'Banjo' Bill Cornett. He turned out to be a giant of old-time banjo playing and singing. I traveled around, asking where I could find banjo players. I'd stop at gas stations and get names, visit people, and film. In the middle of my traveling, I came across [Daisy, KY-born banjo player/fiddler/singer] Roscoe Holcomb [1912-81]. He was only forty-eight but he seemed like a very old man to me. His body had been beat from working in the mines and sawmills. When I met him, he was working in construction, pouring concrete. He was bent, and almost broke, but his singing was 'the high lonesome sound.'"

Cohen met Archie Green, a labor historian who collected hillbilly records, when the New Lost City Ramblers played in CA in 1960. "He connected us with many people," he said, "and we became a funnel, with people pouring their musical riches into us. We brought them forward as best we could and always credited our sources."

In 1961, Rinzler, Cohen, and Izzy Young organized Friends of Old Time Music. The group would produce the first NY concerts by Monroe, Holcomb, Ashley, Watson, the Stanley Brothers, and Dock Boggs. "It was the first time blues and old-time artists were presented by themselves," said Cohen, "and not as guests of someone else. We had that influence on the Chicago Folk Festival as well."

The New Lost City Ramblers continued for a half-century. "When we started," said Cohen, "none of us thought we could make a living playing music. It became a possibility but Mike had a family and he had a desire to play solo. On our first record, there's a tune, 'East Virginia.' Mike did it by himself. He overdubbed all the parts. He could be very funny but chose not to be. He took the role of the educator/narrator but Tom and I developed things to say, and he'd quip back. We became almost funny onstage. We were playing the Ash Grove. Tom was having tuning problems. I said to him, 'Your guitar is flat, Lester.' He said, 'Well, your banjo is sharp, Cecil.' Mike said, 'Don't be such a child, Francis.' It was brilliant. We did a lot of parodying and ridiculing the academics but we appreciated them. Tom would get into a tuning frenzy and I'd make up folklore. We knew how to make it sound educational."

After Tracy Schwarz replaced Paley in 1962, the New Lost City Ramblers "traveled across the country," said Cohen. "We played regularly at the Ash Grove, Berkeley, Chicago, Minneapolis, and then, we'd go to Washington and Philadelphia. We planted seeds. When we'd come back, there'd be a string band discovering the music for themselves. Punk shared many of the same values. It had the same attitude. The Beats were more literary but they also had that attitude. I did photography for *Pull My Daisy*, the film that Allen Ginsberg, Jack Kerouac, and David Amram did in November 1959. It was what the New Lost City Ramblers were about—different things coming together."

Marrying Penny Seeger in 1965, Cohen and his bride "homesteaded" in Putnam Valley, NY. They would have two children (Sonya and Rufus) and two grandchildren. For a while, Cohen played in the Putnam String County Band with Jay Ungar.

The New Lost City Ramblers were celebrating their fiftieth anniversary

Mike Seeger, 1988

when Mike Seeger died in August 2009. "We were playing one or two concerts a year," said Cohen, "but I was pushing to keep it going. It wasn't a smooth ride but I felt it was important."

"I was determined," said Schwarz, "but not as much as Mike or John. They were very principled and driven. They would argue before a concert but they shared a common interest in the music."

Schwarz had been frequenting hoots (open mics) in Washington, DC when he met Seeger. "I was playing my guitar," he recalled, "and Mike walked over with his mandolin and joined in. It wasn't more than two years later that, by chance, he and his love interest rented an apartment two doors from where I was living. That was a big shot of energy for me."

Conflicts within the New Lost City Ramblers intensified. Seeger began thinking of Schwarz as a replacement for Paley. "When the final explosion happened and Tom left," said Schwarz, "I was in the army. I got a letter from Mike asking if I'd like to join the New Lost City Ramblers when I got out in four months. I had been playing with musicians in the army. We were planning to try to make it as a group but the mandolin player divulged to me that he wanted to go back to KS. The very next day, I sent my answer to Mike on an official sheet for important messages (I was a teletype operator) saying, 'Hell, yeah!' We presented old-time Southern music in a way that urban audiences could understand. It was well thought out before I joined. They had a concept and we followed it."

As the popularity of old-time music spread, fiddles "started popping up at festivals," remembered Schwarz, "first one and then two and three. Boy, did they need help. It was something I could do, get them over the basics—how to hold the bow, how to pull it across the strings without sounding like a dying cat. The idea of an instructional album [*Learn to Fiddle Country Style*] was intriguing. I talked it over with Mike and John to see what they thought. I threw caution to the wind and took the idea to Moe Asch. He said yes and I went to work on it. I fell in the outhouse and came out smelling like a rose." A second instructional album, *Traditional Cajun Fiddle,* with Dewey Balfa, released in 1976.

A third-generation fiddler, Schwarz bought his first fiddle in a pawnshop. "It was a piece of junk," he remembered, "but it was something I could start with. I couldn't be blamed for playing bad music on a good instrument."

Schwarz grew up in NJ but spent his summers much differently. "My mother was my dad's second wife," he said, "and he was careful about her health. They bought a place in VT. I don't remember them ever talking about living there all the time—my dad was an investment banker—but we spent our summers there. Farms were right up the road and I learned the milking process. My younger brother and I were into cowboys and Indians and I started listening to country music for that reason. When I heard the themes, and connected it with the backwoods, I was a goner."

A classical pianist, Schwarz's mother noticed his fascination with music and "marched me off to piano lessons when I was six," he said. "Radio gave me everything I wanted to hear. I'd search for rock and roll and end up listening to the blues. I kept following sounds that meant something to me."

Although he dabbled on guitar, the fiddle captivated Schwarz. "I had access to my grandfather's fiddle," he said. "We had the Irish on my mother's side and the German on my father's. My musical drive came through the Irish side."

When the New Lost City Ramblers' schedule slowed down in the mid-seventies, Schwarz joined Seeger, Seeger's then-wife Alice Gerrard, Hazel Dickens, and Lamar Grier as the Strange Creek Singers. "We came together at jam sessions," remembered Schwarz. "There were plenty of parties around the DC area. After a while, we noticed that the same five or six people were playing together the most. It took a while to record an album. I don't know who first talked about it. It might have been Mike; he was often the instigator. It was never certain whether Strange Creek would continue, but when we got together we were always laughing and having a great time."

Meeting at Ashokan music camp in Olivebridge, NY (twenty minutes from Woodstock), in 1988, Schwarz and Ginny Hawker married and relocated to Hawker's home in WV two years later. "We were attracted to each other," remembered Schwarz, "and we started spending more and more time together. Music was a major part of her upbringing."

"My dad [Ben Hawker] sang with his brothers on WBTM radio out of Danville, VA," Hawker said, "and he was an outstanding singer, storyteller, and poet. He also played guitar, banjo, and mandolin." *Good Songs for Hard Times*, Schwarz and Hawker's first album, came out in 2000. *Draw Closer* followed four years later.

Kingsport, TN-raised Ralph Blizard (1918-2004) was "the missing link between old-time and bluegrass." The second-generation fiddler's Southern Appalachian longbow fiddling was "planted firmly in the old-time world but he played with such a style that he could have been a bluegrass fiddler," explained Jamison. "He played as a kid and a teenager

Tracy Schwarz, 1993

before bluegrass existed and put the fiddle in the closet for twenty-five years. Bill Monroe and others came along and developed this new style of music. Ralph took his fiddle out when he retired, looking to play old-time music. We were the people he met. Ralph was in his sixties when he had this second career. We were in our twenties when we played with him at the Smithsonian Festival, the Library of Congress, and folk festivals around the country from Florida to Alaska."

Mt. Airy-born Thomas Jefferson "Tommy" Jarrell (1901-85) didn't record until retiring from the NC Highway Department, but he emerged as a lifeline to the music's roots. He hadn't learned Round Top fiddling from old 78s, like the New Lost City Ramblers, but by playing dances with his father (DaCosta Woltz's Southern Broadcasters fiddler Ben Jarrell) and his uncle (Charlie Lowe) more than a half-century before.

Tommy Jarrell employed a "bowing technique [that] was not the smooth long stroke used by many modern fiddlers. . . . His bow stroke was made up of many complex swirls, pull-backs, and triplets created by using both his wrist and his elbow."[1]

Aspiring fiddlers and clawhammer banjo players, including Tommy Thompson (Red Clay Ramblers), Al Jabbour, Bruce Molsky, Bob Carlin, and Judy Hyman (Horse Flies), flocked to Jarrell's home to learn from a master. "He was a grandfather to all of us," said Jamison.

"[Jarrell] was an old, crusty, country fiddler," remembered Molsky. "He played music that he learned from his father and his father's generation. He settled down, raised a family, and worked for the state for forty-one years. After his wife passed away, he had a new life. I met him after it happened. People were converging on his house but he was always welcoming. He showed me tunes and we played. Years after his death, I took a detour past his house. It was just this tiny, nondescript, frame building on a corner next to an open field. Without his spirit, it was like the rest of the world. It made me realize how special those times were."

Chapter 15

The Big Apple

"There were fiddlers everywhere for dances," said Phil Jamison, "even New York City. The music was different in an urban setting. It wasn't people playing with their families and neighbors at a barn dance."

Folksingers and musicians have gathered in Greenwich Village's Washington Square Park on Sunday afternoons since the early 1940s. Roger Howard Sprung (1930-) was seventeen when his brother George brought him to check out the scene. For the Manhattan-born boogie-woogie piano student, it would be life changing. "The piano went out the window," he said, "and I went to my grandfather's pawnshop and got myself a guitar. For three months, I played the guitar. Then, I heard Pete Seeger and some other people play banjo. I got myself a banjo. Billy Faier told me about Earl Scruggs but he showed me with two fingers."

Discovering country singer Rosalie Allen's record shop, the Hillbilly Music Center, on West Fifty-Fourth Street, Sprung "bought Flatt & Scruggs' 78-RPM records and analyzed what I heard, especially 'My Georgia Rose,'" he said. "My first banjo was a tenor but I tuned it like a five-string."

There were few banjos in NY. "I tried selling my albums at a flea market," recalled Sprung, "but people didn't even know what a banjo was. They'd come over and ask me what I was playing."

Making several trips to the Southeast since 1950, Sprung learned from Appalachian musicians, including Buell Kazee and Jean Ritchie. Named "world champion banjo player" at the Union Grove Fiddlers Convention, in NC's Blue Ridge Mountains, he was the first Northerner to appear at Bascom Lamar Lunsford's Mountain Dance and Folk Festival, an honor he renewed annually for nearly a quarter of a century. "[Sprung] is an unusually adept banjo picker," said the *NY Times*, "who adds a few extra dimensions to the cleanly articulated lines and flowing beat that one might expect. He occasionally goes into a high register to get a sound that resembles a mandolin. . . . He also made an interesting use of glissandos produced by twisting the string pegs."[1]

119

Sprung's nearly four dozen albums included three under the *Progressive Bluegrass* banner (1964-65). "Bluegrass is instrumentation," he said. "You can play any kind of music. I did a Mozart piece, a rag by Scott Joplin, and 'Hello Dolly.'"

Doc Watson featured on the first volume. "Doc and I were at Gerde's Folk City in 1960," recalled Sprung, "and we played a couple of songs together. He loved it and I loved it. I asked Moe Asch if he wanted a record and he said, 'We'll call it "Progressive Bluegrass."' We did the whole album in an hour and a half."

Sprung has taught banjo since 1950, counting Pete Wernick, John Stewart, Harry Chapin, and Erik Darling among his students. "Erik and I were in the Folksay Trio with Bob Carrier," he said.

Joining John Cohen's guitarist brother Mike and washtub-bass player Lionel Kilberg as the Shanty Boys, Sprung frequently guested on Oscar Brand's *Folk Song Festival* (WNYC). Performing at Carnegie Hall's Thanksgiving Eve concert in 1959, they appeared a few months later at the Newport Folk Festival.

Sprung teamed with Hal Wylie (1930-2014), a Bronx-born vocalist/guitarist he met in Washington Square Park, in 1975. As Roger Sprung, Hal Wylie, and the Progressive Bluegrassers, they played weekly at a Newtown, CT pizza place until 2000. Sprung continues to play the first Saturday of each month at a United Methodist church a quarter of a mile away.

The Washington Square picking sessions spurred Anton Robert "Bob" Yellin, Paul Prestopino, and John Herald to form the Greenbriar Boys in 1959. Eric Weissberg replaced Prestopino in 1960, with Ralph Rinzler replacing him a few months later. One of the first urban bluegrass bands, they would be the first Northerners to place first at Union Grove (with Yellin scoring top prize for banjo playing). They backed Joan Baez on her second album, teamed with vocalist Dían for an album, and recorded three albums of their own. Woolwine, VA-born fiddler Buddy Gary Pendleton (1935-2017), who played on their debut album and with Baez, went on to play with Monroe in 1962.

Injecting new life into traditional tunes including "Nine Pound Hammer" and "Stewball," the Greenbriar Boys introduced irreverence to bluegrass with ditties such as "Love Bug," "Coot from Tennessee," and "You Need a Whole Lot More Jesus and a Lot Less Rock & Roll." Linda Ronstadt and the Stone Poneys reached number thirteen on *Billboard's* pop charts with Herald's arrangement of Mike Nesmith's "Different Drum" in 1967. Ronstadt would cover Herald's "High Muddy Water," written with Yellin and Frank Wakefield, and Maria Muldaur recorded his "Jon the Generator."

Roger Sprung, 1993

Reviewing the Greenbriar Boys' show at Gerde's Folk City (with opening act Bob Dylan), in May 1961, Robert Shelton of the *NY Times* wrote, "This band whips up some of the fastest, most tempestuous bluegrass music this side of Nashville."[2]

Six years before, while strolling through Greenwich Village, Yellin stepped into Washington Square Park and saw Eric Weissberg, Marshall Brickman, and Roger Sprung playing bluegrass. "That got me going every Sunday," he said.

Yellin's classical-pianist mother gave up her concert career "when she and my father married," he noted. "My father was an NBC studio pianist until he passed in his eighties. I took cello lessons, violin lessons, piano lessons, and vocal lessons. My parents took me to Carnegie Hall to hear concerts. I studied classical music and played trumpet in the orchestra at the High School of Music and Art. Peter Yarrow's sister was in my class. He was one class below."

In his senior year (1954), Yellin "got into bluegrass at a party," he recalled. "Somebody played a tape of a Flatt & Scruggs concert and I heard 'Flint Hill Special.' That was it for me; that banjo bowled me over. I had to learn to play it. Eventually, my girlfriend bought me a banjo. I started getting records and slowing them down so I could learn the banjo. I never took a lesson. There was nobody giving lessons. Pete Seeger's book, *How to Play the Five-String Banjo*, was the only method. It wasn't bluegrass but I learned what I could."

Weissberg (1939-) spent summers at Camp Woodland, in Constantia, NY, where Pete Seeger's father-in-law, Takashi Ohta, was caretaker. "When Pete started writing his banjo instruction book," Weissberg told me in 2015, "Mr. Ohta put a group together. They handed me a banjo and I started noodling with it. I got instruction from the school music teacher.

"I played a Thanksgiving pageant, at Elizabeth Irwin High School, when I was in the seventh grade. We had a square-dance trio and played for dancers onstage. I played fiddle. My friend, Nicky, played guitar. They put someone behind us, playing banjo. He was picking individual notes; he wasn't strumming. I almost wet my pants. I had never heard anything like it. I told him that he had to show me how to do it. He refused but he had shown his girlfriend and she showed me the rudiments and told me to get Flatt & Scruggs records. My dad collected early Dixieland jazz records—he had thousands—and had a variable-speed turntable. I put on one of Flatt & Scruggs' albums, and as soon as it started to play, I thought, 'I'll never do this.' The notes went by like a machinegun but I said, 'Wait a minute; I'll slow it down.' When you slow it down, however, you're no longer playing the banjo in the same place on the neck. I had to invent all kinds of ways of playing. I learned Scruggs' solos note by note. Roger Sprung showed me a few things. He wasn't a great banjo player but he had his own style. There was also someone at Washington Square—Willy Dykeman. My dad took photographs of me watching their fingers. That's how I learned."

Weissberg attended the University of Wisconsin because "my old friend, Marshall Brickman, was going there," he recalled. "He had an apartment with an empty room and said I could stay. My first night, I went to the freshman mixer, but I was very shy. I pressed my backbone against the wall, trying to hide. I saw someone looking at me. He came over and said, 'Are you Eric?' 'Yes.' 'I listen to you in Washington Square every Sunday. I love your playing and the way you sing.' It was John Herald. I invited him to my apartment to hang out and showed him some things on the mandolin."

Robert Shelton described Greenwich Village-born Herald (1939-2005) as "a leather-lunged tenor whose athletic, high-range country yodeling is a thing of wonder."[3] Dylan called him "the Stevie Wonder of country music."[4]

"I was glad there was someone who played guitar [Herald] so I could play banjo," said Yellin. "I loved John's sweet, near-tenor voice."

Armenian poet Leon Serabian Herald's son discovered bluegrass at a Buck County, PA boarding school. Becoming an entomology student at the University of Wisconsin, he spent most of his time listening to bluegrass records and picking with Weissberg and Brickman.

When Erik Darling replaced Pete Seeger in the Weavers, in November 1959, Weissberg took Darling's place in the Tarriers. "Folk groups like the Christy Minstrels had a banjo," he said, "but nobody was playing bluegrass."

On January 26, 1960, Herald, Yellin, and Rinzler played at Folk City's grand opening. "We didn't even have a name yet," remembered Yellin. "We were just going to get together at Washington Square. There was no formal group. Eric's mother gave us our name; she liked the song, 'The Girl on the Greenbriar Shore.'

"[The performance] got our career started. The president of Vanguard Records heard us and asked us to record a couple of tracks for an album he was making with folksingers Jackie Washington, Hedy West, and Dave Gude, called *New Folks* [1961]."

The Greenbriar Boys recorded their first full album as Joan Baez was preparing *Joan Baez Volume II* (1961). "Joan heard us do 'Stewball,'" said Yellin, "and wondered if we could accompany her on a couple of cuts. I had a copy of a songbook so we went through it and picked 'Banks of the Ohio' and 'Little Pal of Mine.' It was pure chance. Vanguard put us in touch with Joan's manager [Manny Greenhill], who took over our management. He put us on tour with Joan and we did eight concerts together."

The Greenbriar Boys were competing at a fiddlers' convention in NC when "somebody came over to Ralph and said, 'There's an old-time band in one of the classrooms warming up,'" recalled Yellin. "He went to hear them and there was Clarence Ashley with his group. Clarence told him about Doc Watson, who was playing in a bar in Deep Gap, NC."

Jody Stecher filled in during the summer of 1963. "We had a few days off in New England," he recalled. "John and I caught a bus to Boston and then hitchhiked and got to Newport. That's when I saw Dock Boggs. His music hypnotized me. I saw him again in 1965 when Friends of Old Time Music put on a concert with him and Mississippi John Hurt. Hurt's music was like a soft breeze on a warm night—delicate and enchanting—but Dock scared the pants off me."

Stecher bought his first banjo (a fretless Gatcomb) in a pawnshop for two dollars when he was twelve. "I had aunts, uncles, and cousins who played mandolin," he said. "My great-aunt Gussie had a mandolin made by Raphael Ciani, uncle of Johnny D'Angelico, the jazz-guitar maker. She gave it to me. It was very fancy with angels inlaid on the pickguard and pearl buttons and it sounded very, very good. During the 1989 San Francisco earthquake, it fell off a bookshelf. Three hundred books landed on it. I have all the parts in a cardboard box."

One of Stecher's cousins, (Eric) Jay Feldman, played in what may be NY's first bluegrass band, the Kings County Outpatients. "Herb Solomon was the guitar player," said Stecher. "He attended West Point for a year and roomed with a bluegrass fanatic. He brought back reel-to-reel tapes of tunes we couldn't get on records.

"Rock and roll was everywhere but I liked hillbilly rock the best. I loved Chuck Berry, and the Everly Brothers appealed to me, but I was listening to everything—folk music, symphonic music, jazz, and Puerto Rican music. All I had to do was move the dial. I could pick up country-music stations. WWVA had a bluegrass show after the jamboree on Friday and Saturday nights."

At fourteen, Stecher formed a band to play what he heard on the radio. "People called us the Little Outpatients," he remembered. "We were four years younger than my cousin's band. A supermarket chain paid us fifty-one dollars to record an album, *Banjo Time*. We recorded it in one evening. I've never seen a copy. I played mandolin and rhythm guitar. The other musicians were Eric Nagler and Steve Arkin. Sometimes we had two banjos and guitar, sometimes banjo, guitar, and mandolin. Steve's a born-again old-time banjo player. He was the second Northerner to be in the Blue Grass Boys. He's played clawhammer for the past fifteen years. Eric moved to Toronto and became a star of children's TV music shows."

David Freeman started Charlottesville-based County Records in 1963. "We were listening to those records," remembered Stecher, "and learning the tunes to the best of our abilities.

"Anyone interested in bluegrass would go to Washington Square on Sunday afternoons from two to six. We'd gather around the fountain and pick and sing. I met David Grisman there. We were fifteen and sixteen. He's a year older than I am. He was living in Passaic, NJ. He had heard about me. He figured we'd never be in the same band—he couldn't imagine me wanting to do anything but play mandolin—but I just wanted to play. We wound up in several bands together including the NY Ramblers. I joined in the spring of 1965. I mostly played guitar but I sometimes played bass. It was just pickup gigs. Winnie Winston was a great banjo player and David a very rhythmic mandolin player. We had a lot of oomph in that band. I did most of the singing but we all sang. Gene Lowinger played fiddle. He would be the first Northerner to play fiddle with Monroe. Fred Weisz played bass. He had played with David in the Garrett Mountain Boys. The first guitar player was Eric Thompson from Palo Alto. He was a friend of David's. I played with him and Jerry Garcia in the Asphalt Jungle

Mountain Boys in 1964. Eric went back to CA and Jim Field became our guitar player. We did some good duet singing and his rhythm playing freed me to play lead."

The summer Stecher joined, the NY Ramblers made their second appearance at Union Grove. "We won a couple of prizes," he said, "but it would be our last formal gig. Within a few months, David left for CA, Gene moved to Nashville to play with Monroe, and Winnie took a job as a designer for Creative Playthings. Years later, the Grisman Bluegrass Experience's guitarist, Jim Nunally, wasn't always able to go out on weekend tours so I filled in on guitar and sang."

Stecher met Philadelphia-born David Bromberg (1945-), in 1963, backstage at a *Sing Out!* hootenanny at Carnegie Hall. "I had begun attending CCNY [City College of NY]," he remembered, "and the school wasn't far from where David was living on the Upper West Side. I dropped by often and we played together, learning from each other. His approach was different from mine. If he studied Django Reinhardt, he'd get every album he could and try to replicate exactly what Django played. When he tried to play like Doc Watson, he played from the elbow because Doc played with a stiff arm. He didn't move the pick with his wrist; he used his forearm. David specialized in being an accompanist, having a wide range of colors and approaches, and trying to find a way to fit in. Later, he focused on being a bandleader and creating a theatrical experience. He created sets that had an arc and built to a climax. His instrument became the audience."

Stecher's replacement in the Greenbriar Boys, Franklin Delano Roosevelt "Frank" Wakefield (1934-) was "the real deal." Born in Emory Gap, TN, and raised in Dayton, OH, the son of a potato farmer played guitar from the age of six and switched to mandolin at sixteen. "[My brother-in-law] showed me a mandolin," Wakefield recalled, "a tater bug, and showed me some chords."[5]

Forming the Wakefield Brothers with his brother Ralph and sister-in-law, Wakefield "mostly sang in church," he said. "We didn't actually go in bars."[6]

Signing on with Red Allen and the Blue Ridge Mountain Boys in 1952, Wakefield moved on to the Chain Mountain Boys three years later and recorded several tracks, including his show-stopping "New Camptown Races." After a short stint with Jimmy Martin, he joined Allen's new band, the Virginians, in 1958. He relocated to Washington, DC with the group two years later, supplementing his income by teaching. Among his students was Grisman.

Leaving the Greenbriar Boys before it "really broke up," Yellin moved to Israel in 1969. "I wanted to hook up with my Jewish roots," he said.

David Bromberg, 2006

"My grandfather lived in Israel and I wanted to go. I had a family—two children—and a house that I wasn't able to afford as a Greenbriar Boy. My children joined me; my first wife and I split up. I remarried and brought up our children on a kibbutz."

Forming Israel's first bluegrass band, the Galilee Grass, Yellin "turned many people on to bluegrass, but it wasn't my career," he said. "I was an engineer in a cable-wire factory. On the weekends, we'd go out and perform."

The Greenbriar Boys limped along without Yellin. "Wakefield did all kinds of antics onstage," he said, "and they weren't always in the best taste. In Canada, he was egging John on. John told him, 'If you don't stop, I'm going to walk off the stage and never play with you again.' Frank wouldn't stop. John walked off and that was that."

Wakefield would master classical mandolin sonatas and arrange classical pieces for bluegrass instruments. Occasionally performing with Ralph Stanley, he joined David Nelson, Don Reno, and Chubby Wise to record the Garcia-produced the Good Old Boys' *Pistol Packin' Mama* (1975). He moved to San Francisco the following year and toured with the Good Old Boys until 1983.

Frank Wakefield, 2013

Cohen reunited with Herald and Rinzler at the 1982 Philadelphia Folk Festival. "I asked if anyone knew bluegrass players in VT," he said, "and Mark Greenberg introduced himself. He didn't sing but he played guitar. We formed John Cohen & the Joint Chiefs of Bluegrass and stayed together into the nineties."

Herald played guitar on records by Ian & Sylvia, Ramblin' Jack Elliott, and Doc Watson. His own releases, including a solo album (1972) and a country/bluegrass effort with the electric John Herald Band (1976), failed to draw much attention. Active on Woodstock, NY's music scene, he joined Happy and Artie Traum, Maria Muldaur, Jim Rooney, Bill Keith, and John Sebastian to record *Mud Acres: Music Among Friends* (1972). An expanded group, augmented by Paul Butterfield, Eric Andersen, and Paul Siebel, recorded *More Music from Mud Acres* (1977). *Pretty Lucky* (1978), their third album (and their first as the Woodstock Mountain Revue), added Caroline Dutton (fiddle/vocals) and Cyndi Cashdollar (Dobro). Dutton and Cashdollar joined an acoustic John Herald Band in the early eighties.

Herald's struggles ended on July 18, 2005, at his West Hurley, NY home (just outside of Woodstock). Many suspected suicide but there was

John Herald, 1982

no official cause of death. "[Herald] was one of the greatest singers and most creative people we've ever had," said Stecher, "but he was so self-defeating. He was older than I was; I had just turned seventeen. Bob Yellin was twenty-seven. It made a difference. He was more formal. John used to see my friends and me on the street and approach us to talk. He wanted to know our favorite tunes. He introduced me to Cantonese food [and wrote the autobiographical 'The Chinatown Kid']. I spent a summer living in his trailer, in 1967, helping him arrange songs. I brought instruments I had collected to give him new sounds and new ideas."

A reorganized NY Ramblers played Carlton Haney's festival in 1965. "There were only 200 people at Cantrell's Horse Farm," remembered Stecher, "but it was amazing. I came all the way from CA for it. It was so much fun, such a good feeling. At first, I remembered it being more organized than it was. Years later, I saw films and the stage was just a bunch of boards nailed together. I can't remember where or what I ate, but I didn't sleep out in the cold. A bunch of us shared a hotel room—four to a bed.

"Don Reno said something at a banjo workshop that made a big impression on me. Someone asked for advice for people learning to play and he said, 'There's no musician, no matter how sorry, that you can't learn something from. Everybody has natural creativity and plays differently.'

"Later, when I studied Indian classical music, my teacher came from a family that had been court musicians in northern India. He had a student who was having difficulty going up and down the scales stand in front of the class and try. Afterwards, he asked another student what he thought about it. 'It was unbearable,' the student replied. 'Yes, but did you notice,' said the teacher, 'he started with one note, and when he got an octave higher, he managed to be exactly a half-step higher? I'd like to see you try that.'"

Stecher graduated from CCNY in January 1968 with a degree in English. "It took me four and a half years," he said, "but I was so fortunate to have had that extra half-year. That was the semester when Ravi Shankar taught a class. That gave me a theoretical basis for Indian classical music."

Four years before, Stecher visited his cousin who had been in the Kings County Outpatients and was, at the time, a University of CA, Berkeley graduate student. "I liked it better on the West Coast," Stecher said, "so I moved the spring after I graduated. I was in Mendocino County for a while, then came back East again. Then, I lived in Seattle and pre-Microsoft Redmond. It didn't have paved streets; it had a movie theater, a dentist, and a Western-wear shop. The cost of living was low. It was possible to survive doing occasional gigs. We'd play on the Berkeley campus and pass the hat. If you made ten dollars, you could live for a week."

Stecher connected with old-time musicians. "They were ten years later than I was musically," he said, "even though we were roughly the same age. They weren't into singing. It was mostly instrumental but that would change."

Stecher met his wife, Kate Brislin, at Expo '74 in Spokane. A former member of Eric Thompson's Blue Flame String Band, Brislin "was playing with the Arkansas Sheiks, and I was playing with a band from Seattle, Houseboat Music," Stecher remembered. "We used to play on a friend's houseboat on Lake Union. Kate isn't a virtuoso player but she's super steady on the guitar and she sings very purely, without a lot of ornamentation. The kickass side of my music isn't encouraged when we play together. I pare it down and get straight to the heart of the song. She also brings out a part of my voice that's softer. I was a tenor singer in bluegrass bands. Kate can sing a few notes lower than me. Sometimes, we cross our parts. I was comfortable being part of a band. It took longer to be comfortable as a soloist. It was even hard to be in a duo but Kate and I worked it out. She was shy in a duo, not when she was in a band, but she began to talk more. She could be very funny. She started to expand and grow."

Stecher joined Peter Rowan's Bluegrass Band in 2006. "It was such a unique experience," he said. "I had been with the Perfect Strangers with [ex-Blue Grass Boys] Bob Black and Forrest Rose and [ex-Laurie Lewis Band members] Chris Brashear and Peter McLaughlin for seven years. Most of my life, I'd been the one on the edge. I wanted to be a pathfinder, be creative, and play tonight differently than last night. Peter is much more that than me. Compared to him, I was conservative. He'd do a song in a different key every night, changing the words. It wasn't tidy but it was always alive. The other singer, Keith Little, was extremely flexible. He had played with Vern Williams, sung harmony for Dolly Parton, and played banjo for the Country Gentlemen. We all sang lead, tenor, and baritone. On slower, softer songs, I sang below Peter and Keith sang above. On hard-driving bluegrass songs, I had more edge in my tenor, so I sang above Peter, and Keith, who's one of the most creative baritone singers, sang low. We practiced from time to time but not too often. Peter said, 'If you practice and get really polished, then you have what's known as an act.' He wasn't interested in having an act. He wanted uncertainty onstage. It creates energy."

Stecher resigned from Rowan's band in 2011. "My mother was dying," he told me in 2016, "and I wanted to be with her. My sixty-fifth birthday was approaching. I wanted to spend time with my wife, Kate, who was also having some health concerns. I gave my notice and played out the rest of the summer."

Retirement is not in Stecher's future. A longtime music teacher, he's become "more available" to his students. He continues to explore his own musical path as well. "I've been practicing Indian music," he said, "and studying Middle Eastern music; I'm learning the oud. I'm exploring Persian music, which I've loved for fifty years. I'm a year and a half into a four-year project. I'm writing a book and starting a website about modal music in America and the way it connects us to the rest of the world. Why did old-time fiddlers play pitches that didn't correspond to frets? Could it be that they were all wrong at the same time? Why was it that Rufus Crisp pulled out the frets from his Sears & Roebuck banjo? He did it so he could play in tune. Modal music is microtonal. It doesn't use the pitches devised for European harmony. Rock and roll and blues have always been microtonal, played between the frets. I understand it from learning raga music. I want to explain it so everybody could understand it. I hear it in the oldest levels of America's traditional music."

Chapter 16

The Hub

"There was Harvard Square in Cambridge with beatniks," remembered Peter Rowan, "and hip things going on, good coffee, and jazz musicians playing conga drums in the cafés. Then, we'd go over to Kenmore Square in Boston to the Jazz Workshop or Paul's Mall."

In 1939, an immigrant from northern Italy, Frank Segalini, opened a restaurant between Boston's Park Square and the edge of its "Combat Zone." It did well at first but began to struggle during the mid-1940s. Unsure of what to do, Segalini was encouraged when a friend suggested he reinvent the space as a country and western club; there were Southerners at the nearby Charlestown Navy Yard. The Mohawk Ranch had been the first Boston club to present "hillbilly music," but Segalini's Hillbilly Ranch quickly took over as New England's bluegrass center. "Folks like Jim Rooney, Bill Keith, Peter Rowan, and Joe Val got through the door if they were old enough," said Gerry Katz of the BBU (Boston Bluegrass Union), "or they perched by the door listening to the Lilly Brothers. They got an education that was first rate."

"Hillbilly Ranch was a wild scene," remembered Rowan, "with sailors dancing in their uniforms and women all dressed up. I was too young to understand what was going on."

Home to a house band that included Tex Logan, the Lilly Brothers, and Don Stover for nearly two decades, Hillbilly Ranch cast ripples that continue to resonate. Closed after a January 29, 1980, fire, and razed a month later, John Lincoln Wright memorialized it in "They Tore Down the Hillbilly Ranch."

Coahoma, TX-born Benjamin Franklin "Tex" Logan (1927-2015) assembled Hillbilly Ranch's house band. Initially dubbed the Confederate Mountaineers, they were later renamed the Lilly Brothers. Influenced by Tommy Magness's fiddling with Monroe (1940-41, 1942-43), Logan leaned closer to mountain fiddling than the styles of his native Texas.

Music represented only one path for Logan. Eventually possessing a bachelor of science degree in electrical engineering from Texas

Joe Val and the New England Bluegrass Boys (Joe Deetz, Eric Levenson, Joe Val, Dave Haney), 1983

Technological College, a master's degree from Massachusetts Institute of Technology (MIT), and a PhD from Columbia University, he worked as a research assistant for MIT until joining Jerry Howarth and Schuyler "Sky" Snow's band, the Melodymen, in 1946. Their early publicity claimed TN origins, but Howarth and Snow hailed from Portsmouth, NH and called Boston home. Recording yodel-heavy tunes such as "Sparkling Brown Eyes" (1947) and an explosive "Orange Blossom Special" (1947), they produced some of New England's first country records.

Returning to TX, Logan played with Western swing fiddler Hoyle Nix and worked in an oilfield. He continued on to Wheeling, WV, where he teamed with Finley "Red" Belcher & the Kentucky Ridge Runners on the WWVA *Wheeling Jamboree*. The Lilly Brothers—guitarist Michael Burt "Bea" (1921-2005) and mandolinist Everett (1924-2012)—joined Belcher's band. Already bluegrass veterans, they had been playing church and school dances since Everett's ninth birthday. They made their radio debut on WCHS's *Old Farm Hour*, in Charleston, WV, in early 1938 and hosted their own show on WJLS, in Beckley, WV, by the end of the year. After two years with Belcher, Everett left to join Flatt & Scruggs in 1951.

Moonlighting with the Coal River Valley Boys, Logan met an Artie, WV-born coalminer whose mother had taught to play banjo, Don Stover (1928-96). They would remain in touch. Returning to his assistant researcher job at MIT in February 1949, Logan spent the following summer break with Wilma Lee & Stoney Cooper. When it came time to go back to his day job, he was having too much fun. He resigned from MIT and continued with the band until October 1951. Their final concert, in Baltimore, was a package show with Monroe, Flatt & Scruggs, and Cowboy Copas. Backstage, Logan played Monroe his new song, "Christmas Time's A-Comin'." Recording it with the Blue Grass Boys, Monroe transformed it into a Yuletide classic covered by Johnny Cash, Emmylou Harris, Patty Loveless, Sammy Kershaw, Rhonda Vincent, and Peter Rowan. Charlie Daniels recorded it with the Grascals.

Logan joined the Lane Brothers on WCOP/Boston's *Hayloft Jamboree* but the group disbanded after harmonica player Frank Lane received his draft notice. Traveling south in search of Curly Seckler, Logan and guitarist Pete Lane ran into Everett Lilly. Lilly shared his plan to leave Monroe and rejoin his brother in Boston. Logan remembered this conversation when Segalini asked him to put a band together for Hillbilly Ranch.

Logan not only played up to seven nights a week at Hillbilly Ranch but also worked for Bell Laboratories, in northern NJ, from 1956 until his retirement in 1993. "His studies helped make it possible for chemists and astronomers," said the *NY Times,* "to draw accurate interpretations from incomplete data."[1]

Sitting in with Wilma Lee & Stoney Cooper, in West Grove, PA, in 1959, Logan caught the ear of Mike Seeger, who invited him to record a track ("Natchez Under the Hill") on *Mountain Music Bluegrass Style.* He would go on to appear at the Newport Folk Festival, backed by the New Lost City Ramblers, in 1963, guest on a record by New England's first in-grown bluegrass band (Charles River Valley Boys), and become a member of the White Oak Mountain Boys. Recording a solo album, *Things in Life* (1972), with help from Grisman, he played with Lamar Grier (banjo), NJ-born Barry Mitterhoff (mandolin), and Roger Mason (bass) in Peter Rowan's Green Grass Gringos.

Hillbilly Ranch fit in with the Boston/Cambridge folk-music scene. In January 1958, Brandeis University graduates Joyce Kalina (Chapra) and Paula Kelley rented space on the outskirts of Harvard Square and turned it into the eighty-seat Tulla's Coffeehouse. Opening with the Steve Kuhn Trio, they intended to focus on poetry and jazz. Local laws, however, prohibiting more than three stringed instruments in a place with food and beverages, forced it to close. Reorganizing as the nonprofit Club 47, it would be a mecca for folk music, including bluegrass, for a decade. A year after its April 1968 closing, transplanted Chicagoans Bob and Rae Anne Donlin opened a card and gift shop in the subterranean site where it had relocated in 1963. Informed of its legacy, the Donlins rechristened the space "Passim's Listening

Room" and presented music until 1994. Evolving into Club Passim after Donlin's passing, it is now a thriving educational organization spurred by its nightly shows. Club Passim's inaugural executive director, Betsy Siggins Schmidt, attended Boston University's School of Fine and Applied Arts in the late fifties. A classmate of Joan Baez, she was friends with Robert L. "Bob" Jones, an electrician's son and folksinger from West Roxbury who became a director of the Newport festivals, pre-Jug Band Jim Kweskin, and Robert "Bob" Siggins, whom she would marry, in 1961, and later divorce.

OK-born banjo player Bob Siggins came East as a scholarship-funded student at Harvard University. On the train, he met Clay Jackson, a scholarship student who had played ukulele and sang with his sisters in Kerrville, TX. The duo recruited a Harvard student who played guitar and mandolin (Eric Sackheim), and a MIT student who played guitar, mandolin, and autoharp (Ethan Signer), growing into the Charles River Valley Boys. They became regulars on Harvard's WHRB-FM (whose Saturday show, *Hillbilly at Harvard,* has aired since 1948).

Debuting as Baez's opening act at Dartmouth College in January 1961, the Charles River Valley Boys performed weekly at Club 47. *Bringin' in the Georgia Mail* (1961), recorded in the WHRB studio and London, England, released on the UK Folklore label. The group hooked up with record store clerk-turned-producer Paul Rothchild for their second effort the following year. Initially releasing it on his Mount Auburn label, Rothchild reissued it as *Bluegrass and Old Timey Music* after signing with Prestige Records. He also produced *Bluegrass Get Together*, featuring Logan on fiddle.

John Cooke, British-American journalist Alistair Cooke's son, replaced Sackheim. Future Kweskin Jug Band washtub-bass player Fritz Richmond joined. Siggins continued to reorganize the band, adding ex-NY Ramblers singer/guitarist James "Jim" Field, Everett Allen Lilly (the Lilly Brothers mandolinist's son), and Joe Val in 1966. "[Val's] piercing tenor was so high," said Cooke, "we did what the Osbornes did with Bobby's leads, we put two harmonies below him, myself (baritone) and Bob Siggins (a lower tenor than Joe), but when I sang lead, we did the reverse, stacking two harmonies on top of the melody."[2]

Augmented by Buddy Spicher (fiddle), Craig Wingfield (Dobro), and Eric Thompson (guitar), the Charles River Valley Boys recorded the album that would forever etch their place in history. Released by Elektra in 1966, and reissued by Rounder in 1995, *Beatle Country* transformed songs by the world's most popular rock band into true-to-form bluegrass tunes.

The Charles River Valley Boys reunited at the twenty-fifth annual Joe Val Bluegrass Festival, in Framingham, MA, in February 2013.

Boston-born and Dedham-raised guitarist/vocalist Jim Rooney (1938-)

met Brockton-born banjo player William Bradford "Bill" Keith (1939-2015) during his junior year at Amherst College in 1959. Forming a lifelong bond, they recorded *Livin' on the Mountain* (1963) with Val, Richmond, and Herb Applin. In addition to playing as a duo, they played with Red Allen's Kentuckians (with Wakefield), the Woodstock Mountain Revue, the Blue Velvet Band (with Eric Weissberg and Richard Greene), and Partners in Crime (with Everett and Tennis Lilly and Val).

Collaborating with the dean of the Harvard Square scene, Eric Von Schmidt, Rooney wrote *Baby Let Me Follow You Down: The Illustrated Story of the Cambridge Folk Years* (1979). His autobiography, *In It for the Long Run: A Musical Odyssey,* came out in 2014. His first book, *Bossmen: Bill Monroe & Muddy Waters,* published nearly forty-five years before. "Bill Monroe wasn't easy to interview," he remembered. "Asking him questions, it was 'yes, sir,' 'no, sir.' I didn't know how it was going to work until I got very lucky. I was traveling with him when the bus broke down. We took it to a garage near Roanoke but we were there all night. Bill and Kenny Baker started talking. They knew I was there with a cassette recorder but they didn't pay any attention to it. That gave me information I wouldn't have gotten by asking questions."

Eric Von Schmidt and Jim Rooney, 1994

Rooney first heard bluegrass in 1951. "A friend told me I had to listen to this group [the Confederate Mountaineers] on the radio," he recalled. "He told me that it was the funniest thing he had ever heard."

Becoming a nightly listener of *The Hayloft Jamboree,* along with a show that played records by Hank Williams, Lefty Frizzell, and Hank Thompson, Rooney dug deeper into the music. "Once a month, *The Hayloft Jamboree* presented a concert at Symphony Hall," he recalled, "with local musicians dressed in cowboy regalia. There was a weird Western swing band with Armenians from Providence—Eddie Zack and the Dude Ranchers. Joe Val was on that show with the Radio Rangers."

Seeing him strumming a tennis racket along with the radio, Rooney's uncle bought him a ukulele. "I played it for a year," he said. "I subscribed to *Country Song Roundup,* which gave me lyrics to songs. In late 1953, a friend sold me a plywood guitar for twelve bucks. I'm left-handed but I played it backwards."

Successfully auditioning for *The Hayloft Jamboree,* Rooney debuted in early 1954. "I had been listening to bluegrass for a couple of years," he said, "and taken piano lessons. Miss Davis would come to my house, once a week, and give me a lesson. It was dreary and didn't engage me (I learned to read music so it wasn't a total waste). Roxbury Latin School had a glee club. I got in and started singing some challenging works by people like Aaron Copeland but it had no effect on my life in country music."

Rooney met the Lilly Brothers at the WCOP studios. "They were very nice to me," he remembered, "and my pal Dick Curley. We went with them to a bar afterwards. It was the first time I was in a place like that. I was only fourteen or fifteen. There was nothing like it in Dedham. It was another world and it very much appealed to me. It was exotic but so friendly and inviting that it made me want to come back. The night that my brother graduated from Harvard, in 1953, we went with Dick and his brother, who also graduated, to a hillbilly bar, the Mohawk Ranch, on the edge of the black part of town."

When they met, Keith "had a long-necked Pete Seeger-style banjo and Pete's instruction book," Rooney recalled. "There were a couple of pages in the back about Scruggs-style picking. He got Flatt & Scruggs' first album, *Foggy Mountain Jamboree.* 'Bluegrass' had just become a term. I didn't think of myself as singing that type of music. I was into Hank Williams songs. I bought every one of his records. Then, he died and that made it even more exotic."

Rooney took Keith to Hillbilly Ranch to see Don Stover. "He was the first banjo player Bill ever saw," he remembered. "Don was an extraordinary banjo player. When you play in bars and clubs every night, you have to be inventive to keep yourself going and he was. He could play old-time clawhammer and the Scruggs style but he could also play steel-guitar-like licks behind ballads."

Keith liked to tinker on cars with his friend, Loring Hall. Afterwards, they'd sit in Hall's kitchen and pick. Hall's wife, June, who came from Nova Scotia, would take out her fiddle. One night she played "The Devil's Dream" and "The Devil's Hornpipe." "[Keith] wanted to play them note for note," said Rooney. "Scruggs had his three-finger roll but he only played one melody note out of three. Bill wanted every note to be a melody note. As time went on, he got fascinated with the Circle of Fifths and turned the banjo into a true musical instrument. It wasn't a novelty anymore or limited to bluegrass. As a result, you get Béla Fleck and Tony Trischka. Keith opened that door. He was the least flashy person; he wasn't trying to show off. When his style started coming around, and other players started throwing it in all over the place, traditional players didn't like it. I agreed with them; it didn't belong everywhere. Keith got a lesson in this from Bill Monroe. He threw it in Monroe's ragtime song, 'Nola.' Monroe didn't say anything. He just stopped at the end of the verse; that was it. Bill got the message. Monroe didn't like telling people things directly. He'd find some indirect way to let you know if you were doing good or not."

Accompanied by Richmond, Keith and Rooney "played folksongs adapted to the bluegrass style, country songs, and straight-ahead bluegrass songs." The trio was playing in a Boston church when Val and Applin showed up. "I had seen Joe on *Hayloft Jamboree* and a couple of bluegrass shows," said Rooney. "I knew he was a great singer. We started talking. We had just started playing one night a week at Club 47. I told Joe and Herb, 'We're going to rehearse to play at the club. Why don't you join us?' They did and right away, it was fantastic; we could do Monroe trios and gospel quartets. Joe was a pro. He had just taken up mandolin. When I saw him at *Hayloft Jamboree,* he was playing guitar. Herb was a good fiddler and could sing tenor—we had two tenors. We made our first album with Paul Rothchild, who was working in a Boston record store. He started coming around to the club. It didn't take him long to figure out a scene was happening. He talked to the board of directors about starting a record label, MTA Records, named after Boston's public transportation system."

The first group recorded by Rothchild was the Charles River Valley Boys. "Eric Von Schmidt did the cover," Rooney remembered, "but it didn't sell well. We were next on the list. Paul hired a classical-music recording engineer, got some good microphones, and rented a room in a Beacon Hill townhouse, owned by Harvard, with parquet floors and high ceilings, a good natural, acoustic sound. We set up in a circle.

"We hired a fiddle player. Herb Applin was okay but Herb Hooven was from NC and played on Jimmy Martin's *Good 'n' Country,* which was one of the first great bluegrass albums. We cut everything live in one afternoon, and two or three weeks later, Bill, Fritz, and I went in to record the folksongs like 'One Morning in May,' with Keith playing autoharp, and 'Moonshiner,' with him on acoustic guitar.

"The tape just sat there because the label's deal with the club had fallen apart. A month or two passed and nothing was happening. Keith got an offer to go to Washington to play with Red Allen and Frank Wakefield. He took it because it was a chance to get with a 'real' bluegrass band.

"Bob Weinstock ran Prestige Records, which had been a jazz label. I had their records by Miles Davis and Milt Jackson. He was branching into folk music and put out albums by Ramblin' Jack Elliott and Dave Van Ronk. He came up to Boston to talk to Manny Greenhill about the 'Boston scene.' Manny played him the Charles River Valley Boys' record. Weinstock hired Paul Rothchild to be an A&R person for him. Paul went to NY and our records came out on Prestige. He went on to record Tom Rush, Geoff Muldaur, and Eric Von Schmidt."

Funded by a Fulbright Scholarship, Rooney studied at the American School of Classical Studies, in Athens, in 1963 and '64. Keith joined the Blue Grass Boys (as Brad Keith). His melodic picking featured on their recordings of "The Devil's Dream," "The Sailor's Hornpipe," and Monroe's instrumental, "Santa Claus."

Returning to the States in 1965, Rooney succeeded Byron Lord Linardos as manager of Club 47, remaining in the position until the end of 1967. It was a tough time for folk-music coffeehouses. "We had all these incredible artists," explained Rooney, "but opportunities were opening for them to make more money at other places. The Boston Tea Party opened so Paul Butterfield and the Chambers Brothers went there. Richie Havens, Arlo Guthrie, and Judy Collins became concert artists and weren't playing hundred-seat coffeehouses anymore. Music scenes come and go; they have an organic life. The book that Eric Von Schmidt and I did covered from 1958 to '68 and that was it—the whole scene from beginning to end."

The Club 47 experience came in handy after Rooney became a director of George Wein's Newport Folk Festival. "We put on major artists," he said, "James Taylor, Van Morrison, and Kris Kristofferson, but the crowd wasn't out of hand. Bars and restaurants were happy to have all these people in town; they sold a lot of liquor. The trouble started when George Wein booked rock acts—Ten Years After, Led Zeppelin, Sly & the Family Stone, and Jethro Tull—for the jazz festival in 1969. Seventy thousand people showed up and we could only handle 18,000. We had 50,000 people on the hill. It was cold, the fog was rolling in, and people started building fires to stay warm. They tore the fence down and used the wood. Eighteen thousand wooden chairs made good firewood too. Two weeks later, the folk festival was supposed to happen. The town forced us to build a chain-link fence around the site and hire every police officer in the state. That cost us an extra $40,000 and put us out of business. We tried to find another site but, after Woodstock, no town wanted to hear the word 'festival.' We took a year off and finally talked Newport into letting us back. We had a very small, low-key festival scheduled for 1971—Rosalie Sorrels and Bruce Phillips, no hint of rock and roll. George had B. B. King, Ray Charles, and four of five major R&B acts on the jazz festival. The riots happened all over again. That was it. The festival didn't come back until 1985. Keith and I played that year with Mark O'Connor. We had just come back from England and Ireland. We took him out of the country for the first time. Peter Rowan and New Grass Revival were on that afternoon, too."

For a while, Rooney lived in the coastal village of Green Harbor, MA. "My family had a cottage," he said, "and I needed a place a roost, so I stayed there. I went to Passim's and Joe Val was playing. Everett Allen and Tennis Lilly, Everett Lilly's sons, were there. Everett said, 'Why don't we get together and pick some?' Amos Garrett came over from Woodstock. He had been playing with Ian and Sylvia, an exceptional guitar player. He was living in Scituate, ten miles north of Boston. We started hanging out, going fishing and whatnot. I went to Passim's one night and John Nagy was there. He had started producing records for Rounder. He said that we should make a record. 'Why don't we do a night here at Passim's?' We got Bill Keith, Jim Colgrove, who played bass for the Great Speckled Bird, and guitar player Stephen Bruton, and recorded half of the album. I finished it at a four-track studio with Joe Val, Everett, and Tennis, and a Dobro player, Roger Williams. It's never come out on CD and it's impossible to get."

By the summer of 1969, Rooney was out of work and running out of money. "I had the idea for a book," he said. "I woke up in the middle of the night and wrote down what became the introduction. I wasn't working for George anymore but I was still on the board of the folk festival and still going to the office. I called a couple of people and found a publisher. I got a little advance but it wasn't going to be enough. I went to Albert Grossman to see if he needed a tour manager. A couple of his acts played at Club 47 and I had gotten to know him. He managed the Kweskin Jug Band. At one point, I presented Dylan's film *Don't Look Back* in Boston. I took a bit of a bath doing it and he let me off the hook. When I put on the Bauls of Bengal at Club 47 for Sally, his wife, he said, 'I'm building a studio in Woodstock; why don't you come up and run it?' He said that the Band was going to be involved and he played me *Music from Big Pink*. It had just come out. It was great. Albert said, 'Maybe, you should go on the road with the Band and see if you get along.' I went out a couple of weekends with them. They were playing colleges. They were at their height."

Rooney and his wife visited Woodstock a few times that winter. "We needed a place to live," he said, "so I talked Albert into giving me money for a down payment. I never saw the studio because the road was always snowy and unplowed. All that I got was a report from Robbie Robertson. I asked him how the studio was coming. He said, 'It's great,' and that was it. My wife, our dog, and I moved from NY. We got to the house and unloaded. I said, 'I'm going to go up to the studio and take a look.' I went up and saw Albert and Sally walking up the hill. I got out my car and we walked together. The trees were just budding so you could see through them. There was this huge cinderblock wall. There was no roof. Albert said, 'What do you think?' I said, 'Well, it's big.' It turned into a construction job, which was okay. My dad was in that business and my uncle was an architect. I used to draft plans for him."

Blues-harmonica player Paul Butterfield was living in Woodstock. "Paul and I became very good friends," said Rooney. "He had played Club 47 several times. It was the first time in his and his wife's lives that they weren't living in some cheap hotel. Van Morrison was up there with his band. Dylan was just leaving. Happy and Artie Traum had moved up. Happy and his wife, Jane, had started Homespun Tapes. John Herald was up there. Shortly after I moved there, Bill Keith moved over from Cambridge and got a house. Then, Geoff and Maria Muldaur came. We had this group that was just like Cambridge all over again. We continued playing music and jamming together."

The informal jams evolved into *Mud Acres: Music Among Friends*. "Artie Traum got us into a four-track studio near Albany for a weekend," remembered Rooney, "and we recorded. It's a sweet album. That led to the Woodstock Mountain Revue. We did a lot of playing and traveling together and put on some good shows with straight-ahead bluegrass. John Herald was the highlight. He had that spark. It's sad that he never found where he fit. He was a very lovable person but he was bitter. Woodstock was a one-horse town. Instinctively, I knew that I had to get out of there."

Grossman finished Bearsville Studio, the Bear Restaurant, and the Bear Café, but "the construction never ended," said Rooney. "We were turning houses into apartments and houses into offices."

Then, Janis Joplin died. "That really took the wind out of Albert's sails," recalled Rooney. "He wasn't paying attention to business. Paul Butterfield came to my office over the Bear Restaurant. He was talking on the phone with our travel agent. His airline tickets for that weekend hadn't arrived. Paul had a big band with horns. They were working every weekend and making good money. I overheard the conversation. 'You'll get the tickets when we get paid.' That was the tip of the iceberg—hotels, rented cars. Paul didn't go out that weekend and they didn't go out the next weekend. Before you knew it, his horn players went to Stevie Wonder. It's the saddest story in the world. He went down, down, down after that. He was brilliant, a great musician. He never blamed Albert. He did the band with Geoff Muldaur—Better Days—but it never flew. All the promoters wanted his name on top. It was supposed to be a democratic band. Without him, it didn't mean anything to anybody, but Paul's heart wasn't in it. That band was Geoffrey's idea."

Working "night and day," Rooney was exhausted. "I told Albert I couldn't keep doing it," he said. "I had a big ache in the back of my head and I knew what was causing it. I pulled the plug on everything—my marriage, everything. Albert was fine. We never had a problem. He got me an assistant, a booking agent from NY, but half of my job was construction and he had no idea about that world."

Leaving Woodstock, Rooney headed to Nashville. "Because I worked for Albert," he said, "I got a mortgage and paid it off. Nobody knew that I wasn't working for him anymore. At an RV dealership, they asked me what I did for a living. I told them that I was a record producer in Nashville. They gave me the loan. Keith and I used to go to Nashville, every year, for the DJ convention. It was just a big party. You'd go from suite to suite and people would be jamming all over the place. Bill had just taken up the steel guitar. We knew all the bluegrass musicians—Jim & Jesse, the Osborne Brothers, Monroe. It was so much fun."

Hooking up with ex-Sun Studios engineer "Cowboy" Jack Clement, Rooney played three nights a week at George Jones' Possum Holler club with Clement's Ragtime Band. "We didn't play bluegrass," he said, "but we did 'Rocky Top.' It started as a rhythm section, Peace and Quiet, playing with Crystal Gayle on the road."

Taught recording by Clement, Rooney produced albums by Iris DeMent, John Prine, Hal Ketchum, Townes Van Zandt, and Tom Rush. He scored a Grammy for his production of Nanci Griffith's *Other Voices, Other Rooms*. "[Rooney] encouraged me to use what was already there," DeMent told me in 2012, "to be real, to be who I am, and not feel as though I have to put on some face not my own. I took that to heart and that has carried over to all of my records, regardless of who produces them. He was a huge mentor to me."

Chapter 17

Stringbender

During an all-too-short career that spanned from his debut with his brothers Eric (1943-2011) and Roland (1938-) as the Three Little Country Boys, in 1954, to his tragic death before his thirtieth birthday, Clarence White (born Clarence Joseph LeBlanc) (1944-73) brought a new direction to bluegrass flatpicking. Inspired by Doc Watson, Django Reinhardt, and blues, he was as proficient at lightning speeds as he was at flatpicking melodies. He looked stoic onstage but his tone spoke volumes. "He brought a kind of swing," said Jerry Garcia, "a rhythmic openness to bluegrass, and a unique syncopation."[1]

"He didn't play rhythm like Jimmy Martin," remembered Tony Rice. "He didn't play rhythm like Lester Flatt . . . it was just in his DNA."[2]

"As a country player, he was a monster," added Marty Stuart. "As a rock and roller, he was so original . . . he would have been the greatest guitar player there ever was."[3]

Banjo player, guitarist, and ex-Byrds/Flying Burrito Brothers drummer Gene Victor Parsons (1944-) (no relation to Gram) met White in 1966. "I was working in a country band, the Fabulous Reasons, with [Cajun fiddler/guitarist] Gib Guilbeau," he remembered. "Gib and I had been in the Castaways with Darryl Cotton. Darryl wasn't playing with us anymore but we were recording at his studio. Clarence came to play. I was a fan of the Kentucky Colonels' instrumental record. He was playing a Telecaster electric guitar; he had just started playing it. He was using a capo but he was burning it; it sounded great."

The Fabulous Reasons played seven nights a week at the Jack of Diamonds in Palmdale, CA. "We'd go in at nine," said Parsons, "and play until two; five sets a night. On Sunday, we'd come in at lunchtime and play until dinner, take a break, and play until two. We were using anyone we could get to play guitar, people like [pedal-steel player] 'Sneaky' Pete Kleinow. Clarence was looking for work—bluegrass wasn't going to support his growing family—so he went to work with us. We moved to another club, the Nashville West, in El Monte, and played there for quite a while. We became the Nashville West."

Parsons designed a "stringbender," enabling White to play steel-guitar licks. "Clarence was already one of the innovators on the Telecaster," he said, "chiming the B or high E string to make it go up a full tone. On 'Nashville West ('Hong Kong Hillbilly'),' you could hear it. He wanted to do it in the second and third positions up the neck but needed a third hand. We fooled around, trying it, and recorded it. It sounded like a pedal steel or concert harp. Clarence looked at me and said, 'You're a machinist. Figure a way to do it.' I said, 'It's no problem; we'll put pullers on the back of your guitar and run cables to the floor.' He said, 'If I wanted to play pedal steel, I'd play pedal steel. I want it all in the guitar. I want to be able to put it in its case when I'm done and I don't want it to take my hands out of their stance when I am.' I thought about it and came up with using the shoulder strap to pull a spring-loaded lever. I did some drawings and got some steel-guitar parts from 'Sneaky' Pete. I took Clarence's Telecaster and cut an inch-and-a-quarter square out of the body behind the bridge to fit the wires. After a few weeks of machine work and experimenting, I got it to work. I put it in Clarence's hands and he came up with a way to play it."

White played on records by the Everly Brothers, Rick Nelson, the Monkees, Randy Newman, Linda Ronstadt, and Jackson Browne. He played on Gene Clark's first solo album, *Gene Clark with the Gosdin Brothers* (reissued as *Echoes*), and contributed to the Byrds' *Younger than Yesterday* (1967). He returned for *Notorious Byrd Brothers* (1968) and *Sweetheart of the Rodeo* (1968) (John Hartford played fiddle). "I wrote a country-rock song ('Time Between')," said Chris Hillman, "and brought in one of my friends from my bluegrass days—Clarence White—to play electric guitar."

"We were never under pressure from Columbia to do anything," recalled Roger McGuinn. "That's why we were able to play folk, country, and whatever else we wanted; it was a pretty free environment."

Clark's resignation was the first step to the dispersion of the original Byrds. Differences between David Crosby and Michael Clarke continued to intensify until late 1967 when "[Crosby] was fired," said McGuinn two years later. "He just wasn't making it, man. He's a great talent . . . and a nice cat . . . but he was getting a little too big for his britches . . . trying to rule the machine . . . getting hard to work with . . . it was by mutual consent . . . the three remaining Byrds got together, and decided that it would be better if he wasn't around anymore."[4]

Crosby hooked up with Stephen Stills and Neil Young of Buffalo Springfield and Graham Nash of the Hollies to forge one of folk-pop's most successful collaborations. The country influence within the Byrds would increase with the arrival of Hillman's cousin Kevin Kelley on drums and Winter Haven, FL-born and Waycross, GA-raised Ingram Cecil "Gram Parsons" Connor III (1946-73) in 1968. Parsons had come North four years before. Enrolling at Harvard University as a theology student, he "was hell bound to concentrate on what [Richard] Alpert and [Timothy] Leary were up to with LSD," he told *Rolling Stone*, "but they'd left [Harvard by then] . . . I lasted four or five months by playing music and having good times."[5]

Forming the International Submarine Band in Cambridge in 1965, Parsons moved the group to the Bronx and then to Southern CA, where they broke up in 1967. The Buck Owens-influenced singer-songwriter would meet a musical compadre while waiting in line at a Beverly Hills bank. Invited to a Byrds' rehearsal, "Gram picked up a guitar and started singing country tunes," said Herb Pedersen. "That appealed to Chris."

"Gram was a great artist," remembered Hillman, "and it was meant for him to be in the Byrds. We hired him as a backup player but he got us going. He motivated us to record in Nashville. Herb and I still do a song or two from *Sweetheart of the Rodeo* and a couple of the songs that Gram and I wrote for the Flying Burrito Brothers."

Sweetheart of the Rodeo included Parsons' "Hickory Wind" and "One Hundred Years from Now." His stint with the Byrds, however, ended abruptly. Irked that they were booked to play in segregated South Africa, he resigned two hours before the group's flight. When they returned, Clarence White replaced him.

Roland White was ten years old when he taught the basics of guitar playing to his six-year-younger brother. "Clarence was the best guitar player ever," the Madawaska, ME-born mandolinist/guitarist told me. "When we first got to CA, we'd watch Joe Maphis on *Town Hall Party*. He played electric and acoustic guitar and banjo. Later, there was Doc Watson. When he saw Doc, Clarence knew what he wanted to do and how he wanted to approach it. Doc came to the Ash Grove a couple of times and Clarence would go and watch him play."

Roland "was an infant when we moved to Lewiston," he said. "Joanne was born there and then, Eric and Clarence. Lewiston [ME's second most populated city] was much smaller than it is now."

Hailing from New Brunswick, Canada, the Whites' father, Eric LeBlanc, Sr., moved below the border in the mid-1930s. "My mother's from Van Buren," said White, "but her parents were from New Brunswick. Dad played old-time fiddle tunes like 'Ragtime Annie,' 'Soldier's Joy,' 'Saint Anne's Reel,' and he strummed guitar and sang country songs. I started playing rhythm guitar to back him up. My brothers took it up later. By the time I was eleven, Clarence and Eric were old enough to play. Joanne and I sang at family functions, in the summer, under a big oak tree."

Relocating to Southern CA in 1954, the White brothers entered a talent show on KCLA, in Pasadena, and won. "They put us on *Town Hall Party*," remembered White. "That was our first gig. I was sixteen, Eric was eleven, and Clarence was ten. We weren't singing, just playing instrumentals. Eric played tenor banjo, Clarence played guitar, and I played mandolin."

Four years later, the "Queen of Hillbilly Swing" Rose Maddox invited the teenagers to her club to meet Monroe. "She told us to bring our instruments," recalled White, "and said that she'd get us up to play, but I didn't bring my mandolin. When we got there, Rose introduced our dad to Monroe and he introduced us. Rose had us sit where they couldn't serve alcohol; we were underage. The Blue Grass Boys did a set and then, Monroe said, 'We have some boys who are going to play a few tunes for you; they're going to use our instruments.' I said, 'Oh, no,' but we went up and played. The next time Monroe played the Ash Grove, we invited him to the house for dinner."

The Country Boys was one of the West Coast's first bluegrass bands. "There were just us," said White, "and the Golden State Boys with Don Parmley, Vern Gosdin, and Hal Poindexter [who would be replaced by eighteen-year-old Hillman of the Scottsville Squirrel Barkers]."

The group continued to expand. "We met banjo player Billy Ray Latham at a music store in Glendale," said White. "Dobro player Leroy 'Mack' McNees joined us around 1959. We toured the US four times, playing in Boston, NY, Chicago, and Washington, DC. On our first trip, we stayed at Ralph Rinzler's place in Greenwich Village. He had a party and we met Grisman and that crazy mandolin player, Frank Wakefield."

Latham, McNees, Roger Bush (bass), and the White brothers' Country Boys became the first bluegrass band to appear on *The Andy Griffith Show* in 1961. "Steve Stebbins called me," remembered White. "He booked national country acts. Desilu Productions had called him looking for a young string band for a TV show. Steve told them that he knew this family band. Somehow, he got our number and called us. He told us to get in touch with Desilu Productions so we did. I thought it was a local show. They said, 'Why don't you come down next week.' I said, 'How should we dress?' 'No suits, just nice slacks and shirts.' We went to the studio and they led us to the green room and told us to wait. In a few minutes, Andy came in and shook our hands. He had a guitar and started singing a song. We joined him but we didn't get into it very long before he stopped and said, 'That'll do, boys. We'll record Saturday.' When the show aired, in early '61, we got calls from cousins saying they saw us on TV. I realized it was nationwide. The band did another episode but I wasn't in it. I was drafted into the army in September."

Before releasing Joe Maphis-produced *The New Sounds of Bluegrass America* (1963), Briar International persuaded the Country Boys to change their name to the Kentucky Colonels. Their next album, *Appalachian Swing,* produced by Jim Dickson (The Byrds), followed in July '64. Recorded at the Newport Folk Festival, and unreleased before 1991, *Long Journey Home, 1964* includes seven Clarence White and Doc Watson duets, two tunes spotlighting the White brothers, and fifteen tracks by the Kentucky Colonels, four with Bill Keith.

Calvin Scott "Scotty" Stoneman (1932-73) joined the Kentucky Colonels in March 1965. A five-time fiddle champion, Stoneman had played with his parents, sisters Donna (mandolin) and Veronica Loretta "Roni" (banjo), and brothers Gene (guitar) and Jim (bass) since the mid-1940s. His father, Ernest or "Pop" Stoneman, had scored country music's first million-selling hit ("The Sinking of the Titanic") in 1924 and played an important role in Ralph Peer's 1927 Bristol recording sessions. Hard hit by the Great Depression, the family began to bounce back after Pop formed a family band with his wife, Hattie, and their large brood. Winning a talent-show prize of a twenty-seven-week stint at Constitution Hall, broadcast on local TV, they became fixtures of Washington, DC's bluegrass scene. Pop's good fortune reached its apex in 1956. In addition to winning $10,000 on NBC-TV quiz show *The Big Surprise,* he and Hattie recorded for Mike Seeger and Folkways. Taking first place on *Arthur Godfrey's Talent Scouts,* the Stonemans became regulars on Godfrey's CBS-TV show.

Scotty and younger brother Van cohosted their own show on Washington, DC's WTTG. Augmented by Jimmy, Donna, and Roni and banjo player Porter Church, they won the band contest at the Warrenton National Championship in 1962. The Hotel Charles hired them to perform six nights a week as "The Blue Grass Champs."

Guesting on CBS-TV's *Jimmy Dean Show,* in October 1964, the Stoneman Family debuted on the *Grand Ole Opry* a few months later. Their performance inspired a twenty-minute standing ovation (the first in *Opry* history), which "did not go down too well with the established stars of the day," recalled Roni.[6]

"Some people thought [Scotty] was great," said fiddler Alex Tottle, "others thought he was crazy. . . . He'd play without a chinrest . . . he'd break strings—so ferocious was his attack . . . sounds leaped out while the bow shuffled; the player contorted, sweat on his forehead, and blood on his face."[7]

Plagued by personal demons, Stoneman left the Kentucky Colonels after seven months. He would succumb to alcohol poisoning in March 1973. "I thought he should have stayed with the Kentucky Colonels," said Lamar Grier. "He told me that he didn't quit them, they quit him, like it was his band or [he was] the star—too bad for Scott."[8]

Selling his Martin D-18 acoustic guitar to a liquor-store tycoon, in the mid-1960s, Clarence White bought a Fender Telecaster and amplifier from Don Rich, guitarist for Buck Owens' Buckaroos. Tony Rice would acquire White's D-18 in 1975 for $550. "Clarence's father bought that guitar from McCabe's for thirty-five dollars," he said.[9]

With the Kentucky Colonels switching to electric music, Roland "played an electric mandolin my dad made," he recalled. "Billy Ray played a Gibson archtop guitar. Roger Bush had a new Gibson electric bass. We added a drummer, Bart Haney."

After they rejected Jim Dickson's suggestion to record "Mr. Tambourine Man," the Byrds recorded it. It would sell more than five million copies within weeks and top the charts in twenty-six countries. The Kentucky Colonels would perform their final show on Halloween 1965.

Two years later, Monroe "was flying in with his new fiddler [Byron Berline]," White remembered, "and he needed a band. Ed Pearl [owner of the Ash Grove] called me and I told Clarence. He was busy doing sessions; James Burton had given him work. I called Ed back and told him that I'd do it. I asked if he needed a bass player. He said, 'Yeah,' so I called Eric. He was available. Bob Warford had been playing banjo with me. We got together with Monroe and Berline and played Tuesday and Wednesday. On Thursday, Bill said, 'I want to settle up with you,' but he told me, 'Roland, I want you to stay on.' I said, 'Don't you have a guitar player?' He said, 'We could use some help.' His guitarist, Doug Green, was leaving to become Ranger Doug of Riders in the Sky."

White played guitar on "Train 45," "Walls of Time," and "Sally Goodin'." "If we weren't traveling," he said, "we were on the *Opry*. The first time, in June 1967, I was nervous. Bill went, 'Howdy folks, how ya all doing? We're going to do a couple of songs for you.' I wasn't looking at the audience—this was at the Ryman, where you could see the first rows. When I finally looked up, I saw that everybody had fans bought for fifty cents when they came in. They needed them. There was no air conditioning."

White continued to work on his mandolin playing—"the Monroe style." He recalled, "Every time I came home, I'd take my mandolin out and practice. When I started, I didn't have the drive; I couldn't get it. We were on the bus. Bill told me to play a tune and handed me his mandolin. I played something and he said, 'That's wrong.' I knew it was. He told me that I had to practice his way of playing, which I did. By the time I went to work with Lester Flatt, in 1969, I had it down. Lester was like Monroe; very easygoing as long as you showed up on time, could drive the bus, and didn't drink. I treated both of them with respect and they returned it. Lester didn't want to play new grass."

Leaving the Nashville Grass in 1973, White rejoined his brothers and Herb Pedersen as the New Kentucky Colonels and went to Holland and Belgium. "Herb's wife wanted him to go to France," he remembered, "and hook up with Johnny Rivers, so Alan Munde came in on banjo. That's when we went to England and Wales."

White, Guilbeau, and Parsons had previously auditioned for Gram's new band with Chris Ethridge and Kleinow, the Flying Burrito Brothers. "Gram was very distant," remembered Parsons, "and in his own bubble. I never had a harsh word with him, we even had a few laughs, but I never got close to him. I rehearsed with the Byrds for a few weeks, played two or three gigs, and then Chris Hillman left and joined the Flying Burrito Brothers."

"The Flying Burrito Brothers were the classic longhaired honkytonk band," remembered Jeff Hanna. "Those guys were stone country. The way that Chris and Gram sang together, and with Bernie [Leadon] . . . it was super cool."

Replacing Parsons with Clarence White wasn't the Byrds' only change. Informed that McGuinn and Hillman had fired Kelley, Gene Parsons "auditioned and got the gig," he said. "I was never much of a schooled drummer. With my broken wrist, I could never do double strokes very good. It was single-stroke Neanderthal style but I had a good feel. Clarence was my inspiration for rhythm. He used to say it's not what you play but what you don't play."

Dr. Byrds & Mr. Hyde (1969) included a remake of "Your Gentle Way of Lovin' Me," which Parsons and Gib Guilbeau had released as a single in 1967. The album also included White and Parsons' instrumental "Nashville West." A live rendition featured on double-album *Untitled* (1970). "The studio disc was one of our best," said Parsons, "but the live side was done at Carnegie Hall at the end of our tour. We were dead tired and it was one of our worst shows. Jim [Dickson] performed miracles."

Byrdmaniax (1971) flopped. "I attribute that to [producer] Terry Melcher," said Parsons. "We recorded the tracks before a European tour. Terry finished the album while we were gone. He was supposed to wait for us to get back but he was under pressure to get it done. It had nothing to do with us. The original takes were good; he ruined them. The mixes were terrible.

"The Byrds were already becoming disenchanted, mostly between Roger and me. CBS told us that we had to sign with them. Roger, with the advice of his manager, said, 'Don't do that. That will limit you if you want to do other recordings. We'll do a profit-sharing deal.' We were gullible and went for it. We got some money but, all of a sudden, there was no profit. We were noticing that Roger was buying toys. I had just gone through a divorce and I was financially strapped. My ex-wife took me to the cleaners. I had two kids to support. I told him that he had to come through and he fired me."

After playing, with White and Ry Cooder, on Arlo Guthrie's *Running Down the Road* (1969) and Randy Newman's *12 Songs* (1970), Parsons was invited to join a band that Russ Titelman, president of Warner Brothers, was producing. He turned it down. "I had songs that I had written," he explained, "and I wrote some more. I recorded on a Teac four-track and sent the tape to Russ. He got me a contract. We recorded *Kindling* [Clarence played acoustic and electric guitar and mandolin and sang 'Drunkard's Dream' with Ralph Stanley]. It got really good reviews. We were on the right track; everything looked good. Clarence signed with WB and started working on an album with his brother, Byron Berline, Roger Bush, Herb Pedersen, Ry Cooder, and Leland Sklar. Gram Parsons & Emmylou Harris and Country Gazette also got contracts and we all did a promotional tour. It was leading to a massive European tour. Then, Clarence was killed."

"We were at a club in Palmdale [BJs]," remembered Roland White. "It was Clarence and Gib's show but I played a couple of tunes with them. Eric played bass. After the show, we opened the back of Clarence's car to load his amplifier and guitar. A car came close and Clarence said, 'We need to be careful.' Uncle John was across the street in his truck. We were going to his house. It was one-thirty in the morning but Aunt Jeanette was fixing us breakfast. I got up to the car and Clarence said, 'Here're the keys.' I turned around to get the keys and this car struck him, threw him into me, and knocked me over onto the sidewalk. When he hit me, it pushed him back into the car. The car went twenty-five or thirty feet and ended up across the street on the sidewalk. The woman who hit him had been drinking. Uncle John went over and took Clarence's boots off. He tapped him on the cheek and blood started coming out of his mouth and nose. A paramedic pulled up and said, 'Don't touch him. He's hurt bad.' They called an ambulance and took him to the hospital. I went with them. I called my mom. Someone brought her to the hospital but Clarence was braindead. His heart stopped about three in the morning. That was the end of that. I had a disconnected shoulder put back in place."

"It was a real tragedy," remembered Parsons. "Clarence had been messing with drugs—he and Gram had a party—but his wife had had enough of it.

She moved back to KY and took their kids. It was a wakeup call. Clarence got off drugs and booze. He wanted Susie to take him back; he loved her so dearly. She would have and she was ready to. It just about killed her too. She got in a car crash, not long afterwards, and had severe head trauma. It took her years of therapy to get through it. She called me on the phone and said, 'Gene, this is Susie. I've got my brain back together.' I said, 'That's wonderful.' It wasn't a week before she got in another car crash. She and Clarence's son, Bradley, died. The only one left was his daughter, Michelle; she still suffers."

Acquiring Clarence's Telecaster, and assorted memorabilia, from his widow for $1,400, Marty Stuart continues to feature it during concerts. He spotlighted it on his 2010 Grammy-winning instrumental, "Hummingbyrd." "I consider it my B-bender recital piece," he said.[10]

At Clarence's funeral, Roger Bush spoke with his brother. Bush had recently launched Country Gazette with Byron Berline. "He asked if I was going back with Lester Flatt," White recalled, "and I said, 'No but I'll do something.' He said, 'We need a guitar player.' I called my wife and asked what she thought. She said, 'Try it; see if you like it.' I did it until 1984."

Gram Parsons' hard living caught up with him two months after White's death. Overdosing in the Joshua Tree Motel, he was only twenty-six. "He died

Marty Stuart, 2016

Roland White, 1986

where I grew up," noted Parsons. "My dad called and said, 'I'm glad to hear your voice.' The local paper ran a picture of me with a headline saying, 'Local musician commits suicide.' That wasn't me; that was Gram—senseless."

The Nashville Bluegrass Band ruled the bluegrass world when White replaced mandolinist Mike Compton in 1985. "Not every tune was ninety miles an hour," he said, "and we did a lot of country tunes bluegrass style. We rehearsed twice a week at Alan O'Bryant's house and played the songs on the road. When they sounded good, we recorded them. We didn't have to run in and record any old thing."

Since leaving the Nashville Bluegrass Band in 1996, White has fronted the Roland White Band. "We have my wife [Diane] on guitar and vocals," he said, "Brian Christianson [fiddle], Jon Weisberger [bass], Rich Bailey [banjo], and me. When Diane and I got together, twenty-seven years ago in 1990, she played guitar and we started singing together. It works really well."

White had a cameo in *O Brother, Where Art Thou?* "In the scene," he said, "they're at their cousin's house having supper. Someone is singing 'You Are My Sunshine,' in the background, and I'm playing mandolin."

Chapter 18

The Darlings

The Dillards appeared in six episodes of *The Andy Griffith Show* (1963-66) and the *Return to Mayberry* TV movie (1986) as hillbilly family band the Darlings. The music played by Douglas Flint Dillard (banjo), his brother Rodney (guitar/Dobro/lead vocals), Dean Webb (mandolin), and DJ-turned-bassist/emcee Mitchell Franklin "Mitch" Jayne lives on in reruns. "The Darling family was treated with such respect," said Maggie Peterson (Charlene Darling). "These could have been ridiculous characters without Andy's respectful reaction to us."[1]

As teenagers, Doug, Rodney, and Webb recorded ten tracks that would release as *Early Recordings 1959* (2006). "I went up to this boy's house in St. Louis . . . ," recalled Webb. "He had a bunch of recording equipment upstairs. We cut this first basic album of stuff on banjo, guitar, and mandolin . . . later I went back over and overdubbed bass fiddle on everything."[2]

Hammond, IN-born Jayne (1930-2010) taught at the University of Missouri-Columbia before taking a position in a one-room school in Dent County, MO, close to the Dillards' home. "He liked the sound of our tape," remembered Webb, "and said, 'Hey, I want to join up with you guys. I'll learn to play bass enough to play with you and I can tell funny stories and be the emcee.' We found him a bass, and Rodney helped teach him how to play it."[3]

Jayne learned to play bass while driving to the West Coast. As emcee, he opened shows by saying, "Hi, we're the Dillards and we're all hillbillies. I thought I'd better tell you that because you probably thought we were the Budapest String Quartet."[4]

The Dillards' show at St. Louis's Washington University, in 1962, released as *A Long Time Ago—The First Time Live!* (1999). Heading West, they would guest on nationally broadcast shows hosted by Judy Garland and Tennessee Ernie Ford and tour with rock acts, including the Byrds. "People saw something in us," said Rodney Dillard. "Otherwise, they would have gotten bored and looked for the next thing."

Humor sparked the Dillards' performances. "Other bluegrass bands did bathroom jokes, the old vaudeville and medicine-show gags," said Dillard, "but we poked fun at ourselves from a different perspective. I played the foil. Mitch and I kept this banter going on. We spoon-fed our music to urban folks who weren't chasing tradition. They were trying to get away from the outhouse in the back, but here we were, playing places like the Hungry I, giving them subtle humor, and having the music come through— education through entertainment. Comedians Gabe Kaplan [*Welcome Back, Kotter*] and Pat Paulson opened for us. Lily Tomlin would come to the Icehouse when we played and use our audience to test her material."

The son of a gas-station operator and a county nurse, Webb "was a big fan of Homer & Jethro." "They were a comedy group," explained Dillard in 2016, "but they put out *Playing It Straight* [1962]. Dean was the first to play anything like Dawg music. Grisman picked up a lot from him. He played a lot of tremolo, single-note runs. He still plays every Saturday, on a flatbed truck, for tourists."

Leaving the Dillards in 1968, Doug Dillard (1937-2012) released *The Banjo Album* (1969). The Byrds founding member Gene Clark, John Hartford, Byron Berline, Vassar Clements, and future Eagle Bernie Leadon backed Dillard's banjo. In his liner notes, Joe Foster wrote, "Eclectic is certainly a good description . . . jazz drums, harpsichord, djembe, tabla, and various sound effects, as well as a manic attack poised somewhere between Earl Scruggs and The Ramones."[5]

Dillard and Clark would form the genre-bending Dillard-Clark Expedition. Leadon joined soon afterwards. After Clark departed for a solo career, the band continued as the Doug Dillard Expedition, providing the soundtrack of *Vanishing Point* (1971). Forming the Doug Dillard Band in the early eighties, Dillard rejoined his brother in the Dillards by the end of the decade.

Rodney continued to break new ground with the Dillards. With Herb Pedersen replacing his brother, their 1968 album, *Wheatstraw Suite,* remains a masterpiece. Buddy Emmons (pedal steel), Joe Osborn (bass), and drummers Jim Gordon (CSNY, Mad Dogs & Englishmen, Derek & the Dominos) and Toxey French augmented the sound. "It was purely what was in our heads," said Dillard. "Herb added a lot with his harmonies. I started the basic tracks on my tape recorder at home. It had an orchestra, drums, pedal steel, things no one else was doing."

Opening and closing with a thirty-eight-second snippet of Albert E. Brumley's "I'll Fly Away," *Wheatstraw Suite* presented a folk, bluegrass, rock, country, and pop mosaic that included Tim Hardin's "Reason to Believe," Jesse Kincaid's "She Sang Hymns Out of Tune," and the Beatles' "I've Just Seen a Face." "We tried to keep it subliminal," Dillard told Richie Unterberger, "yet give it a depth that the music might not have had . . . the heart and the content. Any kind of sweetening, you do just the salt, you don't overuse it . . . it was where the organic raw met the orchestrated structure . . . it didn't come out like Muzak because you heard the guitar and you heard the squeaks. You know, there're a few mistakes . . . it was okay."[6]

Wheatstraw Suite got rave reviews. "There was maturity in the lyrics," said Dillard. "I wanted to say what was in my heart."

Seventeen years before (1951), third-generation fiddler Homer Dillard ordered a banjo from a Sears & Roebuck catalog and presented it to his fourteen-year-old son, Doug, for Christmas. Younger brother Rodney (1942-), who had been playing ukulele, received a guitar. "Dad wanted a backup band," he said. "My brother and I were always playing with him. When you're a kid, you accept things as they are. We just played and played and played. Until he died, whenever we'd visit, Dad would pull out his fiddle and we'd play. There was a tune I remember very well, 'High Dad in the Morning,' which he wrote. John Hartford, Norman Blake, and Kenny Baker covered it. My dad played old fiddle tunes but he always had new names for them. Bill Monroe did the same thing. Change a couple of notes and it's a new tune. You heard the same thing repeatedly. Douglas and I added our own personalities. Every artist should be able to do that."

Oldest brother Earl played "hokey songs like 'Roll Out the Barrel'" on piano and organ and "was the squarest musician you'd ever hear but an electrical-engineer genius," remembered Dillard. "He worked for McDonnell Douglas. He designed the simulator for the Gemini space capsule and worked with the Stealth helicopter. He came up with the first speech computer system. He got it to sing 'Dooley.'"

Determined to meet Scruggs, the youngest Dillard brothers "went to Nashville, found out where he lived, drove to his house, and knocked on his door," recalled Dillard. "He was gracious and invited us in. He sold Doug tuners for his banjo and put them on right there in his living room. When Doug and I went to CA, we had a PR booklet printed. Earl wrote a piece for it. I saw him over the years and played a couple of songs with him at the *Opry*. He called me, in 1980, and asked me to go on the road. We had a blast. My wife, Beverly, saw us when she was in college. I sang lead on two songs on Earl's *Sittin' on Top of the World* ['Caroline Star' and the title track] and toured for three years on his bus. He told me about his childhood. He had a tough time growing up but he persevered."

Then Bill Keith came along. "Bill and I were jamming at my house in L.A.," said Dillard, "and he told me 'Banjo in the Hollow,' the first thing Doug and I recorded, inspired him to create chromatic banjo playing. I was in high school when we recorded it. Doug was in college. We went to a studio in Belleville, IL and cut 'You Were On My Mind' on one side and 'Banjo in the Hollow' on the other. I remember Douglas coming back after working in the city for the summer. He said, 'Listen to this tune I came up with,' and he played this lick. I had never heard anything like it.

"When folks from the city started listening to old records and imitating them, you could sense—growing up in the Ozarks—the difference between the revivalists and the originals. My dad was an old-time fiddle player. The Oral History of the Ozarks Project produced *Precious Memories: The Musical Life of Homer Dillard* [1992] about him. He taught John Hartford to clog dance. My mom, Lorene, played guitar. She got us interested by putting it behind the couch and saying, 'Don't touch that guitar while I'm gone.' For Douglas and me, you could imagine what that was like."

The Dillards had no interest in the Nashville scene. "The dials seemed rusted on the boards," Dillard said. "Everything sounded alike. It was cookie-cutter and it's still cookie-cutter—manufactured music."

Opting for L.A., the Dillards "walked into the Ash Grove, took out our instruments, and started playing," recalled Dillard. "We were tired, broke, and sick. We had worked our way across the country. Ed Pearl came

Bill Keith, 2000

out and said, 'You can't do that here.' We were in the lobby playing. He said, 'Do it onstage.' That was our introduction. Jim Dickson, the Byrds' manager, was there. He told us he'd produce us. Somehow, Jac Holzman, owner of Elektra Records, got involved. He hadn't moved to L.A. yet."

Back Porch Bluegrass released in 1963. *Variety* reported that Elektra had signed a bluegrass band from MO. Andy Griffith was preparing for an episode ("The Darlings Are Coming") when his manager, Richard "Dick" Linke, saw the report. "We went to audition at Desilu Studios," said Dillard. "We walked in and everybody stopped what they were doing. Andy pulled up a folding chair, and he and Bob Sweeney, the director, sat in front of us and said, 'Show us what you've got.' We started playing 'Reuben's Train.' Andy got up in the middle of it and said, 'That's it.' I thought he was kicking us out but he said, 'You've got the job.'"

During a script reading, "Andy came up to us and said, 'Boys, we're paying you as musicians because you're not going to say anything,.'" recalled Dillard. "There were no residuals but he said, 'I'll get as much of your music on as I can.' He did us one of the biggest favors in the world. They could have had us do traditional tunes. They could have taken money for the arrangements but we had four songs per show and he made sure we did the music the way we wanted. I have transcriptions of us backing him on songs. He didn't care for many people but he sure loved pickers. When we were shooting the movie, he brought in a National steel guitar. He hung it in the cabin scene when we played. The last time I saw him, TV Land dedicated a statue to him in Mt. Airy. He walked up to me in the dressing room, took the guitar from my hands, and strummed it—the same Martin D-18 I played on the show.

"Those writers knew how to write and, of course, Andy grew up in the mountains. They were as close to mountain people as you could get. *The Beverly Hillbillies* went in another direction—it wasn't representative of anything. When we were guests on television shows, they'd want haystacks and dancers with painted freckles and blackened-out front teeth. We'd say, 'No thanks, let's have some reality here, some integrity.'"

Songs heard on *The Andy Griffith Show* were prerecorded. "We'd go to Glen Glenn Sound in Hollywood," said Webb, "and figure out exactly how many seconds or minutes they wanted of whatever song. Then we'd play it specifically to the clock where it came out exactly that way . . . we would 'fake it' to the disc as it was playing."[7]

Dillard wasn't quite ready for the Beatles. "I didn't awaken to them until *Rubber Soul,*" he said, "but we were managed by the same people as the Byrds and we toured with Mitch Ryder, Sam the Sham, and the Sir Douglas Quintet. We were in the middle of the rock and roll world."

The Dillards documented their show on their second album, *Live!!!
Almost!!!* (1964), recorded at popular L.A. nightclub the Mecca. Opening
thirty-two concerts for the Byrds, "there were philosophical differences
between David Crosby and me, though Chris Hillman was cool," recalled
Dillard. "Our drummer, Dewey Martin, was a real piece of work. When
we came back after the Byrds' tour, I got a call from Stephen Stills. He had
stayed at my house when he was broke. He was putting Buffalo Springfield
together and was looking for a drummer. I sent Dewey over."

Pickin' and Fiddlin' with Byron Berline (1965) was "an esoteric but
traditional album," said Dillard. "People crucified us for the first album.
Sing Out! asked, 'When do they have echo chambers on the back porches
of the Ozarks?' I thought, 'Step on my back porch and yell; see what
happens.' It has one of the coolest echoes you've ever heard. We moved to
fiddle tunes to give purists what they wanted."

Jayne and Rodney penned "Dooley," "The Old Home Place," "The Whole
World Round," and "There Is a Time." A real-life moonshiner, Dooley
appeared in the John McEuen-produced *Night in the Ozarks* (2006). "We
changed his name to protect ourselves," said Dillard. "Ebo Walker's real
name was Tarzan Golden. He repeatedly stole the same watch from a
sporting-goods store. They'd throw him in jail and get the watch back.
He'd spend a couple days in a cell and have a place to sleep. When he got
out, he'd steal the same watch and start the process all over again. It was
like an *Andy Griffith Show* episode."

The song is "about a man who died from drinking tractor radiator
alcohol," Dillard told Jeremy Roberts. "He was our town drunk in Salem.
By the way, there is a real Ebo Walker, but he's not the town drunk—he
was a standup bass player for New Grass Revival."[8]

Booked to play on a movie soundtrack with Glen Campbell, Rodney
and Doug walked onto a soundstage and saw Warren Beatty, Faye
Dunaway, [director] Arthur Penn, a European conductor, and an orchestra.
Of course, the movie was *Bonnie and Clyde*. "They sat us in front of the
orchestra," remembered Dillard, "and handed us sheet music. I can't read
music. 'Oh crap, what am I going to do?' I had to go to guitarist Tommy
Tedesco during breaks and say, 'What does this note mean?' He'd show
me. I'd practice it and, after the break, play it. One day, I felt this tug.
It was Warren Beatty. He was concerned about the music. I told him he
needed traditional bluegrass music in the chase scenes. I was hoping he'd
let Doug, Glen, and me do it, but he didn't. When the movie came out, I
went to a special screening. I was walking into the theater when Warren
came over and said, 'I got traditional music in the movie.' It was 'Foggy
Mountain Breakdown.'"

Webb remembered a rehearsal at Rodney's house. Doug got very angry and announced he was just going to quit. When Doug walked out, Webb followed him to his car to try to talk to him. "I said, 'If you come back in now, we'll resolve everything. This doesn't have to go down this way.'"[9] Doug would not listen.

Rodney's split with Doug "wasn't pleasant," he said. "We were still brothers. We went to dinner and spent Christmas together. We just drifted apart. I wanted to experiment and Douglas wasn't fond of where my music wanted to go. If I came in with a different rhythm, or wanted drums, he wasn't into it. He wanted to stay in traditional bluegrass but he and Gene Clark didn't do traditional bluegrass, so go figure. He felt comfortable that he could make his banjo work in any situation."

Doug ran with a wild crowd. "The Troubadour was the Algonquin Round Table of the West Coast," said his brother. "John Lennon, Eric Burdon, and Phil Ochs hung out there. Lennon walked in one night with a Kotex taped to his forehead. Douglas was there. They kicked him and Harry Nilsson out.

"He told me about recording with Phil Spector and Lennon at Wally Heider Sound. He liked calm and hated intensity. Spector and Lennon got into this screaming match. Douglas got up and walked out. He was walking up the street when he heard someone calling, 'Dillard, Dillard, come back; come back.' It was Lennon."

Following *Wheatstraw Suite* with the similar *Copperfields* (1970), the Dillards released their highest-charting album, *Roots and Branches,* in 1972, produced by Richie Podolor (Three Dog Night, Steppenwolf, Ringo Starr). "Somebody thought that putting us together with him would be a big deal," said Webb, "but that was the only one we did with him. . . . He owned his own studio, American Recording. He always wanted us to come in there and record into the night . . . [Pedersen] had just gotten married, and he was not about to stay all night at a studio."[10]

With Billy Ray Latham replacing Pedersen before the album's completion, the Dillards toured with Elton John. "Elton came to our early show at the Troubadour," Dillard remembered, "and then came back for our late show. After *Roots and Branches* came out, his management asked if we wanted to go out with him for his *Honky Château* album. He was so gracious. His band had protocol and respect."

Reconnecting in 1989, the original Dillards performed 132 shows in England, Ireland, and Japan. They added Steve Cooley on banjo, guitar, and upright bass. The lineup's final show came as Pete Seeger and Arlo Guthrie's opening act at Carnegie Hall. "Mitch Jayne had lost his hearing," said Dillard, "and Douglas was very sick. It was a sad time; I knew what was coming."

Dillard's friendship with Guthrie grew over the years. "Arlo called me in 2008," he remembered, "and told me he wanted to do an album of Woody Guthrie tunes [*32 Cents Postage Due*]. I have a state-of-the-art studio, and I've produced Roy Clark and Pat Boone, so I said, 'Why don't we do it here?' He came with a busload of people and stayed at my house. We spent two weeks cutting that album and had a blast. Arlo is very loose about how he records. He just goes in and starts picking. It comes out naturally."

Dillard met his wife, the former Beverly Cotten, at an international music festival in Edmonton. "I was jamming with Steve Goodman and Jethro Burns," he remembered, "and Steve said, 'We've got to get together and write.' 'Yeah, we've got to do that,' but, before we did, he was gone [stilled by leukemia on September 20, 1984].

"There were 10,000 people at that festival including a half-Cherokee girl, in a white dress, with long black hair. She was playing clawhammer banjo and had people clogging. I thought, 'Oh my God!' That was it; I was smittened. She had grown up in NC and gotten her master's in psychology. She was dancing with the Green Grass Cloggers when she got interested in the banjo. She studied with Tommy Jarrell and Doc Watson's cousin, Willard. She became friends with Merle—they dated—but then we got together and married in 1983. It's coming up on thirty-four years of pure bliss."

Between 1982 and 1988, Dillard and his wife played nightly, with Webb, at the 400-seat Silver Dollar City amphitheater in Branson. "Beverly played with Buck Trent [inventor of the electric banjo] for years," Dillard said, "and she had a career of her own before we met. She was doing public TV and was artist-in-residence at a NC college. John McEuen told me she was the best timekeeper he ever met."

On the Nitty Gritty Dirt Band's *Will the Circle Be Unbroken—Volume III*, Dillard revived "There Is a Time," which Maggie Peterson (Charlene Darling) had sung on *The Andy Griffith Show*. "Ricky Skaggs sang it with me," he said. "As I was getting ready to go to Nashville to record it, John McEuen called and asked me to write another verse. I sat down and started writing verses on a napkin. I picked up the phone, called Mitch, and said, 'I've got forty-five minutes to finish writing. You write a verse and I'll write one. We'll compare them and take the best.' He called back in ten minutes. The first two lines, we had written the same: 'Like a rolling river, with no regrets as it moves on, around each bend, the shining morning to greet the friends we thought were gone.' It's so hopeful for life after death."

Alan Jackson covered "There Is a Time" on *The Bluegrass Album* (2013). "He promoted it at Carnegie Hall," said Dillard, "and talked about our inspiration on him. I knew my songs weren't picked flowers of the day."

The last time they spoke, the brothers talked about "everything from aliens to God," Dillard remembered. "The last thing I said was 'I love you, Doug.' He said, 'I love you too,' and that was it. Bernie Leadon produced his funeral. We all had something to say. I told a story ['The Cowboy Angel'] about seeing patterns that the Christmas-tree lights created on the ceiling. I remembered lying on the floor, looking at the ceiling, and pointing out different pictures. Doug said, 'Look, there's the cowboy angel,' and sure enough, there it was, as if Andrew Wyeth had drawn it. Bernie bought a beautiful headstone—it has carved banjos on it—and he wrote the words on the tombstone. It was a celebration of life."

An ordained minister of the Assembly of God since 2001, Dillard isn't "a conventional church person." He explained, "I believe America is destroying the concept of Christianity. I was as bad as Paul against Christians. I made fun of them. My life changed when I met my wife. It was a salvation experience. She and I have a ministry, Mayberry Values in Today's World. I do concerts to support it."

Dillard produced television shows for controversial Assembly of God evangelist Jim Bakker. "I was prepared to dislike him," he said, "until I brought him to my office at the studio. I realized that if I couldn't forgive him, how could anyone forgive me for all the crap I've done? We became friends and I learned the inside story. He built five hospitals in Europe; his naivety got him in trouble."

Reunited with Holzman, Dillard is working on a new album, *Old Road New Again*. "It's the bookend of *Wheatstraw Suite*," he said. "We recut 'The Whole World Around.' Don Henley sang on three songs. Bernie Leadon played banjo on a couple of tunes. Sam Bush played on it. The Whites sang background. I didn't want to make it an event—Rodney Dillard and friends—but I got people I respected. It's the best thing I've ever done. It has a song Beverly wrote with a preacher in MS, 'Tearing Our Liberty Down.' Ricky Skaggs sang it with me. Beverly played banjo on a version of 'Cluck Old Hen' that we called 'Funky Old Hen' and she sang harmony, with Henley, on 'There's Always Going to Be You.' The title song tells the Dillards' history in four verses and talks about the Eagles, the Byrds, Emmylou Harris, and Linda Ronstadt. If we don't perpetuate the truth, young people will never know it."

Chapter 19

Gentle on My Mind

The NY-born and St. Louis-raised son of an infectious-disease doctor, John Cowan Hartford (Harford) (1937-2001) was a child of privilege. He was a descendent of Patrick Henry, the great-grandson of the Missouri Bar Association's founder, and a cousin of novelist Tennessee Williams. Growing up in a gated community, he dressed formally for dinner. Bluegrass and old-time music drove him in another direction.

A high-school friend of Doug Dillard, Hartford often joined with the banjo player and his five-year-younger brother, Rodney, to "play music all night long" and record "reams and reams of reel-to-reel tapes." After the Dillards headed West, Hartford "saw us on TV, and it inspired him to go to Nashville and start doing what he did," Rodney recalled. "When he came to L.A. to be music director of *The Glen Campbell Show,* I helped him get his apartment."

Motivated by a Flatt & Scruggs concert, in 1953 or '54, Hartford bought a banjo and taught himself to play. "I started playing at dancehalls where they did square dancing," he told me in 1988. "The next thing I knew, I was in a full band [the Missouri Ridge Runners]."

Inheriting the aesthetics of his painter mother, Hartford balanced music and art. He recorded an EP, *Backwoods Gospel Songs,* with the Ozark Mountain Trio, in 1960, the same year he graduated with a BFA from St. Louis's Washington University. "Everyone is familiar with Dad's fun side," Hartford's daughter, Katie Harford Hogue, told an interviewer, "and his sense of humor, but not everyone realizes that he was well-educated, a deep thinker, and obsessed with information. He considered himself a frustrated librarian. When he was interested in something, he researched it extensively, inside and out, taking notes and looking for connections to other things. His extensive book collection is evidence to that."[1]

Hartford steeped in bluegrass and old-time music, but his songs were poetically sharp and extremely poignant. "He was musically curious," said Bob Carlin, "and always looking for new ways to do things. He lived music. He studied, listened to, and analyzed it. He was an experimenter but he was very rooted in tradition."

A year after moving to Nashville in 1965, Hartford was signed by Chet Atkins to RCA Victor. (Atkins suggested adding the *t* to Harford.) "Felton Jarvis produced my early records," he recalled, "but Chet oversaw them. Felton also did Mickey Newbury's records and became Elvis Presley's producer. I was interested in putting the banjo into different settings. I had strings and even brass on my records."

Hartford's debut album, *Looks at Life* (1967), opened by asking, "Who's this demon commercial?" and added humor to the bluegrass realm with "I Shoulda Wore My Bathing Suit," "Man with a Cigar," and "Eve of My Multification." "Instead of telling people that I was a bluegrass musician," said Hartford, "I told them I was a folk musician . . . the changes weren't so much in the music as in the packaging."[2]

Earthwords & Music, a few months later, included "(Good Old Electric) Washing Machine (Circa 1943)" and "Naked in Spite of Myself" and introduced "Gentle on My Mind." "John came over to my house after he recorded it," remembered Dillard, "and showed me the lick."

"People want to know what inspired 'Gentle on My Mind,'" Hartford said, "but I'm still not sure. It just came pouring out."

"He told me he wrote 'Gentle on My Mind' after he had watched *Dr. Zhivago,*" Ronnie McCoury told *Rolling Stone,* "and he said, 'I wanted to drink Julie Christie's bathwater.' He sat down at a picnic table and wrote the song in twenty minutes. He said it went against every rule that could be a rule in music. It didn't have a chorus, it had a banjo on it, and it was four minutes long."[3]

Hartford's single began getting airplay on country-music radio stations. "Douglas and I were sitting with Glen Campbell during a break from recording the *Bonnie and Clyde* soundtrack," remembered Dillard, "and he said, 'John Hartford has a song, "Gentle on My Mind." I really like it. I'm going to cut it on Monday.' John's record would have been a hit but Glen Campbell took it away."

Recorded with the Wrecking Crew, including Leon Russell, and Doug Dillard on banjo, Campbell's single became a worldwide phenomenon. He received Grammys for "Best Country & Western Solo Vocal Performance, Male," and "Best Country & Western Recording." Hartford's recording received "Best Folk Performance" and "Best Country & Western Song" awards. Campbell's top-ten hit would only be the beginning. Artists including Aretha Franklin, Dean Martin, Frank Sinatra, Elvis Presley, and Patti Page covered Hartford's tune. Alison Krauss included it on her chart-topping *Windy City* (2017). BMI placed it in the sixteenth position on its

"Top 100 Songs of the Twentieth Century." Six-digit annual royalties gave Hartford the rare freedom to write songs he wanted to write, record what he wanted to record, and play with the best musicians in the business. "All he had to do was play music," said Bob Carlin (the John Hartford Band). "He had people making his lunch, people mowing his yard."

Relocating to CA in 1968, Hartford became music director and onscreen performer on *The Glen Campbell Goodtime Hour* and *The Smothers Brothers Comedy Hour.* He narrated Ken Burns' *Civil War.* Artistically, he hit his stride with his first album for Warner Brothers (and fifth overall). *Aereo-Plain* (1971) would sell more than three million copies. Produced by David Bromberg, with accompaniment by Vassar Clements, Tut Taylor (Dobro), and Norman Blake (guitar), it planted the seeds of newgrass. "Up On the Hill Where They Do the Boogie," "Boogie," "With a Vamp in the Middle," "Holding," "Tear Down the *Grand Ole Opry,*" "Back in the Goodle Days," and "Steamboat Whistle Blues" were bookended by two versions of Albert Brumley's "Turn Your Radio On." "First off, only one guy in the band had to know a song all the way through in order for it to be allowed into the repertoire," explained Hartford to Skip Heller. "Secondly, nobody was allowed to discuss any of the arrangements except to say what key the song was in, in case you needed to move a capo or something. The arrangements were largely a matter of conscience. . . . We went in, played it, and I told David to put it together then call me when it's done."[4]

An album of outtakes, *Steam Powered Aereo-Takes,* released in 2002. *Aereo-Plain/Morning Bugle: The Complete Warner Bros. Recordings* (2012) included both albums and eight previously unreleased tracks.

The inventor of the twelve-string Dobro, Robert Arthur "Tut" Taylor, Sr. (1923-2015), played sessions with Porter Wagoner and released his solo debut in 1962. Hearing Roy Acuff on the *Grand Ole Opry* as a youngster, Taylor "couldn't figure out what he was doing, so I wrote to him about the instrument he played," he told an interviewer. "He wrote me back on a one-cent postcard, saying it was a Dobro. . . . I rushed to a bookstore . . . there weren't any music stores. . . . I looked for a catalog. I couldn't even find one. . . . I [finally] got one a few years later. . . . I had an electric steel [guitar] which had the same tuning [before that] so I was able to play Dobro immediately."[5]

A former member of Hylo Brown & the Timberliners and June Carter and Johnny Cash's band, Norman Blake (1938-) played guitar on Dylan's *Nashville Skyline* (1969) and *Will the Circle Be Unbroken* (1971). He would work with Tony Rice, contribute to *O Brother, Where Art Thou?*'s soundtrack, and record with his Independence, MO-born cellist, Nancy, whom he married in 1975. Their band (1978-86), the Rising Fawn Orchestra, included fiddler James Bryan.

Chattanooga-born, Sulphur Springs, AL-raised, and Rising Fawn, GA-based Blake started out playing "mandolin with a flat pick [and] picked the guitar a little bit that way, too," he said. "Then I heard [Doc Watson and] thought, 'Well, I can do this.' . . . When I got to Nashville, the whole thing opened up. . . . I played with a flat pick part of the time—did that with John Hartford—then I also played alternate thumb and finger style . . . single string . . . ended up finally just . . . flatpicking."[6]

"I was raised in a very rural environment," Blake told Terry Gross, "no electricity, no real modern conveniences, no telephone . . . the highest-tech thing that we had was a battery-powered radio . . . we ran that on a car battery that my father rigged up . . . we had windup phonographs and things and a few old records. The railroad train running through Sulphur Springs, AL was the biggest excitement. They ran twenty-two steam locomotives through a day, passenger and freight trains . . . it was just a real simple upbringing . . . and I've never lost the feel for that. That always appealed to me."[7]

Norman Blake, 1988

Hartford continued to roll out one great album after another. *Morning Bugle* (1972), produced by John Simon, included "Howard Hughes' Blues" and "Nobody Eats at Linebaugh's Anymore." *Nobody Knows What You Do* (1976) introduced "In Tall Buildings," "Granny Wontcha Smoke Some Marijuana," and "The Golden Globe Award." Grammy-winning *Mark Twang* (1976) included "Don't Leave Your Records in the Sun," "Trying to Do Something to Get Your Attention," and an ode to bluegrass, "Tater Tate and Allen Mundy." Songs such as "Skipping in the Mississippi Dew," "Long Hot Summer Day," and "Let Him Go On Mama" reflected Hartford's love of the river and the people who lived along its banks. Acquiring a riverboat pilot's license, he piloted the *Julia Belle Swain*. "The river was my chosen profession," said Hartford. "Music was actually a second choice. I was tickled to read that was the case with Jimmie Rodgers, too! He really wanted to be a railroad man but he wound up being a guitar picker."[8]

Produced by "Cowboy" Jack Clement, and featuring Sam Bush, Jerry Douglas, Marty Stuart, Mark O'Connor, and Roy Huskey, Jr., *Gum Tree Canoe* (1984) maintained the momentum. "Way down the River Road" and "Take Me Back to My Mississippi" extended the river theme, while bluegrass versions of the Janis Joplin-popularized "Piece of My Heart" and the Rolling Stones' "No Expectations" added to Hartford's hipness.

Hartford accompanied his banjo, fiddle, and guitar by clog dancing on an amplified four-by-eight sheet of three-quarter-inch "A"-grade plywood. "It started as a joke," he told me. "I used to sit down to play. Norman Blake used to kid me. He'd say, 'Boy, if you could learn to play like that and dance at the same time, you'd really have something.' I woodshed it for a year."

Concerts by Hartford were anything-goes experiences. Concluding his 1986 set at the Philadelphia Folk Festival, he walked through the audience as he fiddled and led the crowd singing, "Hey, babe, you wanna boogie?" When it seemed as though nothing could top his performance, he returned to the stage, accompanied by Tom Smothers of the Smothers Brothers. Doing yo-yo tricks as Hartford played, Smothers called it "folk yo." It electrified the crowd. "You didn't want to follow John," Ricky Skaggs told *Rolling Stone*. "If John was playing from nine to ten, you could forget about playing after that because the crowd was his. Moments like that showed John as the brilliant entertainer that he was."[9]

Diagnosed with non-Hodgkin lymphoma in the 1980s, Hartford refused to let it slow him down. He collaborated with his son Jamie (*Hartford & Hartford,* 1991), guitarist/mandolin player Mark Howard (*Cadillac Rag,* 1992), and fiddler Jim "Texas Shorty" Chancellor (*Old Sport,* 1995). Grammy-nominated *Retrograss* documented a live-in-the-studio session with David Grisman and Mike Seeger.

John Hartford, 1991

Working with historian Brandon King on a biography of longtime Roy Acuff fiddler James Edward "Ed" Haley (1885-1951), Hartford covered King's tunes on *Wild Hog in the Red Bush* (1996) and *The Speed of the Old Long Bow* (1998).

In *O Brother, Where Art Thou?* Hartford sang in the chorus of "Man of Constant Sorrow" and played a fiddle tune ("Indian War Whoop"). He co-headlined the *Down from the Mountain* tour, his final performances.

In his later years, Hartford played with NY-born clawhammer banjo player Robert "Bob" Carlin (1953-), Matt Combs (fiddle), Mike Compton (mandolin), Mark Schatz (bass), and Chris Sharp (guitar). *Good Ol' Boys* (1999) and Hartford's final album, *Hamilton Ironworks* (2001), were group projects. On the latter, "Hartford takes these wonderful fiddle tunes, virtually all instrumentals, and, when the feeling hits him, he chants out a story or remembrance he associates with the song," said Doug Blackburn. "Could be about Roy, who gets drunk at an all-weekend party and falls face first into the woodpile and skins up his nose or maybe about Chester

Arthur, the one-armed fiddler who played the hell out of 'Woodchopper's Breakdown.'"[10]

Hartford's fiddle and Carlin's banjo featured on the duo album, *The Fun of Open Discussion* (1995). "We put it together right after I learned to read music," Hartford said. "My son taught me. I got to where I could write out fiddle charts. I had just moved to Nashville and had learned to play country music. [Carlin and I] got together and started playing and it sounded good. We played some show dates, but hauling a band around was pretty expensive."

"I had a traditional-music show at WHYY in Philadelphia," Carlin remembered, "and did interviews for *Fresh Air* before it went national. Terry Gross didn't feel comfortable interviewing bluegrass musicians so she asked me to interview Hartford. I was used to seeing him at the Philadelphia Folk Festival, running in with his equipment, playing his set, running through the audience, and then leaving. We sat down to do the interview and the first thing out of his mouth was 'I'm a big fan of your music.' It knocked me for a loop and we became friends. I started guesting on his shows. When he put a band together, he asked me to be part of it.

"John gave me permission to develop a personal style and find a way to integrate it into his music. He'd say, 'I'm going onstage to do my solo act. I want you to fall in behind me and figure out something to do.'

"When he was healthy, we had no set routine. We knew what we might start with and what we might end with, but in between, he'd call stuff that some of the band hadn't heard before. I was conversant with his recorded repertoire but there were songs that I didn't know. He'd pull something out onstage and we'd look at each other."

Things changed in the late nineties. "Doctors had been successful in treating his cancer and getting it into remission," said Carlin, "but he had recurrences the entire time I knew him. It came back and he went downhill."

"When his illness had to be factored into every aspect of how he lived his life," recalled Jamie Hartford, "he made up his mind to deal with the things that were the most important. Certain songs he wouldn't do anymore because they referred to illegal substances and he wanted to be able to play for your whole family."[11]

"I was at the hospital with him at the end," remembered Carlin. "It might have been morphine-induced but he was in a coma. He was very agitated. He didn't want to go; he fought it. I could tell that it was getting near the end. I left so that he could be alone with family; that was the most respectful thing I could do. I drove twenty minutes to George Gruhn's Luthier Shop. I was walking into his office when the call came.

John's funeral was very sad but it was a big celebration. Chris Sharp and I put together a concert, with direction from John's widow, Marie, on the grounds of his house. Earl Scruggs played and then we backed up Marty Stuart, Connie Smith, Sam Bush, and Jerry Douglas. We shot a video but I've only watched it once. It's too hard. I couldn't watch D. A. Pennebaker's *Down from the Mountain,* the video of the concert that John hosted. It was hard for all of us. He came off the road the middle of April 2001 and died six weeks later. I was at the house three of those six weeks, doing things with him and hanging around."

Carlin organized tributes, including one in conjunction with Elderly Instruments at the IBMA Conference and another for the crew of the *Julia Belle Swain.* Jamie Hartford recorded an album (*Part of Your History*) of his father's material.

In 2012, Chris Sharp reassembled Hartford's band. "We went into the studio," said Carlin, "and recorded *Memories of John.* We toured for a year. It was important to keep John's music alive."

Bob Carlin, 2016

Carlin published his book, *Banjo: An Illustrated History,* in 2016. "I have two books about banjo players in the works," he said. "One is a biography of Bill Keith, who was the link between Scruggs and Béla. The other is a memoir, based mostly on my interviews with Eric Weissberg. It's also about growing up in NY, taking lessons from Pete Seeger while he was writing his instruction book, and hanging out in Washington Square."

Chapter 20

Fox on the Run

The Country Gentlemen had it all—superb musicianship, solid material, humor between songs, and smooth harmonies. Joinerville, TX-born guitarist Charles Otis "Charlie" Waller sang in a pure, clear baritone while mandolinist John Humbird Duffey, Jr., the Washington, DC-born son of an opera singer, ranged from high tenor to a glass-shattering falsetto. Adding the visionary banjo playing and strong, but warm, vibrato of Eddie Adcock, and the steady bass playing of Tom Gray, the Country Gentlemen became "an important bridge between hillbilly bluegrass and what could be called urban or suburban or collegiate bluegrass," said Wernick. "It wouldn't be off to refer to them as the fathers of modern bluegrass." The IBMA Hall of Fame would induct the Duffey, Waller, Adcock, and Gray configuration as the "classic" Country Gentlemen in 1996.

Bluegrass standards, traditional folksongs, and reworked Dylan, Lefty Frizzell, and Manfred Mann tunes mixed with originals, including the haunting title track of *Bringing Mary Home* (1965), co-written by Duffey. The diversity was intentional. "We never wanted to do the 'same-old, same-old' stuff," said Adcock.

Waller (1935-2004) divided his early years between Lake Charles, LA, where he moved at two, and Baltimore, where he relocated at ten. His mother ran a boardinghouse; his father worked for the Potomac Electric Power Company. Quitting school in the eighth grade, Waller worked at a gas station/body shop by day and played music at night. After a stint with Earl Taylor and the Stoney Mountain Boys, he headed to CA, in 1956, and hooked up with Buzz Busby and the Bayou Boys. "Charlie was one of the sweetest people in the whole world," recalled Jerry Douglas, who toured with the Country Gentlemen in the 1970s. "He was so nice to me, so complimentary. He was the top of the heap, and even though he's been gone since 2004, he's still highly regarded. He did everything right."

"You could understand everything Charlie sang," added Pat Enright. "He had a clear, bell-like voice and he used it really well."

Eddie Adcock, 2000

Gray's bass playing reflected the influence of Keter Betts of the Charlie Byrd Trio and George and Ron Shuffler. "I sat in with George when he played guitar with the Stanley Brothers," recalled Gray. "He was powerful as a bass player—playing walking bass lines much more aggressively than anyone before or after—but he also had a unique style on guitar. He played rolls on his guitar. They were similar to what banjo players were playing with three fingerpicks but he used a flat pick. Patterns of threes against four-four time gave it a natural syncopation."

Born in Chicago, and relocated to Washington, DC at the age of seven, Gray (1941-) played accordion, piano, and guitar as a youngster. "I wanted to play bass before I put my hands on one," he said, "and played bass runs on my guitar. One day, after a jam session, Tom Morgan left a bass in my parents' basement overnight. That was my chance. I bought one soon after that. Like any young picker, I wanted to show everybody my chops. I was playing bass runs all the time, overplaying a lot."

A member of the Rocky Ridge Ramblers in high school, Gray joined bandmate Jerry Stuart (mandolin), future *Bluegrass Unlimited* publisher Pete Kuykendall, and Smiley Hobbs to record Stuart's "Rocky Run" for

Mountain Music Bluegrass Style (1959). Gray met Waller and Buzz Busby "when I went to hear them play in barrooms in Washington, DC and the weekly lawn parties at public radio station WMRL," he recalled. "That was an important venue. Every year, during the warmer months, there were weekly lawn parties in the back of the radio station. Local bands played. That's where I met John Duffey, Bill Harrell, and the Stoneman Family. I played with Bill Monroe when he came to a lawn party. He had a bass player who wasn't doing well. It was embarrassing to watch him try. Bill's banjo player was Porter Church, who I had met in the bar scene. I went to him and said, 'I know you're playing tomorrow at New River Ranch. If you want a real bass player, I'm available.' Porter talked to the boss and got the word to hire me. I was thrilled. I was eighteen years old and just out of high school."

Returning to Washington, DC in 1957, accompanied by Busby, Waller teamed with Bill Emerson (1938-). "A neighbor who had Monroe and Flatt & Scruggs records" introduced the Buick dealership owner's son to bluegrass before his sixteenth birthday. "When he played them for me," he remembered, "I thought they were cool and wanted to do it. I had a guitar and could play simple tunes but I traded it for a banjo. It was easy to make the transition; the chords are similar. I thought that, if I could play just one song [Reno & Smiley's 'I'm Using My Bible for a Road Map'], I'd be satisfied, but it snowballed from there."

Emerson grew up about a mile from Duffey (1934-96). "There was a drive-in restaurant where teenagers gathered on the weekends," he remembered. "John would be sitting in his car playing his mandolin; that's how I first saw him. When I traded my guitar for a banjo, I put my banjo across the handlebars of my bicycle and rode to his house. I said, 'John, how do you play this thing?' He said, 'Put this pick on that finger and that pick on that finger.' He drew some patterns on a piece of paper and showed me how to play a roll.

"[Duffey] was an imposing presence. He had an air of arrogance about him but he was a brilliant musician and visionary. He saw all this unfolding before anyone else. As talented as the Country Gentlemen were, he was the driving force. He got them off the ground and took them in the right direction."

"[Duffey] wanted to convey an image of somebody who's smart-alecky and belligerent," remembered Gray, "but when he got off the stage, he was quiet and didn't want to socialize with people. It made him look unfriendly. You had to appreciate his strengths and accept his fallacies."

Emerson met Waller around the same time he met Duffey. "Charlie was just a country boy," he recalled. "He used to hang out at places where I hung out. He always had his guitar. He sang and played like Hank Snow. When the Country Gentlemen formed, he caught on with bluegrass. He could sing anything. He was one of a kind; there was nobody like him."

Busby and the Bayou Boys "had an afternoon TV show in DC," recalled Emerson. "I'd walk to a bowling alley during my lunchbreak at school. They had a snack bar with a TV. I'd cut the rest of school and watch the show."

By June 1957, Emerson was a member of the band and playing a longtime engagement (with Adcock on guitar) at the Admiral Grill in Bailey's Crossroads, VA. After their final set on July 3, Busby, Adcock, and bassist Vance Trull "wanted to go to North Beach, MD, where there was legal gambling and bars stayed open all night," said Emerson. "They got into a car with one of their friends and headed to North Beach."

They never made it. "The driver ran off the road," said Emerson, "and they all wound up in the hospital. As soon as I heard about it, I went to see Buzz. He said, 'Get some people together; keep that job for me.' I needed a mandolin player to replace Buzz so I called Duffey. We played together [with bassist John Leahy] while Buzz was in the hospital. When he got out, we decided to stay together—that was the beginning of the Country Gentlemen. Our first show was July 4, 1957. John came up with the name. People called Chet Atkins 'the Country Gentleman' and John lifted that."

Gray played for Busby from 1959 until joining the Country Gentlemen a year later. They would briefly reunite in 1967. "The accident almost killed him," he said. "The car crashed into a utility pole at seventy miles per hour. He was riding shotgun and got the worst of the accident. Duffey came along and replaced him. Buzz tried to hide his bitterness but it was hard. I don't blame him for resenting Duffey. He was never rude about it but it took the steam out of his career."

The Country Gentlemen played the Shamrock Inn, in Georgetown, for twelve years, touring widely on weekends. "We just wanted to play music and have fun," said Emerson. "We didn't worry if we became famous or made records. When we started, we played songs by the Stanley Brothers and Flatt & Scruggs. We didn't have anything our own. As time went by, we came up with more and more songs identified with us."

Winning the national banjo championship, and yearning to "do other things," Emerson left the Country Gentlemen in 1959. Banjo players including Pete Roberts (Kuykendall) and Porter Church replaced him until Adcock (1938-), who had gone to play banjo with Monroe following the auto accident, took over. "I insisted on playing [banjo] my way," Adcock said, "and I demanded we do material that wasn't identified with anyone else."

Adcock would be essential to the Country Gentlemen's sound, encouraging their use of unusual arrangements and songs from non-bluegrass sources. "We were all partners in the band," he said, "but John and I were the main song-finders. They had been doing traditional material but I knew that wouldn't get us anywhere. We had to go further; it had to be more creative."

"Emerson was a strictly bluegrass-style banjo player," explained Gray. "He had an open mind for material, but once he got it, it sounded like bluegrass. Eddie was much more radical. He did plenty of three-finger rolls but he also did Travis-style picking with single- and double-note melodies. He didn't sound like any other banjo player."

A Scottsville, VA-born ex-semi-pro boxer and racecar driver, Adcock had apprenticed with Smokey Graves & His Blue Star Boys in 1953 and gone on to play with Mac Wiseman and Bill Harrell. He was a Blue Grass Boy from April to July 1958. Leaving the Country Gentlemen after eleven-plus years, he moved to the West Coast in 1970. He grew his hair long and formed a jazz band, the Clinton Special. Returning East the following year, he formed II Generation with Bob White, A. L. Wood, Wendy Thatcher, and Jimmy Gaudreau.

Adcock met the former Martha Hearon in 1973, and they married three years later. Trained in classical technique, she played piano for more than a decade before turning to folk and string-band music. She started out by running the soundboard for II Generation, then took over guitar duties when the slot opened. "We were the first newgrassers," she said, "open to a more progressive, inclusive bluegrass."

"We were free spirited," Adcock told the *Frederick (MD) News-Post*. "You would get up onstage and play your thoughts the way they were coming out at the moment, all of us would at the same time; you would do anything you want."

"Eddie's unique musical wizardry is frequently mind-blowing . . . ," said his wife in the liner notes of *Eddie Adcock—Vintage Banjo Jam* (2017). "His ideas and methods have infiltrated, influenced and inspired the entire genre, which has quoted him endlessly, and usually unknowingly, for many years."[1]

The Adcocks formed Talk of the Town with Short Gap, WV-born bassist/vocalist Missy Raines in 1985. "I grew up playing bluegrass," said Raines, "and the real traditional stuff is at the core of my very being, but I enjoy having a way and a venue to explore different stuff."[2]

Experiencing hand tremors, Adcock underwent deep brain stimulation (DBS) surgery in 2008 and twice in 2011, playing banjo while doctors at Vanderbilt University Medical Center operated.

Adcock told *Bluegrass Today* that receiving the $50,000 Steve Martin Prize for Excellence in Banjo and Bluegrass in 2014 meant more "recognition for what I've tried to do in music all my life . . . be myself and find new paths."[3]

After leaving the Country Gentlemen, Emerson played with Del McCoury, Red Allen, and Bill Harrell before joining Jimmy Martin's Sunny Mountain Boys in 1962. Over the next four years, he appeared on twenty-nine tracks, including the million-selling "Widowmaker." "You had to play Jimmy's music his way," he recalled. "I got a good education but it wasn't easy. He was a stern master. His music needed to be good but it also needed to be different. It wasn't the same old songs about cabins on the hill."

Emerson hooked up with Cliff Waldron, the Jolo, WV-born son of a preacher, in 1967. Tom Gray joined a year later. "I took what I learned with Jimmy and applied it to what Cliff and I did," Emerson recalled. "He was a good, straight-ahead lead singer and guitar player. We played 'Proud Mary,' 'Midnight Special," and Bob Wills' 'Faded Love.' We did a James Taylor tune. We used to do 'Country Comfort,' which we got from Elton John. We weren't limited to bluegrass; everything was fair game. We were city boys. We did things no one had done before and we had our own identifying sound."

Emerson & Waldron's Shades of Grass was the first to reinterpret Manfred Mann's "Fox on the Run." "We wanted to be different," said Emerson. "I recorded it off the car radio with my tape recorder and took it to Cliff. We worked it out and recorded it. When I went back to the Country Gentlemen, they wanted to do it as well."

"The first time we played it as a bluegrass tune," Gray remembered, "was in my basement during a rehearsal with Cliff Waldron and Bill Emerson. I was resistant but I grew to like it. It was boring the way Manfred Mann did it."

An early recruit, Mike Auldridge (1939-2012) was "a local kid playing at parties [and the brother of guitarist Dave Auldridge]," remembered Emerson. "Nobody else had a Dobro player. We paid him more. We knew we had something great."

Auldridge "changed what was possible on the Dobro," said Rob Ickes. "He cleaned it up so much; he had such a good ear. He was a real trailblazer."

"Mike developed this smooth style," added Ben Eldridge, "totally different from what was being done. Listen to him and then listen to the people who influenced him—Buck Graves, Bashful Brother Oswald—it's a dramatic difference. He changed the music and made it more appealing."

"Buck Graves helped him buy his first Dobro," said Gray. "I was still in high school when we met. His voice was the kind that blended well with other people's voices. He made everyone sound better. When we were in the band that became the New Shades of Grass, he was a banjo player. He had never picked up a Dobro. He became so excited when he heard that Flatt & Scruggs hired a Dobro player [Graves]. Mike had an uncle, Ellsworth T. Cozzens [composer of "Treasures Untold"], who played slide guitar for Jimmie Rodgers. Cozzens held an acoustic guitar horizontally and played it with a bar. It didn't have the metal cone, or resonator, of the Dobro. Blues players and Hawaiian musicians played like that."

Gray was still in high school when he began frequenting the Country Gentlemen's shows at Bailey's Crossroads. "Charlie recognized me," he remembered, "as the kid who used to stand down in the front to watch the bands up close at outdoor shows he had played with Buzz Busby. . . . I was now a bass player and he invited me to get up and play with the band. In a few years, when bassist Jim Cox became ill, I was asked to join. . . . I was 19 years old."[4]

The classic lineup of the Country Gentlemen—Waller, Duffey, Adcock, and Gray—would be together for less than a half-decade. Gray resigned in 1964, replaced by Ed Ferris. "We got into an argument about politics," Gray recalled. "I objected to a protest song they were recording that talked about racial hatred ['Cold Wind a Blowin']. I didn't think we should be singing it. It cast a bad image of our country. Duffey said, 'Look, this is the most commercially successful thing we could be doing. You're either going to play this song or leave.' I'd been thinking of leaving anyway. My first child had just been born and we weren't making much money. I needed to go back to my day job [as a cartographer for *National Geographic*] and earn a decent living with benefits."

Citing a fear of flying, Duffey left the Country Gentlemen in 1969. RI-born Jimmy Gaudreau (1946-) took his place. Adcock left a year later, suggesting Emerson as his replacement. "We played Oberlin College," Emerson recalled, "and we got a big hand. They said, 'If you come back, we'll form a partnership.' I thought that was a good deal. Cliff and I were struggling, trying to make a name for ourselves. They already had a name."

Gaudreau relinquished the mandolin slot to Doyle Lawson in 1972. "Doyle was a Jimmy Martin alumni," said Emerson, "and we thought alike musically. He moved here from Lexington, KY with his wife and son, Robby."

Ricky Skaggs and Jerry Douglas joined a year later. "Mike Auldridge played a little with the Country Gentlemen," said Emerson, "until I ran into Jerry playing in his dad, John Douglas's band. I saw that he really had something and convinced Doyle, Charlie, and [bassist] Bill Yates to hire him. He's absolutely the greatest Dobro player who ever lived. I met Ricky when he was with Ralph Stanley. He was working at a power plant and living in Manassas, VA. I figured we ought to hire him so we did. I brought Jerry Douglas, Ricky Skaggs, and Doyle Lawson into the band—not bad."

Scoring a second consecutive "Banjo Player of the Year" award in 1973, Emerson resigned from the Country Gentlemen for a second time (with James Bailey replacing him). "We were playing the same old festivals year after year," he said, "and living on a bus that was hot, cold, and dusty. Looking at audiences with the same faces, doing the same songs, I got tired of it. There was also the security issue. There was no retirement. When I got the offer to join the US Navy Band, with all the benefits, I accepted."

Remaining in the navy until retiring as a master chief musician in 1993, Emerson helped introduce bluegrass to the military. "They wanted country music," he recalled, "so we had Country Current. As time went by, and we got new people, we got more into bluegrass. Wayne Taylor [not the Blue Highway bassist] came in the band, a versatile singer who could sing bluegrass. We started playing festivals and became much in demand."

Reuniting on several occasions, Duffey, Waller, Adcock, and Gray recorded a live album, *Classic Country Gents Reunion* (1989), and filmed a video at the Woodstock '92 festival in Woodstock, VA. "We always had fun," remembered Gray. "We enjoyed playing together. Charlie loved singing with Duffey and vice versa. Eddie was a powerful baritone singer; he broke the rules. He was so good—nobody could fault him."

Randy Waller assumed leadership of the Country Gentlemen after his father's August 2004 passing. The group has since veered towards a more commercial country sound.

Besides playing with his wife, Adcock continues to work with North Kansas City, MO-born and Belt Buckle, KY-based Valerie Smith & Liberty Pike. "For years, Valerie hired the hottest pickers in Nashville," he said, "but she had a hard time keeping the band together. In 2014, she was booked to play at the Wind Gap Bluegrass Festival in PA. A Baltimore band I had been playing with [Appalachian Flyer] backed her. She liked playing with us and suggested we make it permanent. Our album, *Small Town Heroes,* came out in 2016."

Duffey hated traveling as much as he despised practicing, but after leaving the Country Gentlemen, he didn't give up playing music. A jam at banjo player Ben Eldridge's Bethesda, MD home with Auldridge, Gray, and guitarist/vocalist John Starling evolved into the Seldom Scene. "We didn't start with the idea that we were going to make money," recalled Eldridge. "Mike said that it was our Monday-night card game. Instead of playing cards, we'd go out and pick."

The Seldom Scene planned to play local places such as the Red Fox Inn and the Cellar Door, and later hosted weekly Thursday-night shows at the

John Duffey, 1986

Birchmere, but the high caliber of their music, and the richness of their harmonies, couldn't stay hidden. Once word got out, promoters started calling to book them for prestigious clubs, theaters, and major festivals. "The Seldom Scene was one of the first bands to bring pop influences to bluegrass," said Rob Ickes. "They did James Taylor songs, Merle Haggard songs, Dylan songs, Eric Clapton songs. They were definitely an urban bluegrass band. Traditionalists didn't like them but everyone else went nuts over them."

"For years, I pinched myself," said Gray. "I was the luckiest person in the world. I was playing with the best bluegrass band. We played only eighty shows a year but they paid well. Duffey had a good instinct for demanding top dollar and getting it. He was negotiating on my behalf. All I had to do was work my day job and play music on the weekends. We were lucky to come along when we did. Bluegrass was in a doldrums. The first generation was still playing but without the excitement of their younger years. We were more creative about it and programmed our music to urban audiences. We weren't alone in making bluegrass contemporary."

Duffey's stage patter surprised even his bandmates. "There were times when he'd say something," remembered Eldridge, "and we'd wish we could sneak off the stage. He scared me before I knew him. I used to see the Country Gentlemen in the early sixties. I wasn't worthy to go up to him and start talking. I started to know him when I taught banjo at the music store where he had his instrument repair shop. Between lessons, I'd chat with him. It turned out that, once you got through that veneer, he was a pussycat, a very smart person. He was nothing like his stage persona but he'd get onstage and the Duffey that most of us think of would show up—wisecracking and cocky."

"He could be extremely funny at times," added Phil Rosenthal, "but extremely caustic at others. In San Francisco, it was suggested that, maybe, he shouldn't use his exaggerated gay persona. Of course, that was the first thing he did in the show. John didn't treat Monroe like a god. At one festival, he had us come onstage, with our instruments, push the Blue Grass Boys from the mics, and take over the song. He tilted Monroe's cowboy hat forward so it covered his eyes. Monroe loved it."

"Duffey intimidated the hell out of me," remembered Dudley Connell, "but he was a shy person and the bravado was a cover for his insecurities. He had a voice that projected like a trumpet. His father taught him to sing from the diaphragm and not from the chest or throat."

Duffey "didn't want to sing about cabins and mountains," added Eldridge. "Before I knew him, he spent a lot of time at the Library of Congress looking for material. We played what we liked. We'd hear a good song and say, 'We can do that.' Duffey wasn't much of a radio listener but the rest of us listened to pop music and rock and roll. Some of that leaked into our repertoire. My son Chris's band, Punch Brothers, with Chris Thile, Gabe Witcher, Noam Pikelny, and Paul Kowert, is the same way. They can sound like a bluegrass band but they don't do it very often."

The Seldom Scene's last founding member, Eldridge retired in July 2015 after forty-four years in music. "I talked my dad into buying me a banjo [a Gibson RB-100] for my sixteenth birthday," he remembered in January 2014. "I had been playing guitar since I was ten but I didn't even know what bluegrass was until hearing 'Foggy Mountain Breakdown' on a local radio station. I thought, 'This is so cool; I've got to learn how to do it.'"

Eldridge's father "hated the way a banjo sounded," Eldridge recalled. "I had a room off my bedroom where I shut myself in and practiced. I learned by taking 45s and slowing them down to thirty-three. I had to tune the banjo down; it was a whole process. My dad came back there one night, while I was practicing, stood in the doorway, and gave me the most disgusted look. He said, 'Son, buying you that banjo is the biggest mistake I've made in my life.'"

A year after graduating from college, Eldridge met Auldridge in 1961. "Tom Morgan was fixing and selling banjos in Severna Park, MD," he remembered. "I started going over and doing menial labor, learning how to repair banjos. Tom had taken a flattop Gibson guitar and put a resonator cone in it. That's what Mike was playing. It was amazing how good he was; he had all of Buck Graves' licks down."

Eldridge hosted regular Monday-night jam sessions. "John Starling lived across the street," he said. "We'd pick for two or three hours and Mike would come over. At first, he wasn't comfortable in anything other than the key of G. I liked to play 'Farewell Blues,' which is in C. He could play it but he'd complain every time we played it. Once he got better, it didn't matter what key you threw at him."

Everyone in the Seldom Scene had a full-time job. Starling was interning at Walter Reed Hospital. Auldridge was doing graphic design for the *Washington Star.* Eldridge was a Johns Hopkins Applied Physics Laboratory mathematician and Duffey repaired instruments. "It wasn't easy," remembered Eldridge, "but we did it. We practiced several nights a week. We didn't get Duffey out much; he didn't like to practice. Starling was married to Fayssoux ("fay-*sue*"), who sang on a couple of Emmylou Harris's albums. She'd sing tenor, when we worked up harmonies, and show her part to Duffey. He'd pick it up in no time."

Starling's schedule as a new doctor became so erratic that he reluctantly left the Seldom Scene in 1977. Replacing him, Guilford, CT-born Phil Rosenthal sang lead and played guitar until 1986, adding folk-music influences and encouraging bluegrass-ized covers of Eric Clapton's "Lay Down Sally" and J. J. Cale's "After Midnight." "The Seldom Scene was recording a gospel album [*Baptizing*]," Rosenthal remembered, "and they saved half of the songs for me. I was inspired and wrote some gospel tunes. 'Brother John,' 'Take Him In,' and 'Walk with Him Again' ended up on the album. I sang 'Were You There?' with Starling. I sang low bass and he sang high harmony. The next album was *Act 4.* I wasn't just taking someone's place but carving my own niche, introducing my own material. I felt more legitimate."

At the Scene (1983) was the last album with Rosenthal singing lead. The Seldom Scene's next album, *Blue Ridge,* featured folk-pop singer-songwriter Jonathan Edwards. "He showed up at the Birchmere one Thursday night," recalled Rosenthal, "introduced himself, and said, 'Any chance I can get up and do a song or two with you?' We found a song that we could do together and it sounded good. He came back a couple of weeks later and we did it again. Then, we thought, 'We should work up some actual material.' We got together and practiced some songs. I have cassette recordings of those rehearsals. I've been listening to them; they're very cool. We started sounding good. Then, we said, 'Let's do a record together.'"

Rosenthal's status became tenuous. The Seldom Scene "wanted someone with a more traditional, hard-edged bluegrass sound," he explained. "When they hired me, they told me I wasn't 'the guitar player' but a full-fledged member. As it turned out, that wasn't the case. They were auditioning people without me knowing. One night, at the Birchmere, they said, 'Phil, we need to get together after the show.' Later, they told me, 'Lou Reid is going to take your place in two weeks.'"

"I saw Lou's band, Southbend, open for Dolly Parton," Auldridge told me, "and they completely knocked me out."

"This was just as the festival season was about to begin," added Rosenthal. "It wasn't a happy parting."

Rosenthal's roots transcended bluegrass. "I grew up listening to my parents' Weavers records," he recalled, "and I liked the sound of Pete Seeger's banjo and voice. I remember going to a record store when I was twelve and getting his latest album. I became curious about other kinds of music that used the banjo and bought an album with two people in suits on the cover. One had a guitar and the other a banjo. It turned out to be Flatt & Scruggs' classic first album, *Foggy Mountain Jamboree*. I loved the sound of Earl's playing. The singing didn't draw me in as much. Someone in the next town was offering banjo lessons. For the first time in fifty years or more, an ad ran in the local paper for banjo lessons. He showed me the three-finger roll."

Rosenthal taught himself guitar and mandolin, and his "goal was to write a song someone recorded," he said. "I used to pretend that I was running my own record label when I was fourteen. I recorded hours and hours of traditional songs using sound-on-sound recording."

In high school, Rosenthal started a band with Dave Kiphuth, a banjo player he met at a hootenanny in a local church. Kiphuth knew mandolinist Nick Barr. "It was the first time any of us played bluegrass in a group," said Rosenthal.

Rosenthal frequented weekly shows, in Yale University's Enormous Room, by Billy Hamilton and the Ohio River Boys. "Billy was a great mandolin player in the style of Bill Monroe," he remembered. "When he got out of college, he got a job teaching and left the area. The rest of his band [Apple Country] wanted to stay together but they didn't have a mandolin player.

Banjo had been my first love but I was good on mandolin. I thought, 'Here's my opportunity.' I stayed with them from 1970 until 1975. They were a very traditional group. Kiphuth was the banjo player. Mark Rikart played guitar. We had a great fiddler, Bud Mornsroe. Gene LaBrie played bass and I played mandolin and wrote songs. I'd been writing since I was fourteen. After a few years, we went into a local studio and recorded *Apple Country Bluegrass*. It had three of my tunes—'Because of Love,' 'Apple Country Breakdown,' and 'When a Girl I Know Gets Back to Town.'"

A half-hour of Apple Country's weekly Thursday-night show at the Enormous Room broadcast live on a country-music radio station. "It was a break for us," said Rosenthal. "It brought in additional people and the place would fill up."

Continuing to play with other groups, Rosenthal "had a quartet that was a little more country," he said. "It was acoustic but there was no banjo. One of the members, photographer/record producer Jim McGuire, moved to Nashville and said, 'If you want to pursue songwriting, this is the place to do it.' By that point, I had had a couple of songs recorded by the Seldom Scene. Jim and I had gone to see them at a festival, in Gettysburg, in 1972. He had just produced Mike's first solo album [*Dobro*] and hooked me up with Mike. Ben Eldridge came over. I played songs for them. They said, 'Those are pretty good. Why don't you put them on a cassette and mail them to us? We're looking for material.' 'Muddy Water' became one of their most requested tunes [they also did 'Willie Boy']."

Rosenthal met his future wife, Beth Sommers, in 1973. "She came up to me after a show looking for a mandolin teacher," he remembered. "Her father played mandolin and banjo—1930s-style music—with the Eastern Banjo Society. When we got married, we had two mandolins on the cake."

Yearning to play more of his own material, Rosenthal resigned from Apple Country and formed Old Dog with Sommers and the Stockwell brothers, Bruce and Barry. "I played mandolin and some lead guitar," said Rosenthal. "Bruce, to this day, is my favorite banjo player. He and Barry were from VT but they were going to Yale. Beth played bass. I was very excited."

When Old Dog played at the Birchmere, "Mike came backstage after the show and he said, 'This is the best band I've ever heard,'" Rosenthal recalled, "He was getting ready to do another solo album and suggested we do it together. It could be half instrumental and half vocal."

Work began in early 1977. "We were in the studio," recalled Rosenthal, "when I noticed, through the glass of the control room, the rest of the Seldom Scene checking us out. I thought, 'That's very nice; they want to see what Mike is up to.' When we took a break, Duffey said, 'Phil, can we talk to you?' We went into another room—the Seldom Scene and me.

John Starling was about to leave and they asked if I wanted to audition for the spot. I was flabbergasted but I had major reservations. I didn't want to move to Washington, DC. I'm from a small town in CT—Guilford. My parents had a chicken farm and I don't like living in the city. I was very excited about Old Dog. We were doing my material and I had my musical stamp on the group. We were finally going to do a record. I said, 'I'm flattered but I'll pass.' They looked at me as if I was nuts. Duffey said, 'Think about it, Phil.'"

After the session, Rosenthal drove to where he and Sommers were staying. "I was going through the pros and cons," he recalled, "and I realized that, rather than being in a group that might get some success, I'd be the lead singer and chief songwriter for a band already at the top of the heap. As soon as we got to our friends' apartment, I called Mike and said, 'I'll try out for that spot.' He said, 'I was hoping you'd say that.'"

The job wasn't Rosenthal's yet. The Seldom Scene "wanted to see if my voice blended with theirs," he said, "so I picked out ten songs and learned their arrangements. Three weeks later, they were playing in New England. We got together in a motel room and sang. Three or four nights later, I got a phone call. They were all on the line, on different extensions, to let me know I was the one they had chosen. I moved to Washington, DC and, a month later, I was with them at the Birchmere. When we got onstage, there was silence. The third song we did was 'Muddy Water.' I got rousing applause. For the first six months, I was scared. Audiences were checking this new person out. It took a year before I felt accepted."

Leaving the Seldom Scene in 1986, Rosenthal was a featured guest on *Scene 20* (1991), recorded during their twentieth-anniversary concert at the Birchmere. "I'd been out of the group for five years," he said. "It was fun being in the band but I never cared for the traveling. When you're in a popular band, every time you do a show, you do the songs everybody wants to hear. They're great songs but, after a while, you can't be creative."

The idea of a bluegrass album for kids sparked while Rosenthal was still in the Seldom Scene. "I didn't want to release it on a bluegrass label," he said, "but on a bigger label like Disney Records or Sesame Street Records. If they wouldn't do it, I was going to start my own label, which is what happened. I started American Melody and put out *Turkey in the Straw: Bluegrass Songs for Children* [1985]. It did really well. It won a Parents' Choice Award and got great reviews in the national media."

Rosenthal discussed his new label with Jonathan Edwards. "One of the songs on *Blue Ridge* was 'Little Hands,'" he said, "a beautiful song about Jonathan's daughter. I asked if he'd do a record with 'Little Hands' as the title track. We started it before I left Washington.

"For the next few years, I focused on getting records done and putting them out. I did well. I produced albums by storytellers but it was mostly folk music and bluegrass for kids."

Finding more of a bluegrass scene in his hometown than before he left, Rosenthal started a band with Stacy Phillips, Phil Zimmerman, and his old friend Dave Kiphuth. He also began performing with his family. "Naomi was twelve years old," he said. "Daniel was ten. My wife played bass; we performed as a duo too. Naomi started playing guitar and writing songs in high school. Daniel came home one day when he was in the fifth grade. His teacher had demonstrated different instruments and he had decided to play the trumpet. I had to hide my disappointment. I had envisioned my son and daughter playing bluegrass guitars, banjos, fiddles, or Dobros, but Naomi has recorded wonderful singer-songwriter albums and Daniel has taken his music to a level I never could. When he started playing, we did some shows together. He'd play solos with a jazzy feel and I'd say, 'See if you could put a little more melody in there.' Over time, he adapted his trumpet to what I was doing."

Father and son toured Great Britain in 2011. "I was going to do it myself," said Rosenthal, "but I had horrible back pain. I thought of canceling—going over in the airplane was torture—but I convinced Daniel to come along and do the driving. When we got back, he had the idea of doing an album [*Fly Away* released in 2013]."

Rosenthal taught privately for decades, and his "latest idea was folk and bluegrass ensembles for musicians who hadn't had the opportunity to play with other people," he said. "I have three groups, two that meet at my home and one that we do at a music school in New Haven."

The Sommers-Rosenthal Family Band's *Down the Road* (2016) "is the best thing I've ever done," Rosenthal claimed. "Of course, I've said that before, but this is a great album. It's a blend of the acoustic roots of the music and originals—folk, bluegrass, and more progressive influences. We did songs from my past, such as 'Muddy Water,' and Daniel added a jazz element on trumpet. We're mining traditional sources but we're also adding something new to the music."

Doc Watson's longtime electric bassist T. Michael Coleman replaced Gray in October 1987. "Mike pushed for that," recalled Eldridge. "He was getting into playing pedal steel and doing country music. Tom wasn't happy playing electric bass so he bailed out."

"There were suggestions that I switch to electric bass as early as 1977," said Gray. "I tried to ignore it for years, but after Lou Reid joined, he and Mike kept getting on my case that we needed to update our sound and our image, looking straight at me. The message was very clear but I'd been playing standup acoustic bass all my life. There were listeners who believed in what I was doing. If I changed what I was doing, it would be a disappointment to them. I kept mulling it over. I had three choices. I could have switched to electric and probably hated myself. I could have demanded that things remain the same. I think Duffey would have backed me up. The third option was to quit the band and have them hire someone who wants to play electric bass. That's what I did. It broke my heart to leave the best job in the world."

"It was awkward at first," remembered Auldridge. "Fans came to shows and didn't like it. Fortunately, we didn't have to go in the studio right away and could take time to get it to gel."

"There were grumblings," added Coleman, "but they eased because of where I came from. They were accepting of me because I had played with Doc and they saw the relationship I had onstage with Duffey. We were a comedy team. I was his jester. I would make him laugh until he couldn't breathe.

"You would think there would be a lot of drive behind a bluegrass band but I almost fell off the stage the first time I played with them. The drive I experienced with Doc and Merle was not there. I had to cover a lot more ground. What made the Seldom Scene so good was they were different and had a very loose rhythmic flow. They were more a folk band than an in-your-face, driving bluegrass band, which made them more appealing. There was a finesse."

Auldridge, Reid, and Coleman released an offshoot-trio album in 1989. Adding Gaudreau and replacing Reid with classically trained singer/ guitarist Moondi Klein, they evolved into Chesapeake. "It snowballed into something very exciting," said Auldridge, "two or three steps ahead of the Scene. The drums are out front. The material is very contemporary sounding."

"Chesapeake was a very creative environment," recalled Coleman. "It cut Mike loose to do things he had always wanted to do, like playing pedal steel. I love traditional bluegrass and I love pushing the envelope using traditional instruments. It all comes from the same pond."

"They weren't happy that the Scene wasn't working enough," said Eldridge, "but Duffey didn't like breaking his neck playing music and I couldn't get busier."

The Seldom Scene continued to go through changes. "Lou Reid left to play with Vince Gill and Vern Gosdin," said Coleman, "and then he formed Carolina with Terry Baucom. Starling came back for a while. Moondi was in Chesapeake so it made sense for him to do double duty when he left."

Auldridge, Coleman, and Klein planned to play in both Chesapeake

Mike Auldridge, 1989

and the Seldom Scene but a scheduling conflict arose in mid-1995. "It was the straw that broke the camel's back," remembered Eldridge. "We agreed to disagree and go our own ways. The last time I heard Chesapeake, at MerleFest, they had a drummer and they sounded great. They broke up after that."

"We couldn't find an audience," explained Coleman. "We were ahead of our time. Our ages had something to do with it. We were playing young music but three of us were in our fifties. Mike was pushing sixty."

Auldridge surrendered after a lengthy bout of prostate cancer on December 29, 2012, a day before his seventy-fourth birthday. Released two years later, Chesapeake's *Hook, Live & Sinker* included tracks with Tony Rice, Sam Bush, John Cowan, Larry Atamanuik, Sammy Shelor, Rickie Simpkins, and Doc Watson.

Auldridge, Coleman, and Klein passed the Seldom Scene torch to Fred Travers, Ronnie Simpkins, and Dudley Connell on New Year's Eve 1995. "Tom Gray recommended Fred and me," said Connell. "I recommended Ronnie; they were familiar with him from the Tony Rice Unit.

"Duffey intimidated all of us. Ronnie and I didn't want to be late but we didn't want to be early. I got to a rehearsal a half-hour early and parked in a church parking lot. I snuck my car a little closer every five minutes. I looked up and noticed another car doing the same thing. It turned out to be Ronnie. He brought his electric bass, thinking that was what John wanted."

Simpkins and his brother Rickie grew up playing in a family band. Recording as Upland Express in the seventies, they separated in the early eighties. Rickie joined the McPeak Brothers while Ronnie worked with the Bluegrass Cardinals. Reuniting as Heights of Grass in 1982, they joined Mark Newton (ex-Knoxville Grass) and Sammy Shelor as the Virginia Squires the following year. They would go on to play with the Tony Rice Unit and Claire Lynch. "Rickie came in with a great knowledge of music," said Connell, "and a desire to make it work. Not only is he a great banjo player but we do a lot of slow ballads and he plays fiddle. The Seldom Scene recorded with Ricky Skaggs on *Old Train* but we've never had a touring fiddler. We've got a darn good one now."

Travers played with the Fred Atkins Band and, with Gray, in the Larry Ferguson Band. "He knew Mike's Dobro breaks," said Connell, "but he did his own thing. Fred first heard the Seldom Scene at a concert they did with Doc Watson. He loved slide guitar players—Duane Allman and Merle Watson. The moment he heard Mike play, he said, 'That's what I want to do.' One Christmas, his wife gave him a couple of lessons from Mike. That was the kickoff point for his Dobro playing."

The reorganized Seldom Scene continued to draw songs from a variety of places. "I introduced Muddy Waters' 'Rollin' and Tumblin' to Duffey," said Connell. "John Starling showed up with James Taylor's 'Sweet Baby James' and we tried to make it our own. We did Dylan songs."

Sandy Springs, MD-born Connell (1956-) "became aware that music was a powerful medium when the Beatles came in 1964," he said. "I really liked the rock music of the sixties, but when the seventies came along, music drifted into disco and heavily produced synthesizers. I found myself getting into Dylan, John Prine, and Neil Young. It wasn't much of a leap to the Stanley Brothers. I found comfort in that lonesome, mountain sound."

Connell's father, George, played tenor banjo but "didn't play jazz or ragtime style," Connell said. "He did some crosspicking to make it sound like a roll, but he never mastered the three-finger roll. He loved that sound. I grew up with Reno & Smiley records. They were my dad's favorite. He was into Reno's single-note picking. We also had Monroe and Stanley Brothers records. Mom and Dad listened to a radio station from GA that played country music—Buck Owens, Ray Price, and Hank Williams. It was my parents' music but it was in my head."

Connell spent his childhood in a subsidized housing complex. "My folks were never poor," he said, "but they didn't have a lot of money. There was no air conditioning in the summer. People listened to music with their windows open and you could hear what everybody was playing.

"It changed from a lily-white neighborhood to almost all black but that only added to my musical growth. It went from Buck Owens and Ray Price to James Brown and Otis Redding. There was a black family living caddy-corner to our apartment. They took me under their wing and introduced me to soul music and R&B."

Attending his first bluegrass festival, Connell was "waiting on line to get a hot dog" when he looked in front of him "and there was Bill Monroe in a cowboy hat," he remembered. "He had his mandolin tucked under his arm. I thought it was cool. I was used to seeing rock stars in limousines and buses; something about the accessibility was refreshing. Bluegrass musicians were regular people like me."

Gathering his rock and roll records, Connell "sold them to finance my bluegrass habit," he said. "I was driving a truck for Montgomery County Schools, and my income was limited, but there was a record store in Langley Park [the Music Box] that had plenty of bluegrass records. Its owner bought surplus stock from King/Starday; there were Stanley Brothers and Reno & Smiley albums. I'd go on Friday and buy everything I could find. I started seeing Gary Reid, who had written a wonderful discography of the Stanley Brothers, there. He approached me. 'I see you like the Stanley Brothers.' 'It's my new favorite music.' He told me he had 78s and 45s. This was before reissues of the Stanley Brothers recordings. I made a date to go to his house with my Akai reel-to-reel. I spent hours recording things I couldn't find at the Music Box. I remember going home, putting on my headphones, and listening until the sun came up."

Accompanied by guitarist Ron Welch, Connell attended Ralph Stanley's memorial festival for Carter. "I could hear this unearthly voice coming from out of the hollows," he recalled. "It was Ralph singing 'Man of Constant Sorrow.' I've pursued the emotional feeling I got ever since."

Connell played banjo and sang tenor. "Ron and I played a handful of paying dates," he said, "but mainly we played open mics. From the late forties to the early fifties, people from Appalachia transplanted to the DC/Baltimore area looking for work—factory jobs, government work—and there were places to play bluegrass. You could hear it in bars seven nights a week. Music was my total passion. Ron loved it but it wasn't all he did; he worked for Sears. We were moving too fast so he quit."

Shakey's Pizza Parlor presented bluegrass every Wednesday. The host band, the Country Clan, led by Benny and Vallie Cain, had a long history in the area. "The day Ron quit, I went to their show," recalled Connell. "Vallie put her arm around me and said, 'You're not much of a banjo player but you have a pretty good voice. If I were you, I'd play guitar and concentrate on singing. Let the banjo go.' She was totally right. I found a banjo player [Frannie Davidson] and a mandolin player [Eddie D'Zmura] that I knew since high school. I pulled in Gary Reid to play bass. He had never played any instrument. That was the early Johnson Mountain Boys. We recorded the first record in somebody's kitchen for Gary's Cooper Creek label."

Gaithersburg-born Eddie Stubbs (1961-) brought solid grounding as a country fiddler. "When music gets inside of you," the future WSM announcer and voice of the *Grand Ole Opry* told the *Washington Post*, "and gets a part of your heart, and a part of your being, and a part of your soul, for those who experience it at that depth, there's nothing quite like it."[5]

"We started covering people like Webb Pierce, Hank Snow, and Johnny & Jack," recalled Connell, "and I was writing songs in the Stanley Brothers tradition. I was trying to write story songs. I wrote 'Now Just Suppose' off Dylan's 'Positively 4th Street,' 'Weather Greystone' off the Blue Sky Boys' 'The House Where We Were Wed.'"

The Johnson Mountain Boys' timing was perfect. "People were listening to bluegrass with a more urban sensibility," said Connell, "and we were the antithesis of that. We played at places like Pip's Country Palace. It wasn't a palace but a dive bar. We played from nine to two in the morning—five sets a night. We'd get $150 to split five ways but it was a great proving ground. When we first came there, people would ask for 'Rocky Top,' 'Fox on the Run,' and songs that were popular at parking-lot jam sessions. When they found out we didn't play any of them, and were adamant about it, they left. Crowds coming to see a bluegrass band dwindled but we started drawing people who came because we didn't play those songs. We were different."

The Johnson Mountain Boys worked over two hundred dates annually but Connell "can't remember a year we made more than twenty-two thousand dollars," he said. "We lived in one of the most expensive counties in the country. I had a wife and a kid, a mortgage, and a car payment. I started thinking that I should go back to school and do something else, play music on the side. Eddie tried to hold us together but he went to work with Kitty Wells and moved to Nashville. We did some shows in the early nineties but it was different. There was never a blowup; it just dwindled away."

Connell heard WV-born Hazel Jane Dickens (1935-2011) on the radio and "loved her roughhewn voice and the level of her writing." The eighth of eleven children raised in an impoverished mining town, the Baptist preacher's daughter left home at sixteen and settled in Baltimore, where she worked in factories and shops, getting by "from pay to pay." She turned to traditional Appalachian music and began performing with her brother in clubs and bars. Briefly playing with a pop band, she "didn't find a home there anymore than they found a home trying to do my kind of music."[6]

Dickens met Mike Seeger through her brother, a patient at the Mt. Wilson Sanitarium where Seeger worked. Through Seeger, she met other musicians including Alice Gerrard, with whom she recorded four bluegrass albums: *Who's That Knocking?* (1965), *Won't You Come and Sing for Me* (1973), *Hazel and Alice* (1973), and *Hazel Dickens and Alice Gerrard* (1975). She recorded *Hard Hitting Songs for Hard Hit People* (1980), *By the Sweat of My Brow* (1983), and *It's Hard to Tell the Singer from the Song* (1987) on her own. Collaborating with Seeger on *Strange Creek Singers* (1970), she joined Carol Elizabeth Jones and Ginny Hawker on *Heart of a Singer* (1998).

The Johnson Mountain Boys "were playing in a bar on Sunday afternoons" when they met Dickens. "[*Bluegrass Unlimited* scribe] Walt Saunders talked Ken Irwin into coming to see us," recalled Connell, "and Ken brought Hazel. Not only did we have the pressure of hoping to impress one of the Rounder Records owners, Hazel was with him. We passed the audition and ended up recording for Rounder. Promoters booked Hazel and us on the same shows. We'd play our set and then back her."

Alison Krauss and Hazel Dickens, 1987

Gray played bass for the Hazel Dickens Band from 1998 to 2003. "I met her when I was in high school," he said. "I was invited to a picking party at her home in Baltimore. She teased me for years because I had to call home and ask permission to stay out late. Hazel and Alice Gerrard were always singing together, which was radical because there were few other women in bluegrass. Mike Seeger was at those picking parties, playing all kinds of traditional instruments. Lamar Grier was always there. He still comes to picking parties but no longer plays banjo."

The Johnson Mountain Boys stopped touring in February 1988. Soon afterwards, "Hazel called me about a benefit for Lee Michael Dempsey," Connell recalled. "WAMU had canceled his bluegrass show. I told her that I wasn't playing anymore but she convinced me. I've been playing since. I played every time she asked and she took me to some interesting places—women's groups, protest marches. She was a deep thinker. She'd call about a date and we'd talk for an hour and a half."

Returning to college, Connell took a class in career development. One of his assignments was to "interview someone with an interesting

The Johnson Mountain Boys (Tom Adams, Larry Robbins, Dudley Connell), 1985

job." Choosing Tony Seeger, director of Smithsonian Folkways, Connell "interviewed him for half an hour, and then he started interviewing me," he said. "I ended up walking out with a job."

Having acquired Folkways in 1987, the Smithsonian was contractually bound to keep the entire catalog in print, regardless of whether it sold or not. "They hired me to figure out how," remembered Connell. "I bought racks of cassette decks, daisy-chained them together, and made cassettes. You could make a single cassette if you had to. The work I do now, archiving live recordings for the National Council for Traditional Arts, is an outgrowth of that job."

During the summer of 1995, Connell received a card in the mail announcing that the Seldom Scene was dissolving. "I called Duffey," he remembered, "and said, 'I'm so sorry.' It was like a condolence call, as though there had been a death in the family. John, in his funny way, said, 'We're not breaking up the band. We're just looking for a guitar player, bass player, Dobro player, and a baritone singer.' I don't know what made me say it—I wasn't looking for a job—but I said, 'Maybe you and I should get together.' There was total silence on the other end of the phone. I thought I had crossed some line inadvertently. Then he said, 'Do you know our songs?' I said, 'No, but I like your music.' He gave me half a dozen songs to learn. I was still playing with the Johnson Mountain Boys so we couldn't get together until September. I wasn't looking at it as an audition but I was interested in the job. It wasn't just because of the music; I had a job and couldn't tour much. The Seldom Scene played on the weekends and spent the week with their families. It was perfect.

"Duffey loved traditional bluegrass. When we got together to rehearse, he was more interested in singing Stanley Brothers songs than Seldom Scene tunes, which frightened me. I had put in a lot of time, not trying to sound like John Starling—no one could do that—but in trying to capture the essence of that sound."

Three weeks shy of the reorganized Seldom Scene's first anniversary, Duffey suffered a fatal heart attack. "He was having a blast," said Eldridge, "loving life. He was notorious for hating to practice. He used to get grouchy about it. After Dudley, Ronnie, and Fred joined, I'd get a call at work every Monday morning: 'Hi, Ben. It's John. Come over Wednesday and rehearse.'"

"I was so sad when he passed away," recalled Connell. "It didn't seem his time. We had played in Inglewood, NJ. On the way back, we sang quartets in the car. He was laughing, cracking jokes, and singing great. We were going to be home on Sunday, but on Monday morning, we were flying to GA to play a private event. We rarely did that. John had his mandolin case, suitcase, and airline ticket waiting by the door so he wouldn't forget anything. We had to make an early flight to get to the afternoon gig. I don't think he had a clue that he was so sick. He had told us, backstage at the Birchmere, that he had gone to the doctor because his energy level was down. The doctor diagnosed him as having congestive heart failure but he didn't seem seriously ill. It was heartbreaking to lose him after only a year. I can't imagine what the band would have sounded like had we had experience under our belt.

"Ben called me—it must have been five in the morning—and said, 'Our boy is pretty sick.' I met Fred, Ronnie, Ben, Ben's girlfriend Barbara, and John's wife Nancy at the hospital but John was gone. He had gotten out of bed, gone to the bathroom, and collapsed from a massive heart attack. He never regained consciousness."

Duffey's funeral was a "bizarre affair," remembered Connell. "His wife couldn't do anything. We ended up the greeters, the current band. The next day, we buried him. A friend of John's from way back said a few words. We sang 'Amazing Grace' and that was it. Nancy's gone too. That whole era's gone."

Dan Tyminski and Mark Newton filled in. Don Rigsby played with the Seldom Scene for almost six months. "I sang with Dudley in Longview," he said, "and he liked what I did."

Lou Reid returned in June 1996. "It fit," recalled Connell. "He knew the style and feel because he played with the band in the eighties."

Eldridge left a decade later. "He's suffering from sciatica," said Connell. "It got to where he couldn't travel. We played with banjo players filling in before he decided he had enough but his playing's tricky. I'd tell him that it was genius but he'd say, 'No, it's not.' The way he looked at his banjo playing was that he played what fit, but what fit the Seldom Scene was totally unique and completely his own. It was easy for him but not for anyone else. Mike was the same way. He listened to Josh Graves but that wouldn't have fit what the Seldom Scene was doing. He had to come up with his own approach to the Dobro. It changed the instrument."

Coleman recorded a CD, *Ready for the Times* (2013), and toured for a year with Bryan Sutton and David Holt, but "Bryan wanted his own band, and David had his thing," he said. "Sutton, Holt & Coleman got in their way but we did play at the Savannah Folk Festival and MerleFest in 2017. It's a lot like playing with Doc and Merle."

The Seldom Scene continues to extend its legacy. The group's 2014 album, *Long Time . . .* , with new renditions of tunes spanning their full discography, included appearances by Emmylou Harris, John Starling, and Tom Gray. "We don't take ourselves seriously," Eldridge told me a few months before his retirement. "In the back of my head, I keep thinking, 'It may be like a Monday-night card game but we've played a lot of Monday nights, Tuesday nights, Wednesday nights, and so on.'"

Chapter 21

So You Want to Be a Rock 'n' Roll Star

Attending a Dillards show at the Ash Grove in 1959, L.A.-born and San Diego-raised Christopher "Chris" Hillman (1944-) realized his future. He convinced his parents to let him travel by train to Berkeley, almost five hundred miles away, where he studied with the Redwood Canyon Ramblers' mandolin player Scott Hambly. After his father's suicide, a year later, he found solace in bluegrass and acoustic music. "It's very simple, honest music," he told me.

The West Coast bluegrass scene was in its infancy. "There were only a few young kids playing," Hillman remembered, "David Lindley, Herb Pedersen, Ry Cooder, Clarence, Roland, and Eric White, and me. John McEuen was five years behind us."

Hillman joined the San Diego-based Scottsville Squirrel Barkers in 1962. The group included future Flying Burrito Brothers/Country Gazette banjo player Kenny Wertz, Larry Murray (Dobro), Ed Douglas (bass), and Gary Carr (guitar). A month before the group's breakup, Wertz was drafted and future Eagle Bernie Leadon replaced him. *Blue Grass Favorites* released the following year. The Scottsville Squirrel Barkers reunited at the San Diego Music Awards in September 2004. "We were all kids in San Diego County," remembered Hillman. "We learned by slowing down records—we didn't have instructional DVDs—and from transplanted Southerners like Vern and Rex Gosdin and Don Parmley."

Playing with Parmley and the Gosdins in the Golden State Boys (1963-64), Hillman appeared weekly on a local TV show, *Cal's Corral*. Together Records released their album in 1969, following Hillman's success with the Byrds, and credited it to the Hillmen.

When the Golden State Boys disbanded, Hillman played with an offshoot of Randy Sparks' New Christy Minstrels and considered going to college. His plans changed when Jim Dickson, a former Golden State Boy, invited him to play bass in a band he was producing—the Byrds. Hillman had never played bass but he jumped at the opportunity. For the next half-

Chris Hillman, 2000

decade, he joined Jim (later Roger) McGuinn, David Crosby, Gene Clark, and Michael Clarke to create rock and roll history. "We were already total Beatle fanatics when we saw *A Hard Day's Night*," remembered Hillman, "but within nine months, we were living it, with girls chasing us and riots stopping our concerts. It was quite exciting."

The Byrds' changing perspective capsulized in McGuinn and Hillman's "So You Want to Be a Rock 'n' Roll Star." "[The song] was a satire of what happened to the culture," explained Hillman. "We had seen how it had changed."

McGuinn kept the Byrds going after its founding members dispersed, but after the disappointing *Farther Along* (1971), his third album with Clarence White, Gene Parsons, and Skip Battin, he dismantled the lineup and reunited the original group. It didn't help. Their 1973 Crosby-produced album "didn't sell that well and didn't get great reviews," said McGuinn. "It was time to hang up the Byrds."

Four years later, Hillman toured with McGuinn and Gene Clark. Joined by Crosby, in 1990, they cut new tracks for the Byrds' boxset. After Clark's passing in May 1991, Hillman and McGuinn scored a minor hit with "Don't You Write Her Off." Their version of Dylan's "You Ain't Goin' Nowhere" on the Nitty Gritty Dirt Band's *Will the Circle Be Unbroken, Volume III* (1992) reached the top ten. "The Byrds didn't know how to play rock and roll when we started," said Hillman. "I played bluegrass but the other guys were folksingers. Our connection with Dylan came later but, when we started, we were trying to play songs that the Beatles did or write songs like them. When we saw *A Hard Day's Night*, we didn't even have equipment yet. McGuinn had been playing an acoustic twelve-string. He saw George Harrison playing a Rickenbacker electric twelve-string in the film and that was it. He said, 'I could do that.'"

The son of journalists (and the authors of *Parents Can't Win*), James Joseph "Roger" McGuinn III (1942-) discovered folk music at a Pete Seeger concert. "Pete had just broken away from the Weavers," he said. "He showed up with a twelve-stringed acoustic, a six-stringed acoustic, a five-stringed, long-necked banjo, and a recorder and told stories between the songs. He got the audience singing in harmony. I went, 'Wow! That's what I want to do when I grow up.'"

A graduate of Chicago's Old Town School of Music, McGuinn joined the Chad Mitchell Trio after high school. "The folk scene was very vibrant," he remembered. "Everybody got fired up when the Kingston Trio had a hit with 'Tom Dooley.'"

McGuinn recorded with Judy Collins and worked as a Brill Building staff songwriter. Between 1962 and early '64, he played twelve-stringed acoustic guitar and sang harmony for Bobby Darin. "Bobby chose ethnic material when he did the folk-music segment of his show," he recalled, "songs like 'It Makes a Good Man Feel Bad,' an old prison song. You don't get a hit record with anything like that but he was sincere about his love of folk music."

Forming Desert Rose with Pedersen, Bill Bryson, and lead guitarist John Jorgenson in 1987, Hillman scored more than a dozen mainstream country hits including "Love Reunited," "One Step Forward," and the chart-topping "He's Back and I'm Blue" over the next eight years. "Desert Rose was John's idea," said Pedersen. "We toured with Dan Fogelberg after playing on his bluegrass album, *High Country Snows* [1985], along with Doc Watson, Ricky Skaggs, David Grisman, Jerry Douglas, Charlie McCoy, and Tracy Nelson. We'd go out as a quartet and play our set. Then, Dan would come out and we'd do the album. It worked well. After the tour, John suggested we plug in our instruments, add pedal steel and drums, and put Bill on electric bass. We went to a rehearsal hall, tried it, and it worked. It was a good run. We still play together. Even if we haven't seen each other for five years, it comes right back. I'd hold us up against anybody, even the Eagles. John makes me play better; he's such a great musician. Desert Rose Acoustic is the four of us—John, Herb, Bill, and me."

Joined by Tony and Larry Rice, Hillman and Pedersen recorded *Out of the Woodwork* (1997), *Rice, Rice, Hillman & Pedersen* (1999), and *Running Wild* (2001). "I'm definitely channeling Earl Scruggs when I play banjo," said Pedersen, "but I listened to anything I could get—Sonny Osborne, J. D. Crowe, and Allen Shelton (Jim & Jesse). I wasn't into melodic banjo players like Bill Keith. I liked straight-ahead, hard-driving bluegrass."

Pedersen grew up in Berkeley, CA. "The Redwood Canyon Ramblers was the band of choice," he remembered. "They were college educated but they loved bluegrass. They were the first live bluegrass band I ever saw. I was in the ninth grade."

Jerry Garcia (1942-95) lived across the Bay. "We both played banjo," said Pedersen, "but we'd see each other from time to time. Six weeks before he died, we did an album with Red Allen, *Bluegrass Reunion*. He played great. I hadn't seen him in forty years but it was as though we were never apart. He was in a great mood."

Pedersen attended school with members of the Pine Valley Boys. "Butch Waller [who's led San Francisco-based High Country since 1968] played mandolin," he recalled. "Rich Connolly, the original guitar player, was a year ahead of us. When he left the band, we got David Nelson and tried to play as much traditional bluegrass as we could. David embraced the Clarence White style, which we all loved. Few people outside our circle were into bluegrass but we'd invite our high-school pals and their girls to see us play and force them to listen."

Pedersen met Grisman in Berkeley the summer of 1964. "David's first night in town," he said, "he came to see us at Tsubo's. Richard Greene was playing fiddle. We got together afterwards and jammed."

In late '65, Pedersen joined AR transplants Vern Williams (mandolin/ high tenor vocals) (1930-2006) and Ray Park (fiddle) (1933-2002). "Their Carroll County Country Boys was Northern CA's first bluegrass band in 1959," he said, "the real deal. Vern was a good songwriter."

When Pedersen appeared on a Nashville TV show, *Carl Tipton and the Mid-State Playboys*, with Vern & Ray, Earl Scruggs was watching closely. "Earl had to go into the hospital for a hip operation," Pedersen said. "He got my phone number through the musicians' union and invited me to his house. He said, 'Make sure you have your banjo.' I got over there and walked in the door, and there he was—the king. We sat down and had a great chat. He said, 'Let's go in the music room and play.' We went in and he picked up a guitar. He wanted me to play banjo. We played Flatt & Scruggs tunes. He wanted to see if my style fit what he and Lester did. He said, 'I got you here under false pretenses. Would you be interested in subbing for me for a few weekends?' I said, 'Are you kidding?' We went to the *Opry* that Friday and he introduced me to Lester and the Foggy Mountain Boys. We did the *Opry* that night and went off to WV on the Martha White bus. The band had been together for twenty years and didn't make mistakes. Lester taught me about phrasing; he would hold a line longer than usual. He was a pro, very gracious to everyone. I never saw him in a bad mood."

A few days after Pedersen filled in for Scruggs, his phone rang. The Dillards' Dean Webb was calling. "Doug is no longer with us," he told Pedersen, "and we're wondering if you'd like to try out." "I was going to be in L.A. to play at the Ash Grove with Vern & Ray," recalled Pedersen, "so I said, 'I'll come a few days ahead.' It worked out and I got the job.

"[The Dillards] had great tunes and Mitch's onstage patter was phenomenal. He was so relaxed, talking about all kinds of things, and throwing in a few laughers. It went smoothly. We weren't musicians standing still, not saying anything, and just playing music."

When the Dillards played the Cellar Door, John Duffey, John Starling, and Mike Auldridge came to the show. "The Seldom Scene was getting ready to cut another album," said Pedersen. "Duffey asked if I had any tunes. I told him that I had just written a couple and he said that he'd love to hear them."

Pedersen sent a cassette with the up-tempo "Old Train" and "Wait a Minute," written after coming home from an eight-week tour with Johnny Rivers. "I got a call to go out on another tour," he recalled. "When I told my wife, she put her hand up and said, 'Wait a minute; this isn't happening.' I said, 'Yes, it is. You know what I do.' The marriage didn't last but the song came out in twenty minutes. The Seldom Scene cut both songs. 'Old Train' was the title track of their album."

Byron Berline, Doug Dillard, and Roger Bush opened for Kay Starr in late 1971. Pedersen got a call from Berline. "He had me join them in San Francisco," he recalled. "Doug couldn't make it but it worked out. When we got back to L.A., Byron said that we ought to put a band together. We got Billy Ray Latham. That was the original Country Gazette. I didn't go on the road with them; I was busy doing sessions. They replaced me with Alan Munde. Later, they hired Roland White to play mandolin."

Pedersen recorded with by Nicolette Larson, Emmylou Harris, the Doobie Brothers, Gordon Lightfoot, Charlie Rich, Kim Carnes, Jimmy Webb, John Stewart, Jesse Winchester, Linda Ronstadt, David Bromberg, James Taylor, Kris Kristofferson, and John Prine. He toured with Jackson Browne when Late for the Sky came out in 1974. "Jackson's one of the greatest American songwriters," he said. "He has such a gift—a great look and great songs. I love his singing."

After playing banjo and guitar and singing on John Denver's 1979 self-titled album, Pedersen was invited "to go on the road to promote it," he remembered. "It was a great band. Hal Blaine was on drums, James Burton on electric guitar, Glen Hardin on piano, and Emory Gordy on bass. Danny Wheetman played fiddle. We traveled all over the world. John took care of all of us. He was excited about getting into bluegrass. He asked me to write a banjo tune so I wrote 'High Sierra.' He learned to play mandolin for that tune. We were passing through Ozark, MO when I saw a record store, Bob's Record Rack. I told the bus driver to pull over and took John into the store. He spent $1,000 on bluegrass albums I told him to get."

Pedersen joined Hillman to record *Bakersfield Bound* in 1996. "That was our tip of the hat to Buck Owens, Merle Haggard, and the Everly Brothers," he said. "How can you deny Don and Phil's influence? They grew up hearing great brother duets. When I heard 'All I Have to Do Is Dream' and 'Wake Up Little Susie,' I recognized their harmonies and knew where they were coming from."

At a jam session at Bill Bryson's house, Pedersen "met this amazing mandolin player, Kenny Blackwell," he recalled. "[Blackwell] had taken lessons from Jethro Burns and had a different slant on bluegrass mandolin. Gabe Witcher, the fiddler, was fifteen. Kenny brought him to a rehearsal and I went, 'Are you kidding?' He played a couple of tunes and I said, 'You're in the band.' He's gone on to bigger, and better, things. He's working with Chris Thile in Punch Brothers and doing sessions. Our guitar player, at first, was Billy Ray Latham. When he left, we got Roger Reed, who was also a great tenor singer. We had it all covered."

Pedersen played with Grisman, Rowan, and Clements in Old and In the Way successor Old and In the Gray. "When [Garcia] passed away," said Pedersen, "David called me to sit in with them. Then, John Kahn passed away and they got Bryn Bright to play bass. We did a couple of enjoyable tours. Deadheads came to see a bluegrass band but the material wasn't all bluegrass. Peter wrote some great tunes—'Midnight Moonlight,' 'Panama Red,' and 'The Land of the Navajo.' The younger generation identified."

Pedersen and Hillman continue to work as a duo. "I'm going to be coproducing a solo album for him [in January 2016] with Tom Petty," said Pedersen. "I worked with Tom on his last Mudcrutch record in 2008 and toured with them. I talked to him about working with Chris and he said that he'd love to do it. He was such a fan of the Byrds; you could hear the influence."

Bidin' My Time released in September 2017. In addition to Petty, (who died shortly after the album's release), guests included Hillman's ex-bandmates David Crosby, Roger McGuinn, and John Jorgenson, as well as Mike Campbell, Steve Ferrone, and Benmont Tench from Petty's band, the

Heartbreakers. Crosby, Pedersen, and Hillman harmonized on a remake of "The Bells of Rhymney" by Pete Seeger and Welsh poet Idris Davies. Playing bass for the first time in three decades on "Here He Comes Again," co-written with McGuinn, Hillman updated Gene Clark's "She Don't Care About Time," the B-side of the Byrds' "Turn! Turn! Turn!" single, and "Old John Robertson" from *The Notorious Byrd Brothers*.

Chapter 22

Baghdad by the Bay

Jerome John "Jerry" Garcia played banjo, guitar, and pedal steel despite losing two-thirds of his left hand's middle finger to a wood-chopping accident at the age of five. That same year, his father drowned. "I get my improvisational approach," he told Elvis Costello, "from Scotty Stoneman, the fiddle player, who . . . first set me on fire."[1]

In early 1961, Garcia joined Marshall Leicester (banjo, guitar) and Dick Arnold (fiddle) in the Sleepy Hollow Hog Stompers. An album of their show at the Boar's Head Coffeehouse, in San Carlos, released more than a half-century later. Meeting San Luis Obispo-born bass/guitar player and lyricist Robert Hunter in April 1961, Garcia embarked on a partnership that would last the rest of his life. Along with David Nelson, guitarists Eric Thompson and Sandy Rothman, mandolinist Ken Frankel, and guitar and Dobro player Norm Van Maastricht, Garcia and Hunter played with the Hart Valley Drifters and the Wildwood Boys. The Hart Valley Drifters' album, *Folk Time*, released in November 2016. "We were into traditional Appalachian folk music," remembered Nelson, "but we were poor beatniks. There was no such thing as hippies yet. We were all scuffling for money. I got a banjo and Jerry got a guitar. He wanted to play banjo and I wanted to play guitar so we traded. We learned to play bluegrass piece by piece."

Nelson was in high school when Rodney Albin (the older brother of his friend, Peter, later with Big Brother and the Holding Company) proposed opening a folk-music cabaret in 1964. "Kepler's Books in San Carlos allowed us to do it upstairs," Nelson remembered. "I learned to play mandolin there. We had a bookcase on the floor with a rug over it. That was our stage. We had a microphone, an amplifier, and a couple of speakers. That was our sound system but we never really needed it. The room was so small."

Fresh from an army stint that included two court-martials and eight AWOLs, eighteen-year-old Garcia was a new arrival to Palo Alto. "We recruited people to play," remembered Nelson, "and Jerry was one of them. He was playing a twelve-string guitar."

Nelson immersed himself in bluegrass. "Anytime Bill Monroe, the Stanley Brothers, or the Country Gentlemen came to town," he said, "I'd see them. My friends and I traded quarter-inch tapes. I knew people in Monroe's band—Peter Rowan, Lamar Grier, and Richard Greene—my age. Richard played in a band I was in from 1964 to 1966 [The Pine Valley Boys]. Herb Pedersen was on banjo and singing in that great tenor voice and Butch Waller was on mandolin. We played in the Bay Area and sometimes L.A. It was an incredible group, strictly bluegrass."

The Black Mountain Boys included Eric Thompson and Sandy Rothman (guitars) and Nelson (mandolin). "We were into all kinds of music," said Nelson, "bluegrass, folk music, old-time music, Cajun music, anything that went way back. I was also into modern jazz."

After playing at places such as the Boar's Head and the Top of the Tangent, Nelson and his bandmates continued partying all night. "We'd end up playing old rock-and-roll songs," he recalled. "Electric guitar was a natural step as soon as I got some money."

Garcia's father "was a jazz musician [for] a big band . . . in the '30s, . . . with strings, harpist, and vocalists . . . ," he told *Rolling Stone*. "I never saw him play with his band but I remember him playing me to sleep at night. . . . I'm named after Jerome Kern, that's how seriously the bug bit my father."[2]

Country music drew Garcia's fascination. "My grandmother was a big *Grand Ole Opry* fan," he said, "I grew up . . . listening to the *Opry* every Saturday night on the radio without knowing what I was hearing. In fact, my first 45 was a Hank Williams record, a song called 'The Love Bug Itch.' It was a really stupid song but, hey, it was Hank Williams."[3]

Fifteen-year-old Bob Weir (1947-) "was wandering the back streets of Palo Alto with a friend when we heard banjo music coming from the back of a music store . . . ," he remembered. "It was Garcia waiting for his pupils, unmindful it was New Year's Eve. We sat down, started jamming, and had a great old rave. I had my guitar with me and we played a little and decided to start a jug band."[4]

Joined by harmonica player Ron "Pigpen" McKernan, Garcia and Weir formed Mother McCree's Uptown Jug Champions in the spring of 1964. *Live at the Top of the Tangent* released in 1999. Adding a bassist (Dana Morgan) and drummer (Bill Kreutzmann), and switching to electric instruments, they performed their first show as the Warlocks at Magoo's Pizza in Menlo Park in May 1965 (Phil Lesh replaced Morgan shortly afterwards). They would be the house band for Ken Kesey and the Merry Pranksters' *Acid Tests*. "I was impressed by Jerry and The Warlocks," Grisman told *Relix*, "as they were incorporating bluegrass, old-time, and other 'rootsy' influences and sensibilities into a rock and roll context. They were also having a lot of fun doing it. It was definitely a departure from most of what was going on at the time and a lot less slick, down-to-earth music with electric instruments. They were playing high school swimming pool parties."[5]

Relocating to San Francisco's Haight-Ashbury, they became the Grateful Dead in December 1965 (Mickey Hart joined in September 1967). Garcia continued to play lead guitar and provide spiritual presence until his passing in 1995. "I'd go with them to places like the Fillmore," remembered Nelson, who played on *Aoxomoxoa, Workingman's Dead,* and *American Beauty,* "just riding along."

In the late sixties, Garcia started playing pedal steel guitar. "He asked me about John 'Marmaduke' Dawson," Nelson said, "and I told him that I knew him. We got together with Phil Lesh and Mickey Hart. That's how the New Riders of the Purple Sage started. Our songs had bluegrass roots; 'Glendale Train' was 'Knoxville Girl' four-four time. They have the same melody. 'Panama Red' is a bluegrass tune. Peter Rowan was one of the people I was trading tapes with."

The Festival Express comprised eight concerts between June 24 and July 4, 1970. Along with the Grateful Dead, Janis Joplin, the Band, and Buddy Guy, NRPS traveled across Canada aboard a chartered National Railway train, stopping to perform shows. "I had a sleeper car of my own," Nelson recalled, "and looked out the window at the beautiful Canadian countryside—lakes and trees. We started in Montreal and went all the way to Vancouver, playing nonstop on the train. There was one car for electric music and another for acoustic."

Nelson recorded the Garcia-produced *The Good Old Boys: Pistol Packin' Mama* in Mickey Hart's barn studio. "Frank Wakefield and I were traveling around playing," he explained, "and he said he could get Don Reno and 'Chubby' Wise to record with us. Sure enough, he handed the phone to me and I hear, 'Hello, David, this is Don Reno.' It was a huge thrill. Jerry and I were like kids.

"Wakefield was a wild man, way out there. We traveled, just the two of us. It was low-budget transportation but a lot of fun. We'd play all night, and after the show, we'd go to somebody's house and play. There was so much enthusiasm."

Garcia remained one of Nelson's closest friends. "I kept going over to his house," he said, "but the New Riders couldn't go on; the music scene had changed. It was the disco dark ages. We had to go to smaller and smaller venues. We'd go back to familiar places and there'd be a big, disco mirror ball in the middle of the room. It was all about disco dancing. We even had tunes with that beat. By 1982, Buddy Cage moved back to the East Coast. I figured it was time for me, too. We'd been doing it for thirteen years."

Reorganized by Dawson (1945-2009) with Rusty Gauthier, Gary Vogensen, Bill Laymon, and others, NRPS continued until 1997. Dawson oved to Mexico and became an English teacher, succumbing to stomach cancer on July 21, 2009.

Mixing bluegrass, blues, rock, and improvisation, Nelson formed the David Nelson Band with John Molo (drums), Barry Sless (pedal steel, guitar), Pete Sears (bass, vocals), and Mookie Siegel (keyboards, vocals) in 1994. He hadn't yet gotten into writing songs. "There were already so many good songs," he said, "but I did it for my own artistic expression. After the Riders folded, I got a DX7 synthesizer and some sequencers. I recorded in digital time, putting in one note at a time, many, many tracks. I started with Dr. John/New Orleans-like music, all this piano stuff. I put a mix on a cassette, with a digitalized flute playing the melody, and sent it to Robert Hunter. It came back with words. He matched my melodies phrase by phrase, beat by beat. It was amazing."

Johnny Markowski and Buddy Cage played together in the early 2000s. In 2004, Markowski asked the pedal steel player, "Where's Nelson? Would he ever think of getting the New Riders back together?" Cage said, "I don't know; call him." "Johnny called me out of the blue," Nelson told me in 2016, "and put forth the idea. I go, 'Really? Are you serious?' He said that we could get guitarist/vocalist Michael Falzarano. The David Nelson Band knew him; he had recorded with us. They shipped me East for a rehearsal and four gigs. We did old New Riders tunes and new songs. We've since broken the record for personnel, eleven years without a change. We finish each other's sentences."

Nelson alternated between NRPS and the David Nelson Band until September 2016. "I broke my shoulder totally off," he said. "It was hanging from the ball socket. I had been running in the dark with two friends, laughing and giggling. We were heading to the hotel, running faster and faster. I tripped on a tuft of grass or something and went down—bam! I hit my face. My teeth broke. Luckily, I didn't get a concussion. That was the first thing they checked at the emergency room—my skull. My left hand is still strong—I'm flexing right now—but the shoulder is painful. I had surgery but it takes so much energy to heal."

Nelson's shoulder was the least of his worries. In a February 2017 message to fans, he revealed that doctors had diagnosed colon cancer. "I'll need to be focused on my treatment," he wrote, "and healing over the next few months."[6]

Concluding on a hopeful note, he said, "Not to worry—I'm in good hands and looking forward to playing with the boys and seeing you all again in the not too distant future. Love, David."[7]

Chapter 23

Will the Circle Be Unbroken

Picking sessions at McCabe's Guitar Shop, in Long Beach, CA, led Jeffrey "Jeff" Hanna, Jimmie Fadden, Germany-born Jackson Browne, and Les Thompson to form the Nitty Gritty Dirt Band in early 1966. Three months after their May 13 debut, Oakland-born John McEuen (1945-) replaced Browne. In addition to his mandolin, guitar, and fiddle playing, McEuen's five-string banjo would be the heart of the group's best recordings. "The Nitty Gritty Dirt Band got very lucky," said McEuen. "Nobody wanted to work for a living. We wanted to play music and go on the road."

McEuen's earliest influence came from Doug Dillard, who "made playing banjo look easy, like it was fun," he said. "He was precise and exciting. I understood what he was doing. It got me out of Orange County instantly. The Dillards played clubs around L.A. and Southern CA, usually five days at a time, and I got a chance to see good banjo up close. They were a combination of the Smothers Brothers and Flatt & Scruggs. They should have gone further than they did. They should have gotten *Paint Your Wagon*, not the Dirt Band. It would have helped their career. It certainly helped ours."

Working at Disneyland's magic shop as a teenager, McEuen demonstrated tricks that he sold. "It didn't matter if you failed," he said, "because twenty minutes later, you'd have a new crowd. Sometimes, it'd be fun all day long. I could do twenty-five pitches in a day's work."

The West Coast's music scene "was more powerful than what was going on in Greenwich Village," claimed McEuen. "I could see Lightnin' Hopkins and Blind Lemon Jefferson at the Ash Grove and between sets run over to the Troubadour and see the Stoneman Family, Judy Collins, or the Smothers Brothers. I could go the Strip, where the Byrds were playing, or the Whisky a Go Go, where it was the Mothers of Invention. There was the Ice House in Pasadena, the Paradox in Preston, and Ledbetter's in West L.A. Jimi Hendrix might be at the Golden Bear in Huntington. We played on a high-school football field with the Byrds, the Jefferson

Airplane, Buffalo Springfield, the Doors, and the Association. It cost six dollars to get in."

One night, instead of seeing John Mayall at the Roxy, McEuen headed to the Ash Grove. "I ended up sitting in with Bill Monroe," he said. "I had seen Flatt & Scruggs and Mother Maybelle Carter do two songs at the *Grand Ole Opry* when I was nineteen. The show sold out but I could see through a window from the outside. They were extremely professional, tight as a drum; they sounded just like the records."

McEuen played on Doug Kershaw's Cajun anthem, "Louisiana Man." His next session was for Richie Havens' "Eleanor Rigby." "Michael Martin Murphey had me play on 'Carolina in the Pines,'" he said, "a pop hit in 1975."

Smaller than the legendary Santa Monica location, McCabe's Guitar Shop in Long Beach "had a coffee table surrounded by racks filled with folk-music, bluegrass, and acoustic-music records and banjos, guitars, and mandolins on the walls," remembered McEuen. "People sat around a coffee table, playing music, not wanting to go home. A group of these people became the Nitty Gritty Dirt Band."

Recruiting the newly formed group to back him at a banjo contest, and winning, McEuen "figured I'd play with them a little longer," he said. "I wanted to be on the radio and needed a band."

Jackson Browne's early involvement is "a historic footnote, but he was never on their records, never made money with them, isn't in any photographs, and he isn't mentioned in reviews," said McEuen. "I was in the dressing room of the Paradox, playing for no money with the Nitty Gritty Dirt Band. It was Jackson's last show. He said, 'Listen to this,' and he played me a song. I said, 'Where'd you get the words?' He said, 'I made them up.' 'Where'd you get that funny chord?' He was playing an F major seventh. He said, 'I thought it sounded better than an F.' The song was 'These Days.' I was the first to hear it. He went onstage that night and played it."

Within seven or eight months, the Nitty Gritty Dirt Band inked a deal with Liberty. Their debut album included Browne's "Melissa" and "Holding." "These Days" and "Shadow Dream Song" appeared on their second release.

Released February 7, 1967, the Nitty Gritty Dirt Band's first single, "Buy for Me the Rain," "was a regional hit, but some radio stations determined that its flipside ['Candy Man'] was a drug song," recalled McEuen. "It killed the single but we kept busy. Our booking agent told promoters that we had a record on the radio. It made it possible for us to get jobs opening for Bobby Sherman, the Doors, and even Jack Benny. We played clubs in Kansas City, St. Louis, Denver, and NY."

The group's music fit with the contemporary scene. "The Band's *Music from Big Pink* and the Beatles' 'Hey Jude' had just come out," McEuen remembered. "Jeff and I spent a lot of time listening to those records, going, 'Gee, they're using mandolin, accordion, and acoustic guitars, along with drums.'"

After the Nitty Gritty Dirt Band appeared as a jug band in *For Singles Only* (1968), Paramount Pictures tapped them to record the soundtrack of *Paint Your Wagon*. They spent four months on the Oregon set. "It was great fun," Detroit-born Jeff Hanna told *No Depression*, "but it was a bunch of kids from Los Angeles being plucked out of Hollywood and dropped into this beautiful national forest."[1]

The Nitty Gritty Dirt Band received positive press for *Paint Your Wagon* but "it actually broke up the group," claimed McEuen. "Jeff didn't want to continue and said, 'I'm quitting.'"

Attending a show by Poco at the Golden Bear six months later, McEuen ran into Hanna, who had been playing with Linda Ronstadt. Agreeing to reunite, they "got together with Jimmie Fadden and Les Thompson and hired Jim Ibbotson as our singing drummer," remembered McEuen. "*Music from Big Pink* was still on our minds. It showed that you could use these instruments with a different feel; half-time drums in a four-four song made it a folksong with a rock-and-roll beat."

"Jimmie and I played washtub bass," said Hanna, "and washboard on some of the bluegrass stuff, which was a nod to our jug band roots . . . we had the five-string banjo, a little mandolin, a little dobro, some fiddle. . . . I think the mountain sound in our music is what set us apart from Poco or the Burritos. There was plenty of room on that musical bus."[2]

Uncle Charlie and His Dog Teddy (1970) mixed songs by Buddy Holly, Kenny Loggins, Mike Nesmith, and Jerry Jeff Walker with bluegrass classics ("Billy in the Low Ground," "Chicken Reel," "Clinch Mountain Backstep," and Scruggs' "Randy Lynn Rag"). "'Mr. Bojangles' made the difference," said McEuen. "It enabled us to play much better venues. We wanted to record in a way that other people didn't, and for that album, we found it. It reached young people—the children of Flatt & Scruggs, Jimmy Martin, and Doc Watson—who played it for their parents, who liked it because it sounded familiar. I tried to record *Made in Brooklyn* in that style—with no three songs alike but a thread running through them—the connectedness of musicians working together."

Uncle Charlie led to *Will the Circle Be Unbroken*. "We owed the [pioneers] because they gave us their influence," said McEuen. "Vassar Clements told me many times, 'I'm so glad the *Circle* album came along because now I have a career of my own.' Merle Watson told me that after the album released, his dad made three times the money. Earl got a lot of work out of it. I asked him to record with us. I asked Doc Watson. I gave Maybelle Carter her first gold record. I went to her house."

McEuen's brother (the Nitty Gritty Dirt Band's manager), Bill McEuen, produced the historic summit meeting. "We had Merle Travis singing 'I Am a Pilgrim' with just his guitar," said John McEuen. "That wasn't followed by something similar like 'Dark as a Dungeon' but the Carter Family's 'Wildwood Flower.' *Circle* sucked you in because it had variety. The talking between the tracks felt like you were watching it happen.

"It was a time of peaceniks versus warmongers, hippies versus the shorthaired, and North versus South but music bridged the gap. The first time we went to the South, Jeff cut his hair short. He was worried about the *Easy Rider* thing. My feeling was that people were just people; give them a chance. Besides, I played the banjo and I was going to go to the South. When I drove a rental car, I kept my driver's license in my banjo case. Police pulled me over at least three dozen times. I told them, 'My license is in the trunk in my instrument case.' 'Oh, are you a musician?' 'Yes sir, I am.' I'd open the banjo case, and immediately, I wasn't a longhaired, speeding hippie anymore; I was a banjo player. I'd take the banjo out and play. The officer would say, 'Slow down,' and not give me a ticket."

Headliners at Stompin 76, near Galax, VA, in August 1976, the Nitty Gritty Dirt Band became the first American band to perform in Russia, Armenia, Georgia, and Latvia the following May. The Russian government "came to see us four times before they chose us," remembered McEuen. "All twenty-eight shows sold out. Our music went over so well that they wouldn't let another American group in for eight years. People were standing up and rushing the stage, dancing in the aisles, things that were illegal at a Russian event. Musicians weren't supposed to incite the audience. In Moscow, there were timeshare tickets. People in the auditorium got up and ran out after twenty or thirty minutes. Somebody else ran in. We weren't a big group. They didn't hear us beyond Voice of America radio shows that got through the signal jamming."

Returning to the States, Hanna and Ibbotson dropped "Nitty Gritty" from the band's name. "I voted against it," said McEuen. "I didn't want to see twelve years of marketing go out the window, which it did. Then, Jeff produced three albums, including *Jealousy*, which was an embarrassment. It was the Nitty Gritty Dirt Band trying to be a rock-and-roll group, which we weren't. Each album was less successful until the point of 1980 when my brother resigned as manager. We called Chuck Morris, president of AEG. He was running Tulagi's when we first played there in 1970. He asked if I was going to stay in the band. I told him I would if we were the Nitty

Gritty Dirt Band, if we had Jimmy Ibbotson, if we recorded for a Nashville label, and if it was acoustic, country-driven music. He agreed and he got us a deal with Warner Brothers. We had number-one country hits with 'Long Hard Road (The Sharecropper's Dream)' in 1984 and 'Modern Day Romance' a year later."

McEuen often found himself at odds with Hanna and Fadden. "They started the group," he said, "but within the first month, Les Thompson was in it. He and I had played in the Wilma City Moonshiners for six months. I wasn't even playing banjo yet. Les called me, a year later, and said, 'Hey, you should come and play with Jeff, Jimmy, and me.' It was all a foggy time."

Conflict intensified in the mid-eighties. McEuen "didn't like the way the band's music was going or the way I was edged out of decisions," he said. "I'd go into the studio to add my banjo and they'd tell me, 'Don't worry about it; Steve Gibson already did it.' 'What!' I've spent my life promoting the banjo and they're putting someone else there. The same year, they told me that the band wasn't going to record my instrumentals, even if I did them by myself, which I usually did because I couldn't get anyone to play with me."

Within a week, McEuen resigned, separated from his wife, and severed ties with his manager, record company, accountant, and agent. "I was living in a friend's basement," he said. "I had child support and legal fees to pay. I had no band, nothing but a car to drive the kids around on the weekends. It took me about a year and a half, maybe two years, to recover. That's when I put *String Wizards* [1991] together. I wanted to make it in two days, with as many first takes as we could get, like a Flatt & Scruggs album. I went to Nashville and we rehearsed for five days. I couldn't have made that album with the Dirt Band."

During his hiatus, McEuen scored eight soundtracks, recorded four solo albums, produced albums for others, and booked acts for music festivals. "When Jimmy [Ibbotson] started having trouble with the Dirt Band," he said, "we did shows together."

In McEuen's absence, the Nitty Gritty Dirt Band recorded a second volume of *Will the Circle Be Unbroken*. Scruggs, Acuff, Johnny Cash, the Carter Family, Emmylou Harris, Ricky Skaggs, John Denver, Levon Helm, and John Hiatt made appearances. Released in 1989, it scored two Grammys. The Byrds' Roger McGuinn and Chris Hillman's redo of Dylan's "You Ain't Goin' Nowhere" broke into the top ten. A third volume released a year after McEuen's 1991 return.

Remastering the first volume of *Will the Circle Be Unbroken* for CD, McEuen "thought it might be a good time to get back with the band," he said. "Sadly, we did 'Walking Shoes' and 'Circle' and that was it. I suggested 'Way Downtown' and they told me, 'We're not doing that anymore.' I knew

John McEuen, 1992

why—I sang it. I asked, 'Why don't we do "Earl's Breakdown"?' and Jimmy said, 'I hate that song.' 'Why don't we do "Tennessee Stud"?' 'That's boring.'"

Problems intensified. "I was told I'm not a member of the band anymore," said McEuen. "I'm an employee. The other three voted me out of the corporation. It's frustrating yet there's a magic in our combination that isn't replicated by anyone else, despite my problems with it or their problems with me."

McEuen's eleventh solo album, *Made in Brooklyn* (2016), featured David Bromberg, John Carter Cash, John Cowan, Martha Redbone, Jay Ungar, and Steve Martin. "I didn't want any tension," McEuen said, "or have to listen to opinions I didn't want. We recorded in an old church in Brooklyn because we wanted natural echo. We gathered in the main sanctuary—[producer David] Chesky set up in the room next door—and we recorded fifteen songs in two days. People ask me how we did it. I tell them that Flatt & Scruggs recorded eighteen songs, including 'Foggy Mountain Breakdown' and 'Roll in My Sweet Baby's Arms,' in three hours and set the standard for bluegrass. They knew their music."

Steve Martin, who played banjo on his original tune "My Dirty Life and Times," worked with McEuen at Disneyland as a teenager. "My brother managed him," said McEuen, producer of Martin's *The Crow: New Songs for the 5-String Banjo.* "I used to back him up on his magic shows. We played together a few times. He played with the Dirt Band and we played on 'King Tut.'"

During the session, Martin "looked at me and said, 'Why don't you call it *Made in Brooklyn?*'" McEuen remembered. "I had been trying to come up with a title for six months. That was a good one. Brooklyn is a cultural crossroads between Jewish, Catholic, B'hai, and Buddhism, a place where ethnic groups get along. All these musicians have different paths. David Bromberg is an East Coast folk-music icon. Martha Redbone lives in Brooklyn but represents Native America and the blues of West Virginia. John Cowan is from all over the place but he's mostly Southeastern-bluegrass influenced. Skip Ward is a NY bass player who doesn't miss a note. Kevin Twigg is a drummer from Manhattan. He's friends with David Amram, who lives in upstate NY but is really from the world. Matt Cartsonis fit right in. John Carter Cash brought a lineage going back to the first *Circle* album, singing his dad's 'I Still Miss Someone.'"

Made in Brooklyn spanned a wide range of influences. "'My Favorite Dream' has a nostalgic sound," said McEuen, "kind of like a 1947 Hoagy Carmichael record but it's a song that nobody's heard before. I needed to record 'She Darked the Sun' and John Cowan needed to sing it. It's a hippie country-rock anthem of the late sixties by Bernie Leadon and Gene Clark before the Eagles existed."

The album included a new rendition of "Mr. Bojangles." "It's a song that everybody connected with," McEuen explained. "It was the very last one we did. We had done seven songs a day for two days. They were long days. Here we were, at the twelfth hour of the second day, and David [Bromberg] started talking about it. It was important to both of our lives. He said that he had a guitar solo that he had always wanted to record with it but hadn't. We didn't have to rehearse it."

In October 2017, McEuen handed in his resignation. "After fifty years, the time has come for me to bid adieu to the Nitty Gritty Dirt Band stage," he said in a press release. "I will move forward with great pride in my personal and musical contributions to NGDB and now can fully concentrate on my independent endeavors. I have much to do, many more creative ideas to pursue."

Chapter 24

Ashokan Farewell

Few tunes spread as quickly, or as widely, as "Ashokan Farewell," the theme of Ken Burns' 1990 PBS *Civil War* series. It may have sounded at least a century old, but Bronx, NY-born fiddler/mandolin player Jay Ungar composed it in the late 1970s and included it on Fiddle Fever's second album, *Waltz of the Wind* (1984). "We were finishing the album," he remembered, "and there was a slow tune not up to par. We were thinking that we should record something else. Russ Barenberg had heard 'Ashokan Farewell,' but when I played it for him, it didn't have a name. He said, 'Let's try that new waltz of yours.' The recording came together fast. It was one take. It felt very powerful. 'Ashokan Farewell' is so simple beginners can learn it and feel a great sense of accomplishment. Music teachers use it; that's so gratifying. It has a life of its own."

Barenberg and Fiddle Fever bandmate Matt Glaser had worked with Burns on a PBS documentary about the Brooklyn Bridge in 1981. "Matt knew Ken from college," said Ungar, "so he gave him an advance copy of our album. He was so taken by 'Ashokan Farewell' that he used it in his next film, *Huey,* about Louisiana politician Huey Long. Matt played a solo version. Molly Mason and I did the music for Ken's short films about painter/muralist Thomas Hart Benton, the US Congress, and early radio broadcasting. He started working on *The Civil War* in 1988. It took years to complete. He had us do most of the traditional string-band music."

A banjo-less, triple-fiddle band featuring Glaser, Ungar, Evan Stover (fiddle/mandolin), Barenberg (guitar), and Mason (bass), Fiddle Fever obscured the lines between bluegrass, old-time, and world music. "Jay's the strongest old-time player," Boston-based Glaser told me in 1989, "and he usually plays melody. Evan's playing is very weird but he thinks he's playing straight bluegrass. With three fiddlers, we try for a wall of sound."

"Matt loved to play high harmonies," remembered Ungar, "and Evan enjoyed playing a looser, underpinning part where he would find the low harmony but also have freedom. It was a natural sound and so exciting."

Matt Glaser, 1988

The Brooklyn-born son of an opera singer, Glaser studied piano from the age of nine. He was playing folksongs on the guitar within a year. Hearing a "scratchy old-time fiddle" on a TV commercial, he pleaded with his parents to get him a fiddle for his thirteenth birthday. He took lessons from John Burke, "a banjo player who also played fiddle," at the Fretted Instrument School in Greenwich Village. Moving with his parents to Katonah, NY, Glaser continued studying with Paul Ehrlich. "He was very open-minded to me playing other kinds of music," Glaser recalled. "He turned me on to Byron Berline. He took me to Union Grove and to hear Stephane Grappelli at a club in NY."

Vassar Clements' fiddling made a life-changing impact. "I didn't know how to begin to sound like Vassar," said Glaser. "It was like hearing a completely new language."

Glaser's influences expanded to include "the great Western swing fiddler Johnny Gimble and jazz violinists—Svend Asmussen, Stuff Smith, Joe Venuti, and Stephane Grappelli."

Barely "squeaking" into the Eastman Conservatory, Glaser quickly dropped out. "I wanted to play music for a living," he remembered.

The Central Park Sheiks provided Glaser's first exposure to jazz. "Richard Leiberson, the guitar player and bandleader," he recalled, "very patiently taught me tunes."

Glaser forged a partnership with Bronx-born fiddler Kenny Kosek, and they "played in brain-damaged avant-garde bluegrass bands and recorded together," Glaser said. "We even did a McDonald's commercial in Spanish."

Glaser and Kosek's collaboration culminated in the NY All-Stars, with Andy Statman, Trischka, Barenberg, and Roger Mason (bass). Trischka and Glaser would form a progressive bluegrass band, Heartlands, in 1977, and back Barenberg on his debut solo album, *Cowboy Calypso* (1979).

Ungar, Kosek, and fiddle/banjo player Bruce Molsky grew up in the same Bronx neighborhood. "We didn't know each other," Ungar said, "but there was something driving us to similar music. I spent my summers in the country; my parents had a bungalow. I've never enjoyed the city. I grew up in a crappy neighborhood so I'm not nostalgic about it. I went to the High School of Music and Art and played in the orchestra and string quartet. The string quartet was the most enjoyable. It was four people working together, listening to each other, and communicating. When I heard bluegrass and old-time music, they had an extra level of freedom. There was room for creativity, playing by ear, and improvising."

Ungar's father emigrated from Hungary. His mother came from a Turkish city now part of Macedonia. "My dad was an Ashkenazy Jew," said Ungar, "and my mom was Sephardic. There were cultural differences but we had music in the house. I heard 78s of folk music—Burl Ives, Pete Seeger—classical music, and popular music. My dad sang Hungarian folksongs when we took long drives. 'Ashokan Farewell' doesn't sound Eastern European but there's sadness and poignancy similar to what my father sang. I've started writing tunes that sound Eastern European. I call it 'Celtic Klezmer music.'"

Ungar drifted to Greenwich Village in his teens. "David Bromberg was on the scene," he remembered. "We became friends and jammed together. I wasn't thinking of becoming a professional musician. My chosen path was to become a veterinarian and live in a rural area. I wandered in other directions, including anthropology, in college. Music is such an integral part of people's personal, social, and cultural life."

Roy Michaels, who had played with Stephen Stills and Richie Furay in the Au Go Go Singers, and Bob Smith formed Cat Mother and the All Night Newsboys in late 1967. "I was in the band the summer they formed," Ungar said, "but I decided to finish my last year in college. They wound up hooking up with Jimi Hendrix and getting a Polydor Records contract. When I left college, they asked me to rejoin. They had a charting single ['Good Old Rock and Roll'], an album, and they were about to record another. I went back for a year and a half. We moved to the West Coast together."

Cat Mother's manager, Michael Jefferey, also oversaw the careers of Hendrix and Eric Burdon and the Animals. "I have an uncle who's an entertainment lawyer," noted Ungar. "I showed him the paperwork and he said, 'This isn't good. Don't do it.' I remained an independent contractor, but for all practical purposes, I was a band member. My experiences over that year and a half drove me from that world."

Returning to the East Coast with his first wife, Lyn Hardy, Ungar met Pete Seeger and became involved with the sloop *Clearwater* and the Hudson River Revival. Together with Seeger's brother-in-law John Cohen, Ungar and Hardy formed the Putnam String County Band. "We started as a square-dance band, the Putnam County String Band, in the early seventies," said Ungar, "to raise money for the McGovern campaign. When we made the smaller version of it, John came up with the idea of reversing the words String and County."

Ungar hosted an annual holiday show at the Towne Crier Café in Pawling, NY. During the 1978 show, he met Molly Mason. The Washington-born bassist had played with Laurie Lewis, Cathy Fink, Marcy Marxer, and Sally Van Meter in Blue Rose. "They only did one album," said Ungar, "but it affected people in a big way. She was doing a guest set with Suzy Thompson when we met. Over the following year, she played a few shows with Lyn and me. She went back West and toured with Benny Thomasson and then went to Minneapolis, to join the *Prairie Home Companion* house band."

After Mason's departure, Ungar joined Bromberg's band. "David's amazing abilities and repertoire made it fun," said Ungar, "and there was a lot of experimenting. Peter Ecklund was a great improviser who played fiddle tunes on trumpet. I got to be part of a sound always on the edge."

When they met, Glaser "was living with his family in Katonah, NY," Ungar recalled. "He came to a square dance where I was playing and sat in. He was into harmonies. I had heard about a fiddler in Poughkeepsie [Evan Stover] so I got the three of us together at my house. I started finding gigs for us, using fill-in guitar players."

Returning East, Mason joined Fiddle Fever, along with Barenberg, in 1980. "We didn't know that was going to be the band," said Ungar, "but it clicked. Russ was creative and solid. Tonally, he had such a great sound it elevated what we were doing. Molly was the grooviest bass player on the planet. She understood all the idioms."

A decade later, Ungar and Mason turned to orchestral music. "We worked with an amazing arranger/conductor, Paul Gambrill," said Ungar, "on a twenty-minute orchestral piece, 'Harvest Home Suite,' and recorded it with the Nashville Chamber Orchestra. The album featured small-group folk arrangements leading up to that piece."

RCA (BMG) teamed Ungar and Mason with Irish flutist James Galway in September 2001. "We spent an afternoon jamming in NY," said Ungar. "I brought sheet music, things we could try. We recorded *A Song of Home: An American Musical Journey,* with mandolinist Peter Ostroushko, in six days at a mountaintop retreat [Allare] near Woodstock, NY.

"Nine-eleven was the day after James arrived in NY. He had an orchestral session early that morning. We were scheduled to record on the twelfth but there was no way; transportation shut down. The world was waiting for the next shoe to drop. He came up on the thirteenth and we spent six days on this isolated mountaintop, in idyllic late-summer weather, checking the newspaper at the end of each day and talking about what was going on in the world. We really bonded."

Jay Ungar, 1992

Much of Ungar's energy is reserved for the workshops and festivals he and Mason host at the Ashokan Center. "I had been involved with a music and dance camp in PA," said Ungar in 2016. "It moved to a college campus in Putnam County for a year, but that winter, the college's main building burned down. If we wanted to do it again, we had to find another place. One of the attendees knew about Ashokan and took me to see it. As I entered the property, I felt something special.

"We've been here forty years. We started with a long weekend and we're running nine camps now. In 2006, SUNY New Paltz sold the property. It was going to end our camps, and the outdoor education programs that started in the sixties, but we formed the Ashokan Foundation and saved it. 'Ashokan Farewell' connected us with people who made it possible.

"When these camps are doing their job, the community feeling, the beautiful utopian experience, stay with you for a while. I was at the tail end of that, feeling a sense of loss and yearning to be back. That brought about the tune. It was a natural flow. I felt something important happening and turned on my tape recorder to capture the moment. We started to use it at the end of each camp. It provides closure."

Fiddle Fever reunited at the Ashokan Center in 2015. "It was twenty-five years since we had played together," said Ungar. "It went well but it was a lot of work. Those arrangements are complex. We spent two days trying to put it back together but we got it going."

Ungar's passion is shared by his daughter. "Ruthy picked up the fiddle as a small child," he said, "but she gave it up after a couple of years and drifted off into other directions. She got into the world of acting; that was her major in college. She went to NY around 1996 and met Mike Merenda in the world of acting. They ended up playing music together, first with the Mammals, then as Mike + Ruthy, and now as the Mammals again. It rekindled her interest in the fiddle and writing songs. I'm so happy to see her play."

Chapter 25

Fluxology

Leaving J. D. Crowe & the New South on Labor Day weekend 1975, Jerry Douglas and Ricky Skaggs played with banjo player Terry Baucom in the short-lived Boone Creek. When Skaggs joined Emmylou Harris's Hot Band, Douglas signed on with Buck White and the Whites and moved to Nashville. It wouldn't take him long to become one of the city's busiest musicians. A member of the house band for TNN's *American Music Shop* (1988-93), he joined Sam Bush, Béla Fleck, Mark O'Connor, and Mark Schatz in Strength in Numbers. He recorded with Russ Barenberg and Edgar Meyer (*Skip, Hop, & Wobble*), Peter Rowan (*Yonder*), and Celtic fiddler Aly Bain (*Transatlantic Sessions*) and played on nearly two thousand records by everyone from Ray Charles and Eric Clapton to Elvis Costello and Mumford & Sons. His twelfth solo album, *Traveler* (2012), featured Paul Simon, Eric Clapton, Alison Krauss, Dr. John, and Mumford & Sons. Douglas's producer credits include albums by the Del McCoury Band, the Nashville Bluegrass Band, the Steep Canyon Rangers, and Krauss, whose band (Union Station) he joined in 1998. The recipient of fourteen Grammy Awards, Douglas is a three-time CMA (Country Music Association) "Musician of the Year."

"Jerry was influenced by Josh Graves and Mike Auldridge," said Rob Ickes, "but he brought an attack that wasn't there before."

Gerald Calvin "Jerry" Douglas's father played Dobro in a bluegrass band with "West Virginians who came to OH to work in the steel mills," Douglas noted. "They were topnotch players, but they couldn't make a living doing it. Bluegrass wasn't popular, not the way it is now."

Dabbling on his father's Silvertone before his twelfth birthday, Warren, OH-born Douglas (1956-) picked up the instrument quickly. By thirteen, he was playing with his father's band. "I went off with the Country Gentlemen during the summer," he said, "but when I came back for school, I played with Dad's band. I had a good time but friends from school, and people I knew who had already graduated, found out I was a bluegrass musician

Jerry Douglas, 1991

and it wasn't the most popular thing. Everybody else was listening to rock and roll. Bluegrass and country music were uncool. I never told anybody I was a musician until I was on the road."

An avid radio listener, Douglas grew up "listening to Flatt & Scruggs in the morning and the Rolling Stones and Creedence Clearwater Revival at night," he said. "It all crept in and had an influence."

It would pay off. Playing three sessions a day, six days a week, Douglas became so busy doing studio work he stopped touring. "The things I brought to recordings," he said, "were exactly what Nashville wanted."

Fifteen years at this pace, however, took their toll. Douglas felt "burnt out" and feared that he was playing the same Dobro part he had played the day before. Alison Krauss put him back on the road. "She didn't play the kind of bluegrass I started with," he said, "but it's not healthy to stay the same. If we wanted to do a down-and-dirty bluegrass song, Dan Tyminski could deliver anything anyone could have wanted. The die-in-the-heart bluegrass fan, we had them in our quiver, too."

Douglas's Dobro powered the *O Brother, Where Art Thou?* soundtrack.

"We worked a full day with a lot of waiting," he said, "but we knew which songs we were going to play.

"We were too bluegrass for country radio and too country for bluegrass. *O Brother, Where Art Thou?* didn't get country-radio airplay but that CD sold ten million through word of mouth and good, honest music."

Douglas was a constant presence on the Nitty Gritty Dirt Band's *Will the Circle Be Unbroken II* and *III*. "We got to be in the same place," he said, "sitting in the same chair, every day. It was a treat to play with Mark O'Connor and Roy Huskey, Jr. I loved the first volume and was honored that the Dirt Band asked me to play on the second and third. I got to play with icons and up-and-coming people at the same time."

The Telluride Bluegrass Festival has been an annual destination since 1981. "That's a full-grown adult," said Douglas. "It's a beautiful, storybook-looking place at the end of a canyon. You have a waterfall [Bridal Veil Falls] coming from the snow melting at the top of the San Juan Mountains. You're at an elevation of 9,000 feet in a town that usually holds about 1,500 people but you're with 10,000 people. Everything is overrun but everybody is happy. It's humanity at its finest."

The Great Dobro Sessions (1994), which Douglas produced, featured ten Dobro players. "The first calls went to Brother Oswald and Josh Graves," he said. "They wrote the book and were the reasons we all played. The rest were players like Mike Auldridge, Stacy Phillips, Gene Wooten, and Tut Taylor. Rob Ickes was the youngest."

Douglas continues to honor the roots with Flatt & Scruggs tribute band the Earls of Leicester, but he keeps his "ear to the ground, listening to all kinds of music and getting influence from everything," he told me in 2016. "The latest version of the Jerry Douglas Band has horns, which leads to a Dixieland and jazz influence. It's not for every bluegrass fan and not meant to be. It's a showcase of what this group of musicians can do, the Dobro being the main thread."

Chapter 26

Walk the Way the Wind Blows

Arriving in the central NY city of Ithaca (about 250 miles from Manhattan) as a Cornell University graduate student, in 1971, Pete Wernick brought a link to the bluegrass world. A Scruggs-influenced banjo player, he had honed his craft in Washington Square Park and hosted what was, for seven years, the only bluegrass radio show in the Big Apple.

Wernick (1946-) discovered bluegrass around 1960. "Friends in the Bronx played folk music," he recalled, "and I wanted to join them. We had a banjo at home. My dad bought it at an auction and put it into playable condition. A friend showed me a few things. After a couple of weeks, I was able to play with friends. I learned to play rhythm and change chords. For my fifteenth birthday, a friend gave me a songbook."

Two months into playing banjo, Wernick saw Flatt & Scruggs at NY's Fashion Institute of Technology in January 1961. "The opening act was Joan Baez, who was nineteen," Wernick remembered. "She played with Flatt & Scruggs towards the end of the concert. I heard Scruggs talk as he was signing autographs after the show; that was a big deal for me. I had heard him on records and it seemed too good to be true that someone could play the banjo that well. I was bewitched, bothered, and bewildered."

Wernick saw Flatt & Scruggs again "at another auditorium and then at Carnegie Hall [on December 8, 1962]," he said. "The audience was much bigger." (*The Beverly Hillbillies* premiered September 26.)

Afterwards, Wernick tried imitating what Scruggs had been doing. "I had the Pete Seeger instruction book," he said, "but it was the edition before he included any teaching or tablature of Scruggs' style. I didn't even have the means of slowing down a record. I just messed around and tried to play. What helped me was that I had good ears. I could duplicate notes I heard. When he played 'Earl's Breakdown' or 'Shucking the Corn,' I could hear the chord progressions. I slowly pieced together the melody notes and figured out how to move my fingers. It was a puzzle but I was extremely determined."

By sixteen, Wernick was playing banjo in a folk trio. "It was mostly Pete Seeger-style," he said, "but whenever I could, I played three-finger. I graduated high school and my parents helped me buy my first good banjo, a Gibson Mastertone.

"Scruggs advertised a Vega so I figured that was what he was playing, but the first time I saw a Gibson Mastertone, at Manny's, it looked like Scruggs' banjo. It was $395 marked down to $345. That was way out of my price range. They let me try it. I hit one of the strings and as soon as I heard the sound, I said, 'This has to be what Scruggs is playing.' That was my breakthrough but it was still too expensive. I heard that Roger Sprung was selling the same banjo for $235. That became my heart's desire. The only banjo lessons I took came from Roger but I already knew what he showed me. My eight dollars an hour wasn't the best investment. I quit after two lessons."

Towards the end of his first year at Columbia University, Wernick discovered Washington Square Park. "I started going every Sunday," he remembered. "I'd watch great musicians assemble around the fountain and play. Eventually, I was able to join in. I started at the lower level but got to where I could fit in with some of the better players."

One Sunday, he jammed with some good musicians, and they offered him a ride. "Instead of taking me to the subway," he said, "they told me they were kidnapping me and taking me to be in their band—the Orange Mountain Boys. Hank Miller, the guitarist, who later became a psychologist, was a great flatpicker and banjo player and he played pedal steel. I learned a lot from him; we wrote a tune that later got on a record. Bob Applebaum was the mandolin player. He lives in L.A. now and plays jazz, but at the time, he was into bluegrass. We got gigs and played on the radio. I taught myself to sing baritone in three-part harmony. They wouldn't have asked me without that skill. We stayed together for a few years. It gave me a chance to work up solos. We played a couple of original instrumentals. I was acquainted with David Grisman; we played one of his tunes. We learned 'Cedar Hill' and wrote 'Orange Mountain Special.' Both got on my first album."

Wernick's life had changed in the fall of '63 when a fellow student suggested they start a bluegrass radio program. The range of the school's AM station was limited to its dorms, but Wernick thought it would give him a chance to learn more about bluegrass. The other student quit almost immediately. "I had to learn to talk on the microphone," said Wernick, "which was very scary, but I could get records from the bluegrass record companies. I built up a collection of albums. I studied them carefully and played them on the air. The following year, I moved to the FM station. It was a big deal. It reached the entire metropolitan area. There was a country music show on Saturday mornings and they put me on afterwards. Eventually, they expanded my show to two hours. I had that show for seven years."

Two people stepped up to mentor the young broadcaster. "I wasn't as knowledgeable as they wanted me to be," he said, "and I was eager to be mentored."

Those two people were David Grisman and Jody Stecher. "They were the stars of NY's bluegrass scene," said Wernick. "They made sure I knew the facts and, in Grisman's case, that I didn't just tolerate Monroe but understood him in a deeper way. I did an entire hour program with Monroe and the Blue Grass Boys in February 1966. They invited me to Ralph Rinzler's apartment, where they were staying during a weeklong run in NY. They didn't have a bass but they had all their other instruments. Grisman brought a portable tape recorder and recorded that program."

A month later, after Grisman joined the Kentuckians, Wernick hosted a performance by Red Allen. "I found out that morning they were coming to my show," he said. "It became a bootleg in Japan and came out on Grisman's Acoustic Disc. I bought a prewar Gibson banjo from Red's banjo player, Porter Church. That became my banjo for the next twenty-something years."

Wernick brought a tape recorder to Carlton Haney's first bluegrass festival in 1965 and interviewed Don Reno, Jimmy Martin, Ralph and Carter Stanley, and Mac Wiseman. "I could go up to any star of bluegrass," he said, "and they were happy to answer my questions. It meant exposure to them in NY. I was thrilled to be there. Looking back, it was when my life's path was set."

On Sunday afternoon, Haney presented *The Story of Bluegrass,* featuring Monroe and people who had played with him—Clyde Moody, Larry Richardson, Mac Wiseman, Carter Stanley, and Jimmy Martin. "They were reminiscing," said Wernick, "and I was being exposed to first-generation bluegrass. It was just too good to be true."

Few people attended that first festival but Haney "had deep pockets," said Wernick. "He was managing Conway Twitty. He had a second festival a year later, much to everybody's amazement. Carlton loved to talk. When the show was over at night, he'd hang around mainstage and expound on his ideas to anybody who would listen. I was always there to listen. He talked about microphones, presentation, and how a bluegrass festival should be built over time."

Wernick "couldn't go anywhere without finding people to play with," he said. "After my freshman year, I went to CA. My father was working on a math book at Stanford University. He was a mathematician. That was another watershed time. I played good enough to be in a decent bluegrass band. I met people from Palo Alto, one of whom was Jerry Garcia [a year before the Grateful Dead]. He had short hair and thought of himself as a bluegrass banjo player. He and I got a group together. He switched to mandolin so I could play banjo."

As a graduate student, Wernick "rented a room in the student union to be isolated from other people and practice," he said. "I got into guitar fingerpicking, which was quieter. I was trying to become a good enough singer so I could perform as a singer-songwriter."

Wernick met his future wife, and Country Cooking's lead vocalist, Nondi Leonard (Joan Wernick), during a road trip following the oral exams for his doctorate. "I had a Triumph Spitfire," he said, "and drove all over the country. I had a friend [Fred Weisz] in Boulder who was a bluegrass musician I knew from NY. I met Nondi through him. Fred and I continued West but I stayed in touch with Nondi. Before the summer was out, I drove back and we became a couple—August 1969. She came East when I resumed my studies. We got married a few years later in Ithaca. She wasn't a musician when we met but she was a very good singer. She became the lead singer in Country Cooking; we could harmonize. Years later, she picked up a guitar and started to play.

"When we arrived in Ithaca, I looked for a band to feature my singing and songwriting. Tony Trischka was a pedal-steel guitar player, as well as a banjo player, from Syracuse. Russ Barenberg wasn't playing acoustic guitar when we met. He was playing electric guitar in a blues band but he was willing to play country-style guitar. Our first gigs were at a country bar, Tweetman's Halfway House. We got on the stage with pedal steel and electric guitar. We did that for a while.

"Tony and I started working out twin banjo pieces for fun. We had enough that I approached Rounder. I knew Ken Irwin and Marian Leighton. They had been producing local concerts and they were catalysts in the old-time world. There wasn't anything like us in the bluegrass world."

Adding "some ringers," Country Cooking recorded its first album, *14 Bluegrass Instrumentals*—Rounder 006, the label's third release. "Rounder asked us to be Frank Wakefield's band," said Wernick. "We went to where Frank was, in a different part of NY State, and recorded. Nondi sang on Frank's record [*The Frank Wakefield Band*].

"We made one more record [*Barrel of Fun*] for Rounder, emboldened by the success of our first. Our mandolin player [Harry Gilmore] had been straight-ahead bluegrass but he was no longer around. We brought Andy Statman up from NY. He was quite a hippie, very adventurous musically."

Nancy Talbott was producing bluegrass concerts at Harvard University's Sanders Theatre. Country Cooking opened for the New Lost City Ramblers.

Scores of musicians "in their early twenties" were catching the bluegrass bug. "They weren't on the singing level of Monroe or the Stanley Brothers," said Wernick, "but good picking styles were being developed; that's what Country Cooking represented.

"Tony wrote a banjo tune at the last minute. It got on the first record but not the CD. By the second record, everybody was writing. Andy Statman and Kenny Kosek, one of our ringers, wrote a couple."

When Flying Fish Records started in 1974, Country Cooking switched to Bruce Kaplan's Chicago-based label. Trischka had departed for NY and the group recorded their last album with an altered lineup. "It was right before my wife and I decided to move to CO," said Wernick. "I was working in the international population program at Cornell and writing my doctoral thesis, which surveyed youngsters about the number of children they wanted when they grew up. In the midst of this, someone suggested I write a banjo book; I had been teaching banjo lessons. One of my friends had put out a clawhammer banjo book, so at someone's suggestion, I went to his publisher [Oak Publications] and proposed a bluegrass banjo book. They told me they had no need for such a book. Luckily, I persisted. I ended up with a contract for a banjo instruction book that sold incredibly well. It was the first book to unlock the style. Scruggs' book sold well but it was mostly transcriptions of what a brilliant player was doing. I learned from my students that it was over their heads but I was able to break it down. Within a few years, my book sold 100,000 copies. I was getting healthy royalty checks. They asked me to do another book, *Bluegrass Songbook*. I finished it as we were leaving Ithaca. I knew that, with the royalties, I didn't need to work."

Leaving his researcher job at Cornell, Wernick, and his wife, started looking for a place where "we would be for the rest of our lives," he explained. "We moved in 1976, the year I turned thirty. By the end of that year, we settled on this lovely homestead in Niwot [about thirty miles north of Denver]. Nondi grew up in a large family in Denver. We came to visit and the weather enthralled me. It was so much better than in Ithaca, a lot sunnier and less humid."

Initially concerned that there would be enough of a music scene, Wernick found a home at the Denver Folklore Center. More than an outlet for guitars and instruction books, it was a record store, bead shop, concert hall, and music school. "I knew I would meet musicians," said Wernick. "Tim O'Brien and Charles Sawtelle were already living in CO. Nick Forster had just moved there."

"I met someone from Boulder visiting friends," remembered Wheeling, WV-born O'Brien (1954-), "and we played some music together. He said,

Pete Wernick, 1987

'You ought to come to Boulder and play in our bluegrass band.' I was planning to spend the winter in Jackson Hole—I wanted to be a ski bum and play music—but it was a small community and it was hard to find people to play with. I started looking for other places and stopped in Boulder to see my friend. There was quite a scene, a lot more than in Jackson Hole. I moved the following September and got a job in a music store teaching lessons. I played in a band organized around people at the music store."

O'Brien's older siblings had introduced him to music. "When my ten-year-older brother came back from college," he recalled, "he had Ray Charles, Miles Davis, Peter, Paul and Mary, and Odetta records. On Joan Baez's record, there were a couple of tracks with the Greenbriar Boys. I heard bluegrass and it whet my appetite."

As a teen, O'Brien frequented broadcasts of WWVA's *Wheeling Jamboree.* "There was a house band," he remembered, "and regulars would play. On most shows, there'd be two or three headliners like Charlie Pride or Merle Haggard. It evolved into visiting artists with their bands. I'd pay $2.50 and get a balcony seat."

Seeing Doc Watson on TV was revelatory. "He was definitely eclectic," said O'Brien. "He gave me the roadmap to liking different music and still appealing to an audience that likes acoustic music and bluegrass."

From the age of twelve, O'Brien "played other people's guitars until I bought an electric guitar with paper-route money," he recalled. "I got a good acoustic guitar when I was fourteen."

Adding mandolin, fiddle, banjo, and bouzouki, O'Brien expanded his musical scope. "I became aware of the Peter, Paul and Mary," he said, "and the songs Dylan had written."

O'Brien recorded Dylan's "When I Paint My Masterpiece" with Del McCoury and a complete album of reinterpreted Dylan tunes, *Blonde on Red*. "My appreciation of Dylan grew gradually," he said. "Charles Sawtelle was a big fan. When *John Wesley Harding* came out, that's when I started listening closer. I was into the Beatles. 'Norwegian Wood' is a Dylan song that he didn't write. Dylan always had a new slant on things. He was a poet."

O'Brien wrote songs for the local Catholic church's folk mass when he was fifteen. "A parish priest and a woman big in the Catholic organization wrote plays," he said, "and I collaborated with them."

Dropping out after a year at Colby College, O'Brien took to the road. The first stop was Chicago. "I had an audition at Somebody Else's Troubles," he said, "and they gave me a night. I got a week at Earl of Old Town. I had a friend from Pittsburgh who had moved to Chicago and I stayed at his house. I thought of staying there, playing solo at the folk clubs. Steve Goodman came to a gig. When he had his second bout of leukemia, Hot Rize's first album came out. I sent a cassette to him in the hospital. He had us play 'Mama Don't Allow' with him at the 1980 Telluride Bluegrass Festival. I looked up to Steve. He was a great performer and songwriter. He gave me validation and told me I should keep at it."

Hooking up with the Ophelia String Band, O'Brien remained with the group for three years. "We played bluegrass and country grooves," he said, "but we mostly played swing music. We wanted to be like the Hot Club of France with vocals or Dan Hicks and His Hot Licks doing old songs. It was a good training ground."

Playing banjo through a phase shifter since 1978, Wernick spotlighted the technique on a solo album, *Dr. Banjo Steps Out*. "I had Tim sing 'Wichita Lineman,'" he said.

"Charles Sawtelle and I decided to start a band but it was going to be very informal and unambitious. We played every Tuesday night, for two years, at the Denver Folklore Center, for forty people or so. The three of us [Sawtelle, Wernick, and Warren Kennison] played with a few different bass players and guest artists. Laurie Lewis showed up with a fiddle and played with us. Tim and Nick played a variety of instruments with us."

Wernick invited O'Brien and guitarist Mike Scap to make a demo with him. When he heard it, Kaplan agreed to release a record on Flying Fish. "We started recording in Boulder," Wernick said.

Around the same time, a local label (Biscuit City) asked O'Brien to record an album. "Tim wasn't known as a singer yet," said Wernick, "but he had been the WY state fiddle champion and they wanted him to make an instrumental fiddle record. I suggested he include some vocals, so he made an album with fiddle tunes on one side and songs, bluegrass style, on the other. He asked Charles and me to be on that side of the record."

Hot Rize nearly fell apart before it started. "Tim eloped," recalled Wernick, "and moved to his wife's home in MN. I said, 'Tim, why don't you move back? We'll put a band together and promote our records.'"

Hot Rize took its name from the secret ingredient in Flatt & Scruggs sponsor Martha White's self-rising flour. "We weren't a bunch of hicks who didn't know anything about bluegrass," said Wernick. "We were deep into it, even if we didn't come from the Southeast."

Scap had returned to NJ but "I still wanted him in the band," said Wernick. "He agreed to come out as Hot Rize's first guitar player. Tim was going to be a lead singer for the first time. Charles played bass. An agent booked some gigs but I could do a better job than he was doing. I took over the agent work, which I had been doing with Country Cooking. I knew how to be persistent and find places that might book a bluegrass band. I got us a very full schedule; we worked every week. We bought a 1969 Cadillac, a nine-year-old car, and after renting U-Haul trailers to carry our sound system, we bought a trailer and painted it to match the Cadillac. That was our traveling rig for two years. Mike didn't like riding in a car. He quit three months in and we got Nick Forster. He had never played bass but we wanted Charles to play guitar."

Wernick had modest aspirations. "My goal was to bring in $100 for each member," he said. "If we got $400, I made it. Some gigs, we got $600 or more. We played for the governor's inaugural ball in 1979 and got a big paycheck. We started to work at hotel parties. They were horrible gigs but they paid bills. We played a festival in SC. We drove our Cadillac across the country, got paid $1,200 to play, and drove back. We came out ahead because gas prices were still low and we stayed in Motel 6s.

"We got very positive feedback. People told us that we had something special. Tim's singing broke through everybody's resistance. He had style and blues in his singing and very good pitch. As soon as people heard him, they wanted to hear more."

O'Brien lobbied for Hot Rize to play more than bluegrass. "Tim suggested

I get a Dobro," said Wernick, "but I saw a six-string lap-steel guitar and bought it instead. We played Jimmie Rodgers songs and it was easy to learn the yodeling lick on the steel guitar. I tuned it at first like a Dobro and then said, 'No, I'll give it more of a country sound.' I learned some Hank Williams chords; I loved the sound of the steel guitar on his records. Nick had an electric guitar and he would switch from bass. Charles would play bass. Now, we had this other configuration. We'd say, 'We're going to play some different-sounding stuff now.' For fun, we started calling it Red Knuckles and the Trailblazers. Tim was Red Knuckles. Charles said that he'd be Slade. I gave Nick the name Wendell Mercantile. He was always thinking of things we could sell. I said that I'd be Waldo Otto. I don't know where that came from. We took it lightheartedly; we were funny."

At the end of Hot Rize's third year (1980), Sawtelle (1946-99) suggested they change clothes when they switched to their alter ego. "We were into experimenting," recalled Wernick, "so we tried it. We had our own mythology, which I tell when the rest of the band goes off the stage and

Red Knuckles and Wendell Mercantile, 1987

I'm by myself. I describe how we discovered the Trailblazers in the border town of Wyoming, MO and how they play old music that nobody likes but they're one of the holdovers so let's give them a chance while Hot Rize relaxes backstage. We've always denied being them. Right now, by talking about it in detail, I'm breaking one of our rules."

"The audience ate it up," added O'Brien, "and we had fun. It was like Halloween. We were two people every night."

Radio interviews further established the Trailblazers' saga. "They asked questions," recalled Wernick, "like 'where's Red Knuckles from?' and 'how did they learn music?' We made stuff up and had to remember what we said."

Red Knuckles and the Trailblazers opened for Ernest Tubb without Hot Rize but "the audience didn't laugh," recalled Wernick. "We were just another band playing the same kind of music as Ernest Tubb. It intended to be zany but it was always good music."

Hot Rize continued to develop its own sound. "I was using the phase shifter sometimes," said Wernick. "I worried that people would be turned off by the electronic effect but people I trusted—Norman Blake, Pete Kuykendall, and [Jim & Jesse's fiddler] Joe Meadows—told me they liked it. That gave me the courage to use it sparingly. I wasn't trying to be the next Don Reno or Earl Scruggs; I had my own thing. I wasn't tempted to go in the newgrass direction. We had done that with Country Cooking but we had our own recipe."

"We tried to emulate the masters," added O'Brien, "but other things went into it. Red Knuckles and the Trailblazers were there so we made a decision to keep Hot Rize in the traditional bag as far as instrumentation and groove. New Grass Revival was a big inspiration to all of us. They could do rock and roll with bluegrass instruments but we didn't want to do that."

Reviews for Hot Rize's first record were sensational. "We were featured in the *Philadelphia Enquirer* and *Kansas City Star*," Wernick noted, "and I was able to put together a promotional sheet that said something like: 'Hot Rize is incredible, the best thing to hit bluegrass since sliced bread.' I got a call from Europe. The promoter wanted us to perform there. I asked how he knew about us. He said, 'I heard the record.' We did a three-week European tour. We were getting all kinds of validation before we got money. We were scraping by but we were busy."

Signing with the Keith Case Agency, Hot Rize toured nonstop. "Keith really pushed us," he said. "He was also booking New Grass Revival and John Hartford so we started doing shows with them. We got into the fraternity of top-level acts. There was a continuous buzz. When TNN [The Nashville Network] started, Keith had a connection and we got onto Ralph

Emery's show. We switched to Sugar Hill Records, who was eager to have us. When the Grammy Award added a category for 'Best Bluegrass Album,' they nominated our album, *Take Me Home* [it lost to Alison Krauss's *Every Time We Say Goodbye*]. Our songs were always on the bluegrass chart for airplay, often with the number-one song, and we noticed our songs played at parking-lot jam sessions. That defines success in bluegrass."

O'Brien's ultimate dream, however, wasn't Hot Rize. "He's a very broadminded musician," said Wernick. "He's played jazz and taken music lessons. He wanted a band with a drummer and a pedal-steel player. I thought, 'Okay, just keep playing bluegrass until that happens.'"

Wernick encouraged everyone to write. O'Brien took on that challenge. "The first tune wasn't special," said Wernick, "but the second song he wrote was 'Nellie Kane,' which became a bluegrass standard."

In 1984, O'Brien released a solo album, *Hard Year Blues*. "We participated on a cut or two," said Wernick, "but he liked being captain of his own ship and not just part of a democracy."

A year after the IBMA's founding in 1985, Wernick ran for its presidency. He won the annual election, as he would for the next fourteen years. "It was getting ridiculous," he said, "so they started term limits—three years—I already had fifteen. I took it very seriously to be part of the leadership of the bluegrass trade organization. I got to influence and be of service to the community I felt nurtured by."

O'Brien met country songstress Kathy Mattea at a festival, in Nashville. "She was just starting out," he remembered. "Our booking agent and her manager shared an office. The next time I was there, I got her CD. She did the same thing and we became fans of one another's music. We were on *Mountain Stage* together and got to collaborate on some songs. She was pitched some of my songs, and she liked them, but what tipped the balance was that I was from WV like her."

O'Brien's 1987 duet with Mattea, "The Battle Hymn of Love," by Paul Overstreet and Don Schlitz, broke into the top ten on *Billboard*'s Hot Country chart. Mattea covered O'Brien's "Walk the Way the Wind Blows" and "Untold Stories." "They were already hits in the bluegrass world," said Wernick, "but when she recorded them, they went to the top ten."

"All of a sudden, I was making all this money," remembered O'Brien. "I started writing more and trying to pitch them to other artists. It gave me independence financially but it broke up Hot Rize. I got a record deal with RCA that never came to fruition but I left Hot Rize to do it. I was ready."

"People were asking who the next stars were," recalled Wernick, "and Tim got on the list. Major labels were courting him. We knew it was going on and we didn't hold it against him. It would mean the end of the band but it would be a good opportunity for him. I remember being in Sanders Theatre in Cambridge. During our sound check, Tim got a phone call. He came back and said, 'RCA wants to sign me.' That night, after the gig, we had a bittersweet celebration."

Hot Rize agreed to have one final year together. "We timed it," said Wernick, "so that the first gig we played with Nick was on May 1, 1978, and the last gig was April 30, 1990. We completed exactly twelve years together."

On July 19, 1989, Hot Rize was booked to play at Winterhawk, not far from the summer home of Wernick's parents. "My family and I were heading East, a few days ahead, to visit my parents," he recalled. "The plane to Chicago was a DC-10 that made its last flight. A titanium fan inside one of its engines cracked. The explosion disabled the hydraulics controlling the flaps and rotor of the plane. We were seven miles in the air and the pilot had to figure out how to get us down safely. He did a legendary job. There was no way to slow the plane, going 200 miles an hour. It didn't quite line up with the runway. The plane tumbled over and broke into pieces. One hundred and twelve people died; 184 miraculously survived. The people who were unscathed, including my wife, my six-year-old son, and me, had been sitting in the center of the plane. We were able to get on another plane and continue our journey. We got to my

Hot Rize (Pete Wernick, Tim O'Brien, Nick Forster, Charles Sawtelle), 1987

parents' house without our possessions, totally stressed. The next day, I went to the festival and played with Hot Rize. My heart and soul were right there. I wrote a song later, 'You Never Know (A Day in '89).'"

O'Brien launched his career as a country music star but RCA withdrew his album before it came out. "They paid for the very best musicians," explained Wernick, "over a hundred grand, and then said, 'You don't have any hits on this album; you have to record more songs.' Tim recorded four more songs and they still didn't think it had hits. Then, they dropped him. He had to get untangled from RCA, pay back some of what they advanced."

O'Brien rerecorded the tracks and released *Odd Man In* on Sugar Hill. "It was a better record," said Wernick. "He used people he knew. Relationships between musicians are more important, sometimes, to the final product than the innate skills of the musicians. It has more cohesion and meaning. The soul can emerge."

The opening track, "Fell in Love and Can't Get Out," should have been a hit. "If I had been on RCA," said O'Brien, "they might have released it as a single."

The Seldom Scene covered "Like I Used to Do," and New Grass Revival recorded "Hold to a Dream." "You stick your neck out writing songs and singing them for people," said O'Brien. "The ultimate feedback is when someone records your song."

Hot Rize considered replacing O'Brien. "Some top-level musicians suggested themselves as replacements," said Wernick, "but when Nick decided to be in Tim's band, the O'Boys, it killed any idea of continuing."

Hot Rize "never quit playing, but we took a break from being full-time," explained O'Brien. "Up until that point, it had been the four of us against the world. We were aiming at the same thing, but it changed."

O'Brien recorded three albums with his sister, Mollie—*Take Me Back* (1988), *Remember Me* (1992), and *Away Out on the Mountain* (1994). "Mollie's a cabaret singer," he said, "and can sing anything. It was a way for me to stretch out. We aimed in the Skaggs and Rice direction. Nick played all the instrumental parts. Mollie and I sang."

Three months after Hot Rize disbanded, Red Knuckles and the Trailblazers made a surprise festival appearance. "The next year, Hot Rize accepted a few gigs and continued to play several each year," recalled Wernick. "In 1996, we actually toured."

Sawtelle contracted leukemia, and his "condition at first wasn't bad," said Wernick. "He still looked and sounded like himself. Nick serendipitously recorded the last two nights of the tour at the Boulder Theater. It came out on a record [*So Long of a Journey*]. It was mostly live versions of songs we recorded in the studio but it crackled with excitement. We designated Charles to mix the multi-tracks but nobody could find the tapes. Charles had died. We tried doing detective work, trying to figure out where he might have left them. A year later, they surfaced. They were at Nick's house the whole time. The record didn't come out until 2002. We thought it was Grammy material but it wasn't eligible. Five years had passed since we recorded it."

After the album's release, the surviving Hot Rize members "decided it would be good to get another guitar player," Wernick said, "and play some gigs."

Leaving Ricky Skaggs' band after three years, in 2000, Asheville, NC-raised guitarist Bryan Sutton (1973-) became a highly demanded session player. No stranger to Hot Rize's music, "his father had our tapes in his car," said Wernick. "Bryan met us when he was a teenager and had his picture taken with Tim. He knew our songs and was amazingly quick to learn. He fit right in. He's continued winning awards and bringing us respect for having him."

Sutton and Hot Rize played together for a decade before recording *When I'm Free* in 2013. After its release, "we had our biggest year," said Wernick. "We wanted to make a statement that Hot Rize wasn't just a band that made records in the eighties; we were a twenty-first-century band."

O'Brien dedicated *Chicken and the Egg* (1997) and original songs "Not Afraid of Dyin'" and "Letter in the Mail" to his father, who died at ninety-six. The album also included "The Sun Jumped Up," for which O'Brien supplied music for lyrics by Woody Guthrie. "Woody's daughter Nora has been working for years on getting Woody's catalogue out," he said, "and she offered me a few lyrics. I saw one tune and immediately thought that it had to go with this old melody. I overlaid it and it worked. Woody was writing to old songs, the way Dylan did. I know many songs that have that melody."

On his 2015 album, *Pompadour*, O'Brien performed a Guthrie song with music by Billy Bragg, "Go Down to the Water."

Thirteen years after collaborating on *Real Time* (2000), O'Brien and London, KY-born Darrell Scott returned to the studio. Sitting face to face, they recorded a Grammy-nominated follow-up, *Memories and Moments* (2013). "Before I moved to Nashville in 1996," explained O'Brien, "I'd go to co-write songs. Darrell was one of the people suggested to me. I met him in the basement of a publishing company. He played a song for me and I realized that he was a monstrous singer and player. We wrote a song that day that we both liked. We kept writing more. He was playing with Sam Bush but he was ready to transition out of that. I had him play on

When No One's Around [1997]. I was getting ready to make a trip to the United Kingdom and Ireland and asked if he wanted to go along. He could play a set and we could collaborate on a few tunes after mine. After the first gig, we realized we should play together the whole night."

Joining Steve Earle's Bluegrass Dukes, with Scott, in 2003, O'Brien signed on as a sideman for Mark Knopfler seven years later. He would assume the Curly Seckler role in Jerry Douglas's Flatt & Scruggs tribute band, the Earls of Leicester, in 2013. "It's exciting music," he said. "It's a great thing that Jerry is doing because it puts that sound in front of people. They get to see it live and hear it with modern technology."

When he appeared at *The New Yorker's* Conversations Festival in 2005, Steve Martin brought banjo players including Scruggs and Wernick. Producers of *The David Letterman Show* saw the advance publicity and invited the group, dubbed Men with Banjos Who Know How to Use Them, to appear on the show. "We got together early to rehearse 'Foggy Mountain Breakdown,'" remembered Wernick. "The show was seen by 5,000,000 viewers and the video has gotten 8,000,000 YouTube hits. That's the biggest exposure I've had to a large audience."

Wernick played on two tunes ("Pretty Flowers" and "Words Unspoken") on Martin's Grammy-winning album, *The Crow: New Songs for the 5-String Banjo*. "It was quite an experience," he said, "watching him develop to where he's making everybody proud and doing great things for bluegrass."

The name of Wernick's Live Five "sounded like we were people in straw hats and bowties playing Dixieland, so I took to calling us 'Flexigrass,'" he explained. "I wanted to keep the basic feel of bluegrass but I've always wanted to experiment. I imagined playing with a vibraphone and a clarinet. I heard great players of these instruments sounding like bluegrass soloists. Earl Scruggs was a Pete Fountain fan. I got the best Dixieland clarinet player [Joe Lukasik] and the best vibraphone player [George Weber] I could find.

"Our music intrigued people, and Sugar Hill agreed to an album [*Up All Night*]. Some people loved what we were doing but others thought it an affront to bluegrass. I sent the CD to bluegrass DJs, hoping they'd play it, and they'd say, 'This isn't bluegrass.' I tried to book the band at bluegrass festivals but they'd tell me to try a jazz festival. When I called jazz festivals, they'd say, 'This isn't jazz; it's bluegrass.' Luckily, there were places like MerleFest that booked us in all our ambiguity. We played a festival in Ireland. I made my bluegrass statement as much as I could, through Hot Rize, and now I was back to being Mr. Experimental."

Wernick and his wife have performed as Pete & Joan since 1990. "We played the first Russian bluegrass festival in 2010," he said, "and we've played in Israel, Hawaii, and Ireland. We were on *Good Morning Denmark* in 2015."

As a music-camp instructor/director, Wernick regularly "did three weeks of banjo camps and then do jam camps," he told me in 2016. "I canceled the banjo camps because banjo players need to jam. I couldn't be everywhere so I started teaching people to teach jamming the way I taught it. The first year was 2010. Within a year, we had Wernick Method teachers in different parts of the country. We're up to seventy active teachers; more than five thousand people have attended classes."

O'Brien stepped out with two solo albums in 2005. In the liner notes of *Cornbread Nation,* he explained, "I borrowed lyrics . . . and changed melodies to suit my mood, and put some drums and electric guitars with them. The great purveyors of folk music always put their own stamp on things."[1]

The Grammy-winning *Fiddler's Green* "is best described," O'Brien said, "as the happy land/heaven imagined by sailors where there is perpetual mirth, a fiddle that never stops playing and dancers that never tire."[2]

O'Brien continues to explore America's music through his ongoing Internet series, *Short Order Sessions.* "It doesn't have to be part of a bigger project like an album," he said. "It doesn't need artwork or publicity. It keeps me in the studio making new tracks. I value the freedom and spontaneity. It ranges from folksongs on a single guitar and Irish tunes on fiddle or mandolin to rock-band kind of things."

On his twenty-first solo album, *Where the River Meets the Road* (2017), O'Brien reflected on the history and people of his birthplace. Kathy Mattea and Mark Howard harmonized with O'Brien on Bill Withers' "Grandma's Hands." Mollie O'Brien sang with her brother on "Guardian Angel," an original song reflecting on childhood memories of losing their six-year-old sister. Hazel Dickens' "Few Old Memories" featured O'Brien's partner, Jan Fabricius, and Sutton's guitar playing. Fabricius also sang on A. P. Carter's "Little Annie (When the Springtime Comes Again)." The title track recalled O'Brien's great-grandfather who emigrated from county Cavan, Ireland in 1851. "There was already a paved road going from Baltimore to Wheeling," said O'Brien, "and a river trade up the Mississippi all the way to Pittsburgh. I know details from family lore. He raised twelve children. His father-in-law was a blacksmith from Donegal. He met my great-grandmother in church. He was a straight shooter and made something of himself. He worked for the B&O Railroad as a clerk and later for the post office. He was a customs agent for the Wheeling court. He started a savings and loan business for Irish immigrants. He was a big shot in the community."

Anticipating its fortieth anniversary in 2018, Hot Rize "will be doing

Tim O'Brien, 2017

some special things, like making a new recording," promised O'Brien. Charles is no longer with us but we try to do justice to his memory, keeping the old repertoire alive and expanding it—keeping the vibe that Hot Rize had going."

Chapter 27

World Turning

Tony Trischka played with Dylan tribute band Early Roman Kings in 2016. "My wife and I are big Dylan fans," said the Syracuse, NY-born banjo innovator. "It was his seventy-fifth birthday year and we wanted to honor him. My son, Sean, played drums. We had Stash Wyslouch, a wonderful guitar player and singer from Boston, and a bass player, Jared Engels. Stash is amazing. He's coming out of punk but he's discovered bluegrass. He has very high energy and sings Dylan very naturally, which is not easy to do."

Early Roman Kings enabled Trischka to play pedal steel for the first time in thirty-five years. "I decided to get it out of mothballs," he said, "and reacquaint myself with it. The banjo wouldn't have been as effective on slower songs and tunes with electric guitar and drums. With a pedal steel, you could make a note ring forever compared to the banjo's ping."

Trischka (1949-) started playing banjo in 1963. "The Kingston Trio had a song ['M.T.A.'] about the Boston subway system," he remembered, "and Dave Guard took a banjo solo that was kind of bluegrass-style picking. Those sixteen notes got me so excited I had to play the banjo. I badgered my parents until they bought me a longneck banjo like Dave Guard had. I was already fingerpicking on guitar; it was a relatively easy transition."

A suggestion to "check out Earl Scruggs" became life changing. "That was it," recalled Trischka. "I was gone. I couldn't yet put words to it; it was just the excitement and the speed. I have so much more of an understanding now of what he was doing. The tone—it sounded so good—precision, and timing grabbed me."

Trischka's passion for the banjo confused him. "Here I was," he said, "the son of a physics professor, and I had fallen in love with Southern music."

Trischka wasn't alone. Banjo player and college student Hal Glatzer had "a band that practiced two blocks from where I grew up," he said. "I took lessons from him. He unlocked the secrets of Scruggs-style picking, as well as the melodic style. I was desperate to learn the banjo. I had been working with Pete Seeger's book but couldn't quite get the hang of it. Hal gave me one lesson and all the notes were in my fingers."

Glatzer introduced Trischka to guitarist Harry Gilmore and mandolinist Joel Diamond, who were also college students. "Wes hooked up and put a band together," he said. "We got a bass player who played washtub [Greg Johnson] and called ourselves the Down City Ramblers. We existed from 1963 or '64, under a couple of names, until the early seventies, playing mostly locally."

Bill Keith's playing made a profound impact. "Other people played the melodic style before him," Trischka said, "but no one took it as far. Suddenly, everybody was hearing this revolutionary way of playing the banjo. It was a comfortable way to play. You didn't have to practice for years."

Trischka's path intersected with Wernick's in 1971. "David Bromberg came to Ithaca to play with the Fabulous Torpedoes, who were actually just his bass player," he recalled. "Pete knew Bromberg from NY so he came to the show. That's where we met. We started talking. It turned out that he had a group, Country Cooking. He said, 'Why don't you play with us?' When he played banjo, I'd play guitar. Sometimes, I'd play pedal steel. Guitarist Russ Barenberg was in the band.

"Pete knew Ken Irwin. One day, he told him, 'I've got this band Country Cooking. Would you like to record us?' Kenny Kosek came up from NY to play fiddle."

New Grass Revival started around the same time. "They certainly had a youthful aspect," said Trischka, "but Country Cooking brought an edgy, Northeastern quality to the music, especially on our second album [*Barrel of Fun*]. Some tunes were out there harmonically. We had piano on some tunes and added Andy Statman on mandolin. He could play like Bill Monroe, but Middle Eastern music influenced him more than traditional bluegrass. I was stretching out and taking bluegrass in a slightly different direction. We experimented as a natural outgrowth of who we were. It was the late sixties and all kinds of revolutionary action were going on. The country was going through upheaval and musicians were trying new things.

"I remember hearing the Beatles' 'Strawberry Fields Forever' for the first time and practically falling over. It was the most beautiful thing I had ever heard. It's still my favorite piece of music. I listened to bootlegs of the Beach Boys' *Smile* and the more experimental things that Brian Wilson was doing, along with Frank Zappa and Jimi Hendrix. I got into jazz fusion—Miles Davis, Weather Report, Return to Forever, and the Mahavishnu Orchestra. Not to take anything away from bluegrass, which to this day is at the root of everything I do, and is beautiful in its three or four chords, but we wanted to make our own way with those instruments."

Entering the banjo contest at Carlton Haney's bluegrass festival, in Fincastle, VA, in 1965, Trischka played "Nine Pound Hammer" in an eastern Mediterranean mode. "Don't ask me why," he said. "Considering that one of the judges was Ralph Stanley, I didn't have a chance to win, but I tried all kinds of wacky things. Salvador Dali was an influence, too. I was into surrealism. It got me thinking differently. Taking people to a place that was unexpected appealed to me."

Trischka took his cues from Peter Rowan, Bill Keith, Richard Greene, and David Grisman. "They were the generation of urban, hip players, just barely before our generation," he said. "Grisman gave Andy Statman mandolin lessons. I met Peter in 1964 at the Syracuse Folk Festival. He backed me up in the banjo contest. Richard was stretching the boundaries of bluegrass fiddling. He was using amazing double-stops, almost a classical technique, while still being totally bluegrass. I saw Monroe's band with Peter and Richard on a number of occasions. It was exciting."

At the second Fincastle Festival, Rowan and Greene participated in a duet workshop. "I remember them doing 'Rain and Snow,'" said Trischka. "It was a totally mystical tune. The way they played was so American and so dark at the same time. I got to have dinner with them when they played in Rochester."

Between shows with Country Cooking, Trischka played with guitarist/ vocalist Danny Weiss in a "sports rock" band, Country Granola. "It was a silly novelty band," he remembered. "We did absurd parodies like 'I Am a Lineman for the Giants.' Danny and Greg Root [ex-Down City Ramblers] ended up in the Monroe Doctrine. The banjo player had to leave and they needed a replacement. They had another banjo player but he couldn't join them for two months so I joined until he could. We played around the Midwest. Our bass player, Mark Hembree, wound up with Monroe for a couple of years."

In the midst of recording the first Country Cooking album, Wernick asked Trischka to write some tunes. Trischka had written a few songs that he sent to Bill Keith and offered Wernick one of them, "Theme from Godzilla." He also penned a new tune, "Hollywood Rhumba." "It was nothing great," he said, "but it opened the floodgate for writing tunes. Pete mentioned to Rounder that I had been writing and suggested they put a solo album out by me. They agreed. My first solo album was *Bluegrass Light*. I had Pete on a couple of tunes—double banjos."

On their bus ride back to NY after playing on the second Country Cooking album, Kosek and Statman agreed to put a band (Breakfast Special) together. "They wanted me to play with them," said Trischka, "so I moved to NY in January 1973. I used those musicians on my album—

Andy, Kenny, Dobro player Stacy Phillips, guitarist Jim Toles, and bassist Roger Mason. We added saxophone and drums."

Trischka appeared in *The Robber Bridegroom*, a bluegrass musical based on a Eudora Welty novella set in Mississippi in the late 1700s. Along with some other members of Breakfast Special, he played not in the orchestra pit but onstage. "We started in L.A. for a few months in early 1978," he said, "and then went to Broadway for five months. It was a steady paycheck. I bought my father a color television and stashed money away. It was great—eight shows a week for seven months."

Tony Trischka & Skyline came together in late 1979. "We were at a loose end," recalled Trischka, "Danny, Barry Mitterhoff, and me. Danny and Barry had a newspaper route together. A friend of Barry's mother ran an organization [Project Impact] that brought music to schools in northern NJ. She suggested that we do a bluegrass show. We'd get up at some ungodly hour and do an 8:00 A.M. assembly. It was the three of us and various bass players. Kenny Kosek sometimes joined us. Dede Wyland was playing in Gas, Food & Lodging but she wanted to leave the Midwest. We got her involved and that was the beginning of Skyline. We started getting gigs. It took off from there; we did it for the next nine years.

"We came up with unusual arrangements. We once spent five hours rehearsing one tune. Bass player Larry Cohen was the brains behind Skyline. He's a great arranger. He has an amazing ear and an orchestral approach to string-band music."

"We were out to use bluegrass instruments," Mitterhoff told *Mandolin Café*, "and a fair amount of bluegrass vocabulary, but just stretch it with a lot of improvisation . . . sections in the songs that had been orchestrated within an inch of their lives . . . taking some classical pieces, and making bluegrass out of them."[1]

Trischka & Skyline's shows climaxed with "I Can't Believe," which ran for ten minutes or longer. "We did it at the Winfield, KS Flatpicking Championship Festival," remembered Trischka, "with Alison Krauss and Mark O'Connor."

One of Skyline's last recordings was "The *Wizard of Oz* Medley," on Mitterhoff's solo album, *Silk City* (1992). "We had Rachel Kalem [who replaced Wyland in 1987] on keyboards," said Trischka. "She was just going to fill in on some gigs but we stayed together and did one more album [*Fire of Grace*, 1990]."

Trischka's solo *Hill Country* (1985) featured original instrumentals with the exception of Bobby Osborne's "Sunny Days." "I tried to write bluegrass banjo tunes," he said, "real straight-ahead. I put together a great band with Sam Bush, Tony Rice, and Jerry Douglas. Béla produced it."

Tony Trischka, 1992

Two decades later, Trischka spoke with Ken Irwin about a follow-up. The Rounder Records co-owner suggested a double-banjo album. Comprised of duets with Earl Scruggs, Béla Fleck, Steve Martin, Bill Emerson, Noam Pikelny, Tom Adams, and Alison Brown, *Double Banjo Bluegrass Spectacular* (2007) was the IBMA's "Recorded Event of the Year" and "Instrumental Album of the Year." Trischka also scored a "Banjo Player of the Year" award. "If someone had told me in 1964 that Earl Scruggs would play on my album," he said, "I'd have told them they were dreaming. It was a thrill of a lifetime. I sat knee to knee with him as we worked on 'Farewell Blues,' which he recorded in 1951. He was eighty-two but he still produced a big sound; he hit his banjo heavily. It doesn't get better than that tone and that sound. My life would have been different without that man. I wouldn't be married to the woman I'm married to; I wouldn't have the kids I've got."

Having met Steve Martin in 1974, when Breakfast Special opened for him in NY, Trischka "thought it would be fun to do a track or two together, so I arranged to meet him at his apartment and record," he said. "He was enthusiastic about the banjo. We played tunes he had written—'The Crow' and 'Plunkin' Rag.' He was so cooperative, no star trip; one of the most humble and generous people I've met."

Trischka produced Martin's second banjo album, *Rare Bird Alert* (2011). "He and the Steep Canyon Rangers almost didn't need a producer," he said. "They were already playing those tunes. Steve's an ace banjo player. He can play 'Shuckin' the Corn' and 'Foggy Mountain Breakdown' but feels that other people do that. He wrote all the tunes on the album. He's constantly evolving and coming up with new things. He played 'Drop Thumb Medley' on *Comedy Is Not Pretty!* [1979] and some banjo tunes on *The Steve Martin Brothers* [1981]. Some of those tunes ended up on *The Crow: New Songs for the 5-String Banjo* [2009]. He kept writing more tunes afterwards and Edie Brickell put lyrics to them. I hadn't spoken to him for a few months and they had a whole album worth of tunes [*Love Has Come for You* (2013)].

"The most important part of *Rare Bird Alert* was getting Sir Paul McCartney to sing on 'Best Love.' We went to Long Island to record him. He was in his flip-flops and shorts, having come straight from the beach. He was totally relaxed and made jokes. He sang for about a half an hour and said, 'Can I do some more?'"

Three-fourths of *Territory* (2008), including duets with Pete Seeger, Mike Seeger, Bill Evans, Bill Keith, and Bruce Molsky, were leftovers from *Double Banjo Bluegrass Spectacular*. Pete Seeger appeared on nine tracks. "My mother went to the Little Red Schoolhouse in Greenwich Village with the woman who became Pete's wife, Toshi," said Trischka, "and I grew up listening to his records with the Almanac Singers and the Weavers. I wrote him a letter, when I was thirteen, telling him that he was the greatest banjo player who ever lived. I addressed it to Beacon, NY and it got to him. Two weeks later, he wrote back a postcard that said, 'I'm glad you like my music but music isn't a horse race; there's no such thing as best.' I still have that postcard.

"You didn't have a conversation with Pete; he would just hold forth. He never repeated stories. In his eighties, he was still talking about new things. After I discovered Earl Scruggs, he seemed a little square, but years later, I went, 'What a dimwit I am. Pete is still the best banjo player who ever lived.'"

Trischka's first banjo student in 1970, Susie Monick, went on to play with the Buffalo Gals. "She wanted lessons," Trischka remembered, "but I told her that I didn't teach. She said that was all right, she wouldn't pay me. That made sense."

Soon afterwards, Trischka got a call from a sixteen-year-old banjo player who wanted lessons. "This kid showed up at my apartment," recalled

Trischka, "and he could play. It was Béla Fleck. He grew up on Seventy-Eighth Street and Riverside Drive. I was in the Bronx, not far away. I started giving him lessons. My first album had already come out and he wanted to learn the tunes. I showed him whatever he wanted to know and we jammed on traditional tunes like 'Little Maggie.' We'd play for three or four hours, improvising, and taking break after break. We'd record it and he'd come back the next week, having memorized every single note, and play it back at me. After a while, it was obvious that he didn't need lessons from me anymore. He moved to Boston and started taking lessons with saxophone/clarinet player Billy Novick, who showed him modal and jazz things, and he started playing in Tasty Licks, his first professional group. He wrote everything out in tablature. No one else did that."

After Wernick finished writing his second book, *Bluegrass Songbook*, "he was burned out and suggested that I write the book he was supposed to write," said Trischka. "I ended up writing *Melodic Banjo*, focusing on Bill Keith and others. I've written fourteen banjo instruction books since. I've done things for Happy Traum's Homespun Tapes and I've conducted workshops. I teach at the Berklee College of Music in Boston three times

Béla Fleck and Tony Trischka, 1991

a semester. Artist Works of Napa, CA approached me about doing a banjo school. I went to Napa for four days and filmed 150 lessons."

Trischka made his debut as a lyricist on his fourteenth solo album, *World Turning*, in 1993. Each subsequent album has included at least one song with words. "On *Great Big World*, I wrote about Wild Bill Hickok," Trischka said. "I took Jimmie Rodgers' blue yodel and wrote about a riverboat gambler from the 1850s. Then, I wrote about Union spies hijacking a Confederate train, taking down telegraph lines. I thought this theme could be an entire album. I conceived a story about a woman in Ireland whose husband dies in a mine cave-in in Australia. She comes to the United States, leaving her children behind until establishing herself during the Civil War. I recorded Maura O'Connell as the woman from Ireland. She knocked it out of the ballpark."

Introduced to nineteenth-century minstrel banjo playing at the TN Banjo Institute in 1990, Trischka "bought an instruction book from 1855 and got into the history of the banjo," he said. "I'm not a Civil War buff, but that timeframe is inspiring, even though it was so horrible. Doing research, I discovered that, in 1938, veteran soldiers got together in Gettysburg. Former Union and former Confederate soldiers shook hands over the stone fence they fought over in 1863. I wrote a song about that."

Aspiring to "write an entire album in a single day," Trischka had his son locate a bed and breakfast in CT. "I went there and spent the night," he told me in 2016. "I woke at five in the morning and wrote until midnight. I ended up with twelve songs. I'm thinking of making it my next album, my latest challenge."

Chapter 28

New Grass

Recognizing Bowling Green as "the birthplace of newgrass," KY's House of Representatives passed Resolution HJR 154 on March 30, 2010. In their proclamation, they described newgrass as "(1) instrumentation that frequently includes electric instruments, drums, piano, and other instruments; (2) imported songs of imitated styles from other genres such as jazz, the blues, and rock and roll; (3) nontraditional chord progressions; and (4) lengthy 'jam band' style improvisation."[1]

The proclamation cited Charles Samuel "Sam" Bush (1952-) as "The Father of Newgrass." "To play newgrass," Bush explained to me, "you've got to know bluegrass. Flatt, Scruggs, Benny Martin, and Monroe created the springboard for us. Carlton Haney used to talk to me about it. He liked New Grass Revival; he was always supportive of new bands. He'd say, 'Monroe is bluegrass, the Stanley Brothers are mountain grass, the Osbornes and Don Reno are country grass, and Jimmy Martin is good-and-country grass. You boys are folk grass. There's room for all of it.'

"Flatt & Scruggs didn't call their music bluegrass. That was Monroe's music. Jim & Jesse, the Osborne Brothers, the Dillards, and the Country Gentlemen learned from the master. They created their own style but they knew the rules (even though there are none written down). When youngsters like us came along in the sixties, we learned from people who departed from bluegrass but whose roots were solid. That's one of the reasons the bluegrass establishment accepted New Grass Revival. They knew we respected bluegrass and loved it. We could play it but we were trying to create our own sound."

Raised on a remote, 330-acre tobacco farm with hogs, cows, and beef cattle, Bush grew up listening to the *Grand Ole Opry* and watching Flatt & Scruggs' TV show. His grandfather played old-time banjo and fiddle. His father, Charlie, played fiddle. "My dad liked bluegrass," he said, "but his favorite musicians were Roy Acuff and Hank Williams. He was a big fan of Hawkshaw Hawkins, Cowboy Copas, and Patsy Cline. I remember when

Sam Bush, 2009

he told me, 'My three favorite musicians died today in a plane crash.'"

A rhythm guitar player, Bush's mother, Henrietta, "liked Dean Martin and Perry Como," he recalled "We didn't buy many records. They were few and far between in a poor farming household, but the ones we bought were country-music records. We listened to records by Tommy Jackson, the great *Grand Ole Opry* fiddler. A lot of the way country fiddlers play comes from how he played on Ray Price and Hank Williams records. He made square-dance records—*Popular Square Dance Music*—*Without Calls* [1953], *Square Dance Tonight* [1957], and *Do-Si-Do* [1959]—and my father bought them, each album with five 78-RPM records, ten sides of music. There was a mandolin player playing with Tommy, and the sound of the fiddle and the mandolin together struck a chord in me. My parents got me a Gibson mandolin when I was eleven. The love of that instrument led me into bluegrass."

His father climbed "to the top of the roof to adjust the antenna so we could watch the *Grand Ole Opry*," Bush recalled. "I saw Bill Monroe, Jesse

McReynolds, and Bobby Osborne. I was a quick study but it wasn't until I could see their hands that it made sense. Now, we have teaching videos; I've made some for Homespun Tapes."

Two of Bush's four sisters, Janet and Clara, who played guitar and sang, started a folk duo. "My sisters had to take me," he said, "or they couldn't go. They started singing in a New Christy Minstrels-type band so I made sure I had the mandolin parts down."

By his teens, Bush was playing sessions in Nashville. One of them was with Ray Edenton, rhythm guitarist on Tommy Jackson's records. "I got to talk to him," said Bush, "and I asked, 'Who played the mandolin?' He told me 'Hank Garland [who usually played electric guitar].' I said, 'I didn't know he played mandolin.' He said, 'He didn't but he was such a great musician that, when Tommy wanted a mandolin, he did it.' I grew up copying a mandolin player who didn't really play mandolin. That's why he played differently. Tommy Jackson taught him the tunes right before they recorded them."

The cover of Doc Watson's first album caught Bush's attention. "I had been playing with a blind guitarist," he said, "and their hands worked the same way; he even liked to be led like Doc. Years later, I went on the road with Doc. Merle and T. Michael Coleman were happy for me to lead him. It gave them a break. For me, it was an honored position."

Bush's father took him to the *Grand Ole Opry,* in 1964 or '65, courtesy of former Hank Williams fiddler Jerry Rivers. "Jerry and my dad became friends," remembered Bush. "He got us backstage at the Ryman Auditorium, where I met someone with whom I've been friends since—Peter Rowan. He remembered me the next time I saw him."

Before heading to the Ryman, Bush and his father stopped at the Roy Acuff Museum and Exhibition Hall. Taking admission was Bashful Brother Oswald. "He and my dad hit it off," remembered Bush, "and my dad told him I was a fiddle player. Oswald went and got a fiddle. I played a tune. Oswald got on the phone, called Mr. Acuff, and said, 'Roy, we got a boy who could fiddle. You'd better get on down here.' Mr. Acuff was there within the hour. There I was, playing for the king of country music. It was incredibly intimidating."

Bush continued making regular trips to the *Opry.* "Mr. Acuff owned buildings on Broadway," he recalled. "You'd go out the back door of the Ryman, across an alley, and through a door into a garage. That was his dressing room. Between *Opry* shows, he ran jam sessions. He had one of the greatest fiddlers ever—Howdy Forrester. I was scared to death when he handed me his fiddle and told me to play. I started playing and he stopped me. My body must have been very withdrawn. He said, 'Son, when you play, stand up straight, and act as though you mean it. Be proud.'"

On Labor Day weekend 1965, thirteen-year-old Bush and his music teacher (Wayne Stewart) drove all night to Carlton Haney's festival. When they arrived around 10:00 A.M., there were already jam sessions all over the place. "I read about it in *Sing Out!*" Bush remembered. "I begged my parents to let me go. I went the next year too. They were totally life-changing experiences. I saw Jim & Jesse, Bill Monroe, Clyde Moody, Larry Richardson, Doc Watson, and the Stanley Brothers."

At the festival, Bush "got into a jam with my Gibson A-50 mandolin," he remembered. "I had always wanted to play an F-5. I'd ask people if I could play theirs and they'd say no. All of a sudden, someone handed me a beautiful mandolin, a 1923 Lloyd Loar, and I heard a voice say, 'Play a good one.' That was David Grisman."

Jimmy Martin's performance with Bill Emerson was "just majestic," recalled Bush. "They kicked off with 'My Walking Shoes (Don't Fit Me Anymore),' but right before he sang, Jimmy reared back and spit an incredible wad of chewing gum about twenty rows into the audience. I said, 'Wow! This is for me. This is classy.'"

Bush attended his first mandolin workshop. On the stage were Monroe, Grisman, Ronnie Reno, and Jesse McReynolds. The following year, Bush watched mandolinists Bobby Osborne and John Duffey. "When I do a workshop," he said, "it's not about showing off. It's about teaching and hoping people learn from me the way I learned, sitting there, watching them."

Lonard "Lonnie" Peerce (1923-96) was a distant relative of Bush's mother, whose maiden name was Pierce (Lonnie's father changed the spelling). Garbed in "matching cowboy boots and fiddles," Peerce and Bud Merideth appeared regularly on Bowling Green TV. "Lonnie took an interest in me," said Bush. "Someone sent him a tape of Benny Thomasson, so he turned me on to Texas fiddling. The first times I went to the National Fiddling Championships, in Weiser, ID, I went with Lonnie and Bud. They exposed me to that world of fiddle contests." Bush placed fifth in 1966 and was junior division winner in 1967, '68, and '69.

Bush remembers his ten-year-older sister, Mary Ann, listening to the Everly Brothers, but he "didn't pay attention to rock and roll before the mid-sixties." He said, "I bought *Rubber Soul* and connected with 'I've Just Seen a Face'; I could relate to the Beatles for the first time. I was reading a British magazine this morning that called 'I've Just Seen a Face' 'bluegrass without a banjo.'"

Playing bass and electric guitar in high-school rock bands, Bush became "a big fan of the Jefferson Airplane, especially Jorma Kaukonen's guitar playing and Jack Casady's bass playing," he said. "The Airplane, the Beatles, and Cream—that was it for me. I tried to copy Jorma and Eric Clapton. I started listening to a lot of rock and roll. It permeated into the music that I love and try to play."

Bush met Alan Munde at a fiddle contest. "He was playing Texas-style rhythm guitar for Byron Berline's father, Lue," Bush recalled. "Courtney Johnson had already met him at a folk festival and told us, 'This boy is the best banjo picker I've heard in my life.' Alan wound up moving to Hopkinsville, KY, where Wayne [Taylor] lived, and the three of us started working on fiddle tunes. No one played them on banjo like Alan. We made an instrumental album, *Poor Richard's Almanac,* during Easter weekend 1969, trying to wed Texas fiddle tunes and bluegrass. One record company sent us a letter. They didn't believe we really played it. They thought we taped a record and sent it to them. It ended up coming out, in 1976, on American Heritage, the label that put out the Bluegrass Alliance records."

The Bluegrass Alliance called their second album *New Grass* (1970). "I wasn't there yet," said Bush. "The first person I heard using the phrase 'newgrass' was Walter Hensley, a banjo picker from Baltimore who did a record, *Pickin on New Grass,* in 1969." The title was a spoof of Kenny Price's country song 'Walking on New Grass.'

Bush was working at a Holiday Inn when Peerce and bass player Ebo Walker invited him to join the Bluegrass Alliance. Dan Crary was leaving and they needed a guitar player. He didn't hesitate to accept. "Hell, yeah!" he said. "Get out of being a busboy, I'll do it.'"

Few guitarists could flatpick like Kansas City, KS-born Crary (1939-). Possessing a Ph.D. in speech communications, Crary taught at Cal State Fullerton. "He brought lead guitar to the forefront of bluegrass," said Bush. "Nobody played with his authority and drive. He played like a banjo player. He came from the world of classical guitar and had all kinds of influences."

As Crary's replacement, Bush faced a considerable challenge; he had only been playing guitar for a couple of months. Mandolinist Danny Jones was leaving but the Bluegrass Alliance already had a replacement, Bob Hoban. "I had to learn Dan's stuff on guitar," said Bush. "When I was in high school, I had gone to his studio to put Texas-style fiddle tunes, played on the mandolin, on tape."

At a Reidsville, NC festival, Bush "saw the world's skinniest man, sitting on a Martin case, playing a brand new D-45 and sounding like Clarence White," he remembered." I introduced myself. It was Tony Rice. He knew me as a mandolin player. We started talking and I said, 'Come into the band and play guitar; I'll move back to mandolin.' Unfortunately, it pushed Bob Hoban out of the group."

Bush learned that "someone doesn't invite anyone to join a band without discussing it with the other members, but within three days, Tony was in

Louisville playing with us," he said. "He learned some of Dan's parts but he didn't play that way. The style of the guitar changed tremendously within that band."

An outgrowth of the Bluegrass Alliance (without Peerce), New Grass Revival "was two different groups," said Bush. "The first nine years with Courtney Johnson and Curtis Burch, we may have been a little closer as brothers than the second nine years."

"I saw their tour with John Hartford," remembered Danny Barnes. "You can't imagine the impact they had. Nothing like it existed before."

Inspired by Paul McCartney's bass playing, John Cowan brought a thunderous drive to New Grass Revival in 1974. "I was their third bassist," he said. "They had Ebo Walker and then Butch Robins, the banjo player who introduced them to Leon Russell. They had a drummer when I joined. The next day, they fired him."

Minerva, OH-born Cowan (1953-) had no prior background in bluegrass. "It wasn't on my radar," he said. "I was playing whatever was on the radio, which fortunately was Buck Owens, the Beatles, Ray Charles, Charlie Rich, the Beach Boys, Eric Clapton, Aretha Franklin, Motown, Stevie Wonder, and Jimi Hendrix. I heard John Coltrane and Miles Davis. I was obsessed with the Allman Brothers Band, particularly Gregg's voice. Once I saw the Beatles, like millions of people, I wanted to be a musician."

Cowan's singing was as dynamic as his bass playing. "My dad sang in church," he said, "and with a barbershop quartet. Singing was something I was always doing."

By the time he graduated from Louisville High School in 1971, Cowan had been playing with local bands, including Everyday People and the Louisville Sound Department, for five years. He enrolled at the University of Southern IN but "college was a joke," he said. "I moved back to Louisville and started a band with guys I had gone to high school with. I brought two guys with me from Evansville."

Cowan was working at a carwash and playing with a local band when his telephone rang. It was Sam Bush. "We had a mutual friend from Bowling Green," Cowan remembered, "living in Louisville. When Butch decided to leave and New Grass Revival started asking around about bass players, Sam heard about me. He asked me to come to where they were living—Mammoth Cave—in western KY. I drove down with my bass and auditioned. They hired me. I didn't sing that day. They hired me on my bass-playing abilities."

After retrieving his possessions, Cowan moved in with banjo player Courtney Johnson and his wife, Hazel. "We practiced every day for five or six hours for weeks," he said. "Sam was an Allman Brothers fan and he had Gregg's solo album. It had Jackson Browne's 'These Days.' He had never played it but he was up for it. I said, 'Can I try singing it?'"

Cowan would also sing lead on the classic Bill Monroe tune "Good Woman's Love," on New Grass Revival's second album, *Fly Through the Country* (1975). Over the next decade and a half, he claimed possession of the Staple Singers' "You Don't Knock," John Hall's "Reach," and Dennis Linde's "Callin' Baton Rouge" (New Grass Revival's only top-forty hit). "Sam says when I joined the band, he was the lead singer," Cowan remembered, "but once he heard me, he said, 'I guess I'm not the lead singer anymore.'

"That isn't exactly what happened," he continued. "I was never 'the' lead singer; we shared those duties. I put a lot of work into it."

The collaboration was mutually beneficial. "Sam grew up playing fiddle and mandolin," said Cowan, "but he was also an electric guitarist and he loved rock and roll. I turned him on to Little Feat. He turned me on to all this amazing roots music."

New Grass Revival became Leon Russell's band in 1976. "Leon was one of the few musicians who could jump into the timing of bluegrass," said Bush. "He loved that we didn't have a trap drummer. We had Ambrose Campbell from Nigeria tapping on beaded gourds. We had an extra mandolin player [Bill Kenner] so we always had a mandolin chop. Leon talked to us about the excitement of the Pentecostal Church, how the music got faster and faster. It taught me about audiences. The frenzy Leon would drive them into was like a church service."

An "absolute, diehard devotee," Cowan "discovered Leon in my teens," he said. "I bought his records and went to see *The Concert for Bangladesh* and *Mad Dogs & Englishmen*. I had so much admiration for him that I had the hardest time being around him."

Performing for Russell's audiences was challenging. "We would play forty-five minutes as the New Grass Revival," recalled Cowan. "There'd be a short break and the four of us would come back out as his core band. At the first show, in Houston, we started to play and people shouted, 'Leon, Leon.' The next shows, he got on a mic backstage and said, 'Hey, everybody, it's Leon. I just want to tell you that my good friends, New Grass Revival, are going to play some songs and I want you to give them a warm welcome. They're a bunch of great musicians, and they're going to be playing with me later, so see you in a while.'"

New Grass Revival's two and a half months with Russell came when the Tulsa-born superstar was at his peak. "We were playing for 25,000 people a night," said Bush. "It was rock and roll hysteria; there were people in hotel hallways waiting for Leon. The first night, we were supposed to be playing on the football field at the University of FL in Gainesville. Right before we were to go on, my legs were shaking. We had a little talk among ourselves—'we can do it.' It started raining and raining, then thunder and lightning. They had to call off the show. The next night was in Tampa. We went through the same freak-out."

Traveling on Russell's plane, New Grass Revival experienced royal treatment. "When the downbeat hits," said Bush, "all audiences are equal. The day after the tour ended, we went back to work at Arnie's Pizza King, in Lafayette, IN, playing six nights a week."

A studio album with Russell (*Rhythm & Bluegrass: Hank Wilson, Vol. 4*) didn't come out until 2001. "When Leon presented it to Warner Brothers," said Bush, "they didn't want him doing, in his words, 'hillbilly music' and turned it down. Leon shoved the live record down their throats; he owned the production company. I just saw a video of John, Leon, and me singing 'Amazing Grace'; it was chilling. When Leon was in good form, we were a fifties rock band with bluegrass instruments."

New Grass Revival headlined the second Telluride Bluegrass Festival in 1975. "The promoters [the Fall Creek Band] heard us at Winfield, KS," said Bush. "We were the first band they brought in. Courtney didn't want to go. We had the gig booked and he said, 'I'm not going for one gig.' I said, 'Yeah, we are.' 'No, I'm not.' We had a standoff and couldn't speak for three days. Finally, Courtney called and said, 'Is there a way we could resolve this?' I said, 'We've got to go; we're contracted.' Well, we went and had the time of our lives. Nobody had more fun than Courtney did. It may have been the altitude of the wide-open space but [the audience] was open to anything. We started telling our friends, like Bryan Bowers, Peter Rowan, and John Hartford, and before you knew it, they started coming. Telluride became a club that we went to every year. I still get to go."

New Grass Revival performed for over one hundred thousand people at Stompin 76, near Galax, VA, in August 1976. "We were scared," remembered Bush. "We had to follow Bonnie Raitt."

Three years later, New Grass Revival was opening for and backing up John Hartford in Tulsa. Their repertoire included Hartford's "Vamp in the Middle," "Boogie," "Steam Powered Aereo Plane," and "Skipping in the Mississippi Dew." "We were always doing crazy things," said Cowan, "like covering Leon Russell, Jerry Lee Lewis, Marvin Gaye, and Bob Marley."

Driving by the club with a friend, Leon Russell saw the marquee and remarked, "New Grass Revival, God, I haven't seen them in years. I wonder how they are."

"We were sound checking," remembered Bush, "when in walks Leon. He played with us that night. After the gig, we jammed all night at someone's house. We started recording soon after that and became his group for two years. We got worse at playing our own music but great at playing his. It was hard work but it was surely rewarding."

Johnson and Burch left at the end of the two years. Bush and Cowan stayed with Russell for two months before regrouping with Béla Fleck and Pat Flynn. "It went to a different level musically," said Cowan, "and we had more visibility. I was stunned when I first heard Béla, like everybody else. He had already made his first solo album [*Crossing the Tracks*]. Sam was more familiar with him because he played on Béla's album."

"Courtney was a groundbreaking banjo player," explained Bush, "unlike anyone else, but once Béla joined, it established that there were progressive musicians in this group."

"It made me dig in as a bass player," remembered Cowan. "Béla brought in tunes with odd time signatures. It transcended where we had been."

"We were the best there could be," said Fleck. "We'd show up at a festival on a Saturday night and be loud, intense, and a lot of fun. Our sound emanated from Sam's mandolin chop and rhythmic intensity. He found his match with John. When they got Pat and me, they added fire. We created such a tight grid, everything could sit on top of it—not only the solos but also the singing. It was spectacular."

Named by his classical-music enthusiast father, Béla Anton Leoš Fleck (1958-) was two years old when his parents split. "I didn't meet my father until I was in my forties," he said, "but my stepfather, who came on the scene when I was seven, was a classical cellist. His string quartet got together every Sunday to play Brahms and Mozart. I'd try to read the manuscripts as they played but I usually fell asleep. It never seemed my thing but it got into my system, whether I knew it or not. When I picked up the banjo, I did things other banjo players didn't because it was in my consciousness."

Taking to the banjo with conviction, Fleck "saw it as a cause to fight for the banjo's honor," he said. "I wanted to prove that it was as good as any other instrument and could do anything. Some of what I do is bluegrass and some isn't. People are doing a wonderful job playing bluegrass banjo, which I love to do, but trying to be different and find my own voice, I've found myself interested in other kinds of music as well. When I'm playing jazz with Chick Corea, Stanley Clarke, or Jean-Luc Ponty, I bring bluegrass with me. When I'm playing Indian music with Zakir Hussain, I'm bringing the same. When I write for banjo and orchestra, bluegrass seeps into it. It's who I am."

Fleck's mentor, Tony Trischka, "was doing things on the banjo no one else did," he recalled. "To me, he was a superhero but I got to play with him at parties. I'd only been playing for two and a half years. We recorded *Fiddle Tunes for Banjo* with Bill Keith in 1981. Russ Barenberg, Andy Statman, and Sam Bush played on it. People said, 'I can't tell which one is which,' when it came to Tony and me. I was hungry to learn fast but I realized there already was a Tony Trischka and he was damn good at it. I needed to stop sounding like him and find my own path."

Opposition to bluegrass's evolution disturbed Fleck. "There used to be letters in *Bluegrass Unlimited*," he recalled, "trashing Tony and people doing new things with bluegrass. I didn't want to be a Yankee banjo player. I wanted to go down South and be where people learned things that made them Southern banjo players. I knew there was an emphasis on tone and drive. It was different from what I was learning in NY so I moved to Lexington, KY in 1982 and got under J. D. Crowe's influence. I never took a lesson from him but I'd go and listen to him every night I was touring with my band, Spectrum, with Mark Schatz, Glen Lawson, and Jimmy Gaudreau. Glen and Jimmy had played with J. D. Crowe. I was hoping some of it would rub off on me and I could learn to be a Southern banjo player. Some of it did. Listening to so much of it, I learned about getting a good sound out of the banjo and what drive was. Bluegrass feels like it's leaning forward and speeding up, like it's a train moving fast, but it never quite does. I'll never be J. D. Crowe or Earl Scruggs, in terms of having that sound and drive, but studying it made me a much better banjo player and much better at being myself. I started doing modern things but I did them with a lot more authority and power."

Fleck raised eyebrows when he compared bluegrass singing to "cats being slaughtered." "I got a lot of flak for that," he said, "but my point was that it was jarring for a New York City kid to hear. I had no problem thinking that the banjo was cool but I wasn't so sure about Bill Monroe, the Stanley Brothers, or Jimmy Martin in the beginning. As I got used to it, it sounded so good. It was like drinking coffee when you're a kid. You taste it and spit it out; it tastes so bitter. Years later, it's one of your favorite flavors. That was bluegrass singing to me."

Hearing Pat Enright, around 1978, made all the difference. Reminiscent of Jimmie Rodgers, Jimmy Martin, and Hank Williams, Enright's singing stopped the banjo player in his tracks. "All of a sudden, I got bluegrass," he remembered. "I had never been in a room with somebody singing the old-time traditional sound so powerfully and honest. From then on, I saw bluegrass in a different light. I moved to Boston and joined Pat's band, Tasty Licks (Mark Schatz played bass). We stayed together until 1981."

"Béla could play whatever came to his mind," remembered Enright, "but he hadn't played much bluegrass. He hadn't heard Earl Scruggs. I gave him a cassette of Flatt & Scruggs."

Following the death of his songwriting partner, Steven Brines, in 1983, Bush stopped writing. "I wanted to concentrate on being in the band," he said. "I was the leader but that just meant I was the one who talked to the booking agents and managers."

"Steve didn't just write love songs with simple lines," said Cowan. "He was a good storyteller. When you combined his words with Sam's musical ideas, you got great things."

New Grass Revival inked a three-album deal with Capitol Records in 1985. "[Label president] Jim Foglesong's wife heard us in Nashville," explained Bush, "and told him about us. He came to hear us and said, 'I want you on Capitol. It's your job to play, our job to sell it.'"

Without Bush and Brines' input, New Grass Revival sought material from alternate sources. Pat Flynn wrote four tunes on the band's first Capitol album and six on their second, *Hold to a Dream*. "Pat was a powerful songwriter," Cowan recalled, "but he rarely sang himself."

New Grass Revival struggled to break into mainstream country music. "When you sign with a major label," Cowan explained, "and they want to put you on country radio, you have a responsibility to try to fit in. We did as much as we could, without losing our minds and our integrity, but we were built for art and to have the music and the audience on its own terms, even if that meant cult status, which is what we were."

"There was a public perception that Capitol tried to change us," said Bush, "but we had Garth Fundis, who produced our last album on Sugar Hill, *On the Boulevard* [1984]. Capitol didn't hear our records—*New Grass Revival* [1986], *Hold to a Dream* [1987], and *Friday Night in America* [1989]—until we turned them in already mixed. We were in the top-forty country market but we were trying to crack it without changing much."

"The door was open to us," added Fleck, "but it was frustrating to me. If we recorded a country song, John sang lead and Sam played mandolin but my role was diminishing. People told us that the banjo would keep our records off the radio. Country music was trying not to have a hillbilly element. I started having a recurring nightmare about having a huge hit with a song on which I didn't play banjo and we had to play it for the rest of our lives."

Fleck would play on number-one hits by the Oak Ridge Boys, the Gatlin

Brothers, and Ricky Skaggs featuring the banjo "loud and proud." "Now, people think the banjo is cool," he told me in 2016. "Playing on Dave Matthews' records helped. When I go to colleges, kids are curious and respectful. Twenty years ago, there'd be a lot of 'yee-hawing' and derogatory remarks. I didn't enjoy that."

Participating in Marlboro's 1988 Country Music Tour, New Grass Revival opened for country-music superstars including George Strait and Alabama. "We were getting paid to play for larger audiences," said Bush. "Marlboro sent John and me to media school. Those were logical shows. New Grass Revival had been the longest-running opening band. We opened for Cheech and Chong. Their fans come to heckle them. What do you think they do to a band with a banjo? People threw stuff at us, but after those terrifying shows with Leon, almost nothing could scare us."

"It wasn't the best place for us," recalled Fleck. "I joined New Grass Revival because it was modern, contemporary, and rhythmically powerful. I wanted to be around musicians who challenged me."

"Béla wasn't having it," said Cowan. "He wanted to play bebop and do what he's done, be on the cutting edge. As we tried to get to the center, that's when we lost him."

Fleck formed a jazz group in Nashville but "didn't have people doing things as unique as what I was doing," he said.

New Grass Revival's final album, *Friday Night in America* (1989), their most commercially successful, included three songs by Flynn—"Lila," "Do What You Gotta Do," and the title track, written with Russell Smith—and Fleck's "Big Foot." The album and the band concluded with the Beatles' "I'm Down."

After the breakup, Cowan signed a solo contract with Atlantic. "They sent me to write songs with a lot of people," he remembered. "I made demos but they dropped me before I got to make a record."

Cowan and Bush toured together for a summer. Afterwards, Bush "came to me and said, 'I want this to be my band. Would you be in it?'" recalled Cowan. "I didn't have anything else going on so I said, 'Okay,' but it was problematic. You can't go from being someone's partner to his employee. That's asking for trouble; it didn't work."

Releasing a six-track EP of classic R&B tunes (*Soul'd Out*) in 1986, Cowan added two tracks when Sugar Hill reissued it four years later. "It was me doing music I grew up with," he said, "Wilson Pickett, Otis Redding. After it came out, Michael Bolton covered 'When a Man Loves a Woman' and had a huge hit. I was ahead of the curve."

Hooking up with Rusty Young (Poco), Bill Lloyd (Foster and Lloyd), and Pat Simmons (the Doobie Brothers), in 1988, Cowan formed Four

Béla Fleck, 2005

Wheel Drive. Changing their name to the Sky Kings, they toured until 1996. The first of two albums (*Out of the Blue*) didn't come out until a year after the group disbanded, but through Simmons, Cowan connected with the Doobie Brothers. "I played with them in the early nineties," he said, "and I've been back since 2010. I played their songs in college; it's not a stretch aesthetically."

Wendy Waldman produced Cowan's first two solo albums. His self-titled debut (2000) included Merle Travis's "Dark as a Dungeon" and a jazz-newgrass instrumental ("Sligo") written with Darrell Scott, among ten original tunes. Cowan reflected on the loss of his father on *Always Take Me Back* (2002). Banjo player Noam Pikelny appeared on *New Tattoo* (2006). The seasonal *Comfort & Joy* and *8,745 Feet: Live at Telluride* followed three years later. "I don't mind being a solo artist," Cowan said, "but I grew up playing team sports—baseball and football—all the way through grade school, middle school, and high school and I love collaboration."

A sterling lineup joined Cowan to record *Sixty* (2014). "It was an overview of my whole life," he explained. "It was so wide musically—from a Marty Robbins song to a Fleet Foxes tune—but that's who I am. We didn't start with making [a historic album] in mind. I had been interviewing musicians, at Doobie Brothers guitarist/producer John McFee's studio, for an XM radio show for two years. Eventually, I asked Chris Hillman and Jim Messina to record with me. I started thinking of who else would sound good and thought of Rodney Crowell, Bernie Leadon, John McFee, Bonnie Bramlett, Ray Benson, Huey Lewis, Alison Krauss, John Jorgenson, and Leon Russell."

Cowan has recorded with Delbert McClinton, Rodney Crowell, and Steve Earle. He's been playing with a husband and wife duo from Avery County, NC, Darin and Brooke Aldridge. "Darin plays mandolin and guitar," he said, "and Brooke sings like an angel and plays guitar. We travel with a quintet when I'm not doing the Doobies and do New Grass tunes. They grew up with that music."

In 1986, Bush and Fleck played with Jerry Douglas, Mark O'Connor, and bassist Edgar Meyer at Nashville's Summer Nights festival. They regrouped the following June at Telluride. "We wanted to call the band 'Telluride,'" recalled Bush, "but there was another group that already owned the name. For a tremendous fee, they offered to let us use it. We said, 'Nope.' We were going to call our record *Strength in Numbers*. We just reversed it."

"At first, we played each other's tunes," remembered Douglas, "but after we recorded *Strength in Numbers* [(1989], we started writing together and really became a band."

"It could have been just a hot-licks jam," added Bush, "but I'm proud of our compositions and the way we played together as a chamber-music ensemble."

Fleck's telephone rang in early 1987. Bassist Victor Wooten "had seen a New Grass Revival video and saw things I was doing with my right hand, using open strings and melodic tricks, that he was interested in learning on the bass," Fleck recalled. "I said, 'Sure, come on over.' We had a two-hour jam that was so much fun. He was on my radar from then on. Victor and I were two wacky musicians doing things on our instruments that were unique. When I met his brother [Roy 'Futureman' Wooten], who plays the self-invented, guitar-shaped Drumitar which electronically replicates a drum set, and [pianist/harmonica player] Howard Levy, I had four people who were so good that amazing things could happen and did. I didn't want to leave the top acoustic-music band for an esoteric art band that lasted for only six months. I wanted to keep the Flecktones together for a long time.

"I knew we were awesome musically but I didn't expect people to like us so much. Instead of 'they don't fit our format,' it was 'let's have them back for a bigger show, let's get them on TV, and let's have them open for Take 6 at Carnegie Hall.'

"Sometimes, I felt guilty. I was leaving bluegrass and doing better outside of it. People in the bluegrass world said, 'He's playing rock and roll; he's not part of our fight anymore.'"

Levy left the Flecktones after three years. "It was the first crisis of leadership," remembered Fleck. "We pared down to a trio. That helped Victor, Futureman, and me become better musicians. We had to cover all that territory without a soloist or piano player. After a few years, we were ready for something new. Paul McCandless spent a year with us; Sam Bush came out for a year. Then, we found Jeff Coffin. He's such a phenomenal musician. He ended up staying for fifteen years. We were going to take some time off and regroup. During the hiatus, he got called to join Dave Matthews."

Surviving testicular cancer in 1982, Bush contracted prostate cancer in 2007. "The first meant chemotherapy and surgeries," he said. "The second time, I knew more about dealing with it. I'm one of many people who have gone through it."

Bush's second solo album, *Late as Usual* (1985), was his first with his touring group. "I've been fortunate to play with the same musicians for years," he told me in 2016. "Drummer Chris Brown has been with me for fifteen years, banjo player Scott Vestal for twelve, and guitarist Stephen Mojo for eight. I love playing with them; they're my favorite musicians."

Bush toured with Emmylou Harris and the Nash Ramblers from 1989 to 1994, restoring his passion for music. "I had gone into a bit of responsibility overload in New Grass Revival," he said. "When we broke up, I had no plan other than to stop traveling. Then, Emmylou called and asked if I'd be interested in starting an acoustic band with her. I said, 'No, but I'll play in yours. I can't be responsible for anything right now.' She's the best bandleader I've ever met, a very generous person. I just showed up and played. I was proud of the album we did at the Ryman after it closed. It won a "Best Country Vocal" Grammy. There were holes in the ceiling and the floor but the room was definitely part of the sound."

Bush co-wrote all the songs on *Storyman* (2016). "Transcendental Meditation Blues," written with Jeff Black, "sounds like an old New Grass Revival song," said Bush. "I talked to a lot of people about writing 'Handmics Killed Country Music' with me. The only one who said yes was Emmylou Harris. I went to her house and we had it done in three hours. I knew it was a country shuffle and should involve pianist Pig Robbins. I called and left him a message. Within twenty minutes, he called back and said, 'Country shuffle—I haven't played one of them in twenty years.' He helped guide us in the rhythm. I overdubbed triple fiddle harmonies."

Bush wrote "Bowling Green" in twenty minutes with longtime family friend Jon Randall. "Carcinoma Blues," written with Guy Clark, "is about the patient and the loved ones watching," explained Bush. "There's no light way to look at cancer. A few weeks before Guy passed, I told him I was going to record it but that it might make people twinge. He looked up and said, 'Tough.'"

Bush wrote "Lefty's Song" with Brines in the early seventies. "Steven had a knack for meeting people, hearing their stories, and writing them down," he recalled. "Lefty Clark was a newspaper reporter he knew when he was young. I lost the tape and couldn't find it until 2014. I sent it to Alison Krauss and asked if she'd consider singing on it. She put the capper on it."

Reassembling the Flecktones in 2011, Fleck reunited with Howard Levy. "He does things on the harmonica," he said, "that no one has done before. He was the perfect choice."

Fleck continues to carve his own niche. "I try to be myself," he said, "and not copy anyone, but, inevitably, I do. If you're a banjo player, your fervent prayer is for someone to tell you that you sound like Earl Scruggs or J. D. Crowe. I'm a combination of both of them and Tony Trischka, who's a completely different kind of player, with a different roll, a different bounce. Scruggs did a great job setting the world on fire, but my chances of sounding like him are limited. I decided, early on, to be Béla Fleck and no one else. Everything I do is acoustic, playing with orchestras or with Edgar Meyer. Playing duos with Chick Corea is acoustic."

Collaborating with his Evanston, IL-born wife, Abigail Washburn (1977-), is "the closest I come back to bluegrass and the traditional banjo sound," said Fleck. "It's wonderful to revisit the scene I left with the Flecktones. Abigail plays clawhammer and I play three-finger style. It takes thought and creativity to define our roles. The fact that she's also a great singer certainly helps. She's comfortable being the rhythmic foundation while I'm more of the soloist. Then, she sings her heart out. I haven't supported a vocalist since New Grass Revival."

"I know what makes bluegrass special," said Washburn, who married Fleck in 2009, "but I'm not a member of that streak that started with Monroe. Béla and I were up for a Grammy, in 2015, but not in the bluegrass or Americana categories. Our blend of his more-bluegrass style and my old-time-based picking and original songwriting fit the folk music category. I'm glad about that. I believe in preserving what was originally amazing about bluegrass, but modern times seep in."

Washburn's "brother was into hard-rock guitar," and she sang in the school choir, but she "chose a path towards becoming a lawyer and going to China," she said. "I was learning to speak Chinese. I visited China three times for six months or more by the time I was twenty-one."

Washburn's college boyfriend played bluegrass. "I sold shirts at their shows," she recalled, "but it was his thing. China was my thing. I discovered old-time music because I loved China so dearly and wanted to love America with the same passion. I wasn't in touch with my own culture yet I was exploring this other country intensely. It came to me, one day, when I was in my apartment with my boyfriend. He put on a record of Doc Watson playing 'Shady Grove.' I heard something in it that Béla calls 'the ancient tone.' I heard America, what came before America, and something eternal. Chinese culture is at least a thousand years old. When I heard this music, I knew I came from a country with an old soul too."

Before heading to law school in Beijing, Washburn "bought a banjo and planned a big road trip," she remembered. "I was going to be sitting behind a desk for the rest of my life. Now was the time to do crazy things. I went to the Center for Buddhist Studies, in Barre, VT, and meditated for a week. I went to NY, toured the city, and saw things I had always wanted to see. I drove through the Blue Ridge Mountains and the Poconos. I went to WV to study banjo music. I wanted to bring a banjo to accompany myself on songs for my Chinese friends. 'Hey, check this out. It's very special and it's American. It's Africa, it's Ireland, and it's Scotland—all these things coming together. It's a deep, ancient place.'"

Washburn spent five days at the Augusta Heritage Center in Elkins, WV. "It was an amazing experience," she said. "People thought I sounded wonderful when I played my banjo, people who came from the traditions, from the mountains. I couldn't understand why they would respect the sound I was making. Yet, I found the channel for me to be passionate about American culture. Nothing was holding me back. I was so proud."

Black gospel music helped shape Washburn's playing. "I listened to it through my childhood," she said, "not because of my parents, but I saw movies and got the soundtracks. That led me to Mahalia Jackson and Aretha Franklin. All that happened when I was in high school, before I went to China. I sang in a college gospel choir and the same spirit was there when I started singing mountain music. I wasn't afraid of putting my whole self into it. Old-timers loved it. I thought, 'Maybe I should keep doing this.'"

Washburn's final stop was Nashville, where her boyfriend had moved to play music. "I planned to visit," she said, "but music intervened and I stayed."

Attending the IBMA Convention, in Louisville, Washburn slept in her truck. "I didn't buy a ticket," she recalled. "I just hung out in the hallways. One night, I met a woman [Megan Gregory] who said, 'Let's jam.' I said, 'I only know four or five songs,' but she said, 'I don't care; let's play those.' That's the spirit of bluegrass. People are so welcoming. If you want to play, play. I sat down and started playing. She sang the harmony parts when I played. When she sang, I didn't play. I just sang with her. After twenty-five minutes, we had an audience of thirty-five people. I felt heat in my belly and my armpits were sweating. An A&R person from Sugar Hill said to Megan and me, 'I'd love to have you play for our label president. He's down the hall; come with me.' They offered us a demo deal a week later."

Dreams of stardom faded when Gregory returned to college and joined her boyfriend's band. "It was for the best," said Washburn, "even though it was sad; we still love one another."

Washburn also met Katherine "KC" Groves at the IBMA conference. "We jammed in the hallway," she remembered. "She called a couple of weeks later and asked if I'd play a wedding with her. Again, I said, 'I only know eight or nine songs.' She said, 'That's fine.'"

Within a few months, Washburn was touring with Groves' band, Uncle Earl. "They were my training ground," she said. "I learned almost everything I know about old-time music from KC, Kristin Andreassen, Rayna Gellert, and the many people we met along the way. We enjoyed ourselves immensely. We were about joy and fun, tender moments. Our chemistry was unique."

John Paul Jones produced Uncle Earl's second album, *Waterloo, Tennessee,* in 2007. "He has daughters," said Washburn, "and he knows how to be around women our age."

Meeting the ex-Led Zeppelin bassist at MerleFest, "Rayna connected with him," explained Washburn. "Mountain music was new to him but he was in love with the mandolin. We were starting our second record and said, 'Wouldn't it be wacky if he produced it?' Rayna reached out to him. He had been to a record store in London. My solo record [*Song of the Traveling Daughter*] had just come out. The shop owner gave him my CD and said, 'You've got to hear this; it's really special.' His wife was so supportive. They put us up in their house when we played in London and he played shows with us. If Uncle Earl makes another record, we want him to produce it."

A variety of forces pulled Uncle Earl apart. "All of us had other things we wanted to do," explained Washburn. "I was the first to say, 'I can't do everything. Let me try this other stuff; keep going as Uncle Earl without me.'

"Rayna was part of the purist old-time scene and there was demand for her too. She started seeing herself as a songwriter. Kristin was touring with Sometymes Why and had to plan around Uncle Earl. They were getting more traction. She's also released two solo records—*Kiss Me Hello* [2007] and *Gondolier* [2015]. KC's involved in a variety of projects. I was playing with the Sparrow Quartet and I had a mission to share what I love about China with Americans and what I love about America with the Chinese."

Reunions of Uncle Earl have been "some of the happiest times I can imagine having on this earth," Washburn said. "They were a band before me, and I wanted them to be a band after me, but there was magic with the four of us. The energy was immense."

Washburn was in the midst of "entertaining the idea of the demo deal with Sugar Hill and starting with Uncle Earl" when her boyfriend suggested they go to a square dance. Béla Fleck would be playing. "I really didn't know Béla," she said. "When I was in college, he played. I remember hearing about it but I went to see a Peruvian panpipe band instead. Everybody was excited that Béla was going to play this dance. Our friend, Patrick Ross, was playing fiddle. Russ Barenberg was playing guitar. I love square dances. I danced and had so much fun. Afterwards, Patrick introduced me to Béla. It was brief. There was nothing to it. I remember thinking he was nice looking and had sweet eyes. He sounded great onstage but that's all I took away from it."

Washburn and Fleck continued to run into each other. "I gave him my solo demo," she said, "and he loved it. He asked me to write with him. That was our first real interaction. I went to his house and we tried to write a song. It didn't go anywhere but a few months later, after my boyfriend and I broke up, Béla started courting me. There's nineteen years between us but we work hard to make it work. We hold sacred space between us. I pinch myself every day. I get to be married to this wonderful man, have his child, and make music for a living. It's a phenomenal life."

Washburn has played with kung fu-Appalachian-indie-folk-rock trio Wu-Force. "My best friend in China, Wu Fei, and I had babies around the same time," Washburn told me in 2016. "We had been creating music with Kai Welch, a partner of mine since I started my third solo album, *City of Refuge* [2013]. He's an amazing pop-rock pianist and singer from OR. He learned about the folk community by traveling with me and he's been producing bluegrass bands. Kai, Fei, and I spent time in Beijing playing music and writing. The only time we could record was when Juno was eight months old. My mom and all these women took care of my baby while we went into the basement to play music. Kai and I would rush upstairs to nurse. Our stuff goes from musical theater to punch-drunk punk and bluegrass-sounding tunes. There's a song about censorship, another about a woman forced to sell herself into prostitution in order to help her family survive. Béla is going to produce a record by Fei and me after we finish our second duo record. For us, it's pure, crazy fun."

When Fleck proposed she join him in a duo, Washburn was "nervous," she recalled. "I had a much younger career. Béla is so established. He's becoming an American icon. It took five years longer than Béla wanted but I was touring on my own and finding myself, building my career before playing together."

"I've seen friends touring with a baby at home," said Fleck, "and I've seen the havoc it creates—estrangement between child and father, troubled marriages because of traveling. It's a tough scenario. If we could figure a way to tour together, and take our child, we would avoid those pitfalls, especially when our child was young and needed both parents. I stepped back from everything I was doing and made the duo the focal point. I had a good feeling about it. I have a lot of respect for Abigail's talent. We've developed a sound people love. We bring seven or more banjos onstage and champion the instrument."

Abigail Washburn, 2016

Béla Fleck & Abigail Washburn went to the top of the *Billboard* bluegrass charts and won the "Best Folk Album" Grammy. "It was a big change," recalled Washburn. "I went from driving in a van to riding in a bus that was my home."

Six weeks after their son Juno's May 2013 birth, Washburn and Fleck started their second album. "It was hard to find time," Washburn said, "or for me to find the inspiration. With the first record, we took things we knew or songs Béla or I had already written. We learned them together and influenced each other's compositions. In the case of our second album [*Echo in the Valley*], we started from scratch."

Fleck continues to maintain a feverish pace. Between writing and recording with Washburn, touring with Chick Corea and the Flecktones, and helping to raise his son, he managed to compose and record *The Juno Concerto* (2017) with the Colorado Symphony under conductor José Luis Gomez. "Fleck finds a comfy place among the violins, viola and cello," said Jeff Tamarkin, "and creates with them a new entity that obliterates genre and the roles of the instruments involved."[2]

"I'm working in a duo with Chris Thile," Fleck told me in 2016. "We've played a couple of shows together but it's part-time [Chris has a new child too]. We're going to keep creating new music and eventually make a recording. It'll just have to fit into the puzzle of our lives."

Chapter 29

Up Above My Head

The Nashville Bluegrass Band's Pat Enright (1945-) recorded with Peter Rowan, Jerry Douglas, and the Fairfield Four. He sang on *Will the Circle Be Unbroken, Vol. III,* and accompanied Johnny Cash on the soundtrack of *Dead Man Walking.* "I don't have any particular technique," said the Huntington, IN-born vocalist/guitarist. "What you hear is my natural voice, the same voice I use to speak. I don't have any secrets. I take a breath, open my mouth, and hope something good comes out."

Enright sang for actor John Turturro in *O Brother, Where Art Thou?* and participated in the *Down from the Mountain* tour. He continues to perform as a Soggy Bottom Boy. "You never know what's going to happen," he said. "The Coen brothers and T Bone Burnett came to town looking for singers and musicians versed in old-time music. It wasn't an audition as much as a jam session at a studio on Music Row. Alan O'Bryant, Roland White, Mark Hembree, and I sat around with other people, singing and jamming. They had a food spread that would feed an army. Free food and musicians go well together.

"John Turturro looked like he was singing but it was me. I even did the yodel. They processed it electronically, twisted it around, and made it sound like what they thought he would sound like yodeling. It paid off really well; I still get residuals."

Growing up with a "Philco radio parked in the middle of the living room," Enright "listened to a country-music radio station from Fort Wayne," he recalled. "I didn't think about being a musician or even about playing music."

Becoming a fan of folk, blues, and country music in high school, Enright bought a "cheap little guitar," he said. "I brought it with me when I went into the navy and learned by making mistakes."

Stationed in MD, Enright heard someone playing banjo in the laundry room. "That was my introduction to bluegrass," he recalled. "I went over and asked, 'Do you mind if I get my guitar?' The banjo player looked at me and thought, 'Who's this guy?' but I got my guitar and we played. He introduced himself as Paul King and we became friends."

Enright and King frequented the Country Gentlemen's Wednesday-night shows at the Shamrock Bar. "Charlie Waller was one of the best singers I've ever heard," said Enright. "I sure listened to him a lot and it soaked in."

Enright was in the Philippines when he completed his naval service in 1969. "I flew to San Francisco," he recalled, "and hung out with Paul King, my picking buddy. We put the Tonto Basin Boys together to play at a pizza place. We made seven dollars—for all of us. That was the first time I played for money. It helped me control my stage fright."

Enright's next band, the Phantoms of the Opry, took over Northern CA. "We were voted best bluegrass band in the Bay Area in 1973," he said. "Laurie Lewis and fiddler Paul Shelasky were in it; Gene Tortora played Dobro; Robbie McDonald played banjo. We played loud to get over the audience. It was rough and raw."

"I fell in love with Pat Enright's voice," remembered Lewis. "When he asked me to join the Phantoms of the Opry, I had never played bass, but I said yes. I had to find a bass and learn how to play so I could be in that band."

Lewis (1950-) studied classical violin from age twelve to seventeen but she "had a hard time reading music," she recalled. "My parents thought I was allergic to rosin and I never got past that. I'd become so wrapped up trying to read notes I couldn't hear the music. I loved playing what I heard. I remember being frustrated because my ear was better than my ability."

Berkeley had a thriving music scene. Political songstress Malvina Reynolds ("Little Boxes") called it home. "People were interested in string-band music," remembered Lewis, "and wonderful bands played on the university campus.

"The 1964 Berkeley Folk Festival was the first place I heard bluegrass. Doc Watson was there, the Greenbriar Boys, the Dillards, Jean Ritchie, and great rural blues players like Reverend Gary Davis, Mississippi John Hurt, and Jesse Fuller, who was an Oakland-ite. Pete Seeger and Joan Baez were there and modern singer-songwriters like Phil Ochs."

At fifteen, Lewis formed a duo with Dana Everts. "We both played guitar and sang," she recalled. "Dana loved Irish folksongs. I always had a passion for country music. We did all the classics. We'd go to coffeehouses in Berkeley and play. We opened for Jesse Fuller at the Walnut Creek library. That was our first real show. I'm sure we were cute and not very good."

Lewis acquired a banjo after seeing the Dillards. "I went to see the Byrds," she remembered, "and the Dillards opened. I fell in love with Doug Dillard's playing. It seemed magical, incredibly inventive."

Lewis's father arranged lessons but she soon lost interest. "I didn't have friends who played," she said, "and solo banjo, when you're not very good, is the most lonesome thing."

The fiddle had a more luring appeal. "My dad bought an album by Chubby Wise and the Rainbow Ranch Boys [Hank Snow's band] because he liked its cover," said Lewis. "Chubby played so beautifully, so clean. It seemed foreign but it grabbed my ears."

Asked to provide music for her older sister's wedding, Lewis "had this idea that I could learn a couple of waltzes off the album," she said. "It became eye opening and ear opening—my first foray into playing fiddle by ear."

The Phantoms of the Opry's reign was short. Within a year, Enright moved to Nashville. "There wasn't anything going on in San Francisco," he said. "I had always had a job and played music on the side. The company I worked for went out of business and I was unemployed. I knew somebody in Nashville and he said, 'Come on out; see what happens.'"

Enright wasn't in Nashville long before he had an accident. "I was working on a mandolin and the string snapped," he said. "It poked my eye out. I went back to San Francisco but there was nothing there for me so I went back to Nashville. I've always moved around, not looking for greener pastures but for newer ones."

Relocating to Boston, in 1978, Enright teamed with Jack Tottle (mandolin), Stacy Phillips (Dobro), Robin Kincaid (guitar), and Paul Kahn (bass) in Tasty Licks (soon joined by Fleck). "We would have a bassist play with us," recalled Enright, "and they'd be a student at the Berklee College of Music. They couldn't get gigs playing concerts so they were playing bluegrass. I didn't care for Boston. I stayed a year to the day and moved back to Nashville."

Enright played on Fleck's debut solo album, *Crossing the Tracks* (1979), and the banjo player produced the Nashville Bluegrass Band's *My Native Home* eight years later. Fleck and Enright joined with Jerry Douglas, Blaine Sprouse, Roland White, and Mark Hembree as the Dreadful Snakes in 1983. "That was a Nashville band thrown together to make an album," Enright explained. "Béla and Jerry Douglas produced it. We only played a few gigs, and never traveled, but it was a good record. Later on, I played with Roland in the Nashville Bluegrass Band."

Enright and Alan O'Bryant moved to Nashville around the same time. "Everybody gathered at the Station Inn every weekend to jam," said Enright. "That's where I met Alan and Roland. Alan and I started singing duets and made a tape. We put a band together with Mark Hembree and Mike Compton for a package tour. We were the bluegrass band on the show. It was more like a Broadway revue but it was a complete mess. We spent more time sitting in hotels waiting because gigs were canceled."

Spirituals provided a major part of the Nashville Bluegrass Band's repertoire. "I went through twelve years of Catholic school," said Enright, "and had enough of it, but Alan and I like a cappella gospel music. We heard a lot of it at black churches and outdoor events. You really have to think about the message to pull it off. If you're just singing, you're not doing anybody any favors. The first thing we recorded was 'Up Above My Head.' Sister Rosetta Tharpe recorded it with a seven-woman choir, in the 1940s, but there were only four of us. It was a very slow process, working out harmonies note by note."

Fiddler Stuart Duncan joined in 1985. "Béla told him to check us out," said Enright. "He was so versed in bluegrass; playing with him was what we wanted to sound like. Despite his young age [twenty-one], it took no time to pull it together."

Heading to Winterhawk in July 1988, the Nashville Bluegrass Band's bus sustained a serious accident outside Roanoke. "It almost killed Mark [who was driving]," said Enright. "We thought he was going to die. He broke nearly every bone in his body. It was a rainy night. We went over

Pat Enright, 1989

a hill and couldn't stop. We rammed into the back of a semi. They had to helicopter Alan out, but with the exception of Mark, we went out the following weekend and played the National Folk Festival. We were hobbling—a couple of us could barely walk—but we did the gig. The show must go on, but it was the last bus we owned."

Compton left not long afterwards. "Roland White was the only other guy who could play mandolin with us," said Enright. "He was with us for twelve years. We got a different bass player too—Gene Libbea. It changed our sound. We were smoother and slicker. We were experimenting with material—semi-pop music, country music, folk music. We were an award-winning band for the IBMA and the Grammys. We were on the top."

The Nashville Bluegrass Band toured with the Fairfield Four in 1990, sixty-nine years after the Grammy-winning gospel group launched at the Fairfield Baptist Church in Nashville. "There were ten people onstage sometimes," said Enright, "singing together. Figuring where you fit was a challenge but we pulled it off. There's a Southern taboo about black and white music merging. They've always merged but people won't admit it."

In February 1991, the Nashville Bluegrass Band collaborated with Peter Rowan on the Grammy-winning *New Moon Rising*. "We were going to do a few songs together," recalled Enright, "but we wound up backing him on almost the whole thing."

Seven of the Nashville Bluegrass Band's ten albums garnered "Best Bluegrass Album" Grammy nominations. *Waitin' for the Hard Times to Go* (1993) and *Unleashed* (1995) won. The group traveled the world. "France, Germany, England, and Italy had bluegrass players," said Enright, "but we did a five-week State Department tour of the Middle East—Egypt, Bahrain, Bangladesh, Iraq, and Israel—and people had never heard bluegrass before. We spent hours in Iraq with the minister of culture. He's a world-renowned oud player. He had us up to his sanctorum, where there was a room with 5,000-year-old Iraqi instruments. We were amazed. He told us that our instruments reminded him of his. He took us into his studio and put on a tape he made with musicians playing those instruments. He turned out the lights and turned up the volume. It was a mind-bending experience."

Bassist Gene Libbea moved to CO in 1996. "He had a new girlfriend," explained Enright. "He was thinking he could live out there and still be in the band. We set him straight."

The Nashville Bluegrass Band continued to go through changes. "Roland bowed out to do things on his own," said Enright, "and Mike came back. Roland has occasionally substituted for Mike. Alan lost his voice a few years back. It was a problem. We worked around it but everybody has something else to do. Stuart is 'Mr. Sideman.' Mike plays solo house concerts and teaches. Alan teaches banjo. I thought of leaving before it collapsed but I stayed. It's gotten difficult to tour. The costs have gotten so high we can't get the fees to make up for it. I could see it coming. I'm not going to sleep on somebody's floor or squeeze into a car anymore."

Quantico, VA-born and Santa Paula, CA-raised Duncan (1964-) would not only be a member of the Nashville Bluegrass Band for more than three decades but also boast a discography of hundreds of recordings as a session player. "Jackson Pollock threw paint at the wall," he said. "That's my approach."

Seeing the Dillards with Byron Berline before his seventh birthday "changed everything," Duncan said. "My dad was a soundman at an Escondido folk club, and I saw Sid Page with Dan Hicks and His Hot Licks and Vassar Clements with the Scruggs Revue."

Duncan knocked around on his father's banjo and dabbled on his mother's guitar. "Larry Rice was playing with Aunt Dinah's Quilting Party," he said. "I saw them with fiddler Bill Cunningham. He told my father to get me a fiddle. I credit him with putting the idea into my dad's head. It seemed like a hundred years, but two years into it, I was playing with the Pendleton Pickers. We were hard to listen to but good enough to win a contest that allowed us to play the *Grand Ole Opry* on a Friday night as the prize. It was the year it moved to the Opry House [1974]. It was a huge deal."

Listening to Flatt & Scruggs' *Foggy Mountain Banjo,* twelve-year-old Alison Brown (1962-) found that the banjo "had the sound I wanted to make," she recalled. "I was taking guitar lessons from a University of CT-Stamford law student who also played banjo. My parents told me that, if I kept practicing the guitar, I could take banjo lessons during the summer."

Duncan met Brown at the San Diego Bluegrass Club's monthly meeting at Shakey's Pizza Palace around 1976. "She was already playing fingerpicked guitar," he remembered, "as well as banjo and she was listening to Doc Watson. A couple of years later, we discovered Tony Trischka and started living further from the center in our musical tastes. Tony didn't have the inhibitions that permeated among traditional players. Some people disliked his records but Alison and I were the opposite. We liked them because they were different. They had a sense of humor and good writing at the same time."

"Meeting Stuart was a lucky break," said Brown. "He was in a local celebrity band, the Pendleton Pickers, who had played on the *Grand Ole Opry.* I had a chance to play with him; his dad forced him. It was huge for my learning curve. We played at a Steak & Ale. We played listening rooms like the Troubadour in West Hollywood, the Ice House in Pasadena, the Banjo Café in Santa Monica, the Cave in Long Beach, and the Palomino Club in North Hollywood. We played festivals, fiddle contests, and hippie weddings, where the bride and groom wanted their first dance to be bluegrass.

"Stuart's father, Emmett, took us to see bands we were reading about in *Bluegrass Unlimited*. We were on the road for six weeks, sometimes driving all night. We saw an ad for the Canadian National Banjo Championship and drove up to Ontario. We wrangled winning the championship into an appearance on the *Grand Ole Opry*. Folks with KSON, San Diego, got us the slot. We played five minutes to midnight. It was incredible. I still feel that magic when I play the *Opry*."

Brown "didn't grow up in eastern KY," she said, "but in Southern CA, hearing all kinds of music. My dad loved jazz guitarist Joe Pass's records. That combined with the Earl Scruggs that I loved."

"I wish I had gotten into jazz when I was young," said Duncan. "I'd understand it more now. I didn't have the self-discipline or the right teacher. I can hear the influence it had on David Grisman and Tony Rice. When I listen to Ricky Skaggs, I can see what he got from Jethro Burns, who seems an unlikely source for bluegrass players."

Duncan's first concert as an audience member was George Jones' show at the Palomino Club in 1979. He was fifteen. "A friend snuck me in," he remembered. "I saw it from the first row. Years later, I played with him. I've loved every session that I've done. Being a versatile player, able to come up with something quick, got me in the door."

Attending South Plains College, in Levelland, TX, was "a waste of my dad's tuition money," Duncan said. "I wasn't focused. I left high school a year early. I should have waited to go to college. There are too many distractions when you're seventeen. I was frustrated with not playing so I went on the road with a bluegrass band, Lost Highway. I've been doing it ever since."

Formed in 1975, Lost Highway solidified after Duncan's arrival. "We headed East," he said, "and played festivals."

The group opened for former Clinch Mountain Boy Larry Sparks in 1983. A few months later, Sparks' mandolin player resigned. "Larry called me," remembered Duncan, "and asked if I'd consider moving East. I called him a few days later and said, 'I'm in.' I got in my truck, drove to KY, and stayed with him for a year."

Duncan met Peter Rowan the first time he played with the Nashville Bluegrass Band. "It was after the Don Reno Benefit in Dayton," he remembered. "The Nashville Bluegrass Band was playing at the Canal

Street Tavern. Peter came to sit in; so did I. That's when the conversation started about me moving to Nashville. I liked playing with Larry Sparks; it took a little persuading. A friend in Nashville had an apartment that was cheap and available. Another friend was getting married and he wanted me to be the best man. I asked Larry if he could get someone to fill in for me. He knew I was thinking of leaving and suggested that I stay in Nashville. It took the words right out of my mouth. I ended up quitting a week sooner than I intended."

Two months later, Duncan joined the Nashville Bluegrass Band. "I had been playing at the Station Inn with Kathy Chiavala and Roland White and the New Kentucky Colonels," he recalled, "and Bobby Clark and David Grier, who had also just moved to town, and sitting in with the Nashville Bluegrass Band. Alan O'Bryant said, 'What would you think about joining the band?' I wasn't sure if I was ready to hit the road. I pondered it for a couple of days before telling them, 'I'm in.'"

The Nashville Bluegrass Band's "music affected people the way the first generation of bluegrass musicians affected us," Duncan told me in 2017. "Other than the Johnson Mountain Boys, Hot Rize, and the Nashville Bluegrass Band, there wasn't a revival of the old sounds. Bluegrass was a dirty word in Nashville when I moved here but I sensed a change. Jerry Douglas made his mark on Randy Travis records. Country music started featuring bluegrass instruments, which had been lacking for some time. I saw the acoustic wave as an extension of greater public awareness.

"Béla Fleck was responsible for me having a greater work ethic; he forced me to turn a corner in my playing. I realized I was going to have to do some serious studying. When we did his album *Drive* [1988], I had to learn many tunes outside the norm in a couple of days. It was scary but it gave me that push to become disciplined and inclusive of musical ideas. Banjo music isn't just banjo music anymore, especially in Béla's hands. He produced my solo record in 1992. Maybe I should call him."

Trying to decide between Harvard and Yale, Brown checked *Bluegrass Unlimited*'s listing of upcoming shows to "see how much bluegrass there was in Boston versus New Haven," she said. "It was no contest. The BBU and Nancy Talbott's Boston Area Friends of Bluegrass were putting on shows and running the Berkshire Mountains Bluegrass Festival. It was much more than we had in Southern CA. There were clubs like Passim in Harvard Square and the Idler in Central Square. It was expensive for bands to come West. You might see one national act a year. It was different in

Boston. The night I moved into my dorm, Knoxville Grass played at Paine Hall on campus. I walked to it."

During Brown's sophomore year (1982), Joe Val suggested she connect with Taylor Armerding, a Boston-born mandolin player/vocalist who had played with the original lineup of Northern Lights. "Taylor and I resurrected Northern Lights," Brown said. "It gave me an opportunity to play gigs and festivals around Boston. Taylor's a great singer and the band pushed the envelope. Bob Emery, who was playing bass, wrote some great songs. *Before the Fire Comes Down* [1983] had a couple of Bob's tunes and a couple of mine."

"I hadn't been in a band for two years," remembered Armerding, "but I had run into guitarist/singer Bill Henry. Orrin Star hired Bill and me to back him at a gig. Bill was living in Cambridge in a house owned by the Old Joe Clark organization. I went down a couple of times to jam with him and we started thinking about putting something together. That's when Alison Brown called. She was interested in being in a band. I called Bill and Bob Emery. He had been the guitar player in Northern Lights but I asked if he'd play bass and he said yes. That was the second Northern Lights.

"We were pretty raw. Alison was the class of the band by a long shot. Bill was a good picker but I hadn't started to play mandolin when I was ten. When you start at twenty-six, it really is teaching an old dog a new trick. I got good but I never got any better. Bob Emery wasn't a natural bass player."

Northern Lights didn't play many gigs with Brown. "Every spring, Alison went back to CA," said Armerding, "so we couldn't play all summer, peak festival season. When she graduated [with degrees in history and literature], she left permanently. We were defunct again."

Continuing on to business school at UCLA, Brown earned an MBA. Moving to San Francisco, she worked for Smith Barney in their investment banking division. "I never thought of banjo playing as a profitable profession," she said. "Both of my parents are lawyers. My sister's a lawyer. I figured that I'd be going to medical school but I ended up going to business school instead."

Brown found plenty of open doors. "It's easier to get into a female voice," she said, "than a high-lonesome tenor male. A beautiful-sounding female voice singing bluegrass is relatable.

"Alison Krauss opened the door for people to discover the music because of her voice. She has a great sense for material. You could see a connection with country music and mainstream music but she has so much bluegrass in her heart."

Joining Krauss and Union Station after their second album, *Two Highways* (1989), Brown played on *I've Got That Old Feeling* (1990), their first Grammy winner. "I got to witness and be part of Alison's transition," she said, "from relative obscurity to TNN videos, Grammy recognition, and mainstream-press attention.

"We had an insatiable passion for music. If we were driving somewhere, somebody would be picking. We couldn't play enough. We were continuously coming up with new material and new ideas."

Touring with Michelle Shocked in 1992, Brown played with a rhythm section and electric instruments for the first time. "Alison was about the purity of the tones," she said, "but this was about getting your sound across, more about the rhythm and the groove than the melodic aspects of the music. It was eye opening to me."

Brown married Garry West, a bass player she met prior to the tour. "I was in charge of putting Michelle's band together," she told me in 2016, "and brought Garry in. He had a background of playing bluegrass at the Six Flags Park in GA and had been in Patty Loveless's band. We spent eleven months on a tour bus but we had the luxury of a full crew. We'd pull into a town and the caterers would start setting up for breakfast. Sound check wouldn't be until 4:00 P.M. We had the whole day off. We were in Stockholm one day. Garry and I sat down in a café and started brainstorming on how to construct a life in music. Garry has a deep interest in production. We drew up a business plan for a record label, recording studio, publishing, touring, and a family. We put the pieces together and launched Compass Records in 1995. We put out Victor Wooten's first album, *A Show of Hands,* the next year. It's a must-have for electric bass players. We introduced Kate Rusby to American audiences. We've worked with Colin Hay for thirteen years. He sold twenty-six million records as frontman for Men at Work in the eighties but he had been putting out records on a do-it-yourself label before coming to us. He and Garry brainstormed a record [*Man @ Work*] that put his career back on track."

Many people expected Brown to focus on bluegrass when she started Compass Records, but "it took a while to have the artists I wanted," she said. "I'm proud of what we've been able to do with Special Consensus. I really like banjo player/bandleader Greg Cahill. I was on the IBMA's board of directors when he was president and I appreciated his leadership."

Brown shared a "Best Contemporary Instrumental Performance" Grammy with Béla Fleck in 2000. "I heard Japanese banjo players who figured out my tune 'Leaving Cottondale,'" she remembered, "and I thought it'd be cool to do a harmony version. Béla was the obvious person to call. It's impossible to be a three-finger banjo player and not be influenced by what he's accomplished; playing with him was incredibly easy."

Duncan played on Mark Knopfler and Emmylou Harris's *All the*

Alison Brown, 2010

Roadrunning tour in 2006. "I had worked with Emmylou in the studio," he said, "but it was a treat to be on the road and see how she carries herself and what she brings to the stage. I didn't know much about Mark's catalog. By the time he started making records with Dire Straits, I had become a bluegrass enthusiast. He was hard to understand lyrically but it wasn't hard to listen to him play guitar. I enjoyed being next to that."

Duncan didn't play on Alison Krauss and Robert Plant's Grammy-winning *Raising Sand* (2007) but he participated in their world tour. "T Bone is to be commended for finding songs and for making that first album happen," he said. "We went into the studio and started working on another one but we couldn't find enough songs. It was a very unlikely pairing, but by the end of the tour, we really had something. Robert was wonderful to work for; he's an incredible archivist and appreciator of vintage music, very knowledgeable about American recordings of the 1930s.

"Elvis Costello is one of the most brilliant people I've had a chance to work with. I went into the studio with him before we toured. I didn't have a clear idea of his history. He's another whose lyrics I couldn't understand because of his thick accent. When we got into the studio, they passed out lyric sheets for the songs we were about to record. My perception changed after reading just one verse."

Duncan has been working with Diana Krall since 2013. "I've finished doing four songs with her for an upcoming record," he said. "Tommy LiPuma is producing it. I got into a conversation with him and mentioned Dan Hicks, who had just passed away. Tommy produced the live Dan Hicks record. I had no idea."

Duncan recorded *The Goat Rodeo Sessions* with Chris Thile. "Chris comes from my neck of the woods," he said. "I played on all of his early records when he was a kid. We also had a connection through the Pendleton Pickers. John Moore, our mandolin player, was Chris's teacher."

Twenty-seven years before replacing Garrison Keillor as host of *A Prairie Home Companion* (now called *Live from Here*), Punch Brothers' mandolinist Chris Thile (1981-) started Nickel Creek with Sean (1977-) and Sara Watkins (1981-) and his father, Scott, in 1989. Alison Krauss produced their 2000 self-titled third album, which achieved platinum status and capped a year that included eleven shows opening for Lyle Lovett. Appearing on *Austin City Limits* with Dolly Parton, in 2001, they backed her at the Grammy Awards ceremony. Their fourth album, *This Side,* again produced by Krauss, reached number eighteen on *Billboard*'s Top 200 and the runner-up slot on the country chart and scored a "Best Contemporary Folk Recording" Grammy. Bluegrass chart-topper *Why Should the Fire Die?* followed in 2005. It would be Nickel Creek's final album for nearly a decade. After their *Farewell (for Now)* 2007 tour, they wouldn't reunite until their sixth album, *A Dotted Line,* seven years later.

Bassist Edgar Meyer, fiddler Mark O'Connor, and cellist Yo-Yo Ma recorded *Appalachian Journey* in 2000. After its release, Duncan replaced O'Connor. "They wanted someone who wasn't expected," he said, "and that's where I came in—the non-classical player."

Restoring antique violins has helped Duncan "understand the vibrations involved in making the instrument tick," he explained. "I haven't answered any age-old mysteries but I've figured out some common denominators."

The Song of the Banjo (2015) was Brown's "way to make banjo music accessible to people not yet initiated into the wonderfulness of the banjo," she said. "I've always felt where I could add to music is in the repertoire of the banjo. I write tunes that show off the banjo's lyrical side. Beautiful melodies draw me. I love arpeggiated rolls and do them more than single-string picking. I set up my banjo so it doesn't have that brash, high end. I bring out the mellow mid-tones and make it as sonically pleasing as possible."

Chris Thile, 2001

Following Brown's departure in 1984, Bill Henry persuaded NY-born Mike Kropp to sign on as Northern Lights' banjo player. Replacing Emery three years later, Oz Barron brought a harder edge to the band. Powered by his electric bass, Northern Lights placed third in Kentucky Fried Chicken's band contest. *Take You to the Sky* (1990) included Armerding's "Northern Rail," which was nominated as "Song of the Year." "That kicked off thirteen years of peak performance," recalled Armerding, "after fifteen years of banging around."

The Dixie Chicks covered "Northern Rail" in 1991. "I haven't written a ton of songs," Armerding said, "but I'm proud that one became a parking-lot standard."

Northern Lights performed an intimate showcase at the IBMA conference in Owensboro, KY in 1992. A larger three-day festival was taking place at English Park's outdoor amphitheater beside the Ohio River. On Saturday, the last three performers were to be Emmylou Harris with her Angel Band (featuring Vince Gill and Herb Pedersen), Tony Rice, and Peter Rowan. "Tony got sick," said Armerding, "and, at the last minute, wasn't available."

Having built connections as an independent rep for Fishman, Remo, and Modulus basses, and a liaison among American banjo builders, Asian manufacturers, and Remo, Kropp "arranged for us to fill in for Tony Rice between Emmylou and Peter," recalled Armerding. "I knew Peter by this time. He and Bob Emery grew up in Wayland, MA. We played at our best and the crowd called us back for an encore. After we were done, I went into the tent serving as the dressing room. Peter and Bill Keith were arguing. Bill didn't want the set list changed ten minutes before they went on. Peter turned to me and said, 'Taylor, do you know "Banks of the Ohio?"' I said, 'Of course, I do.' He said, 'Do you want to come up and sing harmony?' We tried a chorus and it worked. He asked if I knew tunes off the album that he had just done with the Nashville Bluegrass Band, *New Moon Rising*. I had that album and loved it. I was familiar with all the songs. He said, 'Why don't you just come up and play the set with us?' The rest of the group was Keith on banjo, Jerry Douglas on Dobro, and Mark Schatz on bass.

"Our manager, Linda Bolton, was in the crowd. Afterwards, she connected us with Peter and we did a couple dozen shows together over five years. We were usually his backup and opening band when he came to New England."

Working with Rowan could be frustrating. "He really was a space shot," remembered Armerding. "We'd rehearse what he wanted to play, but in the middle of the set, he'd play three songs we hadn't rehearsed. I was from the camp where you learn something, get a tight arrangement, and go out and play it. The only change is your solo. Peter's philosophy is that every time you play a song, it's a different experience. I came to understand that's a cool thing to do."

Bolton also connected Northern Lights with Vassar Clements. "The first time we played with Vassar," said Armerding, "he was playing with Tony Rice. Linda got in touch with him and asked if he'd play 'Northern Rail,' 'Winterhawk,' and 'City on a Hill' with us. He said, 'Sure.' Vassar was one of the sweetest people you'd ever meet, like Joe Val. We got on really well."

Northern Lights played two or three long weekends a year with Clements. "He rode with me in my car," said Armerding. "We talked about a lot of stuff but he wasn't a deep thinker. I came away thinking of him as a savant, but put a fiddle in his hands, and it was magic. I'd watch him when he was taking a solo. It was as though he was looking into the sky, tapped into something that nobody else was hearing."

After spending his teens outside of Chicago, and serving two years in the army, Armerding returned to Boston and sought others interested in bluegrass. "I found what evolved into the BBU," he recalled, "the Boston

Area Friends of Bluegrass and Old-Time Country Music headed by Nancy Talbott and *Hillbilly at Harvard* host Fred Bartenstein. They presented a show a month at First Church Congregational in Harvard Square. The first show I went to was Jim & Jesse. The band that became Northern Lights' first gig was opening for Lester Flatt and Nashville Grass in 1974."

Boston University cinematography student, underwater photographer, and banjo player David Doubilet formed the Park Street Undertakers in 1966. The group included racing-car mechanic/guitarist George Nelson; fiddle, mandolin, guitar, banjo, and autoharp player Neil Rossi; and David Bromberg's future mandolinist, Dick Fegy. Traveling to the Union Grove Old Time Fiddlers Convention, in Harmony, NC, they became the Spark Gap Wonder Boys before entering the band competition. They would release Rounder 0002, *Cluck Old Hen, Cluck Six-Ten, the Dow-Jones Average Is Down Again* (1970), at the same time as NC banjoist George Pegram's self-titled Rounder 0001 (purchased by Ken Irwin from Kanawha Records for $125). "I asked George Nelson if he gave mandolin lessons," recalled Armerding. "He said no, but he brought me to the Old Joe Clark house and I took twenty lessons from Dick Fegy; he taught me fiddle tunes."

Skimming the *Boston Phoenix,* Armerding saw an ad: "Established bluegrass band seeks mandolin player." "I was desperate to get into a band," he remembered. "I didn't know a note on the mandolin but I responded to the ad and spoke with Dan Marcus, the banjo player in How Banks Fail. They had been together for six months. Their mandolin player was moving to NJ. I told him that I was new to the mandolin but that I could sing. He said, 'I'm having a party on Saturday night; why don't you come?' I counted the days. In the interim, I bought a stradolin [a pre-World War II plywood mandolin] and taught myself a half-dozen chords. I could play rhythm and do a little flatpicking. At the party, I ended up singing with Joe Val. He went over to Dan, after I left, and told him, 'This guy will learn to play the mandolin but he can already sing—hire him.'"

Armerding's son Jacob "Jake" (1978-) shares his passion for music. "Jake was eighteen months old," Armerding remembered, "when Russ Barenberg came out with *Cowboy Calypso.* It's an incredibly musical bluegrass-meets-jazz-fusion album. I'd help Jake put headphones on and he'd listen to that album all the way through."

Sent for Suzuki violin lessons at five, Jake "wasn't an instant prodigy," said Armerding. "He wasn't good enough to play a Northern Lights show before he was thirteen but he took off like a rocket. Everything that had been building up came out and he could suddenly play. He was in the band through high school."

Replacing Barron in 1990, Jeff Horton "had a much better singing voice," said Armerding. "We started having groove trouble but I don't think we ever had a better vocal sound."

Northbridge, MA-born Dave Dick (John Herald Band, Southern Rail, and Salamander Crossing) replaced Kropp in 1999.

Armerding began playing with the Bluegrass Gospel Project in 2001. Inaugurated for First Night festivities, they played a handful of shows the first year but "weren't really working together or trying to shape it." The turning point came at the 2002 Joe Val Bluegrass Festival. "We played as well as ever," said Armerding, "and sold 120 copies of our first album."

Resigning from Northern Lights the following year, Armerding passed the baton to ex-Sugarbeat mandolinist/guitarist Ben Demerath. "We had done what we were going to do," Armerding said. "We weren't just mailing it in like another day at the office but things had stalled creatively."

Henry kept Northern Lights on track for another seven years. They played their final show, joined by former members, in Mansfield, MA, on March 13, 2010. The Bluegrass Gospel Project concluded their sixteen-year run at the Vergennes, VT Opera House on March 11, 2017. "I have focal dystonia [a neurological disease also known as 'musician's cramp']," explained Armerding. "There's no pain but it affects finger coordination."

Armerding can still sing, though. Since 2008, he and his son have been harmonizing with Boston-born singer-songwriter Mark Erelli in an Americana band (Barnstar!) formed by Ray LaMontagne's double bassist/producer Zachariah "Zack" Hickman. "Mark, Jake, and I," Armerding said, "make one of the better vocal trios around."

Chapter 30

Reassessing Old-Time

Moving to Ithaca in 1972, the Highwoods String Band transformed the college town on Cayuga Lake's southern shore, in central NY, into the center for the old-time music revival. "They were pivotal," said Judy Hyman (Horse Flies). "Their energy was attractive, they were young and adorable, their rhythm solid. The sound of their two fiddles, banjo, guitar, and bass was captivating. They were funny and had a good flow to their shows."

"We never made much money," said Malcolm "Mac" Benford, "and it was a hard life on the road, but knowing we were making an impact kept us going."

The inspiration leading to the Highwoods String Band sparked in San Francisco. Bob Potts stood on stilts as he fiddled old-time tunes with All-Skates. The Columbia, MO-born son of a classical pianist, Walt Koken played fiddle and clawhammer banjo for the Busted Toe Mudthumpers. Woodbridge, NJ-born Benford played banjo with Dr. Humbead's New Tranquility Stringband and Medicine Show, whose specialty "was music we learned from old records by Charlie Poole & the NC Ramblers," he said. "We made a decent living and traveled across the country playing fiddle contests. People who had played with Charlie Poole were impressed with what we were doing."

Connecting as the Fat City String Band in early 1971, Potts, Benford, and Koken appeared at the Smithsonian's Folklife Festival. "The New Lost City Ramblers presented songs as if they were artifacts from the past," said Benford, "but we tried to make it relevant in the present. It didn't have to be handled with kid gloves; it could be a party."

Eleven years before, Benford (1940-) headed to Williams College, in northwest MA, planning to become an English teacher. His path diverted to music. "The New Lost City Ramblers turned me on to old-time music," he recalled, "and I got interested in where that music was coming from. I started collecting 78s and making trips to Galax and Union Grove to hear old-timers."

Benford traveled South when "kids from the North were getting beat up and killed," he said. "We were apprehensive but we wanted to hear the music. At Galax, there were probably thirty people from outside the area. We banded together and formed friendships that go on to this day. Southern people were very welcoming. They were charmed that we traveled all that way just to hear their music."

Clawhammer banjo player Wade Ward (1892-1971) was an early model. "I met him at the Galax Fiddler's Convention," Benford said. "The director's son, Nelson Edmonds, took me around and introduced me to old-time musicians. He was the father of Jimmy Edmonds, who was eight or nine but already playing fiddle with Wade Ward. The elegance of [Ward's] style, the clarity of the notes, was beautiful banjo playing."

Benford shared stages with Kyle Creed (1912-82), who "played in the Camp Creek Boys, the hottest old-time band," and one-handed banjo player Lowe Stokes (1898-1983). "I listened to [Stokes] with Gid Tanner & the Skillet Lickers," Benford said. "Getting to perform with him at Brandywine is a high point of my career. There are many stories about how he lost his hand. They all have to do with a jealous husband and a firearm. When I met him, he had a rig on his fiddle that held the bow in a position perpendicular to the strings. His noting hand was still working fine. He played the old tunes as good as ever."

Benford met Roscoe Holcomb during a Smithsonian tour organized by Mike Seeger. "We were in eastern KY," he said, "and stopped by Roscoe's house. His singing was intense; it could make your hair stand on end."

When he arrived in San Francisco in 1967, "the counterculture was exploding," Benford recalled, "and people were open to all kinds of new stuff. FM radio was just starting. Instead of playing top-forty hits, they were mixing Roscoe Holcomb, Ravi Shankar, the Grateful Dead, Lightnin' Hopkins, Dave Brubeck, and the Jefferson Airplane."

Koken moved East in late 1971. Potts and Benford followed a year later. Adding guitarist Doug Dorschug and fiddler Jenny Cleland, they became the Highwoods String Band. After touring for a couple of years, they "threw a big party and invited all our friends," remembered Benford. "It became an annual celebration. Many people got their first taste of Ithaca."

"We traveled to it when we were still in IN," recalled Hyman. "I was star-struck. It was an opportunity not only to play but to hear what other people were doing."

The Highwoods String Band exported old-time music beyond North America. "In Europe, people were familiar with old-time music," said Benford. "The New Lost City Ramblers toured there. In Latin America, where we did a six-week State Department-sponsored tour in 1974, it was a very different thing. They'd never heard anything like us."

Performing in Carnegie Hall in 1978, the Highwoods String Band appeared on the Grammy-nominated *The New Lost City Ramblers 20th Anniversary Concert with Special Guests Highwood String Band, Pete Seeger, & Elizabeth Cotton.* Turmoil, however, was brewing. "We'd been doing it for seven or eight years," said Benford, "and the most I made was $5,000, the year we did the Latin American tour. We all had families. When we started, we were able to put up with the hardships, compromises, and lack of money. We thought that, if we kept at it, we'd find success, but more and more people got into playing old-time music. It used to be that a promoter could afford to pay us $500 to play a show, but in every town, there were old-time bands happy to play for $100."

As a non-Southern band, the Highwoods String Band faced considerable opposition. "The folk-music establishment made a determination," said Benford, "that we weren't authentic. Government-sponsored folk festivals weren't allowed to hire us anymore."

Traveling became strenuous. "Our bodies could barely keep up with the lifestyle," said Benford. "It was time to call it quits. I got a regular job for the first time. After trying the construction business, and coming home exhausted, somebody suggested that, if I took the Civil Service exam and scored high enough, the government was obligated to offer me a position. I ended up the Tompkins County Medicaid director for twenty-seven years. I retired with Social Security and a pension."

Staying active musically, Benford played solo gigs and started the Backwoods Band. He formed the Woodshed All-Stars with fiddlers Pete Sutherland and John Kirk and vocalist/mandolin player Marie Burns (the Burns Sisters) in 1990. "We played together for seven years," he said, "trying to come up with a style of old-time music true to the roots but also appealing to the bluegrass crowd."

Benford formed the Uncles with Rick Good, Good's girlfriend Sharon Leahy, and fiddler Woody Woodring. "We played Uncle Dave Macon music," he said. "His sound was very different from Charlie Poole but there were similarities in the material they did and they were both entertainers who loved to put on a show. Sharon is an amazing dancer and choreographer. Her four-person dance team, the Footnotes, traveled with us. We played while they danced. The old instrumentals were meant for dancing; even the lyrics have a propulsive rhythm."

The son of an engineer, Bruce Molsky (1955-) grew up listening to NY top-forty radio stations. "If you liked Motown and the Beatles," he recalled, "you had to listen to everything else. The folk-music revival was in full swing—the New Seekers, Barry McGuire, and Bob Dylan—and the sound of an acoustic instrument gave me the bug. I could look at performers with a wooden box and steel strings and say, 'I could do that.'"

Pianist/educator Dr. Billy Taylor brought jazz to NY public schools including P.S. 181, which Molsky attended. "We had an assembly in the auditorium," he remembered, "and Dr. Taylor's presentation enabled me. It's one of the reasons I love teaching old-time fiddle, clawhammer banjo, and fingerstyle guitar at the Berklee College of Music. I went home and asked my mom if I could have guitar lessons. It was the beginning of the end."

Molsky took half-hour lessons until "we ran through all my teacher's books and he threw me out after ten months," he said. "After that, I was on my own."

Molsky's older sister bought him a Beatles fake book and Doc Watson's first Vanguard LP. "I got a copy of Happy and Artie Traum's *Fingerpicking Styles for Guitar,*" he said, "and learned to fingerpick. I ended up in a bluegrass band."

Studying architecture and engineering at Cornell University, Molsky fell in with a group of musicians after classes. "We'd meet at Johnny's Big Rig Grill," he said, "and play all night. There were fiddles and banjos. Howie Bursen was one of the people at those sessions. I watched him play clawhammer banjo on 'Staten Island Hornpipe' and all these New England tunes and I got interested and bought myself a banjo. I liked playing melodies. Six months later, I got a fiddle. It was that time in my life to try stuff. I was hanging out with people who were much older [they were twenty]. In many ways, they were much further along as musicians, but it was a community and I soaked it all in. I heard all this great music; there were parties all the time. The Highwoods String Band was on the scene; Walt Koken gave me my only banjo lesson. He made it sound spontaneous and fun but he knew where it was coming from. I eventually hooked up with the Correctone String Band. It was as much of a social scene as a music scene."

Heading South in the mid-1970s, Molsky "was running away from home as much as anything else," he recalled. "I was enticed by the romance of living in the country, chopping my own wood, shooting a squirrel. I soon found it wasn't an easy lifestyle, especially when you didn't grow up in it. My family worried on my behalf. They came from Eastern Europe and had cultural expectations that we didn't do things like that. They thought I was out of my mind but I have strong memories of places that were so beautiful. I had great experiences but I'll never be a Southerner; I'm a New Yorker. It took me a while to double back but I realized I could have both. I moved to Atlanta with my wife, Audrey, in 1981, lived in the Washington, DC area for many years, and live in Rockbridge County, VA. There are good people everywhere."

Molsky and Mike Seeger recorded *Old Time Music Dance Party: Old Time Mountain Music for Buck Dancing, Flat Footing, Clogging, and Other Activities by A. Robic & the Exertions* (1987) with Paul Brown, Chester McMillian, and Dan Newhall. "Nobody loved the music, performers, and history more than Mike," Molsky said. "He reveled in it. He wasn't a party animal. I'm not either but I love playing sessions. To me, it's all about the music. If you meet somebody with similar musical interests, it's a reason to be friends. It's the same with my students. I hear them at their best when they're playing with their peers—trying to impress each other, making each other sound better, creating a sum that's bigger than the parts. We all look for those musical moments when it's magic, when the rest of the world goes away."

Joining the HillBenders (not the KY-based band) in 1989, Molsky continued to work as a mechanical engineer until 1997. "It was tough to juggle," he said. "I worked a high-pressure, sixty-hour week with deadlines. I tried to play music on weekends and my two weeks of vacation. It all came crashing into itself. Gratefully, I have a wonderful partner who saw it coming and supported me through the whole thing. She was dancing with the Green Grass Cloggers when we met in 1980. Once again, it was a social thing."

Recording *Fiddlers 4* (2002), with Michael Doucet (BeauSoleil), Darol Anger, and Rushad Eggleston, "was mind-bending," said Molsky. "I'm self-taught and I don't read music. I met Darol through Alasdair Fraser, the Scottish fiddler, in the late nineties. We became fast friends. He envisioned an album with jazz, Cajun, bluegrass, and old-time music. We started as a trio and then Rushad came in. It was a terrifying experiment, out of my musical comfort zone, but it afforded an opportunity to play places I couldn't have played on my own."

Mark Knopfler's *Tracker* (2015) featured Molsky on several tunes. "It looks good on my resume," he said. "We connected because I had played on the *Transatlantic Sessions*. Two of the musicians in the house band, Michael McGoldrick and John McCusker, had joined Mark's band. They were playing my CD on the bus and he said, 'Who's that?' When I was in Britain, they contacted me. I went to London and recorded with them for three days. Mark and I hit it off and had great conversations. He writes great tunes."

The Anonymous 4's chart-topping *1865: Songs of Hope and Home from the American Civil War* (2015) was a "meeting of two totally different musical approaches," said Molsky. "Marsha Genensky and I collaborated on all of the material. The classical world is much different from folk music. We recorded in a beautiful, resonant space picked for the acoustics. Everything was done live, no overdubs."

Molsky has been working with Irish multi-instrumentalist Andy Irvine (Sweeney's Men, Planxty). "Mozaik was Andy's brainchild," he said. "He had a trio years before that combined Irish and Balkan music. My wife and I have been friends with him since the early eighties. He wrote me a letter and asked if I wanted to be in the band with Donal Lunny (Planxty), Dutch guitarist Rens van der Zalm, and Hungarian multi-instrumentalist Nikola Parov. We ended up doing a lot of music in Ireland and toured the States."

Molsky has also been collaborating with Scandinavian musicians. He recorded *Rauland Rambles* (2016) with Finnish fiddler Arto Järvelä and Norwegian multi-instrumentalist Ånon Egeland. "Every time I use my musical tools, based on old-time, in another style," he said, "it helps me understand those tools better."

Molsky's Mountain Drifters grew out of his classes at Berklee. "I taught Allison de Groot clawhammer banjo," he said. "She came to me for lessons for three years. We got so into each other's playing that we invited Stash Wyslouch to join us. He's a great singer and we've been doing a lot of harmony singing. Slash and Allison are half my age but they're virtuosos. We've got something that crosses generations."

Sparking a 1990s revival of old-time music, the Freight Hoppers' "trademark sound . . . [drew] upon their personal musical rapport to make a sonic hue that refracts their inspirations and love of Southern American, gospel, blues, punk, and folk music."[1]

The NC-based group "got tunes from old recordings," said clawhammer banjo player Frank Lee. "Collectors hooked us up. The Carter Family was a great source. Uncle Dave Macon had entertaining songs. We had recordings by the New Lost City Ramblers and Harry Smith's *Anthology of [American] Folk Music*. It wasn't hard to find stuff; we were so crazed about it."

Lee (1958-) "grew up hearing about my grandfathers, who both played banjo," he said. "My grandmother and my mother sang in a way that there wasn't a consciousness of even numbers of beats. They were just singing, taking a breath at the end of a phrase. Old-time music is crooked with extra beats added. When I was a young kid, I remember hearing that dynamic. To me, that's what separated commercial music from what was truly primitive."

Lee's neighbor "had a stereo console and really powerful Marantz speakers, and he listened to classic bluegrass records," he recalled. "I could hear them from my yard. By the time I was a teenager, I was seeking how to play the banjo. That's when I heard the Highwoods String Band mixed in with bluegrass on the radio. It spoke to me in a different way.

"The banjo can be very percussive. I mute it with a rag. It takes away the overtones as it would with a drum. It's more poppy and not as harsh."

Lee met fiddler/flatfoot dancer David Bass at an old-time festival in 1993. "On a whim, without any expectations, we started playing," Lee remembered, "just the two of us. We sat there all night playing. He had a style of fiddling people call 'squirrelly.' Unless you're used to it, it's hard to hear the downbeat. You have to know the tune that the fiddler is playing. It set me off to an awareness of syncopated bowing. At the time, David was traveling around the country, trying to busk for a living. He'd spend the Christmas season in NY, playing in the subway, then go to New Orleans and work during Mardi Gras and the Jazz Festival. He didn't have anything to do during the summer so it fit his schedule to come here. He showed up living in a van."

Moving to Bryson City, NC a year before, Lee had played for the Great Smoky Mountains Railroad, a popular tourist attraction. "I didn't like working with the musician I was playing with so I left," he recalled, "but I knew David's fiddling would fit what people expected to hear. I didn't have any intention to get involved—I had other stuff going on—but as soon as the people who owned the train heard us, they offered us a job playing four shows a day at their depot. In fact, they hired the whole band and paid each of us thirty-five dollars per show. It was unbelievable money. We had a chance to rehearse while making a check.

"Our harmonies were comparable to bluegrass acts. I love the New Lost City Ramblers and the Highwoods String Band but their vocals weren't as tight as bluegrass audiences are used to hearing. We were a different-colored fish but people didn't care what style we played; they dug it."

The Freight Hoppers were going full force when Bass experienced a heart attack. "His first baby was on its way when his heart went out," said Lee. "He had to quit touring. By the time we regrouped, six years later, his wife had gone back to school and become a nurse. She works on a swing shift and never knows when she's going to be working. He has to be available; they have two kids. We mostly played festivals on the weekends but it became too much for him.

"After David left, there was no Freight Hoppers. His fiddle playing was so much of our sound but I wanted to keep playing music. I had an interest in country blues, as old as I could find, and picked up a 1932 National Duolian steel guitar. Learning blues was an impetus for playing solo. I had to learn to play that guitar or I was going to sell it. I didn't want to be a hack."

Regrouping in 2008, the Freight Hoppers "tried a few fiddlers before we met Merritt Smith," said Lee. "Andrea Smith, his wife, is our bass player. He likes the Round Top sound, which is contrary to what I do, but those tunes have such drive that it works."

Lee and the Freight Hoppers' guitarist Allie Burbrink have been playing as a duo. "We're setting up a recording room in her new place," he told me in 2016. "We're going to be doing a series of Internet Concert Window sessions. It's outside the box of your typical old-time banjo tunes."

The Brooklyn-based Spirit Family Reunion maintains a homegrown approach to music. "It's honest," said vocalist/guitarist Nick Panken, "and there are no frills. NY has just about everything but it can get a little pretentious and exclusive. Many people are looking for something less offensive and that's driving them to seek deeper roots than high-risers and expensive restaurants. We love old-time music and bluegrass but some of that music is stuck in the past. It's hard to strike a balance, leaning towards the future with our feet in the past."

With an impromptu performance for Occupy Wall Street, Spirit Family Reunion connected with political protest. "It seemed like a natural thing to do," said Panken. "It made for a great video. We had just come home from a tour and we were interested in what was going on downtown. We play for tips on the street all of the time. We went down to play for goodwill. It was a real good feeling. We weren't singing songs with complicated words. When people sing together, it's so unifying."

Spirit Family Reunion emerged out of a growing community of musicians in NYC's most populous borough. "The Jalopy Theater and School of Music in the Red Hook neighborhood has become the central base for the roots-music resurgence," said Panken. "They're a venue, an instrument repair shop, and a music school that teaches classes in banjo, guitar, harmonica, and fiddle."

After attending the Hudson River Revival, and listening to records by Pete Seeger and Woody Guthrie, Panken "just wanted to play music with my friends," he said. "This was the music you play when you're just sitting around playing."

Seeking to immerse himself further in the roots, Panken visited the archives at the office of Guthrie's late manager, Harold Leventhal. "I had read about it in the *New York Times*," he said, "so I went and knocked on the door. They opened it halfway. I ended up doing an internship. They've since moved to upstate NY and they're building a Guthrie Center in Okemah, OK, where he was born."

Spirit Family Reunion traces back to a Creedence Clearwater Revival cover band that Panken formed with washboard player (and future drummer) Stephen Weinheimer, a high-school friend. "CCR's songs are simple, fun, and everybody likes them," said Panken, "metal heads, folk-music enthusiasts, rock and rollers, motorcycle guys, everybody."

The group's scope continued to expand. "After contemplating college," Panken recalled, "we decided that we wanted to have fun and play music, not be caught up in any scene."

Soon after Panken and Weinheimer began writing songs, clawhammer banjo player/vocalist Maggie Carson joined the group. "I called Stephen," remembered Panken, "and said, 'Do you remember that girl in high school who played banjo? Why don't you call her? We have a show booked next week.' She came and played and she didn't want to leave. I figured that was a good sign."

Spirit Family Reunion continued to expand with the addition of fiddler/ vocalist Mat Davidson, drummer/vocalist Peter Pezzimenti, and upright bassist/vocalist Ken Woodward. They had previously played in a "hot jazz" band, the Scandinavian Half-Breeds. "They're NYC transplants," said Panken. "We absorbed them one by one. First, it was their mandolin player. Then, the drummer said he wanted to play with us. Then, it was the bass player. All of a sudden, we were six people with a whole rhythm section. Then, the mandolin player decided to learn fiddle. He was a little too accomplished on the mandolin to play with us."

Spirit Family Reunion released its debut album, *No Separation*, in 2012. *Hands Together* (2015) and *Harvest Festival Live* (2016) followed. "We've been playing shows and touring for the last few years," said Panken, "and we've learned that we could make more money if we have something to sell people after they've seen us play."

The traditional songs of eastern TN and western NC were preserved by the Roan Mountain Hilltoppers, a family band comprised of Joe Birchfield and his son Bill (fiddles), Joe's brother Creed (clawhammer banjo), and Bill's wife, Janice (washtub bass). Joe's wife and Bill's mother (Ethel), who played washtub bass, was a skilled ballad singer. After Joe's passing, his son led the group until 2014.

The spirit of the Roan Mountain Hilltoppers continues with the Nashville-based Hogslop String Band. "We're a square-dance band," said mandolinist Kevin Martin. "That's what sets us apart. It's not that we aren't bluegrass. Banjo player Graham Sherrill is a great caller. His mother is a caller in GA. He learned a lot from her."

Like Bruce Molsky, Atlanta-born Martin (1963-) thought he was playing bluegrass but "was actually playing old-time music," he said. "I had a friend who was a great banjo player. His dad was an old-time fiddle player and record collector. I was interested in mandolin, and itching to play, so we formed a trio."

Moving to Nashville in 2008, Martin got into a jam session with Casey Meikle (fiddle), Gabriel Kelley (guitar), Casey "Pickle" McBride (washtub bass), and Sherrill. "We were sitting around picking," he said, "and someone asked us to play at a square dance. That was our first gig. Since then, every weekend, we've had a gig. We don't spend a lot of time rehearsing."

McBride's washtub bass "is a twenty-five-dollar instrument," Martin told me in 2016. "The Roan Mountain Hilltoppers were real mountain musicians, some of the last around. They had a washtub bass. It was as much a percussion instrument as a rhythm instrument. It has visual appeal and it's a novelty. 'Pickle' is our wildest-looking, wildest-mannered member. He runs around the stage with a washtub with a parachute cord and a broomstick. He's a great electric bass player and toured with rock bands for years. He and Gabriel just played a surf-rock gig."

The Hogslop String Band has filmed two videos—"Reuben's Train" and "John Henry." "The Roan Mountain Hilltoppers played the fire out of 'Reuben's Train,'" said Martin. "We don't do it the same way but it's been extremely popular for us. People think of 'Reuben's Train' [or 'Train 45'] as a rocking banjo tune. We think of it as fiddles, fiddles, fiddles. Maybe that's why people like it. We play it the old way. Modal tunes have their appeal; they're more rocking. 'John Henry' is a classic tale of the common workingman. It is America."

Chapter 31

Wild Rose of the Mountain

Opened in 1969, Paul's Saloon became one of the liveliest venues in San Francisco's Marina district. Buses brought an endless stream of "Japanese tourists." Musicians playing the Great American Music Hall came to hear local bands. "The first time I went to Paul's Saloon," said Laurie Lewis, "was for Styx River Ferry's farewell party. I heard Ingrid Fowler singing and playing the fiddle."

Lewis formed the Good Ol' Persons with Barbara Mendelsohn, Dorothy Baxter, Sue Shelasky, and Kathy Kallick in 1975. Members would include Paul Shelasky, Sally Van Meter, and Todd Phillips. Playing at Paul's Saloon once a week, they "immediately got press coverage," said Lewis. "It gave us a jump start."

The Good Ol' Persons began a lengthy stint at the Red Vest Pizza Parlor, in El Cerrito, in 1976. Leaving after a few months, Lewis hooked up with Beth Weil, Greg Townsend, Tom Bekeny, and Steve Krouse as Grant Street. "It was a cooperative band," she said, "but the shots were mostly called by Beth and me. We wanted to play the best music we could but we didn't have aspirations to tour nationally. We had the usual personnel problems and fell apart. After *The Grant Street String Band* [1979] came out, people started calling us for gigs but there was no band. I took the bull by the horns and put together Laurie Lewis and the Grant Street Band."

Lewis supported her music by working at Marin Violin. Preparing to retire, in 1980, the owner proposed she buy his inventory and take over the shop. "If I didn't take advantage of it," Lewis explained, "I'd always be kicking myself and saying, 'I could have had a violin shop.' I ran it for seven years before deciding to record the songs I'd been writing.

"I was jealous of Kathy Kallick. She wrote songs and brought them to the band. We'd work them out but they were hers. I'd hunt for great old songs. We'd work on them and a month later, it would be on the new Emmylou Harris album. Everybody'd go, 'You're doing the Emmylou song.' I had written prose and poetry as a teenager but hadn't wed lyrics and melodies before the Good Ol' Persons."

Working on her first solo album (*Restless Heart*), in 1986, Lewis heard her songs played by great musicians and "felt alive," she recalled. "That's when I said I was going to be a professional musician. I sold the shop and that was that."

When Lewis met him in the early 1980s, Tom Rozum was playing mandolin for a San Diego-based swing band, the Rhythm Rascals. "They were scheduled to play on KPFA," she said, "and the bass player didn't want to do it. They sent word out among the music community. I was playing bass in a traditional-jazz band so I said that I would play with them. It was very scary. I didn't know their material and had to follow my ears."

Moving to Flagstaff, Rozum played with Flying South. He came to the Bay Area to hang out with the Grant Street String Band's mandolinist, Stan Miller. "They met at my house," said Lewis, "and we played together."

Rozum moved to San Francisco in early 1984. "He was in the band that did my songs from the Flying Fish album," said Lewis, "and he's been playing with me since. Our duo album, *The Oak and the Laurel,* was nominated for a 'Best Traditional Folk Album' Grammy in 1996." (The award went to Ramblin' Jack Elliott's *South Coast.*)

Lewis has produced several projects. "I'm so glad Scott Nygaard asked me to produce *No Hurry* [1989]," she said. "I want to help artists realize their dream of their music."

Lewis was working with Charles Sawtelle when the Hot Rize guitarist succumbed to leukemia on March 20, 1999. "Losing Charles was heartbreaking," she said. "We had been dear friends for many years. He asked me to produce his album but he was starting to be ill. He had a good studio and he enjoyed recording. People would come to town and, after their gig, come to his studio and play. He had fantastic tapes with wonderful musicians—David Grisman, Flaco Jimenez, Michael Doucet, Vassar Clements, and Norman Blake—and he wanted to pull them together for his album. Before he lost consciousness, I was with him in the hospital. He was still saying, 'Let's get Vassar to sing "Mommy and Daddy's Waltz."' My job, after he passed, was to realize his dream. I think he would have liked the way it came out."

Jean Ritchie and Joan Baez sparked Lewis's early fascination with Appalachian ballads. "I loved the stories," she said. "My friend Dana turned me on to Irish ballads. There's a big connection. I heard Hazel Dickens and Alice Gerrard around 1975. Their Folkways album [*Who's That Knocking*] came out ten years before. There weren't many women playing bluegrass. The album had Chubby Wise, my favorite fiddler, Lamar Grier playing

Laurie Lewis, 1996

banjo, a very young David Grisman on mandolin, and two women playing bluegrass. Their voices were different from each other but they had a wonderful blend—the round tone of Alice and the strident piercing of Hazel. Alice's writing blossomed later but Hazel was already writing.

"When Hazel appeared at the National Folklife Festival, she picked people to sing her songs. She gave me two songs—'Beyond the Riverbend' and 'Scars of an Old Love.' That was the first time I had any real interaction with her. She started coming to the Hardly Strictly Bluegrass Festival, in San Francisco, which is put on by [venture capitalist] Warren Hellman, a huge Hazel fan."

Lewis produced Gerrard's first all-original album, *Bittersweet* (2013). "I love that woman so much," Lewis said. "She's incredibly deep and an inspiration for how to grow old without getting old. Our friendship has blossomed."

Accompanied by the Right Hands, Lewis celebrated the music of Gerrard and Dickens on *The Hazel and Alice Sessions* (2016). "We did songs we liked," she said, "and things we thought were underappreciated."

Lewis honored another influence when she and Kathy Kallick recorded

Sing the Songs of Vern & Ray (2014). "Vern & Ray were the real deal," she said. "We were bluegrass neophytes when they were playing festivals and clubs. They were so powerful. I'd go to fiddle contests and Ray would show up and play. When he took the stage, it was a show. I ended up playing bass, and sometimes fiddle, in Vern Williams' band for a year after he and Ray quit working together. It was the best seat in the house."

Except for its theme song, Wayne County, KY-born Don Parmley (1933-2016) played the banjo heard on *The Beverly Hillbillies*. Together with his sixteen-year-old son, David (bass), and Randy Graham (mandolin), the ex-Golden State Boy formed the Bluegrass Cardinals in 1974. "We had it going on," remembered Larry Stephenson, who sang with the Bluegrass Cardinals (1983-88). "We played the *Grand Ole Opry,* all the Nashville Network shows, and flew all over the world."

A five-time SPBGMA (Society for the Preservation of Bluegrass Music in America) "Contemporary Male Vocalist of the Year," Stephenson continues to expand bluegrass with his dynamic vocals. "I can't be New Grass Revival or a progressive band," he said, "but I like making those songs my own yet keeping in a traditional vein so the audience can relate to what I'm doing. I never got into rock and roll, never had any interest in it at all. I was so obsessed with bluegrass and old country music that it was all I wanted to do."

Stephenson's "brother started bringing bluegrass records home, and our mom and dad took us to bluegrass festivals," recalled the King George, VA-born vocalist. "My dad played guitar a little and he taught me. I saw first-generation players and heard them on the radio. I had Jim & Jesse's *Bluegrass Special* [1963] with 'Sweet Little Miss Blue Eyes' and 'Somebody Loves You Darling,' which I recorded when I was seventeen. I also cut the Osborne Brothers' 'Rocky Top.' They were so good vocally and instrumentally. I sang the high lead at first but as I got older, my voice changed."

Frequenting a Methodist church as a youngster, Stephenson regularly attends a Baptist church. "I didn't do a lot of singing in church beyond the hymnal," he said, "but in every band I've been in, gospel music has been a big part. I worked with Cliff Waldron and the Gospel Way after he dropped the New Shades of Grass. When I worked with Bill Harrell and the Bluegrass Cardinals, we cut gospel records. I've had five gospel albums out myself."

Forming a band with his father while still in high school, Stephenson "didn't copy anyone in particular," he said. "I grew up listening to Jimmy Gaudreau, Doyle Lawson, and John Duffey but I just try to play the melody and fit in with the song. I love a good mandolin chop; it defines bluegrass to me."

Stephenson was a Cliff Waldron fan before playing with the singer/

guitarist. "Cliff was borrowing tunes from rock and roll and country music," he said, "and turning them into great bluegrass songs. The music had a progressive edge yet he could do a Stanley Brothers song. I played with him for about a year and loved every minute of it. He was a great singer, a great guitar player, a man of God, and a good person—him and his wife, Nancy—it was a great learning ground."

A stint with Bill Harrell and the Virginians after Don Reno's departure in 1979 was "probably the best four and a half years I've had playing music," said Stephenson. "I loved Bill Harrell. He wasn't drinking and he was taking care of business. He kept us extremely busy. The five of us were together the whole time. It was all new to me. I had only been out of high school for three years."

Stephenson continues to dig deep into the archives. "We did 'Great Speckled Bird' on our gospel CD, *Pull Your Savior In* [2014]," he said. "I grew up with Roy Acuff's record. My mom and dad had it but it took until I was an adult to realize that it was a gospel song. I wanted to record it for eight or nine years before I got around to doing it. I put a different twist on it. As soon as I start singing it, people start applauding and a smile comes to their face."

Stephenson started singing Vernon Dalhart's "The Prisoner's Song" (the flipside of country music's first million-seller, "Wreck of the Old '97") in the late seventies. "It's a fun song for a tenor to sing," he told me in 2016. "I started doing 'Mule Skinner Blues' for fun too. We've been closing shows with it for fifteen years. We have to keep the songs alive. I love those old songs."

"Mule Skinner Blues" was one of thirteen tracks on the guest-laden *20th Anniversary* (2010). "Me and My Old Banjo" featured Sonny Osborne and Ronnie Reno. Connie Smith and Marty Stuart sang on "Talk to Me Lonesome Heart"; Del McCoury added harmony to "Have You Come to Say Goodbye." "It was a scheduling challenge," said Stephenson, "but we got my heroes to sing with me. Everybody was so gracious. Nobody said no. I've known Del since he was living in PA, before his kids could play. Getting to sing with Ricky Skaggs was a treat."

Stephenson knew nothing about Tom T. Hall's wife, Dixie, before they met. "Their assistant came to Ernest Tubb's Midnight Jamboree," he recalled, "and stood in the autograph line. She handed me a CD when she got to the front of the line and said, 'Miss Dixie and Tom T. would like you to record some of their songs.' You could have blown me over with a feather. It didn't take my wife, Dreama, and me long to learn about Miss Dixie. She was a driving force. Both she and Tom T. loved bluegrass and acoustic music. He even had fiddles and banjos on his hits. We became friends and recorded six of their songs. We still do every one onstage. We visited Tom T. when Miss Dixie passed away in 2015. I cherish that friendship."

Stephenson's wife handles everything from booking to designing his website. "Now that we're putting music out on our own label [Whisper Dream Music]," he said, "she's designing CD covers and doing the photography. We've been married seventeen years. I couldn't have done what I've done without her."

Debuting in 1989, the Larry Stephenson Band remains a solid forum for the bandleader's singing. "I've had Kenny Ingram [banjo/vocals] with me for eight years," he said, "and Kevin Richardson [guitar/vocals] for six. Bass player Matt Wright has been here for three. Kenny is one of the legends of the five-string banjo. He played with Jimmy Martin when he was nineteen. He's sixty-four now. He's a pro; leave him alone and let him do what he wants. He gets the job done."

Chapter 32

I've Got That Old Feeling

Alison Krauss's debut on Capitol, her first album of new material in almost eighteen years, *Windy City* (2017) topped *Billboard's* bluegrass, country-music, folk, and Americana charts and reached number nine on its Top 200. "The king of bluegrass is met by a queen who takes it in a new direction," said Abigail Washburn, "full of elegance and grace. It's just as powerful but from a feminine perspective."

Born in Germany, Alison and Viktor's psychologist-turned-real estate broker father, Fred, sang opera at the University of Illinois at Urbana-Champaign. Their mother, Louise, was an illustrator who played guitar and sang harmony. Alison (1971-) started music instruction at five. Viktor (1969-) was already playing piano, "so I took classical violin lessons until I was eleven," she told me in 1989. "I taught myself to play bluegrass."

Competing in fiddle contests from the age of eight (with her brother accompanying her on bass), Krauss won the IL State Fiddle Championship and the National Flatpicking Championship, in Winfield, KS, at thirteen. The siblings recorded *Different Strokes* (1985) with guitarist Maurice Bruce "Swamp" Weiss. "My parents encouraged us to do just about anything," Krauss recalled. "They owned a Flatt & Scruggs record but I didn't listen to it. I listened to J. D. Crowe & the New South."

Kenny Baker and Stuart Duncan influenced Krauss's fiddling. "Kenny's tone was so great," she said, "and his songs were amazing. When Stuart plays a solo, you can't imagine it played any other way."

The SPBGMA's "Most Promising Fiddler in the Midwest" in 1983 and 1984, Krauss caught the ear of Robert L. Jones, who booked her to play the Newport Folk Festival. "[Newport] was incredible," she said, "We'd never played anything like that before. The amount of money we got freaked us out. It was such a prestigious place; it helped tremendously. We got other festivals because we played there."

Rounder signed Krauss on the strength of her demo tape. She recorded her debut album, *Too Late to Cry* (1987), with Sam Bush, Béla Fleck, Jerry

Alison Krauss, 1985

Douglas, Tony Trischka, Russ Barenberg, and Roy Huskey, Jr. Her first album with Union Station, *Two Highways* (1989), included a cover of the Allman Brothers Band's "Midnight Rider."

Coproduced by Jerry Douglas, *I've Got That Old Feeling* (1990) added drums and piano. Selling over one hundred thousand copies, it received a "Best Bluegrass Album" Grammy. Krauss's next album, *Every Time You Say Goodbye* (1992), did equally well. She and Union Station became *Grand Ole Opry* members in July 1993, the *Opry's* first new bluegrass band in three decades.

Released in February 1995, *Now That I've Found You: A Collection* reached the runner-up position on the country charts and number thirteen on pop's Top 200. In addition to nine songs from previous albums, it included Krauss's Grammy-nominated "When You Say Nothing at All" from *Keith Whitley: A Tribute Album* (1994) and covers of the Foundations' "Baby, Now That I've Found You," Bad Company's "Oh, Atlanta," and the Beatles' "I Will."

On the *O Brother, Where Art Thou?* soundtrack, Krauss featured on "Down to the River to Pray" and harmonized with Gillian Welch and Emmylou

Harris on "Didn't Leave Nobody but the Baby." Krauss produced albums by Reba McIntyre, Nickel Creek, and the Cox Family, and she scored a "Best Country Collaboration—With Vocals" Grammy, in 1994, for singing on Shenandoah's "Somewhere in the Middle of the Night." She overtook Aretha Franklin, a decade later, to tie Quincy Jones for the second most Grammy Awards (only Budapest-born classical conductor Sir Georg Solti has more). Placing third in the Kentucky Fried Chicken band contest with Classified Grass in Louisville in 1985, "Alison was fifteen when I saw her and Union Station win [a year later]," remembered Tim Stafford. "She called me a month later and wanted me to join. I couldn't do it; she was living in Chicago. Adam and Tammy Steffey, Barry Bales, Brian Fesler, and I formed Dusty Miller. When Alison had the chance to hire Adam, Barry, and me, I'm glad she did."

Union Station took Stafford to a much higher level. "Our first show was the *Grand Ole Opry*," recalled the Kingsport, TN-born vocalist/guitarist, "the second was Telluride. I didn't know anything about high altitudes. I had never played for that many people; my heart was beating out of my chest.

"Alison liked me singing with her. We blended well. We had epic jam sessions in the early years. We were eaten up by music."

Stafford met Chris Thile, and Sean and Sara Watkins, at a festival in 1990. "Byron Berline wanted Alison and me to come to the campground," Stafford recalled, "and pick with these kids. Chris didn't play mandolin that night; he played guitar. These kids were amazing, the vanguard of young players coming up. Not long afterwards, there were so many great players coming from every direction. Alison was a hero to these kids."

Krauss hadn't yet reached superstardom but Stafford was making a good living. "I didn't leave over finances," he said. "We spent all our time on the road. I was gone 340 days in 1991. It was only going to get busier. I was married and my wife got pregnant. Our son was born in January 1992. It was a tough decision, but if I didn't leave, I was going to regret it."

Stafford remained in music as a DJ and *Bluegrass Unlimited* writer. One of his articles was about the Bristol-based Ken Laughlin Band. "I did an interview and hit it off with their bass player, Wayne Taylor. I thought, 'If he ever leaves that band, maybe we could play together.'"

Stafford ran into Taylor again at the SPBGMA conference in January 1994. "I hadn't seen him in a few years," he remembered. "I said, 'How's the band going?' and he said, 'Well, I'm the only one left. Maybe we should pick some.'"

The group continued to expand. Leaving Ricky Skaggs, Shawn Lane (guitar/vocals) "called to see what I was doing," remembered Stafford. "I told him I was starting this band with Wayne and he said, 'I know Wayne.' So, then, we had Shawn on board. Dobro player Rob Ickes had gone out with Alison and traveled with us. He was friends with Union Station guitarist Ron Block and they had a band for a while, New Wine. I called to ask if he'd be interested in playing and he said, 'I'd love to.'"

"I'm a mix of Mike Auldridge and Jerry Douglas," explained Ickes. "I liked how clean Mike played, that big, warm tone he got, but I like Jerry's energy and blues feeling. The three of us did a record together, *Three Bells* [2014]. Jerry was super nice to me. Mike was the same way, very encouraging. It was a treat to see somebody so excited about music. I picked his brain. He was at the end of his life but he was still fired up."

The band's last piece was banjo. "We held auditions," said Stafford. "Tony Brown was going to be our banjo player. He ended up not being able to do it but he did a four-song demo with us. We auditioned Jason Burleson twice."

Blue Highway's success came unexpectedly. "We were local musicians who played on the weekends," said Stafford, "but we put together a tape and sent it to Dave Freeman of Rebel Records. I had developed a relationship with him when I produced Ricochet, out of NC. We signed a record contract before playing our first show on New Year's Eve 1994 in Kingsport."

Preparing for Blue Highway's first album, *It's a Long, Long Road*, in January 1995, Stafford "tried to get the best material I could," he said. "I knew it was a good record. I remember sitting in the studio, listening to Shawn and Wayne singing the title track. That was the first time I thought we were on to something. The record won the IBMA's 'Album of the Year' and we were 'Emerging Artist.' It spurred us to become full-time. Wayne lost his job as a coal-truck driver so he was free. Shawn was finishing a metals technology degree and was available during the summer."

"Everything fell into place," said Ickes. "Blue Highway had great songwriting, great musicianship, great singing. We added progressive influences, original songs, and covers of songs by Sting and Merle Haggard. Wayne and Shawn singing together had that bluegrass sound. Shawn is from where Ralph Stanley was born. Tim hadn't written much before the band but he started pumping them out."

Born in San Francisco, Ickes grew up a mile southeast of Chico in Mulberry. "It's a musical desert," he said. "There are hardly any places to play but I'd go to bluegrass festivals, where I'd see some great music, get all fired up, go back to the campground, and stay up all night playing. I'd walk around and meet people in the same groove, people playing David Grisman or Django Reinhardt tunes. What a great place to learn."

Ickes' great-grandparents emigrated from Norway. He made his first trip to his ancestral home in April 2016. "Whenever we had family gatherings," he said, "everybody would pull out their fiddle or guitar and play music.

Every time there was a wedding, baby born, or somebody died, there would be a three-day party with a fiddler in the center.

"My grandfather gave me a fiddle lesson when I was seven but I never took it out of the case. I heard Mike Auldridge's first solo record [*Dobro*, 1972] when I was thirteen. I can't even describe how it made me feel. I've spoken to other people who had a similar experience. That record got them, maybe not into playing Dobro, but into playing something and singing. It hit me harder than most. It was like a drug. I had to learn every note. I picked up the Dobro fast. People were impressed with the way I played. The more I kept playing, and the further out I played, the more I realized I might have something special. I knew I wanted to play for the rest of my life. As I got older, I got to work with better musicians."

Moving to Nashville, Ickes played on the Cox Family's *Everybody's Reaching Out for Someone* (1990). The Krauss-produced album received a "Best Southern, Country, or Bluegrass Recording" Grammy. "We rehearsed at Alison's apartment," Ickes said, "the night before recording. She was music, music, music. That was her life. She didn't know how to wash dishes or fold clothes."

Playing with Earl Scruggs between 1992 and 2012, Ickes featured on the banjo player's album with Doc Watson and Ricky Skaggs, *The Three Pickers*. It remained on the *Billboard* charts for 138 weeks. "I've never met anyone as versatile as Doc," he said. "You'd hear him playing the blues and think that's all he'd been doing since he was born. Then, you'd hear him play bluegrass. He did it all well."

Ickes was the youngest player on the Jerry Douglas/Tut Taylor-produced *The Great Dobro Sessions*. It too received a "Best Bluegrass Album" Grammy. "All these great things were happening," he said, "but it was still, 'How do I make a living?' When I started playing on Alison's records, I was, 'Okay, here we go,' but it took a couple of years before people started calling me for sessions. I was broke."

Shawn Lane and Jason Burleson grew up in musical families. "Shawn's grandpa was a fiddler," said Stafford, "and Jason's uncle played banjo. I didn't grow up in that kind of family."

Stafford's earliest influence came from his piano-playing twin sisters. "They're twelve years older than me," he said. "They were sixteen in 1964 and went through the Beatles craze. I had to go through it too. I love the Beatles. I love great songs, great melodies, and great chord progressions."

Stafford discovered bluegrass in high school. "I had a teacher, Wayne Chilcote, who had a bluegrass band, Country Comfort," he recalled, "and a very forceful personality. Students tried to play bluegrass because of him. One of his inspirations was the Country Gentlemen. Doyle Lawson's mother lived near the high school. The Country Gentlemen's bus would pull up and stop. One day, I got the nerve to talk to them. Doyle still talks about it. I remember him asking me what I played and telling him guitar. He said, 'I bet you've heard Tony [Rice].'

"There was a blossoming of music going on. *Deliverance* was in the theaters and people were thinking that bluegrass was 'cool.' It was organic, a fun musical option."

Stafford attended his first bluegrass festival, in Wise County, VA, in 1976. "Everybody went crazy over Ralph Stanley," he said. "He had Keith Whitley with him."

It took Stafford a while to get into the Stanley Brothers but once he did, he totally immersed himself in their music. "I've always loved bluesy sounds," he explained, "and soulful singing. There's no one with a richer tradition of singing than the Stanley family. It filtered down to Ricky Skaggs and Larry Sparks. I love that soulful sound.

"I didn't see Bill Monroe until I had been playing for years. I played with him, in 1979, when I had a local group. I wasn't aware of his status. I had a few of his albums that my dad's friend let me borrow but they didn't hit me as much as more modern things. I was already into Tony Rice and David Grisman. It took a while to appreciate the early stuff."

Country Comfort morphed into the Boys in the Band. Stafford joined around 1980. "We traveled to festivals in Winfield, KS and Peace River, FL," he said. "Adam Steffey [mandolin] joined in '82. I left in '84 to work on my Ph.D. in history, at Miami University, in OH, but I never finished the degree. I finished all the coursework but not the dissertation."

Glen Lawson (who replaced Tony Rice in J. D. Crowe & the New South) filled in for Stafford. Upon his return, Stafford reclaimed the slot. Barry Bales (bass) joined soon afterwards. It wouldn't be the band's last change. "Adam and his wife at the time, Tammy Rogers, wanted to play together," explained Stafford. "They approached Barry and me about joining them in a group with Brian Fesler [who would later play banjo for the Lonesome River Band]. That's how Dusty Miller started. We recorded a self-produced cassette and an album on June Appal and stayed together until Alison hired Adam, Barry, and me in early 1990."

Blue Highway celebrated its twenty-third anniversary in 2017. "We kept the original members together," said Stafford, "until Rob left. Jason left for a couple of years but came back. Wayne's had so many health issues including heart attack and colon cancer, within a few months of each other, around 2000. Fifteen years later, he had quadruple bypass surgery, but everything went well. He's in great shape and has a lot more energy. He's lost weight. He's mean, lean, and still singing great."

Since its second album, *Wind to the West* (1996), Blue Highway has focused on original material. "Our first Rounder album, *Still Climbing Mountains* [2001], was one of the first bluegrass albums of original material," claimed Stafford. "Jerry Douglas produced it."

Ickes played his last show with Blue Highway in November 2015. He "was being pointed in other directions and burning out," he said. "I've always told myself that I wouldn't play music just for a paycheck. That came from watching my dad, who was a cop. He burnt out but had to keep doing it."

Ickes' departure came as a shock. "We weren't expecting him to leave," recalled Stafford, "but we wanted to continue. Jason told me that I had to hear Gaven Largent. We didn't do any other tryouts. He was all we needed; he amazes me every time we get onstage. He's been playing since he was five [he was nineteen when he joined] and he never plays anything the same way twice. He's upped the game for us."

Blue Highway released its first post-Ickes CD, *Original Traditional*, in September 2016. "We wanted to do a traditional album," said Stafford, "but, except for a gospel song ['Hallelujah'], it's all original. The title's a good description. We've always loved traditional bluegrass. Shawn is from Scott County, two counties from where Ralph and Carter grew up. He has that soulful sound."

Blue Highway (Shawn Lane, Gaven Largent, Wayne Taylor, Tim Stafford), 2016

Since leaving Blue Highway, Ickes has teamed with singer-songwriter Trey Hensley. "We definitely love bluegrass," he said, "but we're exploring new things too. Trey's playing electric guitar and I play lap steel. Trey reminds me of Doc. He has a great feel for blues, country, and bluegrass. When the right people get together, it's like a fire."

Joining Alison Krauss and Union Station full-time in 1994, Daniel John "Dan" Tyminski loved that they "wanted to play music all the time." The Rutland, VT-born banjo/mandolin player said, "I don't think you get to their level without that degree of commitment. Those were fun years, when the instruments never went in their cases."

Tyminski (1967-) knew he "wanted to play music as far back as my memory goes," he said. "J. D. Crowe's album with the New South was certainly a spark but I already liked music."

Learning a few chords on guitar at the age of six, Tyminski switched to mandolin within a year. "I played it until I heard that J. D. Crowe record when I was twelve," he recalled, "and my life changed. I knew I wanted to play banjo. I spent my formative years with a banjo in my hands."

Tyminski's greatest influence came from Del McCoury's banjo player Paul Silvius. "He was king to me," Tyminski recalled. "He wasn't playing licks learned from someone else but very melodic, all meat and potatoes."

Forming the Green Mountain Bluegrass Boys, in the early eighties, with his brother Stan on guitar, Tyminski "traveled everywhere we could go," he remembered. "We slept in the car, whatever we had to do to go to festivals. We covered bluegrass tunes, picking songs we liked and doing our versions."

Tyminski joined Sammy Shelor, guitarist Ronnie Bowman, and founding mandolinist Tim Austin's Lonesome River Band in 1988. "Those were some of the most fun years I've had," he remembered. "I was young and free. I had just moved away from home. I slept in my van or on a floor so I could play music. It was a great big beautiful world."

The Lonesome River Band's brand of bluegrass excited Tyminski. "I like high-energy, forceful, and intense power-grass," he explained. "I like to feel the freight train moving. They had that."

Hearing the Lonesome River Band's *Looking for Yourself* (1989), Alison Krauss called Tyminski, offering a job. "This was early on with the Lonesome River Band," he said, "so I turned her down."

Tyminski gradually became a fan of Krauss's music. When he got a second chance to join her band, in 1992, he took it. "I stayed for half a year," he said, "and went back to the Lonesome River Band for another year and a half because I felt like I was letting my buddies down. We had just released *Carrying the Tradition*, the IBMA's album of the year."

It was 1994 before Tyminski heard from Krauss. This time the timing was right. "I don't know how many people leave a mark," Tyminski said a quarter-century later, "but she's at the top of that list. Not all of what she plays is bluegrass but we play bluegrass instruments. We mix different types of music but much of what we do is traditional, hardcore bluegrass."

The addition of Jerry Douglas as a full-time member, in 1998, was a welcomed surprise. "Adam Steffey needed to make a move," explained Tyminski. "We were looking at Jerry to get us through the summer but it worked out so well, he said, 'If you want to do it all the time, I'm all about it.' When I played with my brother in Green Mountain Bluegrass, we had David Bevins, a phenomenal Dobro player. Mike Auldridge's playing was in a different world but when Jerry arrived, the torch passed to him. He took the Dobro and made it cool. We're lucky to have a person who changed the face of his instrument."

Singing for George Clooney in *O Brother, Where Art Thou?*, Tyminski continues to perform with the Soggy Bottom Boys. "I can't explain how I ended up with that gig," he said, "but it was a life-changer. I wasn't keen on how they wanted to record it in one take without overdubs. It made me rethink how I listen to music as to what the best it could be actually is. Since *O Brother*, I think the best it could be is whatever way moves you the most.

"It was amazing to see how that film changed the demographics. Audiences went from doctors, lawyers, and librarians to people in rock-and-roll T-shirts, spiked hair, and fake jewelry."

Krauss's collaboration with Robert Plant, *Raising Sand* (2007), brought bluegrass to the global stage. "When I was a kid," Plant told *The Nashville Scene*, "there was a hit record in England by Lonnie Donegan, who was . . . a skiffle player . . . a combination of bluegrass and folk."[1]

"Any time anyone has a side project," said Tyminski, "it's beneficial to the whole band. Their success trickles down to all of us. It was an awesome thing Alison did with Robert. It allowed me to do things I might not have had a chance to do, like the Dan Tyminski Band."

Tyminski worked with Swedish producer Avicii on an electronic dance track, "Hey Brother," in 2013. A dance-club hit, it reached number one in six countries. "That goes to show you," said Tyminski, "there's room for all kinds of things. That project opened me to music I was unaware of before. Will that affect the next music I play? Absolutely, but am I going to use that as a template? No, not at all, but it adds to my vocabulary."

Chapter 33

Pocket Full of Keys

Few people dominated bluegrass in the early twenty-first century as much as southeastern KY-born Dale Ann Bradley, the IBMA's "Female Vocalist of the Year" in 2007, 2008, 2009, 2011, and 2012. "Some people think I'm too young to have grown up with this music," said the daughter of a coal miner/Primitive Baptist minister, "but I grew up in the coal hills in the Cumberland Gap, where VA, TN, and KY meet, and things haven't changed since my great-grandmother's time."

Bradley (1964-) spent much of her early life without electricity or running water. "We lived in a house with my grandmother," she said. "We finally got a light socket. Everything ran off it with extension cords. Things didn't change until my senior year in high school. That's when we got city water, electricity, and cable.

"We didn't have musical instruments at home and certainly not in the church. It was a lot like how Ralph Stanley grew up. Knoxville and Cincinnati churches had shape notes but we didn't have them in the mountains, where it was modal singing. You could hear it from a distance, ringing out to the hollers from this little brick building. I learned to sing harmony parts."

Acquiring her first guitar at fourteen, Bradley cut a pick from a milk jug. "It was flimsy," she recalled, "but it was all I had."

Hailing from the same hollow as Bradley's mother, Mearl Risner's family "was dirt poor like everybody else, but he put himself through college," Bradley said. "He was the county's band director for many years. During the summer, he worked at Pine Mountain, the first state park in KY, as entertainment director. I'd go and sing with him and his wife. We added Harold McGeorge, who played banjo, and started playing gigs as Backporch Grass."

Playing mostly at private parties and restaurants, Backporch Grass "was a huge starting ground for a young girl," said Bradley, "but it wasn't easy for my parents to accept for the longest time."

Married in 1985 or '86 (she can't remember), Bradley moved to Jacksonville. "My ex-husband was stationed at the Naval Station," she said, "but he was going to be deployed for six months. When I found I was expectant with my son, I went back to KY. After he was born, I knew I was going to have to do something."

Bradley became a regular on the *Renfro Valley Barn Dance*. "I was under a five-year exclusive contract," she said. "I started as a solo act and remained until the early 2000s, even with traveling. They bent with my schedule."

In 1937, ex-*National Barn Dance* producer John Lair assembled the Coon Creek Girls, featuring Powell County, KY-born clawhammer banjo/fiddle player Lily May Ledford, for his Saturday-night *Renfro Valley Barn Dance*. Appearing on the show for eighteen years, the Coon Creek Girls, with Ledford's sisters, Rosie (guitar) and Minnie (stage name: Susie), performed at the White House, along with Bascom Lunsford's square dancers, when Pres. Franklin Roosevelt hosted King George VI and Queen Elizabeth in 1939.

Lair launched the New Coon Creek Girls, with Vicki Simmons, a student of Lily May Ledford, Pam Perry Combs, Wanda Barnett, and Pam Gadd in 1979. Gadd and Combs left to join Wild Rose in 1988 (rejoining in 2014). Bradley auditioned to be a replacement. "They were looking for a fiddle player," she said, "but I didn't play fiddle. Mandolin player Deanie Richardson auditioned around the same time and they hired her [she would leave to play with Holly Dunn]. They called me to play guitar and sing when there was another opening. I was signed to *Renfro Valley* but they let me play with the New Coon Creek Girls. I made decent money playing music and learned a lot."

Produced by Sonny Osborne, Bradley's debut solo album, *East Kentucky Morning*, included a bluegrass version of U2's "I Still Haven't Found What I'm Looking For." "Working with Sonny, I learned things I needed to learn," said Bradley. "One was not to trade emotion for perfection. I learned about tone and mixing, how to balance players. It was invaluable."

Performing together since 1997, Dale Ann Bradley and her band, Coon Creek, didn't make their recording debut until nearly twenty years later. "Pinecastle let me produce *Pocket Full of Keys* [2015]," Bradley said, "and this time, I used my band. Scott Powers [mandolin], Greg Blaylock [guitar, banjo, Dobro], and Tim Dishman [upright bass] are very special. They worked so hard on the songs. It meant a lot to me."

The IBMA's "Fiddler of the Year" ten times between 2001 and 2015, Henryville, IN-born Michael Cleveland played at Bill Monroe's Bean Blossom Festival before his tenth birthday. Alison Krauss introduced him at the *Grand Ole Opry* three years later. By nineteen, he was amazing Dale Ann Bradley's audiences with masterful, straight-from-the-heart fiddling. He would spend three years with Rhonda Vincent before forming Michael Cleveland & Flamekeeper.

Dale Ann Bradley, 2014

During his senior year at the KY School for the Blind, in 1999, Cleveland (1980-) considered what he was going to do after graduation. "I was going to go to college," he said "or find a gig and start playing music. I heard Doyle Lawson might be looking but he already hired somebody."

One day, Cleveland's phone rang. Vicki Simmons, Bradley's bass player, was calling. "Deanie Richardson recommended me," recalled Cleveland. "They were playing at a bar in Shepherdsville, KY every Friday. They sent me *East Kentucky Morning* and *Old Southern Porches*. There wasn't a lot of time. I had to learn the fiddle parts in a couple of days, but whatever they were going to play, I knew. I learned so much about being on the road.

"Deanie Richardson was a hero to me. I jammed with her when I was nine. She had a very aggressive style. My grandparents recorded the jam session and I tried copying every lick she played."

Leaving Bradley after six months, Cleveland teamed with mandolinist/ vocalist Rhonda Vincent. "Rhonda was playing old-school bluegrass," he said. "I wanted to play with her because my friend, Steve Sutton, played banjo in her band. I had gone to MerleFest in 1996 and jammed with him, Roland White, and Brian Allen. I loved picking with Steve. After that jam, he said, 'One of these days, you and I are going to be in a band.' When the opportunity came, he told Rhonda to call me."

Playing with Vincent led to Cleveland's first IBMA "Fiddler of the Year"

Michael Cleveland, 2012

award. "She came out with *Back Home Again* [2000]," he said, "and we were playing everywhere. We were even busier the following year. We'd improvise on 'Sally Goodin' for ten minutes, play 'Fire on the Mountain' at 200 beats a minute. It allowed me to become consistent as a player."

Cleveland scored three "Instrumental Album of the Year" IBMA awards. A duo album with banjo player Tom Adams, *Live at the Ragged Edge* (2004), followed his first solo album, *Flame Keeper*, two years before. "It wasn't intended to be an album," he said. "Tom and I had both left Rhonda Vincent's band. I went back to Dale Ann Bradley. I sent tapes of her music to Tom and we did some shows with her. I ended up going back to Tom's place, in Gettysburg, between shows. We had a few days off. On one of those days, he said, 'I know a coffeehouse where we could play for fifty bucks apiece.' I'm ready to play anytime. There wasn't any talk about an album. I don't think the place could hold more than thirty people, if that. A couple of hours before we were supposed to play, Tom remembered that we didn't have a sound system. We ended up going to a church and borrowing their equipment. It wasn't an elaborate setup. Tom and I recorded it for fun but Tom played great on it. Ken Irwin loved it. It's the cheapest album he's ever made."

"*Let 'Er Go, Boys*," Cleveland's third straight IBMA winner, came out in 2006. *Leavin' Town* followed in 2008 and *Fired Up* in 2011.

Cleveland's playing reflects diverse influences. "You can hear Bobby Hicks, Benny Martin, Scotty Stoneman, Kenny Baker, Dale Potter, and Vassar Clements," he said. "I try to take the approach they would take."

From earliest memory, bluegrass enraptured Cleveland. "My grandparents had a big record collection," he said, "and an eight-track player. I remember turning one of the speakers over, laying my head on it, and going to sleep to bluegrass."

A local bluegrass association presented concerts in Henryville. There was another show fifteen miles away in Scottsburg. "It gave local players an opportunity to get stage time," recalled Cleveland. "Bands would sign up for a thirty-minute slot. There were so many bands, it would go from seven o'clock to eleven and not get in all the bands. There was jamming out in the parking lot."

Cleveland's grandparents started taking him to concerts when he was six months old. "I was at a show when I was four," he recalled, "and heard a fiddler playing 'Orange Blossom Special.' That did it. I knew I wanted to learn to play the fiddle, even if it was only to play that song."

As they were preparing to send him to school, Cleveland's parents heard about a strings program at the KY School for the Blind. "It taught the Suzuki method," he said. "Miss Nolan, the music teacher, asked me why I wanted to play the violin. I told her, 'I don't know much about the violin but I know a lot about the fiddle.' That didn't go over too well. She didn't want me playing bluegrass. She thought it would hurt my playing but she showed me simple versions of 'Boil the Cabbage Down' and 'Old Joe Clark.' Once I got to where I could play, I started going to local shows and jamming in the parking lot."

Mac McBain "was the first person to take the time to play with me in the parking lots," said Cleveland. "He wasn't a fancy fiddler but he knew old fiddle tunes like 'Up Jumped the Devil' and 'Soldier's Joy' and showed me how to play them."

Conflict between classical violin and bluegrass fiddling was inevitable. "My teacher wanted me to go to workshops with a classical instructor," Cleveland remembered, "but there were bluegrass festivals going on. My mom didn't care for bluegrass but my grandparents kept taking me to the festivals. I ended up telling my teacher no and dropping out of the classical program. I came back a few years later and Miss Nolan listened to me play. She said, 'Wow! You're a lot better now—far more advanced. What have you been doing?' 'Well, I've been playing bluegrass.' I started bringing in records by Kenny Baker and Bobby Hicks and she got a new respect for bluegrass.

"I heard hip-hop and rap, and tried to like it, but I always came back to bluegrass. I'd go home on the weekends and go to bluegrass shows. Other kids went home but they couldn't wait to get back to school. They had nothing to do. I was the opposite. I don't think the school understood me all that well."

The "big sound of fiddles" awed Cleveland. "Unless you have a good fiddle," he said, "you can't do that. It took a while before I had a good instrument. My folks didn't know what they were doing. We ended up renting from a local music store. I started on small fiddles. They had to special order a sixteenth-sized fiddle. I moved on to an eighth and then a quarter-sized. John Cikowski saw me playing the rented quarter-sized fiddle and said, 'Man, that fiddle is a piece of junk.' I said, 'Really?' He said, 'Let me get you a good fiddle.' I thought, 'This guy doesn't know what he's talking about,' but when he showed up the next week, he had one for me. It was a lot better than the one I was trying to play. From then on, he's kept finding me fiddles. When I grew into a half-sized fiddle, he found a fiddle for me built in the 1800s. It sounded great, as close to a full-sized fiddle as you could get."

Pete Wernick invited Cleveland to be part of the Bluegrass Youth All-Stars performance at the IBMA Awards ceremony in 1993. The *Washington Post* had claimed that bluegrass was dying off among young people. "Pete wanted to prove that article wrong," said Cleveland. "He got Josh Williams, Cody Kilby, Chris Thile, and me. Chris's mandolin playing blew my mind. I had never heard a kid play like that. He was so far ahead of his age."

Appearing "in front of the bluegrass community," Cleveland "was a kid in a candy store," he said, "meeting Byron Berline and Eddie Stubbs, just about everybody you could imagine."

After the Bluegrass Youth All-Stars' performance went well, a lineup led by Cleveland, Thile, and Kilby organized for a tour. "It was a slightly different configuration than the awards show," said Cleveland. "We got together, practiced, and even talked about recording an album."

Wernick produced Thile's first solo album, *Leading Off* . . . (1994). "He was the only 'kid musician' on the record," Wernick said. "The rest were well-known players."

Wernick would present the *Young American Bluegrass Idols* at the IBMA Awards ceremony in 2003, with preteen artists including Sierra Hull (mandolin) and Sarah Jarosz (bass/mandolin).

During the 1993 IBMA conference, Cleveland sat in with Doc Watson, Tim O'Brien, Pete Wernick, and Dan Crary. "They were jamming as my father and I were walking by," he said. "My dad asked if it'd be all right if I played a couple of tunes with them. The first tune was 'Black Mountain Rag.' We did it just like the *Will the Circle Be Unbroken* album, where Doc starts in the key of D and Vassar takes it to the key of A.

"That's how Alison Krauss first heard me. Not long afterwards, she was playing in New Albany, not far from where I lived. We went to watch her play. My grandparents and I talked to her after the concert. My grandparents might have said something about me having a dream to play the *Opry*. A week after she became an *Opry* member, she called. I had just come home from school. 'Hey, Mike, it's Alison.' I said, 'Alison who?' She said, 'Alison Krauss.' I thought it was somebody messing with me but she asked me to come and play on the Opry. Luckily, I was too young to be nervous. I didn't think of the magnitude of what I was doing."

Invited to appear on *A Prairie Home Companion*, Cleveland was unaware of the NPR program. "Where I grew up," he said, "people listened to old-school bluegrass. I didn't know anything about bands like Hot Rize. When *A Prairie Home Companion* called, I didn't know anything about it; neither did my folks. We didn't listen to the show. They wanted me to come to St. Paul, Minnesota and play. My dad said, 'They're crazy.' Then, we found out that they paid for the flights and hotel rooms, so we went and did it."

Joining the Blue Hollow Band, Cleveland played around the Midwest and competed in contests. "School was always a problem," he said. "The teachers took a sensible look at it and said that I needed to have something to fall back on, but I believed I was a musician. My parents let me miss a day, if it was important, but they kept me in school. I respect them for that. Music would have become a job fast."

Cleveland collaborated with Andy Statman and Tim O'Brien on *Superstring Theory* (2013). "Andy wrote all the tunes," he said, "with the exception of 'Green Rocky Road' and Ritchie Valens' 'Come On, Let's Go.' He books studio time without having an idea of what he's going to record. A couple of weeks before the sessions, he starts writing. If I did it that way, I don't know if I'd have anything or not. It inspired me to write more."

A video of Flamekeeper's mandolinist Nathan Livers playing "Jerusalem Ridge" backstage at the Forrest Fest in Louisville, in early 2016, went viral. "The Inspire channel picked it up," said Cleveland, "and it wound up getting more than six and a half million views."

At the 2017 IBMA awards, Michael Cleveland & Flamekeeper were "Instrumental Group of the Year" and received an "Instrumental Recorded Performance of the Year" award for the title track of the Grammy-nominated *Fiddler's Dream* (2016). A variety of guests appeared on the album. "Sam Bush and Jason Carter sang," said Cleveland. "Jerry Douglas played Dobro and Andy Statman played mandolin. I had played with Sam Bush and [guitarist] Dave Peterson in Nashville. Barry Bales and I worked together in a few situations. I loved playing twin fiddle with Jason Carter. We think the same way. I wanted people to hear Lloyd Douglas, a banjo player from

Michigan who's one of the best-kept secrets in bluegrass. He played with the Warrior River Boys and Jim & Jesse. He's a conductor on a railroad but he's my first call when I need a banjo player. He knows my tunes exactly like the records."

Bush featured on a version of John Hartford's "Steamboat Whistle Blues." "We recorded at Compass Studios," said Cleveland, "which used to be Hillbilly Central, the studio where [Hartford] recorded *Aereo-Plain* in 1971. Hearing Sam tell stories about Hartford and Vassar Clements was a blast."

An original instrumental, "Blues for Bill" paid tribute to the father of bluegrass. "I didn't write it with the name in mind," said Cleveland, "but it definitely sounds like Bill Monroe."

Chapter 34

Genuine Negro Jigs

Appalachian State University (ASU) English professor Cecelia "Cece" Conway's *African Banjo Echoes in Appalachia* (University of Tennessee Press, 1995) stirred interest in the banjo's African-American roots. An Internet group, Black Banjo: Then and Now (originally Black Banjo Players: Now and Then), organized in March 2004. Thirteen months later, Conway helped to stage the first Black Banjo Then and Now Gathering on the Boone, NC campus where she taught. "Just saying the banjo was African-American," recalled Rhiannon Giddens, "you'd be flayed. Many people were holding on to cherished misbeliefs that the banjo was invented in the Appalachian Mountains by Irish people and that black people didn't have anything to do with it."

"There were enough people with questions," added Dom Flemons, who formed Sankofa Strings (the Carolina Chocolate Drops) with Giddens after the conference. "I came as a guest but it changed my life. I met musicians including Mike Seeger, who had always been an advocate for the black influence on country music. He introduced me to the music of Lesley Riddle, a quintessential part of the story."

There had been previous banjo gatherings, but this was the first to focus on the instrument's black roots. "For scholars and musicians, including a handful of black musicians and the elders they brought," said Giddens, "it was validation."

Phoenix-born Flemons (1982-) was two months shy of graduating college when he attended the gathering with Sule Greg Wilson, a percussionist from Washington, DC. "I had been playing with the Wild Whiskey Boys," Flemons said. "The guitar player let me borrow a banjo for the summer. He didn't like the fifth string so he took it off. He was just strumming it, learning jazz tunes. I had been playing guitar. I took what I had been doing and transferred it, in open G, to the banjo. I saw it as being in the same tradition as what Pete Seeger did. He worked with his twelve-string guitar and banjo and came up with creative stuff to accompany the songs. I did the same thing."

316

Seeing him with his crude four-string banjo, an observer handed Flemons a Deering banjo. "He told me to learn clawhammer," Flemons recalled. "I was encouraged to continue moving forward. After I finished college, I sold a lot of things, packed what I had left, loaded my car, and took off for NC."

The recipient of the Steve Martin Prize for Excellence in Banjo and Blue-grass Music in 2016, Greensboro, NC-born Giddens (1977-) grew up with old-time music and bluegrass. "There were still remnants of the traditions like Joe Thompson," she recalled, "and people in the mountains. Northern-ers came to study with people like Tommy Jarrell and stayed. I didn't know the music's history until I was an adult but I knew it was going on."

Trained as an opera singer, Giddens graduated from Oberlin Conservatory in 2000. "Opera taught me to be resilient," she said, "how to breathe, and how to learn an instrument. Picking up the banjo, I went back to how I learned opera, staying with it and being tenacious and repetitive. It's great to go deep in any music.

"Being a classical singer, people expect me to wear heels, but I'm over six feet tall. It's hard to find good shoes. I stressed out about what I was going to wear with my dress but I stopped caring what people thought about my feet. I was barefoot at the White House."

Giddens, Flemons, and Wilson occasionally joined with fiddler/jug player Justin Robinson. "We were committed to the blues," said Flemons, "and the jazzier side of string-band music. We played MerleFest between the Nitty Gritty Dirt Band and Elvis Costello. It was the greatest feeling. There were 40,000 people on the lawn."

Taking their original name (Sankofa Strings) from a word in Ghana's Twi language that translates as "go back and get it," the group became the Carolina Chocolate Drops. *Colored Aristocracy* reissued as *The Carolina Chocolate Drops Presents* (2011). Things skyrocketed. "I could see from the first moment," Flemons said, "that we were destined for greatness but it kept going and going. It was like being in the Negro baseball leagues. Obama was president and we had eight years with him in office. During the primaries, he'd speak in a town and we'd play music. It was an exciting time."

The Carolina Chocolate Drops' debut outing on Nonesuch, *Genuine Negro Jig* (2010), scored a "Best Traditional Folk Album" Grammy. The *Guardian* called it "an appealing grab-bag of antique country, blues, jug band hits and gospel hollers, all given an agreeably downhome production."[1]

"The Carolina Chocolate Drops are . . . revisiting, with a joyful vengeance, black string-band, and jug-band music of the Twenties and Thirties," added *Rolling Stone*, "the dirt-floor dance electricity of the Mississippi Sheiks and Cannon's Jug Stompers."[2]

Rhiannon Giddens, 2011

"We made great strides with old-time music," said Giddens. "It's quintessential American music. It needs to breathe. It should never be a relic."

"People were so ready to see what we were doing," added Flemons. "They wanted to see a black string band that was good and we gave them everything they were looking for. We were young people enjoying ourselves. Rhiannon and Justin were embracing their Southern culture. It was an excellent package. With my knowledge of folklore, and the crisscrossing traditions, we talked our ways into bigger places. I thought of us as the Kingston Trio, the New Lost City Ramblers, and Peter, Paul and Mary but with a variety of sounds and songs."

The Carolina Chocolate Drops spent Thursday nights with third-generation African-American fiddler Joseph Aquiler Thompson (1918-2012). "Joe was a very quiet fellow," remembered Flemons, "but when he raised his voice to tell a story, everybody would stop and listen to what he had to say. He had a stroke a couple of years before I met him and the fiddle was his way of getting back to health. He had treasured memories of playing square dances with his brother, father, and uncle, but he had never played publically in any commercial way."

Dom Flemons, 2013

British folklorist Bruce Bastin was researching Blind Boy Fuller and Piedmont-style country blues, in the early 1970s, when he began recording old-time banjo players. "[Bastin] met Joe's cousin, Odell Thompson," said Flemons, "and then Joe joined him as a folklore package. They hadn't played together before but they knew the same songs."

"Somebody once told me, 'Don't teach [Joe] new tunes,'" Giddens said, "as if the modern world would corrupt him, but he was a musician to the end; he wanted to learn new things. His left hand wasn't as precise as it used to be but his bowing was still amazing. He lived and breathed music. We took the heart of it, not the exact thing. It wasn't about playing the 'right' notes. When I play those tunes with Justin, it's as though we're sitting with Joe. It got in our bones."

Flemons explored roots further with Durham-based bluesman John Dee Holeman (1929-). "He plays in a style that's a combination of Lightnin' Hopkins and John Lee Hooker," he said, "but he also sings 'Down Yonder' and 'God Loves His Children.' He heard them on the radio when he was growing up."

Flemons also spent time with Boo Hanks (1929-), a Piedmont-style guitar player in the Blind Boy Fuller mode. "He grew up playing square dances with his father," Flemons said. "He never played out much but he loved music. He was just a feller who played in the community during the weekends. It wasn't until I met him, when he was seventy-nine years old, that he made a record. I don't think anybody would have seen him if I hadn't started working with him through the Music Maker Relief Foundation."

The Carolina Chocolate Drops experienced change following Robinson's departure, in 2011, and the addition of guitar/mandolin/banjo/bones player Hubby Jenkins and beatboxer Adam Matta. A bigger change occurred two years later, when Flemons announced he would be leaving at the end of November 2013. "I was in a weird spot," he recalled. "Everyone was saying that I had been unreasonable to work with. I started believing them. I decided to be the bigger person and walk away. That's where I've been sitting with it—doing my material and performing solo. I have a clear conscience.

"Playing solo has always been the easiest thing for me. One of my biggest influences as a storyteller and entertainer was Dave Van Ronk. I saw him when I was eighteen. It was right before he passed. He told amazing stories along with his songs. I thought it was the greatest thing. I've applied that to my show. As one of Mike Seeger's students, I started on the guitar, banjo, and harmonica. When I came to NC, I started playing the jug. I got the rhythm bones when I was at the fiddlers' convention in Mt. Airy, NC. I picked up the 'quills,' or panpipes, from a fellow Mike introduced me to."

Giddens participated with an all-star lineup on *Lost on the River: The New Basement Tapes* (2014). "Working with unfinished Dylan lyrics was challenging," she said. "It pushed me in a big way. Elvis Costello, Marcus Mumford, Taylor Goldsmith, and Jim James were all fabulous."

Planning to keep the Carolina Chocolate Drops going, Giddens found an offer from T Bone Burnett irresistible. "I was content to continue with the band," she said, "and so happy to find [guitar, bones, snare drum, cajón, and djembe player] Rowan Corbett and [cellist] Malcolm Parson, but I got the offer to record the solo album and you have to follow where you're being led as an artist. I was able to bring the guys with me to the Rhiannon Giddens Band but we've gone places where the Carolina Chocolate Drops couldn't go."

For her first album as a bandleader, *Tomorrow Is My Turn* (2015), Giddens "wanted to honor women who inspired me and covered tunes by Patsy Cline, Odetta, Dolly Parton, and Nina Simone," she said. "It all came from a common well."

Giddens' second outing, *Freedom Highway* (2017), garnered an "Album of the Year" nomination at the Americana Music Honors & Awards.

Giddens appeared in a recurring role as Hanna Lee "Hallie" Jordan on CMT's *Nashville.* At a dinner party for the cast, she met Scott Borchetta, the head of Taylor Swift's record label, Big Machine. "The conversation got around to me," she said, "and he asked if I had been to Nashville. I was thinking, 'Is he kidding? We were the first black string band at the *Opry.* I bored him to death talking about the banjo. I don't care about the fame or celebrity. I just want to talk about the banjo and American music, the voices that have been lost, this rich tapestry that we keep trying to thin out. That's why I'm on this planet."

Chapter 35

Jamgrass

Merging progressive bluegrass with the spirit of the Grateful Dead and the Allman Brothers Band, a growing breed of bands incorporated mountain music into diverse-as-America palettes. Not everyone was pleased. "Much of what passes for 'bluegrass' these days," wrote Kathy Kallick in a column for the CA Bluegrass Association, "sounds to me like rock bands playing acoustic instruments. The singing has no connection to the bluegrass approach, instruments are plugged in so they have erratic sound quality, and the songs often sound like rootless 'product' rather than expressions based in honest emotion."[1]

Others take a different view. "Bluegrass has improv built into it," said Vince Herman, guitarist/vocalist of Boulder-based Leftover Salmon. "Jamgrass is bluegrass from a jazz perspective and taking it further."

Leftover Salmon fuses Herman's Cajun/Zydeco, old-time, and bluegrass influences with the instrumental explorations of Mark Vann (banjo, vocals) and Drew Emmitt (mandolin). The result is a genre-crossing music dubbed "Polyethnic Cajun Slamgrass." "People have been partying on the bluegrass scene for a long time," said Herman. "John Hartford brought a hippie crowd, open to so many things, yet they held reverence for tradition. We can be party people and still honor that deep bluegrass tradition."

Hailing from Pittsburgh, Herman (1962-) grew up "just forty-five minutes from the Mason-Dixon Line," he said. "West Virginia called to me because of its beauty. I went to college there, and got deeper into bluegrass, but Pittsburgh had a lot of music going on. The Smoky City Folk Festival exposed me to bluegrass. It was the first time I saw people, who had just met each other, standing in a circle, playing tunes, and having a ball. I watched that and wow! I had been learning to play guitar but once I saw that, I was deep down the bluegrass highway."

The youngest of seven kids, Herman "absorbed my older siblings' music," he said. "My ears are older than my age. I was used to hearing diatonic accordion. As opposed to the keyboard accordion, you get a

322

rhythm that's so driving. I grew up listening to Motown, rock and roll, the British Invasion, the Rolling Stones, and Mott the Hoople. All this stuff was in my ears, including polkas. Cajun music made sense to me but bluegrass was the road I chose to go down.

"I came dangerously close to graduating from WV University. By that time, I was deep into bluegrass and old-time and wanted to play with a more-inclusive edge. Once I realized that Hot Rize was living in Boulder, and there was a scene, a buddy and I jumped into a 1956 Volvo wagon and pushed the speed thermometer. It was a good adventure. The very first thing we did when we got to town was pull up to a bar with a sign that said, 'Bluegrass tonight.'"

The group playing that night, the Left-Hand String Band, included Emmitt, Vann, and Glenn Keefe. "I was using Grisman and Hot Rize as my blueprint," said Nashville-born Emmitt, "but as I began writing, my rock and roll ideas kept coming up and I thought, 'What if I could fuse bluegrass and rock and roll.'"[2]

"They didn't have a drummer," remembered Herman. "They were a straight-ahead bluegrass band but they were progressive at the same time and played original tunes."

"When you're playing well," Emmitt told Rachel Steele, "you're Zen and in the moment. You're letting the music come from [inside] you and you let go of your ego and get out of the mind. You calm the inner chatter, and you feel the energy, and you're being one with the environment, one with body and mind."[3]

Acquiring an acoustic guitar one Christmas, Herman had started out by playing Dylan and Neil Young songs. "I didn't know anyone who listened to bluegrass," he said, "but because of Jerry Garcia, I got into it. Talk to anyone on the jam scene, or bluegrassers who didn't grow up with bluegrass, and almost everyone will tell you that Old and In the Way got their attention. Grisman did as well. If you listened to his quintet, you heard Tony Rice and turned on to J. D. Crowe and the New South. Later on, I became friends with Darol Anger. I was five years old when he was recording with Grisman and Rice."

Herman played with the Left-Hand String Band for a year and a half but "they fired me," he said, "and got a better guitar player." After being pink-slipped, he formed a "Cajun jug band," the Salmon Heads. "I really liked Jim Kweskin and the Jug Band," he explained, "and our fiddle player and I had a chance to spend a week a year, for a few years, with Dewey Balfa, the Bill Monroe of Cajun music. When he played, it would be fifty-fifty whether he'd be laughing or crying. Music moved him so much. He was a tremendous influence on us, as was Creole fiddler Canray Fontenot, who we met during the Augusta Heritage Cajun week in Elkins, WV."

Booked to play at Crested Butte nightspot the Eldo, on New Year's Eve 1990, Herman faced a dilemma when members of the Salmon Heads notified him they would be unable to make it to the gig. Remembering the Left-Hand String Band, he placed a few phone calls and put a band together with Emmitt, Keefe, Vann, drummer Michael Wooten, and keyboardist Joe Jogerst. "On our way," Herman recalled, "we came up with this horrible name, Leftover Salmon. If we had known that we were going to last, we probably could have come up with a better one.

"The Eldo was thoroughly insane. We played old-time tunes fast and aggressive and it made people go schizoid. Slam dancing started happening. We had never seen that reaction but we went with it. We kept playing old bluegrass and it worked. That night, we got other bookings. There weren't other bluegrass bands playing the bars. We made our own circuit by winning towns over one at a time."

After two independent albums, *Bridges to Bert* (1993) and *Ask the Fish Live* (1995), Leftover Salmon took things to the next level. Appearing at the H.O.R.D.E. Festival, they signed with Hollywood Records. Their next release (their second studio album), *Euphoria* (1997), added Kent, England-born keyboardist Pete Sears (Rod Stewart, Jefferson Starship).

Regular performers at Telluride, Leftover Salmon "would pick in the campgrounds until the early morning every night of the festival," said Emmitt. "We are the only band [that] has gone to the main stage but still plays in the campgrounds simply because that was such a large part of our musical upbringing."[4]

Americana existed long before there was a term for it. Bluegrass was a melting pot of traditions, but a new generation reared more by Grisman, Rice, and Fleck than Monroe and Flatt & Scruggs and influenced by everything from the Beatles and the Grateful Dead to Zappa and punk rock was playing it. The director of Grisman's Acoustic Disc label, Rob Bleetstein, "walked into the *Gavin* radio office and told them, 'You're missing a whole genre of music,'" said Herman. "He presented such a profound argument that they started the Americana chart, on January 20, 1995, and made him its first editor. He now programs the Pearl Jam and Grateful Dead stations on XM."

Produced by Randy Scruggs, with guest appearances by Del and Ronnie McCoury, Taj Mahal, Béla Fleck, Sam Bush, Jerry Douglas, Lucinda Williams, Waylon Jennings, and Jo-El Sonnier, Leftover Salmon's *The Nashville Sessions* (1999) fused the best of both worlds. "It was a blast to have Earl Scruggs come in the morning," said Herman, "and Taj Mahal in the afternoon. We gave Randy a wish list of people and he made it happen. He and 'Snake,' the engineer, made the process transparent. We just went in and did what we do."

Vann's death from cancer in 2002 "was a major loss," recalled Herman. "We tried to press on, but after a year or two, we required a spiritual break. He was instrumental in making the band work. He took care of a lot of our business and, musically, made us what we were. We miss him all the time."

After playing with fill-in musicians, Leftover Salmon connected with Skokie, Il-born Noam Pikelny (1981-). A student of Greg Cahill (Special Consensus), he played with the John Cowan Band (2004-6). He joined Greg Garrison (bass), Chris Eldridge (guitar), and Gabe Witcher (fiddle) to back Chris Thile on his solo *How to Grow a Woman from the Ground* (2006). Following Thile's farewell tour with Nickel Creek, in 2007, they regrouped as the Tensions Mountain Boys before changing their name to Punch Brothers. The IBMA "Banjo Player of the Year" in 2014, Pikelny scored an "Album of the Year" award for *Noam Pikelny Plays Kenny Baker Plays Bill Monroe* a year later. "The banjo is thought of as such a staccato or tinny instrument at times," he said, "and it works well in a band setting with that kind of timbre . . . but there can be a lot of warmth that the banjo can actually display."[5]

During Leftover Salmon's hiatus, Emmitt focused on the Emmitt-Nershi Band, the group he shares with Billy Nershi (String Cheese Incident). Herman started Great American Taxi. "We did that for four or five years," he said. "There was an overlap between the two bands. It kept me on the road doing what I love."

In June 2007, Leftover Salmon reunited at Telluride as "Drew Emmitt and Vince Herman and Friends." It led to a handful of shows over the next three years. Since regrouping on their twentieth anniversary at the Eldo, the site of their first show, they've remained together. Recommended by Chris Pandolfi [the Infamous Stringdusters], Andy Thorn replaced Pikelny. "Drew and I had a tripod with Mark," said Herman. "Andy brought that back."

Leftover Salmon released their first album in eight years, *Aquatic Hitchhiker,* in 2012. The title "is a warning," explained Emmitt, "to boaters to not pick up 'hitchhikers' or mussels attached to the bottom of your boat . . . that's what Leftover Salmon is—aquatic hitchhikers—traveling around, playing music, leaving little pieces wherever we go."[6]

Drummer Alwyn Robinson joined Leftover Salmon in 2013. Little Feat's keyboard player, Bill Payne, signed on a year later. He would remain for two years (with Erik Deutsch replacing him). "It was cool hearing old stories about Lowell George," recalled Herman, "and about the source of songs. His musical vocabulary is endless. He can take it anywhere, ready to turn it any direction. We played with him whenever we'd see him at a festival. Drew and I went to the twenty-fifth anniversary of the recording of Little Feat's *Waiting for Columbus* at the Warner Theatre in Georgetown.

Watching Bill put that massive jam with forty musicians together made me think that he'd be good producing our record. He produced our last album [*Leftover Salmon*] before the hiatus and we stayed in touch. Little Feat was taking a break so he was available for shows. We kept him interested until Little Feat got back to it."

During a three-night stint at Phil Lesh's Terrapin Crossroads in April 2015, Leftover Salmon jammed with the ex-Grateful Dead bassist. "Phil is fun to ride that groove with," said Herman. "We played with Bill Kreutzmann at the Fillmore the following January. The same thing—that groove is unmistakable. Once you get into the improv of it, it's fun to ride. I played in a Grateful Dead band in college and I played some shows filling in for Dave Nelson in his band. It was a huge honor. That band is amazing."

Bluegrass remains at the core of Leftover Salmon's genre-hopping music. "We like playing bluegrass," said Herman. "It's a good shoe for us. It always fits. We play a lot of it during our shows. It's what people want. We've created a community that mirrors what I saw growing up making my way to blue-grass festivals—that instant camaraderie through music. That's the beautiful thing about bluegrass music. You don't have to be young and 'purty.'

"We're going to make another record. It's harder for it to make economic sense but that's what you do when you're a band. Erik Deutsch brings a different kind of texture, a jazz sense, and a modern keyboard sound. Our rhythm section—Greg Garrison [bass] and Robinson [drums]—play in a progressive-jazz trio. Our next album will reflect some of that. The jazz monster may be creeping in."

The Nederland, CO-based Yonder Mountain String Band (YMSB) was "pretty much the only band playing plugged-in, loud bluegrass without drums," claimed guitarist/vocalist Adam Aijala. "We had a marketability that helped us grow fast; we were different. It helped us get booked into jam festivals and exposed us to more people. On the other hand, we'd play bluegrass festivals and be on the fringed edge."

Banjo player/University of Illinois at Urbana-Champaign student Dave Johnston and singer, songwriter, and guitarist Jeff Austin planted the seeds that grew into YMSB. They would reconnect in CO. "[Bassist] Ben Kaufmann was already there," said Aijala. "I moved to Nederland because my buddy, who I went to college with, told me that the music scene was good. I had been a forester major in college and worked in ID and CA. I thought I could get a job for the forest service or a private forester and work on my music."

It wasn't long before Aijala, Johnston, Austin, and Kaufmann connected. "Jeff played with Dave in a bar," said Aijala, "and met Ben at a show. They exchanged numbers. There was an open pick on Wednesday nights, at the Verve, where the four of us played together for the first time. We sang a few songs. I went to get a Guinness at the bar. I turned around and Dave and Jeff were right behind me. 'Hey, you want to be in a band?' I went, 'All right.'"

YMSB's name has "a kind of trad sound," said Aijala. "You'd equate it with a band out of Nashville. In our eyes, we wanted to be a bluegrass band."

The group, however, has never been a typical bluegrass band. "We don't have a traditional sound," said Aijala, "even though we play traditional instruments. We're on the family tree of bluegrass but none of us grew up with bluegrass. Our influences were rock, punk, reggae, heavy metal, even jazz. For us, it's: 'Let's not have a set idea of who we are and what we sound like. Let's just do what we do.' When I'm writing songs, I don't worry about it."

Aijala "literally went from Metallica to the Grateful Dead," he said. "They weren't what I thought when I heard their name. It sounded like a metal band but someone said, 'You know that song on the radio, "Casey Jones"? That's the Grateful Dead.' 'What! That's them?'

"My buddy was way into it. He went to a boarding school. When he came back, he said, 'You've got to check this out.' I remember not liking it, tripping, and then, all of a sudden, I got it. I remember hearing 'China Cat Sunflower/I Know You Rider' and needing to learn that guitar lick."

YMSB gained renown with tunes from outside the bluegrass canon. "Some of the biggest cheers come with songs that people know," said Aijala, "but we try to pick obscure things. Jake [Jolliff] writes instrumentals and knows bluegrass songs but he's also brought pop tunes to the table. We play Pure Prairie League's 'Amy' and America's 'Sister Golden Hair.' Allie [Kral] sings 'Son of a Preacher Man.' 'Only a Northern Song' is one of my favorite songs because it's so weird. I've always loved George Harrison.

"Some songs, like 'Ever Fallen in Love,' 'Only a Northern Song,' and 'Crazy Train,' translate into bluegrass rhythm, but others we play in the original rhythm. The Talking Heads' 'Girlfriend Is Better' was that way. Sometimes, when you bluegrass it, it totally hokes it up."

Austin's departure, during YMSB's eighteenth year, "was about creative differences and personal happiness," said Aijala. "We weren't feeling it anymore. It was mutual, a long time coming."

Sam Bush, John Frazier, and Ronnie McCoury filled in for Austin. "I'd get the week's set lists done before the gigs," said Aijala, "which we usually didn't do until the last minute. The new members practiced, and then, we'd get together for four or five hours before the show."

Jake Jolliff brought a new dimension to YMSB's sound. "We know a lot of mandolin players," said Aijala, "but he's one of the best, maybe one of the best ever. He started playing when he was six. All he does is practice. He's precise and thoughtful about what he plays. He can play any scale and any mode in any key, up and down the neck, improvising in each mode. He blows me away. He'll play a solo and it'll be different from the last time he played it."

Fiddler Allie Kral joined at the same time. "We had a comfortable thing between Dave, Ben, and me," said Aijala. "Adding these two new folks creates a cool dynamic."

All five members of Canton, NC-based Balsam Range, the IBMA's "Entertainer of the Year" and "Vocal Group of the Year" in 2014—Buddy Melton, Darren Nicholson, Tim Surrett, Caleb Smith, and Dr. Marc Pruett—grew up in western NC's Hayward County, where the Blue Ridge Highway meets the Great Smoky National Park. "The Balsam Range is the range of mountains that make up the backbone of the area," said Melton, the IBMA's "Male Vocalist of 2014."

Balsam Range's members combine extensive experience in bluegrass. "Marc played banjo for Ricky Skaggs," said Melton. "He recorded a solo album in 1981 and played on the Bill Monroe *Bean Blossom Live* album that came out at the same time as *Will the Circle Be Unbroken*. He had his own band. Steve Sutton played in it. He played with Jimmy Martin and turned down Bill Monroe. He played with the Whitewater Bluegrass Company and Rhonda Vincent. Tim was playing upright bass and Dobro with the Kingsmen; he had worked with Tony Rice, Doyle Lawson, J. D. Crowe, and Ralph Stanley. We all got off the road at the same time, and had free time, so we got together to pick for fun. We realized we had something special. We're blessed to have great talent, great singers—a variety of vocal blends."

Releasing their debut album, *Marching Home,* in 2007, Balsam Range "didn't intend to turn into a national touring act," said Melton, "but radio picked up on our music and people started asking us to play."

A pop and rock fan as a teen, Melton (1969-) didn't play fiddle until he was at Western NC University (he received a bachelor's degree in environmental science and went on to study engineering). "My parents had a fiddle hanging on the wall," he remembered, "and I got someone to set it up for me. A fiddler from Waynesville, Bill Phillips, showed me tunes. Bluegrass doesn't take classical training; you don't need to know how to read music. You pick it up by hearing it and watching it played."

Melton's band, Jubal Foster, was "all about original music," he said. "Milan Miller and Mark Baumgartner were incredible songwriters. They've written most of Balsam Range's popular songs."

Melton's 2007 self-titled solo album was the first step towards Balsam Range. "Marc Pruett played banjo," said Melton. "Tim Surrett played bass. We had an incredible time."

Tony Rice made a guest appearance. "I would have never expected to be playing with him," said Melton. "He brought a lot of excitement—he's Tony Rice—and he played exceptionally well. He took more interest in the project than I thought he would. He didn't just play his part, get his pay, and leave. He stayed involved through the mixing. We were world-class musicians brainstorming together."

Shortly afterwards, Darren Nicholson (mandolin/vocals) recorded a solo album with most of the same musicians.

From the beginning, Balsam Range had a distinct sound. "We're blessed to have four singers," said Melton. "I'll sing lead and switch to tenor. Darren will sing lead or baritone. Caleb sings lead or harmony. Tim's a great singer. Musically, they're creditable on their instruments. Tim is a wonderful producer and he hears vocal parts really well. He has a long history in gospel music, singing with the Kingsmen and other gospel groups. Caleb was a member of a gospel bluegrass group for years. It's part of who we are. Faith is important for all of us."

Playing four nights a week "helped us become a cohesive unit," said Melton. "By the time we played outside the area, we had a lot of material."

Songs about working people form the backbone of Balsam Range's repertoire. "Canton is where Champion International Paper started more than a hundred years ago," Melton told me in 2016, "and our families have worked there. *Papertown* [2012] fit that mentality."

The title of *Mountain Voodoo* (2016) projected a darker image. "You could twist it around," noted Melton, "and be scared of that title, but to me, it said a lot. It's intriguing and makes people want to know what it is. Music from our region is magical; it casts an acoustic spell."

Melton continues to explore outside projects. He and Miller collaborated on *Secrets, Dreams & Pretty Things* (2016), which included the bluegrass chart-topper, "Adeline."

Hearing a snippet of a 1973 outtake ("Rock Me Mama") on Bob Dylan's *Pat Garrett and Billy the Kid* soundtrack in 1992, Phillips Exeter Academy student and fiddle, harmonica, and banjo player Ketch Secor finished Dylan's words. "I recorded it with Roger McGuinn, Rita Coolidge, and Booker T.," Dylan told Bill Flanagan, "at a movie studio in Hollywood. That's where they got it; it just had a different title."[7]

Covered by Mumford & Sons, and a top-forty hit for Darius Rucker, Secor's "Wagon Wheel" became a staple at picking sessions. "I knew it was good," he said, "and that it would last. I waited for people to hear it and turn on to it. That took a long time but I didn't stop having faith. I knew I'd be singing it for the rest of my life. I felt, when I wrote it at seventeen, that I was rescuing a Dylan song as good as 'Knockin' on Heaven's Door.' Dylan was dabbling with a magical palette and the things he sketched had as much power as the things he finished. It was up to me to finish it.

"It's got a simple chord structure so it's easy to play and has instant accessibility. It makes you feel good in the right places in a ubiquitous manner. You don't have to be a smart cookie to like it. Dylan didn't claim to write 'Rock Me Mama.' He said that he learned it from Arthur Crudup. It's clearly not the same. Maybe Bob forgot he wrote it or didn't care. I read the liner notes of Crudup's albums and he said that he got it from Big Bill Broonzy. As somebody interested in origins of roots music, to be part of a songwriting chain that stretches all the way back to the Great Migration, the exodus from Mississippi to Chicago, which included Big Bill Broonzy, was unbelievable. Folk music could be so real to my generation."

Dylan remains at the heart of Old Crow Medicine Show's repertoire. On their live album, *50 Years of Blonde on Blonde* (2017), they transformed the fourteen songs on the bard's 1966 masterpiece into their own statement. "Dylan was the super glue between Ketch and I growing up . . . ," said guitarist/banjo player Chris "Critter" Fuqua. "Our tastes differed when it came to music, sometimes drastically, but the one common thread was Dylan. . . . I think Dylan is in the league of Shakespeare and Tolstoy, Hemingway and Beowulf, perhaps even the Bible. His work should be launched into space on a rocket, headed toward Andromeda for some form of intelligent life form to contemplate."[8]

Together with Mumford & Sons and Edward Sharpe & the Magnetic Zeros, Secor and Old Crow Medicine Show traveled on the April 2011 *Big Easy Express.* "It wasn't as wild as the *Festival Express,* with the Grateful Dead, Janis Joplin, and the Band," said Secor, "but it was magical. We covered a lot of real estate—Oakland to New Orleans—but it went by quick. We were the common denominator. Mumford & Sons have a signature sound. The Zeros are the same way. We're in the middle. We might sound like the Mumfords for a song, the Band for a song, or the Dead for a song."

Born in 1971, Secor's first job was shining shoes in a barbershop when he was eleven. "Everybody was talking about VA's colored governor [Douglas Wilder]," he remembered, "the first black governor since Reconstruction. It was a big deal. My region couldn't make up its mind about him. I referenced that with the folk music I was discovering. I heard Pete Seeger sing 'Oh Freedom' on *Carnegie Hall, 1962* and it felt applicable to my life. I remember when they changed Martin Luther King Day at my school to Lee and Jackson Day, celebrating Stonewall Jackson and Robert E. Lee. That said something

Old Crow Medicine Show, 2015

to me. I was political as a child. When they prayed for aborted fetuses, I said, 'Let's pray for the Sandinistas and the Contras.' I learned 'The Ballad of Medgar Evers' by Phil Ochs when I was twelve. Bob Dylan became the voice I paid closest attention to; he talked about things that meant a lot to me. He walked the crossroads between social activism and music."

Secor "got off on playing old-time music on street corners and did it really intensely for a decade in thirty-five American and Canadian cities," he said. "I was playing for money. Joy was what I was selling. The joy came naturally but the money didn't. To me, it was a hustle. I wanted to make dough. The money was the drive.

"I liked the freakiness of it. You're always sleeping at the house of somebody you just met and eating like a homeless person. Everybody was getting drunk, passing the bottle around. There was a wonderful wildness to busking. It was as close as you could get to Woody Guthrie in the late nineties."

Rounded out by Chance McCoy (guitar, fiddle, banjo), Kevin Hayes (guitar), Morgan Jahnig (upright bass), and Cory Younts (mandolin, keyboards, drums), Old Crow Medicine Show came to the attention of Doc Watson. "Doc liked this sandwich joint on King Street, in Boone, where we were playing," Secor said. "His daughter Nancy saw us and liked us. She asked if we were going to be there for a while. 'I want to get my dad; he likes this kind of music.' It was amazing. It felt like Doc was Jesus and we were the disciples.

"I figured we'd be his pals but we weren't. He had other relationships that kept him busy. He wasn't going to hold our hand any longer than the five minutes he held it when he got us the gig at MerleFest, but that gig changed our lives. It led to an ongoing stint entertaining crowds between shows of the *Grand Ole Opry*. We felt blessed by Doc and will always, as long as we're a band."

Old Crow Medicine Show became members of the *Grand Ole Opry* in September 2013. "It's what Bob Dylan listened to," said Secor, "how he knew the Delmore Brothers' 'Freight Train [Boogie].' Nashville resented the hillbillies but couldn't deny the *Grand Ole Opry*. It's been there so long it's the symbol of country music, and that's where its power lies, no longer in the broadcast. When I perform at the *Opry*, I get off on being a link in the chain, part of an institution."

Since 1993, CMH Records' *Pickin' On* series has given the bluegrass treatment to everyone from the Beatles and Rolling Stones to Metallica, Bon Jovi, and U2. There are even bluegrass salutes to the Disney catalogue and *The Simpsons*. Rounder assembled a who's who cast for *Moody Bluegrass: A Nashville Tribute to the Moody Blues* (2004). They followed with a second volume nine years later. "I thought they were crazy," said John Cowan. "What were they going to do, play all these songs with a banjo and record *Hee Haw Salutes the Moody Blues?* But it wasn't done that way. Sam Bush, Alison Krauss, Tim O'Brien, and Vince Gill played on it. It was a very respectful and artful tribute. I later sang on a Van Halen tribute."

In late 2014, the Springfield, MO-based HillBenders began working on a bluegrass version of the Who's 1969 rock opera, *Tommy*. The idea originated with Louis Meyers, late director of Folk Alliance International. "We were friends for years," said mandolinist/lead singer Nolan Lawrence. "He was searching for a location to move the Folk Alliance and had been to MO three or four times. Every time he passed through, he stopped at my house. This time he came for dinner. Towards the end of the evening, he said, 'I've got this crazy idea. I listened to *Tommy* on my way here and thought it'd be cool to do a bluegrass version.' I laughed but tried to get my head around it. It sounded interesting and different but I said, 'Who's going to do that?' He looked me squarely in the eyes and said, 'I thought you would.'"

Winners of the Telluride Bluegrass Band Competition in 2009, and the National Single Microphone Championship the following year, the HillBenders "had done cover songs, but this was a whole other level," noted Lawrence. "I took the idea to the band and got a mixed response. Jimmy Rea, our guitar player, had seen the theatrical version. Everyone seemed interested enough to talk more about it."

Preparing to move Folk Alliance to Kansas City, Meyers was in the area regularly. "He sat down with us," recalled Lawrence, "and talked about the concept. We knew he had a lot of success in the music industry, so we agreed to work up a couple of the tunes. We practiced *Tommy* tunes between working on our own material. We hashed three songs out, recorded them around a microphone, and sent the tape to Louis. It was exactly what he was seeking. We found out later that he had had the idea for twenty years before pulling the trigger."

The HillBenders spent two months in their practice space preparing to record the album. "The vast majority of that time," Lawrence remembered, "was spent listening to the Who's record, any videos we could find, and learning our parts. We worked the songs up in a lot less time than we would have liked but we put our noses to the grindstone and got everything ready. By early December, we were in the studio recording.

"It was a complex undertaking. There're a lot of themes and styles. The chord progressions are very abstract. We decided to record analog and found a studio that had a two-inch tape system. Louis paid to have the equipment refurbished. None of us had recorded analog before. It's a very different approach. You could do a little cutting and splicing but it's not easy. You've got to be a lot more precise in what you play."

The HillBenders recorded the first song in three takes. "Louis came into the tracking room," remembered Lawrence, "red in the face, and screaming angrily. He took us aside and said, 'We have a very short time. You get no more than two takes per song.' He turned around and walked away, left us shaking in the alleyway, but instead of getting scared away, we walked into the studio and nailed the first take. We proceeded to nail every song. In four days, we tracked the entire record. We spent one day in mix-down, getting the takes just right."

Meyers sent a copy of the finished master to Pete Townshend's management. "Within an hour, Pete responded that he loved the project," said Lawrence. "We were invited to meet him after the Who performance in Kansas City, but they canceled the show due to Roger Daltry losing his voice. Louis was vigilant about staying in touch with their management and rerouted the opportunity to Nashville. We were going to be playing at the Station Inn the night before the Who concert at Bridgestone Arena. We played an amazing show that night. The next night, we went to watch the Who. They played a *Tommy* set and the parallels were amazing. After the show, we met Pete. He was very supportive, telling jokes about the project and asking who sang 'Acid Queen.' I raised my hand and he said, 'With a beard like that?'"

The HillBenders Present the Who's Tommy: A Bluegrass Opry premiered, in March 2015, at the Folk Alliance conference. "We performed for 400 people crammed into a room," said Lawrence. "The energy was palpable. We absolutely destroyed it. The crowd went wild. It was a precursor of things to come. We knew we had done something great.

"Writers, publicists, and industry heavyweights came to see us at Threadgill's. *Rolling Stone* said it was one of the best things at SXSW. That gave us a huge amount of publicity. *Billboard* picked it up. We had the attention of the music world and took advantage of it. We pushed and pushed and got the word out."

Corpus Christi, TX-born Lawrence studied vocal performance at Del Mar College. "I spent years singing in choirs," he said. "I studied vocal technique, breathing, and trained to be an opera singer. Around the age of twenty-one, I started losing my lust for classical music and fell in love with commercial country music. TX has a rich tradition of great songwriters and its own style of music. That led me to the mandolin. I walked away from opera and became a singer-songwriter. *Tommy* was the first time that the two worlds—opera and bluegrass—collided. It's not a true opera but it is vocally taxing. My skills came in handy."

Lawrence met Mark Cassidy at South Plains College in Levelland, TX. "They have a highly respected bluegrass program," he said, "and students come from all over the world. Mark was a young kid, very much a punk, but he was an amazing banjo player. We ended up being roommates for a

Nolan Lawrence, 2015

year. Towards the end of school, he started looking for a band and found the Arkamo Rangers. The day he left, he thanked me for being such a great friend and said, 'You and I will play music together in the future.' I said, 'That'd be cool.'"

About a year and a half later, the Arkamo Rangers broke up. "Mark called," remembered Lawrence, "and said, 'We want to pick up where we left off. We need a mandolin player and a singer. You're the best I know.'"

Residing in Austin, Lawrence had been trying to start his own group, but "it hadn't grown legs yet," he recalled. "I told Mark that I'd meet the band, see what it sounded like."

Spending a weekend on the front porch of the guitarist's house playing music, Lawrence sensed "similar sensibilities for sound, harmonies, attack," he recalled. "Three weeks later, I packed everything I owned, stuffed it into my car, and the HillBenders were born—March 2008. We officially launched on April Fool's Day."

Dobro player Chad "Gravyboat" Graves didn't join the HillBenders until they had won their championships. "He left the Arkamo Rangers before they broke up," said Lawrence, "and toured with Valerie Smith & Liberty Pike. He'd come back to visit family. Each time, he'd hang out at our band practice and pick a few songs with us. Eventually, we talked him into playing a couple of shows with us. It was a great fit. We said, 'If you'd like to be a part of the band when you're not on tour, we'd love to have you.' We picked dates around his schedule. That worked for a few months, but we needed to find someone more stable. He made the call to go full-time. All five of us have been together since. He's embraced the Keith Moon role and become a wild man, jumping around, flailing about, and getting into the show."

The HillBenders were in Australia, in March 2016, when they heard that Meyers had died. "We were working on a film about the *Tommy* project," recalled Lawrence "partly organized by Louis. He had all kinds of irons in the fire. There's no telling where we'd be if he was still with us."

Tommy was such a phenomenon that it's going to be a challenge to maintain the momentum. "We're either going to release a new album of originals," Lawrence told me in 2016, "or another themed project. People have suggested *Quadrophenia* and *Jesus Christ Superstar.* Whatever we do, it's going to be big, loud, and bold enough to keep us firmly footed."

The winner of the Steve Martin Prize for Excellence in Banjo and Bluegrass in 2015, Temple, TX-born Danny Barnes followed with a straight-ahead instrumental album, *Stove Up,* in early 2017. Original tracks ("Isotope 709," "Charlie," and "Get It While You Can") mixed with tunes by Grandpa Jones ("Eight More Miles to Louisville") and Earl Scruggs

("Flint Hill Special" and "Foggy Mountain Breakdown"). "I've never done a record like it," said Barnes. "Nick Forster produced it and played guitar. We did it with Del McCoury's bass player [Mike Bub] and fiddler [Jason Carter]. Chris Henry played mandolin. It was my homage to Don Stover."

Stove Up was a departure for Barnes (1961-), who explored a "Bill Monroe goes to CBGB synthesis" of punk rock, country music, and bluegrass with Killbilly, the Austin-based band formed by Alan Wooley. Debuting on Dallas community radio, in 1987, Killbilly played more than six hundred concerts before disbanding in 1994. "We were trying to do something different," said Barnes, "and thought it would be interesting to combine punk rock and experimental music with bluegrass and country music. Our friends were punk rockers and musicians in heavy metal bands. They were our audience—college kids and people who didn't grow up on bluegrass."

Leaving Killbilly in 1990, Barnes and upright bass/tuba player Mark Rubin took things further with the Bad Livers. "My idea was to have a smaller ensemble," Barnes said, "with people who could double on different instruments. Ralph White played fiddle and accordion. I played banjo and guitar and produced the records."

Delivering a hard-driving brand of bluegrass, the Bad Livers bewildered listeners with their more experimental music. When a representative from Sugar Hill came to scout them, he pointed out that their audience "was a different set of people than who they sold records" to, said Barnes. "We wound up doing two records and a gospel cassette [*Dust on the Bible*] for a punk label [Quarterstick/Touch and Go] out of Chicago. We put out a 45 with a cover of Iggy Pop's 'Lust for Life.'"

Sugar Hill released Bad Livers' fourth album, *Hogs on the Highway,* in 1997. "We recorded it on an eight-track analog machine," explained Barnes. "My house in Austin had a nice wood floor and sounded really good."

Mostly comprised of bluegrass/old-time tunes, *Hogs on the Highway* took a different tack with its electronic-mélange final track, "Falling Down the Stairs (With a Pistol in My Hand)." "That song became the harbinger of my entire career," said Barnes, "my raison d'être. I had been in studios because, if you could read music, you could work a couple of sessions a week. I got the idea that you could use the studio as an instrument like Lee Allen and Brian Eno, the experimental people."

The Bad Livers' music became even more outrageous. Produced by Lloyd Maines, *Industry and Theft* (1998) and *Blood and Mood* (2000) emphasized electronic keyboards, electric instruments, and hard-hitting percussion. "If Lloyd put his stamp on it," recalled Barnes, "Sugar Hill would go for it. It was our job to do something different.

"We never thought of how people perceived us. Our records started out with, 'Do you know what would be cool?' It never entered our minds that anyone else was listening; Mark and I weren't wired that way."

Barnes grew up listening to country music. "My dad's from Birmingham," he said, "and my mom grew up in TX. We listened to the *Grand Ole Opry* every week. I remember Hawkshaw Hawkins and Webb Pierce. My dad's favorite singer was Red Foley but he had records by Flatt & Scruggs, Bill Monroe, Bob Wills, and Johnny Cash. Fifty years later, I still listen to those records."

Grandpa Jones and Stringbean's banjo playing during a 1970 *Opry* package show set Barnes on his life's journey, but "I thought of it as acoustic country music," he recalled. "TX was far from the epicenter of bluegrass."

Studying audio production at the University of Texas, Barnes "learned about the early history of recording," he recalled, "and people like Steve Reich and John Cage."

Barnes found a comrade in Rubin. "Mark knew about punk rock," he said, "but he also had Ralph Stanley records. My thing was British and NY punk; his was West Coast rock. He's four years younger. He was into Black Flag while I liked the Clash and the Ramones."

Barnes and Rubin played under a variety of fictitious names. "You could only play twice a year in Austin," said Barnes, "if you wanted a decent crowd. We booked shows under fake names like the Sawdust Boogers so we could practice. Our fans would know and seventy-five people or so would come. We'd play and work on music. There were so many clubs that we made good money."

Barnes has released twenty solo albums on various labels, including Minner Bucket, which he runs from his Seattle home. He recorded *Pizza Box* in Dave Matthews' Charlottesville, VA Haunted Hollow Studio in 2010. Matthews sang on the single "Overdrive."

Since late 2000, Greensky Bluegrass has not only improvised on original songs but also on a repertoire spanning from bluegrass and country classics to tunes by Jimi Hendrix, Lionel Richie, and the Grateful Dead. "We're proud of the bluegrass influence," said Paul "Phoffman" Hoffman (mandolin, vocals), "but we put our own twist to it. Some of our tunes are straight-ahead bluegrass but others are the opposite, thus the transposition of our name. The Seldom Scene, and Old and In the Way, were big influences, as were the Grateful Dead and Pink Floyd. New Grass Revival influenced us to take on weird pop and jazz elements but also be badass on bluegrass instruments.

"We used to say that we're not a bluegrass band. We didn't want to be burned at the stake for doing it wrong, but people encouraged us to do it our way rather than the 'right' way. The bluegrass community is small; we need everybody's flag to fly."

"If we were playing rock and roll on bluegrass instruments," added Anders Beck (Dobro), "and had no idea what bluegrass was, that would be a problem, but all of us studied bluegrass. I could play fiddle tunes. I listened to Flatt & Scruggs' recordings and paid close attention. I learned bluegrass and then decided to meld it with all the other music I love—jam bands, jazz, and rock and roll. Bluegrass is a piece of it but there are a lot of pieces."

Greensky Bluegrass's hometown, Kalamazoo, MI, was formerly the home of Gibson Guitars (now based in Nashville). "Guitars, banjos, and mandolins used to be made here," said Hoffman. "All the bluegrass pickers know about Kalamazoo. Lloyd Loar lived here."

Hoffman started out playing guitar and writing songs. "I bought my first mandolin when I was eighteen," he said, "after seeing David Grisman play and checking into Sam Bush. I was more interested in the instrument than bluegrass. I'm better at crosspicking than Grisman-type playing. My time was better served writing songs, and learning to express my musical ideas, versus learning fiddle tunes."

Hoffman met Michael Arlen Bont (banjo) and Dave Bruzza (guitar) at an open mic. "I suggested that I play with them," he recalled, "and they said, 'Do you know any Bill Monroe tunes?' I said no, and they gave me a Rounder sampler and a Monroe CD and said, 'Listen to these and come back next week.' I've been playing with them since. It was the right time and the right place.

"We were all new to the music. Our guitar player was a drummer and our banjo player was a guitar player. They were just messing around for fun at open mics. We developed a following of people who liked us. Nobody was doing anything like it in Kalamazoo. There was a demand for it. That encouraged us to be better every week."

"I wasn't in the band when they came up with the name," remembered Beck, "but one of their friends said they should call it 'Greensky' because it was the opposite of bluegrass. They started as a traditional bluegrass band, playing around a single mic, but we've grown into the name. We couldn't have picked a better one. We are bluegrass and the opposite at the same time. Bluegrass gave us roots but we branch out from there."

"Bluegrass is a lot like jazz," said Hoffman, "or chamber music. People ask us if we're going to add a drummer. That would take the fun out of it. There's an ebb and flow to five people sharing rhythmic responsibility. I'm the 'snare drum,' an unsung role, but if we're jamming for ten minutes and I'm chopping away, I get great joy."

Beck (1977-) was an electric guitarist when he stumbled onto the Dobro at Telluride. "I was walking by a workshop with Jerry Douglas, Rob Ickes, and Mike Auldridge," he recalled, "and it hit me like a ton of bricks; the instrument I had been looking for—the electric guitar of acoustic music. It has sustaining; that's what I love about it. I bought one the next day and haven't put it down since."

Taking a lesson with Auldridge, Beck "learned his sense of timing and tone," he said. "The Seldom Scene was a big influence. I saw them at the Birchmere and loved their willingness to have fun."

"The Seldom Scene had a bluegrass vibe," added Hoffman, "but they were also playing folksongs and there was a rock-and-roll edge. We came to bluegrass through Old and In the Way. We're Grateful Dead fans who learned that Jerry played the banjo but we came from the rock-and-roll vibe."

"My parents let me go to Grateful Dead shows when I was fifteen," remembered Beck. "They knew how important it was. I thank them but also tell them they were crazy for letting me do it. The Dead's willingness to jump off a cliff improvisationally is what we're after."

"As much as they've been musical influences," added Hoffman, "it was the relationship between them and the fans, the way they cultivated a lifestyle where people followed them, taking risks to make every show something you don't want to miss. It's a trip to be embraced by the community; it's very powerful."

Greensky Bluegrass jammed with Phil Lesh, at Terrapin Crossroads, and played "China Cat Sunflower/I Know You Rider," with Mickey Hart and Bill Kreutzmann, at the Hoxeyville Music Festival. "I've gotten to know Billy," said Beck. "He's like a sixteen-year-old who just wants to play music. He spent time learning our songs and took us on an adventure, pushing boundaries."

Hoffman and Bruzza split the songwriting. "Years ago, I would have said that he wrote the more bluegrass songs," noted Hoffman, "but it's shifted. We're intuitive to each other's style. We trade the same licks and have similar musical approaches. When either of us introduces something new, we pick it up quickly and it becomes part of our music consciousness. We sing differently but I love singing harmony with him. It drew me into the band. I had choral training growing up. When I saw them, I wanted to sing three-part bluegrass harmony."

Greensky Bluegrass's *Totally Bitchin' '80s Dance Party* Halloween shows include tunes by the Police, Paul Simon, Los Lobos, Flock of Seagulls, the Cure, Billy Joel, and Bruce Springsteen. "It took a lot of work," said Beck, "but it's why our fans like us. That level of commitment speaks for itself."

"We goof around," added Hoffman, "but people are drawn to the joy. They want to witness the passion."

Chapter 36

Celebrity Connections

The banjo is more than a prop for Stephen Glenn "Steve" Martin (1945-). Since 1962, the Waco, TX-born and Southern CA-raised comedian/banjo player has played three-finger on tunes that are "driving and staccato" and clawhammer on those that are "moody and melancholy."[1]

"I really appreciate the fact," said 2014 Steve Martin Prize for Excellence in Banjo and Bluegrass Music recipient Eddie Adcock, "that there's someone out there [Martin] who knows the financial realities of bluegrass in a position to help his fellow pickers and take up some of the slack; it must feel great to be Steve."[2]

Participating with an all-star cast on Scruggs' rerecording of "Foggy Mountain Breakdown," Martin shared a Grammy in 2002. Five years later, he introduced an original instrumental, "The Crow," on Tony Trischka's *Double Banjo Bluegrass Spectacular*. His first single since 1978's "King Tut," it spurred him to continue writing. He had enough compositions by 2009 to record the Grammy-winning *The Crow: New Songs for the 5-String Banjo*. "There was a folk-music craze led by the Kingston Trio and Pete Seeger," Martin told ABC News, "and the banjo was introduced in that music, and it quickly led me to bluegrass music. . . . My ear was just transfixed by the sound of the banjo. I got one as soon as I could. . . . I kind of worked out my own style of playing."[3]

Martin continued in another interview, "When I started doing my comedy act, which seemed so—in teen parlance—'random' . . . I would incorporate the banjo . . . to show I could do something . . . it looked like I was goofing off but that was an illusion. It was really well thought out. . . . I played maybe a song and a half or used it for some comedy—and I would always play a legitimate song."[4]

Needing a band to tour, Martin recruited the Steep Canyon Rangers in 2010. They would collaborate on the Trischka-produced *Rare Bird Alert* (2011) and the Peter Asher-produced *The Long-Awaited Album* (2017). "Steve's very unique as a banjo player," guitarist Woody Platt told me in

2016. "He doesn't play a lot of Scruggs licks but he can play fast and he's a great clawhammer player. If our banjo player is taking a break, Steve will frail behind him, He's self-taught and has his own sound based around the melodies that he writes. He's not going to get onstage and play someone else's songs.

"Steve's a very hardworking, focused person. Whatever he does, he wants to be well rehearsed and put on a great show. We've done different shows with him—a Steve Martin show, a Steve and Edie Brickell show, and a Martin Short and Steve Martin show. It's put us in front of a lot of people."

"We need to present it in the best possible light," continued Graham Sharp (banjo), "take out all the stereotypes, and boil it down to the music."

The IBMA "Emerging Artist" of 2006, the Steep Canyon Rangers' connection with Martin "came about very organically," Sharp said. "There were never any producers coming to scout us. He had people and musicians he knew a long time [Wernick, Trischka, and McEuen] who were rightfully protective of him. They wanted to make sure he was in a good situation, but once we passed the mustard, they accepted us. We worked hard on the songs. They sounded like the record. We got on late-night TV shows and played shows that were bigger than we had ever done."

Platt, Sharp, and Charles Humphrey (bass) met at the University of

Steve Martin, 2010

NC at Chapel Hill. A high-school music teacher introduced Sharp to bluegrass. Jerry Garcia inspired him to acquire a banjo. "I picked up a copy of Old and In the Way," he recalled, "and immediately fell for it. I had no idea who Grisman or Clements were but I knew I loved the music. It was different from rock and roll. It felt intimate, like being in somebody's living room. Darrell Scott told me that album got him into bluegrass, too.

"I played the banjo for a couple of years before I felt like I was playing the 'right way' and could keep up. I started going to festivals, taking my banjo out, and playing songs. I was welcome to stay all night."

Platt, Sharp, and Humphrey "started picking together out of the blue and got totally obsessed with music," remembered Platt. "Around us, in the Piedmont and outside Chapel Hill, there were lots of traditional players, festivals, fiddler conventions, and places to immerse in the culture. We'd show up eager to jam and learn. We were longhaired college kids but we were accepted. It's a great community."

Platt recalled that when the Steep Canyon Rangers started, "we were writing our own songs and playing whatever music we could play, but if you have a banjo player, there's a good chance you're going to wind up naturally progressing into bluegrass."

Taking their cues at first from progressive players, the Steep Canyon Rangers realized they needed to go back to the pioneers. "We stayed there for a while," said Platt, "and learned tunes from the root of the tradition."

"Charles and I had a songbook of bluegrass songs," Sharp added. "We lived in a camper in the Outer Banks of NC for a summer. We played that book from cover to cover at least fifteen times, but we realized that we should get back to writing our own tunes.

"I studied literature in college. I don't think about it having a correlation with my songwriting, but I love to read and I know that reading boosts my writing. I try to be a disciplined writer and put in an hour or two every couple of days. It's like a muscle. You have to keep in shape. If it makes me laugh or cry, I consider it a good song."

Sharp is one of the few banjo players who sing. "When I'm singing," he said, "I keep the banjo simple and find space to push the banjo. I'm halfway listening to the band and letting my fingers go, along with the rhythm, while the other side of my brain is thinking about singing."

The Steep Canyon Rangers' first break came as "Curly" Seckler's support band in 2006. "Curly was playing MerleFest," Seckler's biographer Penny Parsons told me, "and needed a band to back him up. We talked about this band and that band. I was friends with the Steep Canyon Rangers. They were going to be at the festival the day before, but when they found out they could play with Curly, they said, 'We'll stay.' I sent them the song list. The night before Curly's performance, they came to his hotel room and rehearsed. He was amazed. They had done their homework and knew his songs."

"We played his music the way he wanted us to play it," recalled Platt. "We had never done anything like that, backing somebody up. It was a real honor. He respected us. He spent so many years chopping the mandolin and singing tenor with Flatt & Scruggs. We played 'I'll Go Steppin' Too' and 'What Would You Give in Exchange for Your Soul.'

"Halfway through the show, we played 'Salty Dog Blues' and got a standing ovation. Curly didn't flinch. He looked at us and said, 'Kick it off again.' I assumed we would play a chorus, he would pick his guitar up, and we would tag it, but he wanted to play the whole thing—all four verses. We played it twice in a row and got another standing ovation."

Platt was working as a fly-fishing guide when he met Martin's future wife, Anne Stringfield. After she connected with the comic, she brought him to vacation close to where Platt lived. "She called me," he remembered, "and said, 'Steve's coming to town with his banjo. Round up some guys and come over to play some music.' It turned out to be a lot of fun and we stayed in touch. When we were in NY, he sat in with us. He showed up at our Mountain Song Festival, in Brevard, NC, and played. Shortly after that, we got a call from his agent. He had just put out *The Crow* and wanted to know if we had interest in being his band. Of course, we said yes. We became known, but it also made us want to forge our own identity."

Recorded in Levon Helm's barn studio, the Steep Canyon Rangers' *Nobody Knows You* (2012) reached the runner-up slot on the bluegrass charts and scored a "Best Bluegrass Album of the Year" Grammy. Larry Campbell produced *Tell the Ones I Love* a year later. "We brought a friend [Jeff Sipe] to play drums on a handful of tracks," said Sharp. "It felt like a natural progression, the right thing for us."

"We had been up to the Midnight Rambles," added Platt, "and Levon invited us to record there. The vibe was so special. They had never made a bluegrass record before. Watching Larry lead Levon's band, play fiddle, mandolin, and guitar, and looking at his producer creds, it made sense. He helped to stretch our music—we brought in drums—but we maintained our integrity."

The Steep Canyon Rangers added Michael Ashworth on "cajón drum kit," Sharp said. "When Steve was recording with Edie Brickell, his producer [Peter Asher] wanted to bring in someone to play drums. We asked if we could give Michael Ashworth, our mandolin player's best friend, a try. It went so well, we said, 'Let's make this all one thing; bring it on.'"

Jerry Douglas produced the Steep Canyon Rangers' first sextet album, *Radio* (2015). "Jerry coached us," said Sharp, "not worrying too much about postproduction but trying to capture the moment."

Steep Canyon Rangers, 2015

"Jerry and Larry are similar producers," added Platt. "They understood where the band was coming from and what we were trying to do."

Sharp has been "trying to write from a hopeful place, but things swing back and forth," he said. "*Radio* had rock elements, but by the time we finished it, I was writing old-time-type mountain ballads. I don't steer it too carefully."

"The Seldom Scene told us we're doing the same thing they did," added Platt, "bending the rules. It's great that people want to preserve the traditions, but it's healthy for music to progress."

The Grascals also parlayed a connection with an entertainment superstar into a pace-setting career. Touring with Dolly Parton in 2004 and 2005, the Nashville-based "Emerging Artist" of 2005 continued its ascent afterwards. "What a great kickoff for a band," recalled seven-time SPBGMA "Mandolinist of the Year" Danny Roberts. "Dolly's an icon, a movie star, and a music star, a female Elvis. She was so good to us and so good for us, too. She never stopped. Every day, she had a new song written the night before.

"When we first got together, we went into the studio, sat in a circle, and learned her songs. She didn't want to use charts. The first year, we'd play our set, change our clothes, and come back to play with her. At the end of the tour, we went back to touring as the Grascals. She called and asked if we'd open her shows. She really wanted us so we went back for another year."

The Grascals' 2005 self-titled debut included the IBMA's "Song of the Year," "Me and John and Paul," by Harley Allen, and a bluegrass rendition of the title song of Elvis Presley's *Viva Las Vegas* (1964), with Parton on vocals. "'Viva Las Vegas' was an odd choice," said Roberts, "but Dolly made it fun. We've been doing 'Last Train to Clarksville,' 'Mystery Train,' and 'Lay Down Sally.' We don't want to be a novelty band, but we have fun."

When the Grascals came together, in 2004, longtime Osborne Brothers guitarist/vocalist Terry Eldredge and bassist Terry Smith had been leading the Sidemen at the Station Inn's weekly Tuesday-night gathering for a decade and a half. "Musicians would come and play with them," said Roberts. "One night, Jamie Johnson [guitar/vocals] and Jimmy Mattingly [fiddle] talked with the Terrys about putting a band together."

The Danville, KY-born son of a square-dance fiddler, Mattingly (1962-) played with Béla Fleck, Jimmy Gaudreau, Glen Lawson, and Mark Schatz in Spectrum, in the early eighties, and was a member of Garth Brooks' Stillwater from 1995 to 2001. He and Eldredge played on Parton's return to bluegrass, *Halos & Horns* (2002). Like Roberts, Mattingly emerged from the music program in Leitchfield's schools. State senators proclaimed the small, tobacco-farming community "fiddle capital of KY" in April 2016. "School superintendent Don Ralph got an orchestra started," remembered Roberts (1963-), "and got all these fiddle players going. Jimmy moved to Leitchfield when he was ten. When he got into the orchestra, he brought a fiddling element no one had seen before. He started going to fiddling contests all over the country and won just about every one, including the U.S. Grand Master Fiddler Championship. He was my neighbor. We met when I was twelve. When I started playing guitar, he helped me. He's as close as a brother would be. My dad was a huge fan of Merle Haggard, Dean Martin, and Jerry Lee Lewis, but nobody in my family played music. When I started going to the contests with Jimmy, that's when I learned about bluegrass."

A year after graduating high school in 1981, Roberts met Fred Duggan at a guitar competition. "He was from Murfreesboro, TN, where I had moved," Roberts remembered, "and we became very good friends. We opened a music store and put a band together [the New Tradition] to play at contests. I was already competing on mandolin, guitar, and beginner fiddle."

Bluegrass gospel provided the avenue for the New Tradition's success. "We played two or three churches a week," said Roberts, "and a bluegrass festival on the weekend. We were on the road two hundred and twenty or thirty days a year.

"We lasted twenty years but we couldn't get into the real bluegrass market—the East Coast, the Carolinas, and PA. We had a great following in the West. We were on the contemporary side, ahead of our time."

Leaving the New Tradition in 2000, Roberts took a job with the Gibson Guitar Company. His hiatus from music would be brief. "Ronnie Reno approached me," he recalled, "and asked if I'd like to play with him. I said, 'I don't want to travel.' He said that he wasn't talking about traveling; he had his TV show. It sounded good. I wanted to scratch that picking itch."

Remaining with Reno for three seasons, Roberts left to join the Grascals. "Jimmy called me," he said, "and told me they were putting the band together. We hadn't gotten to play together since we were kids. We started working on a CD but, in my mind, I was just helping them out."

The Grascals' recording engineer, Patrick Murphy, worked with Parton. "He played her some of the stuff we were recording," said Roberts. "Jimmy had played with her off and on for fifteen years. Patrick told her, 'Here's Jimmy's bluegrass band,' and she fell in love with it. She called Jimmy and said that she was going on the road and wanted us to go with her. Jimmy called me and said, 'You've got a choice to make. Dolly wants us to start next week.' It was such a great opportunity, the greatest thing that's happened in my life."

The Grascals' second album, *Long List of Heartaches* (2006), featured Steve Wariner, George Jones, the Jordanaires, and Dierks Bentley. Released by Cracker Barrel, *The Grascals and Friends—Country Classics with a Bluegrass Spin* (2011) included Bentley, Charlie Daniels, Parton, the Oak Ridge Boys, Tom T. Hall, Brad Paisley, and Joe Nichols. "When George came to record," Roberts remembered, "we were like little kids. He pulled into the parking lot and we were waiting for him. He was in his Cadillac. We had heard that he wasn't drinking, but when he stepped out of the car, he looked straight at us and said, 'You boys want a cold one?' We froze. He raised his backseat, reached into a cooler, and started handing out bottles of George Jones White Lightning water."

Performing to enthusiastic audiences in Belgium, France, and Greece, the Grascals then headlined the 2006 Country Gold Music Festival in Japan. "The audience wore cowboy hats," recalled Roberts. "They were square dancing, line dancing, and single dancing, and having a ball."

Japan would be the original lineup's last hurrah. After their return to the States, Parton offered Mattingly, and banjo player Dave Talbot, full-time jobs. Talbott accepted; Mattingly opted to stay. In the midst of recording the Grascals' *Keep On Walkin'* (with Vince Gill the only guest), however, he found an invitation to rejoin Garth Brooks irresistible. "Jimmy was such a good friend," said Roberts, "it was hard when he left. I still talk to him all the time."

The Grascals' tenth album, *Before Breakfast* (2017), introduced SC-raised Kristin Scott Benson. "She's a big Sonny Osborne fan," said Roberts. "Sonny told us to listen to her. I've known her since she was a teenager. Her first band was with my wife, Andrea Campbell Roberts, Petticoat Junction, when she was seventeen. She was staying at our house on the weekends. She fit perfectly from day one."

Roberts has appeared on the *Grand Ole Opry* over two hundred times. "I played it with Jimmy when I was eighteen," he said, "when he won the Grand Master. Roy Acuff had us play on his portion. I expected that would be it but I've done it with New Tradition and, of course, with the Grascals. I pinch myself every time I'm on that stage."

Chapter 37

Horse Flies, Mammals, and Duhks

Mixing old-time traditions with modern sensibilities, the Ithaca-based Horse Flies "was part of a new wave," said NJ-born fiddler Judy Hyman. "We weren't trying to recreate something old but find old tunes that could be played in a way that felt right."

Studying violin since childhood, Hyman was studying anthropology at the University of Pennsylvania when she heard a schoolmate playing fiddle. Overwhelmed by the melodies, she struck up a conversation and told the fiddler, "I need to do something just for fun." "No problem," said her new friend. "There's a great festival—Union Grove. I'll take you."

Union Grove not only expanded Hyman's musical vision but also altered her life's path. "The driver of the vehicle [Jeff Claus]," she said, "is now my husband and bandmate."

Bluegrass bands dominated the festival, but "there was quite a bit of old-time music," remembered Hyman. "I didn't know the difference, but in hindsight, I was drawn more to the old-time playing. It was very dance-oriented. When I was first attracted to it, and got started, you often got into a jam where a flat-footer was part of it, like a drummer. These people had the most glorious sense of time. They would percolate with the rhythm and weaving of the old-time tune."

Starting out with note-heavy tunes ("I could pick them up quickly"), Hyman moved to the Round Peak style of fiddling. "It's not so note-driven or melodic," she said, "but more rhythmic. To this day, I'm on a hunt for tunes without a lot of notes or harmonic changes. Tommy Jarrell was a great influence. If you hum the melodies he played, you're missing what was so special about it, all those internal rhythms. He learned from black musicians and allowed that rhythmic influence to be expressed in his playing."

After a summer of old-time festivals, Hyman transferred to Indiana University's Jacobs School of Music, in Bloomington, to study violin and classical music. "There weren't many women interested in playing old-time fiddle music," she said. "When I'd go to fiddle festivals, it would be a little disconcerting. There was a lot of sexist behavior. I would sometimes need protection walking around. People would hang over me and say, 'Hey, baby, you play that thing?'

"My professors didn't know I was playing old-time music, and I didn't discuss my classical side with the fiddle players. I had this dual life going on. I did most of my fiddling during the summer and my violin playing during the academic year, except I would go to dances to listen and play. Dillon Bustin and the Bloomington Old-Time Music and Dance Group started a Wednesday-night contra-dance, in 1972, where they played old-time music rather than northeastern Celtic music. It was a very rhythmic style of dancing, all about the groove."

KY-born Strawberry McCloud fiddled at many of the dances. "He was the next generation from Clayton McMichen and Fiddlin' Doc Roberts," said Hyman, "and he was fascinating to all of us."

The Tompkins County Horseflies started as a "traditional acoustic band with a Northern accent," said Hyman. "I grew up in northern NJ and was into soul music. That groove was always in my head."

The group shared their first album (*Chokers and Flies: Old Time Music*) with the Chicken Chokers. "We had one side and they had the other," said Hyman. "The Chicken Chokers also had a Northern inflection. It's harder to get to the South from Boston than it is from Ithaca."

Shortening their name to the Horse Flies, they began to forge their own identity. "We did a cover of Baby Face Nelson's 'Pretty Little Girl,'" said Hyman, "and an original by Richie Stearns, 'Falling Star.' The rest were traditional fiddle tunes with original scat lyrics."

Hyman met Stearns at a "Breaking-Up Christmas" party when he was fourteen. "He was learning fiddle and banjo," she remembered. "We were celebrating the tradition of having parties every night at a different house."

Formed in 1974, Stearns' first group, Bubba George, was "alternative and off the grid," said Hyman. "They were influenced by the Highwoods String Band and John Specker's Correctone String Band and they gave old-time music a reggae inflection. The whole band lived together. Still to this day, they're not conventional in any way."

Shortly after she and Claus moved to Ithaca, Hyman heard that Bubba George was playing at a local "hole in the wall," she remembered. "There were a dozen people there, all friends of the band. As Jeff and I were buying our tickets, someone said, 'Look, it's somebody who's not us.'"

The Horse Flies' first full album, *Human Fly* (1987), took things further. "Jeff, Richie, [ex-Correctones bassist] John Hayward, and I had been getting together," said Hyman, "and not just playing old fiddle tunes. We were creating music that jazzed us up. Rounder wanted a traditional album.

We talked among ourselves and said, 'We don't want to make a traditional album. We want to explore what we've been exploring.'"

Canadian producer Bill Usher (Bruce Cockburn, Zachary Richard) took the reins on *Human Fly*. "We knew he was a percussionist," said Hyman, "and we were interested in fusing our thing with percussion. We went to Toronto and recorded. He connected us with a wonderful engineer, Kevin Doyle, who we've worked with since. It was the beginning of samplers and track beds and we explored that with him. We set lyrics about heavy subjects to traditional tunes and played them in different tunings. We added lyrics from graffiti in West Philadelphia that expressed sobering realities of life."

The Horse Flies got a boost with the addition of percussionist Taki Masuko. "We were part of a dance camp at Pinewoods during the summer," remembered Hyman, "with a Latin band. Taki was in that band. We convinced him to join us. He started on a full drum kit but we discovered that it didn't work sonically with acoustic guitar, banjo, fiddle, and synthesizer and he scaled down.

"We started experimenting with pickups, pedals, and electric instruments. The culmination came with *Gravity Dance* [1991]. By then, we were totally electric." (The album reached the top forty on the *Gavin* and CMJ charts.)

Performing for enthusiastic European audiences, the Horse Flies met a different response in their homeland. "Old-time music fans told us, 'I don't like what you're doing to old-time music,'" remembered Hyman, "and I kept trying to say, 'We're not doing anything to old-time music; we're making music.'"

The Horse Flies felt uncomfortable playing bluegrass festivals. "They hadn't gotten the word that we played old-time yet," explained Hyman. "People were not only confused; they were frightened. We stopped playing bluegrass festivals for many years because we didn't fit. In 2016, we played at the Grey Fox Bluegrass Festival, in Oak Hill, NY, for the first time. A woman who had been working at the record concession came up to us and said, 'I can't tell you how many people said, after your set, "I don't know what it is but I like it."'"

The Horse Flies were close to breaking through, opening ten shows for 10,000 Maniacs, when doctors diagnosed cancer in John Hayward. Intense treatment and surgery followed before it went into remission. "We had been playing loud, electric music for seven or eight years," said Hyman, "and missed playing acoustically. We did an acoustic tour of the Northwest during the summer of 1996 and had an absolute blast. John had an appointment with the doctor that he put off until after the tour.

Judy Hyman, 2014

We all knew this was it. Sure enough, the cancer was back. He died a year later and we hung it up. We had played together for seventeen years and had become family."

Plans for retirement, however, were premature. "We got a phone call from an agent who hadn't gotten the word," remembered Hyman, "asking if we'd be interested in playing Telluride. You don't say no to those things. We got June Drucker to join us on bass and found ourselves back on the map. We recorded *Until the Ocean* [2008] and got going again. By then, June had moved and Jay Olsa was playing bass."

The Horse Flies continue to resurrect between late spring and early fall. The rest of the year, they do other projects. "Richie does quite a bit of playing with fiddler Rosie Newton," said Hyman. "He and I toured and recorded two albums with Natalie Merchant—*The House Carpenter's Daughter* [2003], with Jeff on one tune ['Sally Ann'], and *Leave Your Sleep* [2010]."

The daughter of Jay Ungar and Lyn Hardy, Ruthy Ungar was born into music. "I remember going with my mom and dad to square dances," she said. "Musicians traveling through stayed at our house. The Boys of the Lough and Norman and Nancy Blake spent several days with us. I looked forward to my dad's camp at Ashokan and to spending time with the few kids who were there. My best friend lived in VT but we'd get together at the camp. We'd spend our time in nature but be absorbed by the music.

"I had a fiddle my size when I was a kid but I didn't play more than a couple of tunes. I didn't have the drive to go deep into playing scales. When I was twelve, I picked up the ukulele, which wasn't as intimidating. There was no one in my family already great at it. It was easy and fun; it didn't hurt my fingers. It was great for accompanying songs, and I love to sing.

"I didn't go to my first concert that didn't involve my family [Bonnie Raitt] until I was fifteen. I didn't have a perception of the music scene. For me, it was more about the dance community. My dad published *The Fiddle & Dance News,* which spread the word about regional dances, and he drew a comic, *Fiddle Man,* about the evil Mandolin Brothers capturing Ida Red."

Studying theater at Bard College, Ungar "learned the craft of performing," she said, "stage presence, breathing, storytelling, interpreting language, and connecting with an audience."

Meeting playwright, songwriter, and electric guitarist Michael "Mike" Merenda proved a turning point. "We were both from the theater world," said Ungar of her future husband, "but we shared an interest in songs. That's how I transitioned from theater back into music. I had a small production company, and put on a few shows, but being an actor was even more difficult than the music business."

"I was the new kid in town," recalled Merenda. "I had moved in with theater friends who I met in London doing a Shakespeare program. Two of them had gone to Bard with Ruthy. They invited me to the school's Christmas party in December 1998. That was the night I met Ruthy. We talked about open mics and she mentioned the SideWalk Cafe as a hotspot every Monday night. I remember this lightbulb going off over my roommates' heads. 'Why isn't she singing with him?' That night, there was an after-party at our apartment in Manhattan's financial district. I grabbed a guitar and started singing. Ruthy sang harmony during the chorus. When it ended, she said, 'Sing it again.'

"She hadn't played music with anyone her age before. Here I was, writing songs and trying to figure out what that meant, and this girl comes along and makes my song sound twice as good. She was trying to become an actor but she had a beautiful Gibson guitar that her mom gave her and a fiddle. She wasn't playing them but she was living in a tiny apartment, where space was a premium, and she had these instruments."

"When I started to connect with the traditional music I grew up with," said Ungar, "and playing with people my age, I was suddenly the expert. I pulled my fiddle out of the closet, put it in this old-time A-E-C# tuning, common for 'Rye Whiskey' and 'Hangman's Reel,' and played in my kitchen. My neighbors must have wondered what was going on."

Northampton, MA-born and Durham, NH-raised Merenda had no connection with roots music before meeting Ungar. "My only exposure to music," he remembered, "was what I heard on the radio or my friends shared with me. There was a folk community where I grew up but I wasn't privy to it. My parents weren't artistically inclined. My dad is a UNH business professor."

In addition to acting in high-school musicals, Merenda played with the orchestra and jazz band and participated in sports. "School was a nuisance," he said, "something I had to do to partake in activities."

Listening to the UNH radio station, Merenda "turned on to underground bands and indie labels." During the mid-nineties, he played in a punk-rock/ska band, Skarotum, with his brother Chris. "We had eight pieces," he said, "and a full horn section, very high energy. We were all high-school friends. We grew out of needing to heal after the death of the lead singer's older brother. Our songs were very political."

As he neared his high-school graduation, Merenda "had this idealistic vision of grabbing my guitar and hitting the road like Dylan, but I went to college and parlayed my interests into what I thought would be a theater career," he said. "I loved writing and directing plays. You couldn't pursue songwriting at a university."

Together with Ungar, Merenda formed a trio with Carter Little, a singer-songwriter who lived upstairs from him. "We had gone to college together," he said. "He had a deep awareness of bluegrass and he knew [Ungar's stepmother] Molly Mason. It was the perfect storm pulling us into each other's world."

"Carter was a Norman Blake fan," added Ungar, "and he had a few of my dad's records."

Ungar brought Merenda and Little to her father's music camp at Ashokan in 1999. "She talked her dad into giving us scholarships," said Merenda, "running the sound system for the evening dances."

Ani DiFranco's guitar playing heavily influenced Merenda. "Ani smacked her guitar in a percussively aggressive way," he said. "I appropriated that as a way of articulating melodies and bass lines, striking the strings the way a piano mallet hits a piano string. That became my guitar sound. When Ruthy saw me doing that, she realized I was playing clawhammer banjo on the guitar."

Ungar "put a banjo in my hands, and I was off to the races," Merenda continued. "I took to it immediately. All this muscle memory was already cooking. The banjo opened worlds to me. It's really the quintessential American folk instrument. It became a deep well of musical education."

"The banjo came naturally to him," remembered Ungar. "He showed up at lunchtime playing 'Pig in a Pen.' He was so obsessed he forgot to eat lunch."

Shortly afterwards, Merenda's roommates moved out and he had to find another place to live. "Ruthy was on the road," he said, "performing in schools on the East Coast. One of my bands from college, Spouse, had relocated to Northampton, where I was born. Ruthy's mom was a luthier at the fretted-instrument workshop in Amherst. They were looking for a counter boy. Lyn got me the job and very generously invited me to stay at her place. It was a rude awakening. She was living in the foothills of the Berkshires."

After playing drums for a local band (the Voltage Box), Merenda started a solo record. "I had songs I had written in college," he said. "Ruthy and I were working on separate records. We found our own place in Cummington. She was commuting forty-five minutes to Pittsfield, where she got a job at a photo shop. I was driving forty-five minutes the other way to the music shop. We were playing music at night. On Thursdays, my boss took off and left the shop to me. One Thursday, Pete Seeger's grandson, Tao Rodriguez Seeger, walked in the door. I had seen a poster for a Tao and Pete concert and recognized him. Tao was pulling instruments off the wall and trying them out. I helped him and we talked. I mentioned my girlfriend, Ruth Ungar. He knew her from the folk scene. We ended up swapping a couple of songs and he invited me to a party at his place in Easthampton. Ruthy and I showed up. Tao had a fiddler, Alicia, and we ended up playing old-time fiddle tunes. A band [the Mammals] was born that night."

The Mammals took their name from William Faulkner's 1930 novel, *As I Lay Dying.* "[Faulkner] referred to the shape of a character's wet dress," explained Ungar, "as 'mammalian ludicrocities which are the horizons and valleys of the earth,' mocking human ridiculousness."

"We didn't pander to any trends," added Merenda. "We played a melting pot of music but at the core was the traditional bedrock. We used that as a springboard. To us, the sky was the limit. We had very open minds. *Departure* had Nirvana and Morphine covers, a Spanish antiwar anthem, and an anti-Vietnam War song."

"I had 'The Water Song' years before Standing Rock," added Ungar. "Mike had 'Culture War' before Trump got in office and dropped the arts. The Mammals existed under the George W. [Bush] reign. When the Dixie Chicks got in trouble for talking about politics, we were singing 'The Bush Boys.' We sang it when we opened for Arlo Guthrie's 40th Anniversary tour. His audience loved it but Festival International, in Lafayette, nearly kicked us out when we performed it as an encore. Some people were cheering because they never get music like that, but others freaked out. The next day, the organizers said, 'You can't play that song again.' Sponsors complained and there were death threats. We did 'Fall on My Knees' instead. It has a pro-choice verse but it's more metaphorical. Most people weren't listening close enough to notice."

The Mammals reflected the cutting edge of Americana. "When we wrote, we didn't think about it," Ungar remembered. "It just ended up that way. ABC News said that *Bright as You Can* [2015] had every segment of American music, not just bluegrass but also blues, folk, and old-time music. The freedom of genre that started with the Mammals continued to open doors for us."

"We suddenly had sister bands," remembered Merenda. "The Avett Brothers started as a rock band but they had exposure to Appalachian string-band music. They made the shift to roots music. A lot of us did. We grew up when folk music wasn't on the mainstream radar but we found it and each other."

In 2003, Matt Glaser invited Ungar and Mason to sing with the Wayfaring Strangers. "I wanted to make music I could listen to on my own deathbed," Glaser told *Roots World*.[1]

"We did a gig in a music hall," Ungar remembered, "and Matt started calling me to substitute. I ended up singing on their second record, *Shifting Sands of Time,* with Aoife O'Donovan [Crooked Still] and Tracy Bonham. I met Aoife at the Philadelphia Folk Festival, in 2000, when she was eighteen. We sang 'When Golden Leaves Begin to Fall' as a duet. I had sung it with Molly. We ran through the song backstage. After the first line, we were so relieved. It was so easy and fun. We've been best friends since. She sang on every Mammals record and I sang with Crooked Still.

"Matt joked that we took the bluegrass repertoire and jazz harmony and alienated two audiences. I related. Sometimes with the Mammals, we were too folky for rock audiences and too rocking for folk shows."

The Mammals nevertheless enjoyed special status in the folk world. "Being in a band with Pete Seeger's grandson," noted Merenda, "emboldened me to have the courage to say important things that had to be said."

When the Children's Dance Company of Salt Lake City organized a tribute to Seeger's music in 2002, "Tao got the Mammals to back up Pete," recalled Merenda. "We went downhill skiing with him. He was well into his eighties. We played MerleFest together and a few things around the Hudson Valley. We supported him plenty of times, even if it was just helping him get in tune or setting the microphones at the right height. At his ninetieth birthday celebration, at Madison Square Garden, I was his guitar tech. I shadowed him, helped him stay in tune, and changed a broken string. If he spoke to too many people before a show, he couldn't sing. I made sure he took a nap and didn't lose his voice by talking all day. I made sure he had enough food and that he had his hearing aid. I was part of the family."

The addition of a bass player and drummer, in 2008, provided "the signature Mammals sound, a rock band with old-time instruments," Ungar said. "We never stopped using that formula as Mike + Ruthy. Sometimes, there were keyboards and horns. We were somewhere between a nineties indie-rock songwriter outfit and a traditional old-time band."

Merenda and Ungar have hosted winter and summer hoots at Ashokan since 2013. "It's great to turn people on to music not on their radar," said Merenda, "and create a community spirit. We've had Natalie Merchant, Dan Bern, Loudon Wainwright III, David Bromberg, and Anais Mitchell. It's a juggling act between new and established acts."

"We're certainly not purists or traditionalists," added Ungar. "It's hard to be daring and stay true to the roots but it's a worthy pursuit."

Ungar and Merenda reclaimed the Mammals' name in 2017. "Tao's

The Mammals (Ruthy Ungar, Mike Merenda), 2008

happy not being a touring musician," explained Ungar, "and he was fine with us taking the name back. It's a great name. We started Mike + Ruthy as a duo, but after ten years, we'd grown into a band. We have a better chance of making an impact as the Mammals."

Merenda and Ungar produced *Beyond the Blue* (2014), the fifth album by Winnipeg-based neo-traditionalists the Duhks. "Mike and I are avid writers," said Ungar. "It was great to work with people whose ego wasn't caught up in writing and were open to collaboration. I sang 'Lazy John' on the Wayfaring Strangers album. Leonard [Podolak] had the idea of it as a Cajun tune. We let it grow in the studio. Blake Miller [the Revelers] played accordion."

"We had a history of running into each other at festivals all over the world," added Merenda, "Canada, Australia, Denmark, and the U.S. Because we were the Mammals and the Duhks, festivals paired us at workshops. We ran with that joke. We started calling it 'Platypus, the Duck-Billed Mammal.'

"The Duhks had a much different existence than us. They made some high-budget music videos, ran up debt, and broke up. They were in the awkward position of not being on the road but owing money to lawyers and managers. They started doing gigs with the original lineup to pay back some of this debt. They enjoyed it so much they thought about making another record. That's when they approached Ruthy and me. We have a studio in our house and we've been producing records. By the time the project happened, original members had started bowing out one by one until it was just Leonard, [vocalist] Jessica 'Jessee' Havey, and [fiddler] Tania Elizabeth. They lost their drummer and guitarist but we dove head on into it. It wasn't easy. They didn't have road-tested material. We had to not only make a record in short time but also develop a repertoire for them. Everyone brought ideas to the table. We rehearsed and built arrangements while we were making the record. It was doable—it came out great—but it was hard work and long days."

"I wanted Mike and Ruthy involved," explained Podolak, "because of their ability to make vocals happen in a profound way. They're both great singers. They have a contemporary edge but they're also rooted in traditional music. The Mammals were our sister band. We grew up together and traveled to the same festivals. They brought a serene place to work, a scene outside the scene. It was successful as an artistic endeavor but not commercially. We rushed it out; I wanted it for MerleFest."

Like Ungar, Podolak (1975-) grew up amidst traditional music. His father, Mitch, was an old-time banjo player who ran the Bohemian Embassy Coffee House, in Toronto, in the 1960s. In addition to producing documentaries and hosting a CBC radio show (*Simply Folk*), he was a guiding force behind the Winnipeg, Vancouver, Edmonton, and Calgary folk festivals. "My dad taught me the banjo when I was sixteen," said Podolak. "I told him that I'd learn his old-time stuff—he could teach me the basics—but I wanted to play like Béla Fleck and planned to switch to newgrass. That never happened because I fell in love with old-time music.

"I developed a way to play triplets on a four-string tenor banjo. You could nail the ornamentation playing clawhammer. I'm not impressed by the number of notes but by melody. With old-time music, the joy is easy to transmit."

Podolak's palette continued to expand. "As soon as I started playing old-time music," he said, "I realized how much I also loved Irish, Scottish, and Cape Breton music. That led to Quebecois and Cajun music. I found the fiddle harder than the banjo but I found a way to play Irish, Scottish, and old-time fiddle tunes on the banjo."

Incorporating diverse influences, Podolak formed Scruj MacDuhk in 1995. "The founding band was button-accordion player Geoff Butler," he recalled, "and this freaky dude, Dan Baseley, who played piano accordion and tin whistle. He took Scottish fiddle tunes and played them on a steel drum from Trinidad. We recruited a fiddle player [Jeremy Penner], a guitar player [Joel Fafard], and a bass player [Gilles Fournier]. After a couple of years, [Australian-born vocalist] Ruth Moody [The Wailin' Jennys] came in. I had gone to school with her in Winnipeg. We got a guitarist [Jeremy Walsh] who was a great singer of Irish ballads. He got Oliver Swain to play bass. Christian Dugas, who was in the Duhks for a couple of years, came in on percussion. I was looking for people who wanted to tour. We played all over Canada and started making inroads into the States. That's when we broke up."

Wanting to keep the momentum going, Podolak formed the Duhks in 2001. "We never wanted to be a straight-ahead old-time or Celtic band," he said, "but play creative arrangements that moved. Scruj MacDuhk was a young band. We didn't know what a manager or publicist did. We were a hurricane going down on the road, a bunch of clowns. The Duhks gave more thought to the arrangements. We wanted everything to be thought-out and precise."

The original Duhks included Jordan McConnell (guitar), Elizabeth, and Havey. "I've known Jessica since she was born in 1983," said Podolak. "Her parents are longtime Winnipeg volunteers. Her uncle lived in my parents' basement. When Scruj MacDuhk ended, he said, 'Why don't you give Jessica a call?' I thought it was outlandish but I had no better idea. She was into it. Scruj MacDuhk was a huge influence on her."

The Duhks "came storming out of the gates," said Podolak. "Our first

Jessee Havey, 2014

album [*Your Daughters & Your Sons*, 2003] was nominated for a Juno and our second [*The Duhks*, 2005] won."

Mark Schatz produced the former while Béla Fleck oversaw the latter. "Béla stressed playing new things," said Podolak, "and taking listeners on a journey. He taught me tone and the importance of every note and not repeating yourself. Even if you're not going to have many notes, you want to play in time and have a clear tone."

Tim O'Brien produced the Duhks' third album, *Migrations* (2006). "Tim was all vibe," said Podolak. "He had more to do with song selection and heart and soul, less with technique."

At the height of the Duhks' popularity, Havey departed for a solo career. "It's been a rollercoaster," said Podolak. "The Duhks was never easy, a combination of youth, scheduling, and insecurity. It was Spinal Tap-ian in how the closer we got to making it, the harder it got."

Havey's replacement, Sarah Dugas, was "a stalwart of the Winnipeg folk scene," said Podolak. "Her brother, Christian, was in Scruj MacDuhk. There are four kids and they're all singers and dancers, amazing artists. When Jessica left, I called Christian and told him that I needed Sarah's number. 'Why do you need her number?' I said, 'I'm not calling to ask her for a date.' He said, 'I want to come too.' As it turned out, our percussion player and his wife were having their second child. It got to be too much for him to be on the road. He left a couple of months after Sarah joined and Christian rejoined me. That's when we made *Fast Paced World*. We took a departure from where we were going. We had been working with Gary Paczosa, an amazing engineer, but there was a big change at Sugar Hill and he became our A&R person. He didn't want to produce the record. We were a 'new' band with Sarah, with more of a rock-and-roll influence. We made the record with Jay Joyce, who's produced Emmylou Harris and Patty Griffin. It was a chance to experiment with different sounds, different attitudes, and different concepts of arrangements.

"It pissed off traditional fans—it had drums. We approached it very folky, but it didn't go over and we hit a wall. We decided to take a break. Sarah and Christian got jobs with Zac Brown."

It wasn't the end, however. "I had a big debt to pay," said Podolak. "A booking agency convinced me to keep going, so I tried to reestablish the band. Musically, it was cool, but it didn't pan out. It went from being a collective to me owning it and I couldn't sustain it. I should have just left it as a reunion of the original band but I said, 'This is fun; we should make a new record.' We should have made T-shirts instead. Scott [Senior] and Jordan didn't want to do it but Jessica and Tania were up for it. Halfway through, the Avett Brothers recruited Tania. Trying to find a band that was going to be full-time became impossible. I wound up working with people on a per-gig basis. That wasn't the Duhks anymore. It was my holding on to the concept, desperately."

Podolak's recent focus has been on Home Roots, a network of home concerts started by his father (who required months to recuperate from cervical surgery). "There are two tours," he told me in 2017, "one with French-Canadian artists, and nearly eight hundred gigs a year. My official title is executive producer but we're a team. We're going to be steering the organization in the future and trying to grow it. My goal is to bring it into the States."

Podolak has "been playing with Matt Gordon, a great fiddle player from NY who lives in Ireland," he said. "We're going to record with a rhythm section [New Roads] that plays traditional Irish music with an old-time twist. We're following in the tradition of inclusiveness and eclectic-ness."

Chapter 38

Berklee

The goal of Berklee College of Music, the world's largest independent music college, is to "prepare students for careers in jazz, pop, and commercial music." The Boston school expanded its scope in 1981 with the arrival of fiddler/educator Matt Glaser, who possessed a master's degree in music from Tufts University. "I knew Berklee wasn't just jazz anymore," recalled Ottawa-born fiddler April Dawn Verch (1978-), who attended the school in 1998. "I met Matt at Mark O'Connor's fiddle camp, in Nashville, when I was fifteen, and knew he would encourage me to develop whatever style I wanted to play. He wasn't going to push me in any one direction."

Verch's father played in a classic country-music band, but she "hadn't heard the old-time, Appalachian tradition before the fiddle camp," she said. "It seemed more foreign to me than bluegrass. Old-time Canadian music differs from old-time American music. It's not our oldest style. It refers to the late fifties, when fiddle music broadcast coast to coast on Don Messer's radio and TV shows. He took fiddle tunes from regional styles, played them with a full band, and tried making them accessible for people who thought fiddle music was just for country folk. It was the first time the whole country was hearing the same fiddle styles.

"I didn't think about playing in the 'Ottawa Valley style.' I just played what I grew up around but I loved the fiddle, the music, and the culture and wanted to be part of it. That was a conscious decision."

Natural ability shone through Verch's fiddling. "At first, it came quite easily," she recalled, "I have a good ear. Then, I reached a point where I plateaued and it was hard to get better. That's when a local musician told my parents to get me violin lessons. It was really frustrating, being able to play and having to backtrack."

The step dancing that Verch does while fiddling "isn't part of a tradition," she said. "I saw someone dance like that when I was small and decided I wanted to do it. There's movement in Canadian traditions. You stamp your foot or move with the music. That's typical. It's dance music."

Verch danced "because my sister, Tawnya, who's four years older than me, was dancing," she said. "Our dance teacher, Buster Brown, used to do performances and wanted dancers to take with him. He chose my sister and four others who were quite good. They became the Dueling Dancers. They added me because I was cute.

"Our parents were great at making sure we had opportunities and so, in addition to dancing, we started to do things on our own. Eventually some of the other dancers quit and we ended up four pieces—my sister and I and the Pilatzke brothers—Jon and Nathan. They dance with the Chieftains now. We morphed from step dancers to Jon and I playing fiddle, my sister playing piano, and Nathan playing drums. We all sang. It was a great way to learn and get experience."

Verch was ten when she made her Canadian-television debut on *The Tommy Hunter Show* in 1988. "That was incredible," she remembered. "I had always wanted to be on the show and play with Al Cherny, Tommy's fiddler, but Al passed away and I was heartbroken. A week or so later, my parents got a phone call saying that Tommy had seen a video of me on a telethon and said that he was going to have me on the show to play with him on the tribute to Al Cherny. I was on with all these great fiddlers; it was a dream come true." The following year, Verch and Hunter toured Canada.

Winning over four hundred fiddling and step-dancing competitions, Verch believes "competitions weren't for the competing but part of the fiddle culture," she said. "It was where we could go and be around other kids who loved to play. You didn't feel that way during the school year. In the summer, there was a contest every weekend."

Verch released her debut album at thirteen. "My parents said, 'We'll help you pay for it. You're going to sell them,'" she remembered. "I saved all the money from those recordings, won from competitions, or got paid by performing with the Dueling Dancers, and paid for college."

Strictly instrumental at first, Verch didn't start singing until she was in her twenties. "I wasn't trying to sing like anyone," she recalled. "I was just trying to learn to sing. I've played the fiddle since I was a kid. Singing, I felt more vulnerable. It took me a long time to get comfortable."

Teaching at a fiddle camp in Saskatchewan, Verch met her ex-husband, Marc Bru. "He was a percussionist," she recalled, "but he wasn't playing music for a living. When we got married, in 2000, he wanted to tour with me. He brought bodhrans and spoons, which worked with my music. He was also my first manager and booked my shows. He toured with me for eight or nine years. He decided that the road wasn't for him and stopped touring. Not long after that, we divorced. That was a big change. It meant we were scaling down to three pieces. That's when I started getting into old-time and bluegrass. Cody Walters brought clawhammer banjo to the band in 2007. A lot of things coincided."

Verch tours more in the United States than Canada. "You're more foreign when you're away from home," she said, "and that makes it special. It's logistically harder to tour in Canada. Things are farther apart."

Recent shows have teamed Verch with MO-born and NC-based multi-instrumentalist Joe Newberry. "Even though we come from different traditions," she said, "we approach music in a similar way. We love the melodies and we both play with a drive and groove. It's easy for us to play together. He grew up in the Ozarks but the fiddle players he grew up backing listened to Canadian fiddle tunes. The chord changes are a little different, but when I play Canadian tunes, they sound familiar to him."

Berklee's first banjo principal, Chris Pandolfi (the Infamous Stringdusters), attended from 2001 to 2003. "Matt Glaser helped me to get in," said the Briarcliff Manor, NY-born and Hartford, CT-raised banjo player, "but there were people who weren't supportive of what I was doing. I took a guitar curriculum. I studied what to play, not necessarily how to play it. I had to learn that on my own."

Pandolfi formed the Infamous Stringdusters with Andy Hall (Dobro) in Boston. Relocating to Nashville, after he graduated in 2003, and adding Andy Falco (guitar), Jeremy Garrett (fiddle), and Travis Book (bass), they opened for Jim Lauderdale, Dolly Parton, Ronnie Bowman, and other "traditional voices of bluegrass," he said. "That's how we learned to play our instruments. We were trying to get gigs at the Station Inn and sessions on bluegrass albums. There was only one way to do that. That doesn't mean we're masters but we put in the time."

The Infamous Stringdusters' debut, *Fork in the Road* (2007), tied with J. D. Crowe & the New South's *Lefty's Old Guitar* as the IBMA's "Album of the Year." The title track was "Song of the Year" and the Infamous Stringdusters were "Emerging Artist." "The more confidence we have to go out on a limb," said Pandolfi "the more people sense the risk and reward. Not every show is perfect but we certainly do our best every night. Some nights, it pays off."

Book's bass playing anchors the Stringdusters' sound. "The hallmark of bluegrass," Pandolfi explained, "is that there are no drums. String instruments become rhythm instruments. We don't have a mandolin. The bass takes on an added layer of rhythmic responsibility; it's the rock on which we weave our melodies and musical statements."

Each band member contributes tunes. "We get a dialogue going on about what we like," said Pandolfi, "the feelings and vibes we're seeking, and we decide on the best songs. We arrange them for the band; that's the crucial element in making things quintessentially ours."

Pandolfi inherited his passion for music from his paternal grandparents. "They started the CT Opera Association," he said, "and they were both professional musicians. My grandfather was a voice coach, my grandmother a pianist. I started on piano but I didn't go deep into music until I started playing banjo."

Acquiring his first five-string in 1997, Pandolfi had no idea what bluegrass was. "This is great evidence," he said, "of the modern strains of bluegrass opening the door to the traditional music. I heard Béla Fleck and the Flecktones. My older brother was a bass player so he was into Victor Wooten. When I got my first banjo, I got Pete Wernick's book *Bluegrass Banjo* and started to learn rolls. I tried playing Flecktones tunes but they were too heavy on technique. I was in over my head. It made more sense for me to learn 'Blue Ridge Cabin Home' and 'Fireball Mail.' I didn't get Earl Scruggs' playing right away but after years of listening and absorbing banjo music, I came to understand his incredible intensity. I learned bluegrass out of necessity, but I fell in love with it."

Ladies & Gentlemen (2016) featured guest appearances by Nicki Bluhm, Mary Chapin Carpenter, Claire Lynch, Aoife O'Donovan, Joan Osborne, Sara Watkins, Abigail Washburn, and Lee Ann Womack. "You're a band for so many years," said Pandolfi, "you have to find ways to mix it up. The producers, including Tim O'Brien, helped to line everything up. We handed the reins over more than we usually do and the result was something completely different."

The Grammy-winning *Laws of Gravity* (2017) represented "the pendulum swinging back even more into the Stringdusters' house: our songs, our arrangements, and improvising," said Pandolfi. "Our drive has always been to take what we love about bluegrass—the precision, the feelings you elicit the way those instruments are played—and refining it along the way. That's a big part of the consistency, trying to take those dyed-in-the-wool bluegrass techniques and apply them to a more modern concept of songwriting. We're playing the songs from *Laws of Gravity* on the road and still making new discoveries."

Pandolfi's side project, Trad Plus, is "a much more modern interpretation of what the banjo can do, with samples and beats and real drums," he said. "It's a rethinking of what can be done."

After directing Berklee's string department for twenty-eight years, Matt Glaser became artistic director of its new American Roots Music Program in 2009. Sierra Dawn Hull was already on her way to stardom when she enrolled as the program's first Presidential Scholarship recipient. During her two years at the school (2009-11), the mandolin phenom "did a little of everything, from songwriting to playing with an improv orchestra," she said. "My first semester, I played with a Caribbean hip-hop ensemble. It was good to stretch in different directions and sometimes feel out of place. It expanded my abilities. I lived on campus and was around people constantly working on music. I'd study during the week and, on weekends, jump on a plane and go somewhere to play."

Hull (1991-) grew up in Byrdstown, TN, where "everybody knows everybody," she said. "There's one high school in Pickett County—I graduated with forty-four people. I heard bluegrass gospel music and hymns. Family members would get up in church and sing but I got the bluegrass bug right away. The first ten years of my musical life was nothing else."

Hull's father "loved the mandolin as a kid," she said. "My great-uncle Junior inspired that. He loaned my dad a guitar. After that, Dad got his own mandolin. He's the reason I wanted to play and started going to jam sessions."

Learning her first tune ("Boil That Cabbage Down") at the age of eight, Hull progressed quickly. Her father "showed me what he knew, and he was trying to learn more so he could help me," she remembered. "I was naturally quick but I did a lot of work."

Within two years, Hull was holding her own as a musician. She recorded her independent debut album, *Angel Mountain,* an all-instrumental recording, at ten. "I've always been singing," she said, "but making a mandolin album seemed the easiest way to kick things off."

Alison Krauss captured Hull's attention. "I got one of her albums when I was nine," she recalled, "and I met her very briefly at a festival when I was ten. She was my biggest hero. I drew pictures of being onstage at the *Grand Ole Opry* with her. My parents took me to see her at MerleFest. We had never been anywhere as big. I was just a fan getting a picture.

"I met Ron Block at IBMA and he told Alison about me. The next thing I knew, she called my parents' house and asked me to play the *Grand Ole Opry,* at the Ryman, with her. That was a dream. I've had a friendship with her ever since."

Hull knew how big a deal the *Opry* was. "I spent a lot of time watching my *Grand Ole Opry* heroes on TV with my whole family," she said. "We'd be at jams on Saturday night when it came on but they would re-air the performance on Sunday morning and we'd watch it then.

"Most people get it wrong. I didn't make my debut on the *Opry* with Alison. I actually made my debut a few months before with my brother, Cody. We were invited to play at the Opry House by national banjo champion Mike Snider."

Hull spent the summer of 2003 on the Great Mountain Tour with Krauss and Ralph Stanley. "I was so young," she recalled. "I wish I had the opportunity to do something like that now. There would be things I would appreciate more than a twelve-year-old kid possibly could. Alison was so sweet. My brother, my mom, and I traveled on her bus for two and a half months. I remember waking up the first morning and looking out the window. We were in Chicago and I thought, 'Wow, what a big city.'

"Being around Ralph Stanley was remarkable. In the middle of the tour, we had a week or so off and he had a gig at a festival. He invited me to be his mandolin player; I got to dress up like a Clinch Mountain Boy. Ralph was sweet. He took time to talk to me and be encouraging. Every night, he'd come onstage wearing a rhinestone jacket. He'd take it off and throw it to me. I'd put it on and Buck White and I would go onstage and dance while he played clawhammer banjo."

Hull became serious about songwriting around thirteen. "I'd written a little before," she said, "but I got more interested in writing lyric songs. With every album, I've written more. It's one of my favorite things to do as an artist."

Performing at the IBMA Conference in 2006, Hull impressed Ken Irwin. "Alison had been on Rounder for years," said Hull. "After we became friends, I got to know Ken more. Many of my heroes—Alison, Tony Rice, and Blue Highway—recorded for Rounder. I dreamed it would be the label I got to record for."

Ron Block produced Hull's first Rounder album, *Secrets* (2008). "He was the reason I knew Alison," Hull said, "and I felt comfortable working with him. He invested a lot of time into the project. For him to take a fifteen-year-old girl, like me, and be willing to go the extra mile to make sure the project was everything it could possibly be, was cool. Because of him, we were able to get Tony Rice on the album. I don't think I would have been brave enough to ask those people to take part in the record. Ron's very much a perfectionist. I knew, going in to make the record with him, that it would be an album I'd be proud of making. It reached number two on the bluegrass charts. Every record bumps you up to the next place. I started to tour more. I was in high school when I made that album so there was only so much I could do as a student."

Hull was attending Berklee when she recorded her second Rounder album, *Daybreak* (2011). "It felt like baby steps to me," she said, "rather than something dramatically changed; it was a slow climb. I was still performing and working on music but I wasn't touring as much as I would around the release of an album. I took a little time trying to focus on figuring out what I wanted to do next."

Joined by Krauss and Tyminski, Hull performed at a White House concert on November 21, 2011. "That was surreal," she said. "I never thought I'd get to do anything like that. Again, that goes back to Alison being kind enough to invite me to be part of that with her. It was very cool. Not only were we performing but also a whole slew of people, from Lyle Lovett to James Taylor and Kris Kristofferson."

By her third Rounder album, *Weighted Mind* (2016), Hull "was feeling that next wave and had something to say." Producer Béla Fleck brought out a more intimate side of her persona. "Béla asked me, 'What would happen if you start with mandolin and voice?'" she remembered. "It made me pull something out of myself that I hadn't tried to do before. It was challenging but also super exciting. I identify myself as a bluegrass musician who loves other things too. *Weighted Mind* isn't a bluegrass album but I wouldn't say that it's a folk album either. It straddles different genres with sparseness— instrumentally and with the writing. *Weighted Mind* received IBMA and Grammy 'Album of the Year' nominations in the folk category. I've been accepted in this other world as well."

Taking a brief break from "touring like crazy" with bass player Ethan Jodziewicz, Hull cohosted the IBMA Awards Ceremony with Tyminski. "I was surprised when I was asked to cohost the show," she said. "Dan has so much personality; he made it so much fun. I'd love to do it again."

Since graduating from Berklee's two-year program, Hull has called

Sierra Hull, 2014

Nashville "home," she said. "I grew up two hours away. It's where Alison, Ron Block, and a lot of folk I've spent time with live. I'm a TN girl at heart. I travel enough to enjoy other places but being here, I get to come home."

When we spoke, Hull was preparing for the March 31, 2017, performance of a concertino for mandolin, clarinet, and piano, by Ofer Ben-Amots, at Colorado College's Celeste Theatre. "I've never done anything like it before," she said, "a more orchestral situation. I'm slaving away at it. It's a lot of work being a musician."

Chapter 39

It All Comes Around

Innovation, experimentation, and improvisation push bluegrass and old-time music forward, but many of the best players retain reverence for the roots, loyalty to the founding fathers, and ties to the ongoing stream of tradition. Recreating the magic of Flatt & Scruggs and the Foggy Mountain Boys, the Earls of Leicester with Jerry Douglas emerged as one of the most exciting bluegrass bands of the early twenty-first century. "It's as close as I'll ever come to playing with Flatt & Scruggs," said Douglas. "They were my Beatles."

"I love playing close to the records," agreed Darrell DeShawn "Shawn" Camp (1966-). "I need to be in the character of Lester Flatt when I'm doing these songs, and the only way I could do it is to bend and scoop my notes the way Lester did. He was a real crooner. I hadn't realized what a good singer he was. It was deceptively complicated. I'm playing a role, but when I sing a song, I try to give a truthful interpretation. You have to be yourself when you're throwing emotions out there."

Banjo player Charlie Cushman had been playing Foggy Mountain Boys tunes with Johnny Warren, son of Flatt & Scruggs fiddler Paul Warren. "They asked Jerry to play on their project," explained Camp. "They talked about it and decided that it would be a good idea to put together a whole band. Jerry called and asked if I wanted to be Lester. I said, 'Hell, yeah.'

"In a couple of weeks, we got together for a rehearsal. Eight bars into the first song, we had to stop. It felt so real. We knew we were on to something. The way Jerry digs in, he pushes the bar high as far as musicianship and playing with soul. Everyone came up to that level. Johnny Warren played his daddy's fiddle, the one on Flatt & Scruggs' records. It brought authenticity."

At first, Tim O'Brien assumed Curly Seckler's role. "We played several gigs," he said, "before we went to the studio. It turned into a jam session where we were playing old stuff but feeling like we were stepping into the grooves of old records."

O'Brien made "the perfect Curly Seckler, but he put out a new Hot Rize album [*When I'm Free*] at the same time that the Earls of Leicester's first album came out and he ended up touring with Hot Rize," said Camp. "We had a rotating mandolin slot until we got Jeff White."

Bluegrass drew Camp's interest early. "I'm a country boy," he said, "and bluegrass was always in the back of my mind. It's in my blood from the ground up; I grew up going to bluegrass festivals. I didn't listen to rock and roll outside of Elvis Presley, Jerry Lee Lewis, and Johnny Cash—all the Sun Records stuff. I listened to Merle Haggard and classic sixties country songs. I soaked it all in. I loved the old bluegrass songs, especially the death ballads like 'The Girl in the Blue Velvet Band.' The darker story songs, like 'The Dreadful Snake,' attracted me."

Growing up in Perryville, AR, Camp "lived about ten miles out of town, on a thirty-acre farm with cows and chickens," he said. "We had a couple of catfish ponds. I love NY but you can't go fishing for a catfish anywhere."

Camp's father played guitar and sang country songs with his mother. "I started playing guitar when I was five," he said. "After supper, Dad and I would sit in the kitchen and play old songs. That's how I learned to play— that and picking parties. There'd be people playing and I'd get in the circle. It was a hands-on way of learning. Nobody taught me. I was just around it a lot."

At sixteen, Camp played fiddle and guitar for the Grand Prairie Boys, a six-piece traditional bluegrass band. "I sang a couple songs in the show," he recalled. "I started working with a bluegrass band out of Edmond, OK, Signal Mountain with Freddy Sanders, Virgil and David Bonham, and Randy Latham. It was more progressive and not so straight-ahead bluegrass. Between bluegrass shows, I worked at VFW and dancehalls around Little Rock, keeping my foot in the country world. I played with lots of little bands in AR. I worked the Derby Theater, with Ted Moulinex, across the street from the horse track in Hot Springs. It was a Vegas-style dinner show."

Arriving in Nashville in 1986, Camp signed on as fiddler for the Osborne Brothers. "My dad had their records," he said, "and they were superstars. I only lasted six months. They were waiting on Glen Duncan to quit Jim & Jesse. Glen was notorious for staying with everybody for six months; he was hot as a fiddle player."

Camp's 1993 debut solo album nearly broke into the top sixty. Since then, he's released four studio albums. *Live at the Station Inn* (2004) released on Tim O'Brien's Oh Boy Records. "*Lucky Silver Dollar* [2001] is the solo album I'm most proud of," Camp said, "but nobody picked it up. I put it out on my own label [Skeeterbit]. Allen Reynolds produced it and it had some great sounds. I put out a compilation of demos, *Fireball*, in March 2006."

Camp continues to play with Pat McLaughlin, Greg Morrow, Michael Rhodes, and ex-NRBQ guitarist "Big Al" Anderson as the World Famous Headliners. "I saw NRBQ in 1989," he recalled, "when Big Al weighed about four hundred pounds; sweat was just flying off of him, and he was playing his ass off. It was mind-blowing. I never dreamed I'd be in a band with him."

Co-producer (with Chris Latham) of Guy Clark's final album, *My Favorite Picture of You*, Camp received a "Best Folk Album" Grammy in 2014. "Guy was as much the producer," he said. "He had a real charm in his vocals. The fragile tones, at that point in his life, played in his favor. He had a vulnerability that you didn't hear in his earlier things."

Camp has worked extensively with country-music superstar Loretta Lynn. "We've written songs together," he said, "and I've played on seventy tracks with her."

Written with Sandy Mason and Benita Hill, "Two Pina Coladas" was Camp's first of four chart-topping collaborations. "We didn't have anything to write about," he told me in 2016, "and we were stuck. We went out on the front porch. I said, 'Let's forget this songwriting and go to FL.' Sandy said, 'Well, if I go to FL, I want a pina colada.' Benita added, 'I want one for each hand.' Twenty minutes later, we had the song. Within a week, Allen Reynolds played the demo for Garth Brooks. It was number one six weeks later. I had another one go to the top of the charts that summer ['How Long Gone,' 1998, by Brooks & Dunn]; it was a big summer for me. Josh Turner had a number-one hit with 'Would You Go with Me' and George Strait with 'River of Love.' There was a time when I co-wrote with somebody every day but it burns you out. It's time to play some shows and do a little picking."

Coda

In 1982, Tommy Jarrell received a National Endowment for the Arts National Heritage Fellowship and sat next to Bill Monroe at the awards ceremony. When a reporter asked if he was a "master of the old-time fiddle," he answered quickly, "Now, mister, there ain't nobody mastered the fiddle. . . . There's music in that thing that'll be there when Gabriel toots his horn."[1]

Author Interviews

Eddie Adcock 6/15/17
Martha Adcock 6/14/17
Adam Aijala 11/15/16
Taylor Armerding 3/7/17
Danny Barnes 12/26/16
Anders Beck 3/20/17
Mac Benford 12/15/16
Byron Berline 10/13/16
Dale Ann Bradley 10/26/16
Alison Brown 12/22/16
Sam Bush 11/18/16
Shawn Camp 11/8/16
Bob Carlin 10/17/16
Michael Cleveland 11/14/16
John Cohen 12/5/16
T. Michael Coleman 6/27/17
Dudley Connell 11/29/16
John Cowan 3/10/17
J. D. Crowe 10/27/16
Iris DeMent 11/13/12
Rodney Dillard 11/22/16
Jerry Douglas 12/13/16
Stuart Duncan 1/3/17
Ben Eldridge 1/16/15
Bill Emerson 4/21/17
Pat Enright 12/27/16
Béla Fleck 12/8/16
Dom Flemons 11/28/16
Rhiannon Giddens 11/10/16
Tom Gray 7/19/17

Richard Greene 11/30/16
Dr. Anthony Harkins 4/6/17
John Hartford 3/22/89
Paul Hoffman 3/29/17
David Holt 11/18/16
Sierra Hull 1/17/17
Judy Hyman 10/26 and 10/31/16
Rob Ickes 10/19/16
Phil Jamison 11/16/16
Gerry Katz 10/18/16
Alison Krauss 3/15/88
Jack Lawrence 10/21/16
Nolan Lawrence 12/15/16
Doyle Lawson 11/2/16
Frank Lee 11/30/16
Laurie Lewis 12/14/16
Del McCoury 12/29/16
John McEuen 11/28/16
Roger McGuinn 5/27/14
Jesse McReynolds 10/27/16
Kevin Martin 12/19/16
Buddy Melton 12/12/16
Mike Merenda 1/14/17
Bruce Molsky 12/27/16
James Monroe 10/26/16
Alan Munde 12/1/16
David Nelson 11/8/16
Tim O'Brien 3/15/17
Bobby Osborne 12/28/16
Chris Pandolfi 4/4/17

Nick Panken 3/26/12
Gene Parsons 2/8/17
Penny Parsons 10/11/16
Herb Pedersen 12/7/16
Woody Platt 12/1/6
Leonard Podolak 1/17/17
Ronnie Reno 11/2/16
Don Rigsby 3/1/17
Danny Roberts 2/21/17
Jim Rooney 10/27/16
Phil Rosenthal 10/19/16
Tracy Schwarz 10/14/16
Gary Scruggs 12/22/16
Ketch Secor 10/25/16
Graham Sharp 12/6/16
Ron Shuffler 12/14/16
Roger Sprung 2/11/17

Tim Stafford 3/5/17
Ralph Stanley II 10/6/16
Jody Stecher 11/22/16
Larry Stephenson 10/31/16
Ron Thomason 10/28/16
Tony Trischka 12/6/16
Dan Tyminski 11/30/16
Jay Ungar 10/19/16
Ruthy Ungar 1/24/17
April Verch 2/8/17
Abigail Washburn 12/19/16
Doc Watson 4/25/88
Eric Weissberg 4/20/15
Pete Wernick 10/18/16
Mac Wiseman 11/22/16
Bob Yellin 12/21/16

Notes

Introduction

1. Gaye Thompson, "90 Years Ago: The Grand Ole Opry Begins Broadcasting," *The Boot* (November 28, 2015).

2. Malcolm Jones, "Earl Scruggs, Dead at 88, Pioneered a Banjo Style Imitated but Never Equaled," *The Daily Beast*, March 29, 2012.

3. Curwood Garrett, "Norton's Dock Boggs Has Style All His Own," http://www.angelfire.com/folk/longtimecoming/dockboggs/.

4. Anthony Harkins, *Hillbilly: A Cultural History of an American Icon* (New York: Oxford University Press, 2003), 39.

5. J. E. Lighter, *Random House Historical Dictionary of American Slang* (New York: Random House, 1994).

6. https://exhibits.lib.unc.edu/exhibits/show/hillbilly_music/green_hillbilly/part_two.

7. Ibid.

8. http://www.debed.com/lanham/teocfp.htm.

Chapter 1

1. Richard Thompson, "On This Day #47—Bill Monroe," *Bluegrass Today* (September 9, 2016).

2. Roger Wolmuth, "Bill Monroe," *People* (September 1, 1986).

3. Richard D. Smith, *Can't You Hear Me Callin': The Life of Bill Monroe, Father of Bluegrass* (Boston: Little, Brown, 2000).

4. Ibid.

5. http://www.spbgma.com/bill-monroe---preservation-hall-of-greats-1984--spbgma.html.

6. http://www.npr.org/2011/09/12/140366232/bill-monroe-celebrating-the-father-of-bluegrass-at-100.

7. http://www.spbgma.com/bill-monroe.

8. Danice Woodside, "Lucky from Kentucky: Bill Monroe—The Boy Who Would Become the Father of Blue," *Lovely County Citizen*, August 3, 2007.

9. Kathy and Don Thomason, "Arnold Shultz," *The Amplifier* (July 2006).

10. Woodside.

11. John Lawless, "IBMM Honors the Godfather," *Bluegrass Today* (February 14, 2012).

12. http://www.spbgma.com/bill-monroe.

13. Marshal Wyatt, "Kentucky Songbirds: The Monroe Brothers and Byron Parker in Greenville, SC, 1935-1936," *Bluegrass Unlimited* (June 2017).

14. Wayne Erbsen, "Cleo Davis, the Original Bluegrass Boy," http://nativeground.com/cleo-davis-the-original-bluegrass-boy/.

15. Ibid.

16. http://countrymusichalloffame.org/Inductees/InducteeDetail/arthur-e-satherley.

17. Jeff Nilsson, "The Post Discovers Country Music . . . in 1944," *Saturday Evening Post* (July 28, 2010).

18. Ibid.

19. Paul Wadley, "Obituary: Chubby Wise," *The Independent*, February 5, 1996.

20. Randy Noles, *Orange Blossom Boys: The Untold Story of Ervin T. Rouse, Chubby Wise, and the World's Most Famous Fiddle Tune* (Milwaukee: Hal Leonard, 2002), 9.

21. Ibid.

22. Richard Thompson, "I'm Going Back to Old Kentucky #113," *Bluegrass Today* (January 21, 2011).

23. "When Lester, Earl and Chubby Came to Town," http://www.thebluegrassspecial.com/archive/2011/october2011/bill-monroe-centennial-moment.html.

24. James Rooney, *Bossmen: Bill Monroe and Muddy Waters* (1971; repr., Zurich: JRP Books, 2012).

25. Steve Martin, "The Master from Flint Hill: Earl Scruggs," *The New Yorker* (January 13, 2012).

26. "The Story of 'Foggy Mountain Breakdown,'" *Weekend Edition*, NPR, April 1, 2000.

27. Ibid.

28. William S. Powell, *Dictionary of North Carolina Biography* (Chapel Hill: University of North Carolina Press, 2016).

29. "The Eclectic John Hartford," *Come for to Sing* (Summer 1985).

30. Pete Wernick, *Banjo Newsletter* (September 2011).

31. Lance LeRoy, "Lester Flatt," http://www.flatt-and-scruggs.com/lesterbio.html.

32. http://www.flatt-and-scruggs.com/earlbio.html.

33. Doug Benson, "Bill Monroe: King of Blue Grass Music," interview in

The Bill Monroe Reader, ed. Tom Ewing (Champaign: University of Illinois Press, 2006).

Chapter 2
1. Chris Talbott, "Bluegrass Pioneer Earl Scruggs Dies at Age 88," *San Diego Union Tribune*, March 29, 2012.
2. http://www.voanews.com/a/remembering-earl-scruggs-145197045/179225.html.
3. J. McSpadden, "50 Years of Dirt: Jeff Hanna Treks Across a Half Century of American Music," *No Depression* (December 5, 2016).

Chapter 3
1. Don Bryant, "Mac Wiseman," *Bluegrass Unlimited* (September 1, 2014).

Chapter 4
1. https://web.archive.org/web/20080822231520/http://www.donreno.com/bio.htm.
2. Tony Russell, "Bill Harrell Obituary," *Guardian*, September 25, 2009.

Chapter 5
1. Kent Gustavson, "Dawg DNA: David Grisman and Half a Century of Unabashedly Acoustic Music," *No Depression* (May 31, 2017).
2. http://www.chiefnoda.com/intvw/dgr.html.
3. http://www.cmt.com/news/1473115/son-of-bluegrass-ronnie-mccoury-mandolinist-for-the-great-del-mccoury-band-releases-debut-solo-cd/.

Chapter 6
1. John Lawless, "40 years of Old and In the Way," *Bluegrass Today* (October 2, 2013).
2. Steve Weitzman, "The Grateful Dead Revisited: A 1976 Interview with Jerry Garcia," *Relix* (August 1, 2013).
3. "Vassar Clements, 77, Fiddler Across Many Styles of Music, Dies," *NY Times*, August 17, 2005.
4. Weitzman.

Chapter 7
1. Peter Snick, "Richard Greene on Bill Monroe," *Fiddler* (June 1, 2005).

Chapter 8
1. Jim Rooney and Eric Von Schmidt, *Baby, Let Me Follow You Down:*

The Illustrated Story of the Cambridge Folk Years (Amherst: University of Massachusetts Press, 1994), 259.

2. "Jimmy Martin—In the Hall of the Mountain King," *No Depression* (April 30, 1999).

3. Ibid.

4. "Bluegrass Pioneer Jimmy Martin Dies," Associated Press, May 16, 2005.

Chapter 9

1. Ralph Stanley and Eddie Dean, *Man of Constant Sorrow: My Life and Times* (New York: Gotham, 2009).

2. Derek Hasley, "Bryan Sutton: A Great Guitarist Digs Deep with the Legends," http://www.swampland.com.

3. David Merconi, "The Picker Who Set the Beat," *News & Observer*, October 21, 2007.

4. Chrissie Dickinson, "Ralph Stanley's Long Road Leads to Chicago," *Chicago Tribune*, January 31, 2013.

5. Vicki Dean, "Interview: Ricky Skaggs Is Steeped in Tradition," *New York Herald Tribune*, January 10, 2017.

Chapter 10

1. "Jim & Jesse—You Can Sometimes Get What You Want," *No Depression* (December 31, 2000).

Chapter 11

1. Larry Nager, "Bobby Osborne Original, Unstoppable," *Bluegrass Unlimited* (August 2017).

2. Chuck Dauphin, "At 85, Bluegrass Legend Bobby Osborne Looks Back on Appalachian Upbringing and His Legacy," *Billboard* (May 11, 2017).

Chapter 12

1. Desiré Moses, "Tony Rice on the Legacy and Impact of Tony Rice," *Bluegrass Situation* (September 29, 2016).

2. Bill Nowlin, "The Story of 0044: Part 3," *Bluegrass Situation* (April 15, 2016).

3. http://www.chiefnoda.com/intvw/tr.html.

4. Ibid.

5. Sandra Beasley, "Tony Rice, Guitar Hero," *NY Times Magazine* (February 14, 2014).

Chapter 13

1. http://visitwilkesboronc.com/2013/03/05/special-tributes-to-doc-watson/.

2. Jon Sieverts, "Like Some Kind of Fine," *Frets* (March 1979).

3. Michael Brooks, "Bluegrass Guitar King," *Guitar Player* (July/August 1972).

4. https://www.hcpress.com/news/rosa-lee-watson-passes-away-on-thursday-towards-heaven-she-rises-to-be-with-doc-and-merle.html.

5. "Eddy Merle Watson, Bluegrass Guitarist, Accidentally Killed at 36," *L.A. Times*, October 24, 1985.

6. http://greatinsurancepeople.com/2010/11/02/merle-watson-tractor-rollover-death-famous-son-of-doc-watson/.

7. "MerleFest's Richard Watson Dies Monday," *Wilkes Journal-Patriot*, June 3, 2015.

Chapter 14

1. http://fieldrecorder.org/tommy-jarrell/.

Chapter 15

1. John Wilson, "Sprung Displays Champion's Finesse in Banjo Concert," *NY Times*, April 6, 1970.

2. Ben Sisario, "John Herald, 65, Folk Singer and Guitarist," *NY Times*, July 23, 2005.

3. Ibid.

4. http://www.johnherald.com/home.shtml.

5. http://candlewater.com/interviews/story015.html.

6. Ibid.

Chapter 16

1. https://hillbillyatharvard.wordpress.com/2015/06/02/tex-logan-1927-2015-part-ii/.

2. https://www.mandolincafe.com/news/publish/printer_1297.shtml.

Chapter 17

1. https://www.guitar.com/articles/clarence-white-byrd-who-truly-soared.

2. http://www.thebluegrasssituation.com/read/tony-rice-legacy-and-impact-clarence-white.

3. Ibid.

4. http://die-augenweide.de/byrds/speak/aboutcrosby.htm.

5. http://www.rollingstone.com/music/news/gram-parsons-the-mysterious-death-and-aftermath-19731025.

6. http://www.ronistoneman.com/the-stoneman-legacy.html.

7. http://www.burritobrother.com/KYcolonels.htm.

8. http://www.remembertheaba.com/KY-colonels.html.

9. http://www.chiefnoda.com/intvw/tr.html.

10. http://www.burritobrother.com/afterthebyrds.htm.

Chapter 18

1. http://www.cybergrass.com/node/1450#sthash.RKtQBRqF.dpbs.

2. https://medium.com/@jeremylr/the-dillards-secret-weapon-in-step-with-mandolin-maestro-dean-webb-7a476a27bf7a.

3. Ibid.

4. Brance, "Mitch Jayne Passes," *Bluegrass Today* (August 3, 2010).

5. Joe Foster, liner notes, *The Banjo Album*, Rural Rhythm, 2004.

6. http://www.richieunterberger.com/wheat.html.

7. https://medium.com/@jeremylr/the-dillards-secret-weapon-in-step-with-mandolin-maestro-dean-webb-7a476a27bf7a.

8. Jeremy Roberts, "Reminiscing with Bluegrass Legend Rodney Dillard," *Phoenix Metro County News*, December 5, 2013.

9. https://medium.com/@jeremylr/the-dillards-secret-weapon-in-step-with-mandolin-maestro-dean-webb-7a476a27bf7a.

10. Ibid.

Chapter 19

1. http://www.cybergrass.com/node/3645#sthash.P8GRJCJN.dpbs.

2. "The Eclectic John Hartford."

3. Andrew Dansby, "John Hartford Dead After Cancer Battle," *Rolling Stone* (June 5, 2001).

4. Skip Heller, "A Good Act: John Hartford, Hippie, Eclectic Southern Riverboat Intellectual," *No Depression* (November 2006).

5. http://www.chiefnoda.com/intvw/tt.html.

6. http://www.thebluegrasssituation.com/read/end-road-conversation-norman-blake.

7. "Bluegrass Musician Norman Blake Releases an Album of Original Songs," *Fresh Air*, NPR, March 19, 2015.

8. "The Eclectic John Hartford."

9. Dansby.

10. http://www.soundstage.com/music/reviews/rev405.htm.

11. Heller.

Chapter 20

1. Martha Adcock, liner notes, *Eddie Adcock—Vintage Banjo Jam*, Patuxent, 2017.

2. Vicki Dean, "Interview: Bluegrass Star Missy Raines on Stepping into the Spotlight," *Herald-Tribune*, January 18, 2017.

3. "Eddie Adcock on His Major Award," *Bluegrass Today* (September 9, 2014).

4. http://www.bluegrassmuseum.org/tom-gray/.

5. Joe Heim, "The Old Country," *Washington Post*, July 27, 2003.

6. Rosemary Oxenford, "Going the Mile—A Profile of Hazel Dickens," *The Black Sheep Review* (January/February 1984).

Chapter 22

1. Oliver Trager, *The American Book of the Dead* (New York: Simon & Shuster, 1997), 32.

2. James Henke, "Jerry Garcia: The *Rolling Stone* Interview," *Rolling Stone* (October 31, 1991).

3. Greg Cahill, "High on Bluegrass: Grateful Dead Guitarist Jerry Garcia's Acoustic Side," *Acoustic Guitar* (February 17, 2015).

4. http://www.paloaltohistory.org/the-grateful-dead.php.

5. Josh Baron, "The Thrill Lives On: David Grisman Reflects on Jerry Garcia," *Relix* (August 1, 2012).

6. http://www.nelsonband.com/.

7. Ibid.

Chapter 23

1. McSpadden.

2. Ibid.

Chapter 26

1. Tim O'Brien, liner notes, *Cornbread Nation*, Sugar Hill, 2005.

2. Tim O'Brien, liner notes, *Fiddler's Green*, Sugar Hill, 2005.

Chapter 27

1. https://www.mandolincafe.com/news/publish/mandolins_001437.shtml.

Chapter 28

1. http://www.lrc.ky.gov/Statrev/ACTS2010RS/0052.pdf.

2. Jeff Tamarkin, "Béla Fleck: Juno Concerto," *Relix* (May 17, 2017).

Chapter 30

1. Richard Thompson, "The Freight Hoppers Ride Again," *Bluegrass Today* (March 25, 2008).

Chapter 32

1. Rob Trucks, "Talking with Robert Plant: Touring the South, the Legend Talks About Led Zep and Alison Krauss, Mostly Krauss," *Nashville Scene*, July 17, 2008.

Chapter 34

1. Alfred Hickling, "Carolina Chocolate Drops: Saturday Night Femur," *Guardian*, February 19, 2012.

2. David Fricke, "Fricke's Picks: Maximum Cool, Modern Jug-Band Music and as Strange as 1969 Ever Got," *Rolling Stone* (August 17, 2007).

Chapter 35

1. https://www.cbaweb.org/Welcome/Column/3546.

2. http://www.jambands.com/features/2002/05/21/it-felt-great-to-play-bluegrass-again-an-interview-with-drew-emmitt.

3. https://www.elephantjournal.com/2008/07/interview-with-drew-emmitt-my-favorite-buddhist-mandolinist/.

4. http://www.jambands.com/features/2002/05/21/it-felt-great-to-play-bluegrass-again-an-interview-with-drew-emmitt.

5. theboot.com/noam-pikelny-universal-favorite-interview-2017/?trackback=tsmclip.

6. https://www.telluride.com/blog/interview-drew-emmitt.

7. https://www.bobdylan.com/news/qa-with-bill-flanagan/.

8. Gary Stoller, "Dylan Provides Common Ground for Members of Old Crow Medicine Show," *No Depression* (July 2017).

Chapter 36

1. "Steve Martin: Comedian Takes Banjo Seriously," *All Things Considered*, NPR, February 4, 2009.

2. "Eddie Adcock on His Major Award," *Bluegrass Today* (September 9, 2014).

3. Margaret Aro and Enjoli Francis, "Man and His Banjo: Steve Martin Shares Lifelong Passion," ABC News, October 7, 2011.

4. http://www.thekelword.com/following-the-muse-an-interview-with-steve-martin/.

Chapter 37

1. http://www.rootsworld.com/interview/jewgrass.html.

Coda

1. "Tommy Jarrell and Fred Cockerham: North Carolina Fiddle and Fretless Banjo," *Musical Traditions* (1993).

Index